BIG BLACK
STAND AT ATTICA™

Published by
ARCHAIA™

BIG D
STAND A

Four days in 1971 changed
the course of **American history**.

LACK ATTICA ™

WRITTEN BY
FRANK "BIG BLACK" SMITH
JARED REINMUTH

ILLUSTRATED BY
AMÉZIANE

LETTERED BY
ANDWORLD DESIGN

ARCHAIA™
Los Angeles, California

COVER BY
AMÉZIANE

CREATIVE CONSULTANT
PATRICK KENNEDY

DESIGNER
SCOTT NEWMAN

ASSISTANT EDITOR
ALLYSON GRONOWITZ

EDITOR
SIERRA HAHN

Ross Richie CEO & Founder
Joy Huffman CFO
Matt Gagnon Editor-in-Chief
Filip Sablik President, Publishing & Marketing
Stephen Christy President, Development
Lance Kreiter Vice President, Licensing & Merchandising
Arune Singh Vice President, Marketing
Bryce Carlson Vice President, Editorial & Creative Strategy
Scott Newman Manager, Production Design
Kate Henning Manager, Operations
Spencer Simpson Manager, Sales
Elyse Strandberg Manager, Finance
Sierra Hahn Executive Editor
Jeanine Schaefer Executive Editor
Dafna Pleban Senior Editor

Shannon Watters Senior Editor
Eric Harburn Senior Editor
Chris Rosa Editor
Matthew Levine Editor
Sophie Philips-Roberts Associate Editor
Amanda LaFranco Associate Editor
Gavin Gronenthal Assistant Editor
Gwen Waller Assistant Editor
Allyson Gronowitz Assistant Editor
Jillian Crab Design Coordinator
Michelle Ankley Design Coordinator
Kara Leopard Production Designer
Marie Krupina Production Designer
Grace Park Production Designer
Chelsea Roberts Production Design Assistant

Samantha Knapp Production Design Assistant
Paola Capalla Senior Accountant
José Meza Live Events Lead
Stephanie Hocutt Digital Marketing Lead
Esther Kim Marketing Coordinator
Cat O'Grady Digital Marketing Coordinator
Amanda Lawson Marketing Assistant
Holly Aitchison Digital Sales Coordinator
Morgan Perry Retail Sales Coordinator
Megan Christopher Operations Coordinator
Rodrigo Hernandez Mailroom Assistant
Zipporah Smith Operations Assistant
Breanna Sarpy Executive Assistant

ARCHAIA™

BIG BLACK: STAND AT ATTICA, February 2020. Published by Archaia, a division of Boom Entertainment, Inc. Big Black: Stand at Attica is ™ & © 2020 Frank B.B. Smith, Jared Reinmuth, Hammouche Améziane. All rights reserved. Archaia™ and the Archaia logo are trademarks of Boom Entertainment, Inc., registered in various countries and categories. BOOM! Studios does not read or accept unsolicited submissions of ideas, stories, or artwork.

BOOM! Studios, 5670 Wilshire Boulevard, Suite 400, Los Angeles, CA 90036-5679. Printed in China. First Printing.

ISBN: 978-1-68415-479-1, eISBN: 978-1-64144-637-2

For the 1539,
That their Stand at Attica
Inspires the Spirit of Abolition and Resistance.
And brings Hope and Inspiration to those Incarcerated
In these modern institutions of Inhumanity.

For Mom and Dan,
Who taught me the story of Attica,
Introduced me to Big Black and Pearl,
And with Love and Generosity,
Pursued Justice Relentlessly to the End.

For Pearl,
Big Black's North Star,
Who guided us,
Kept us moving Forward,
And never allowed us to Give Up.

And for Big Black,
The Heartbeat of our Story.

—Jared Reinmuth

For my Love, Syb.

For my boys, Gab & Noé.

For all the ones who
trusted me on this book:
Patrick, Jared, Pearl, Alex, Judy,
Joan, Sierra, and Allyson.

—Améziane

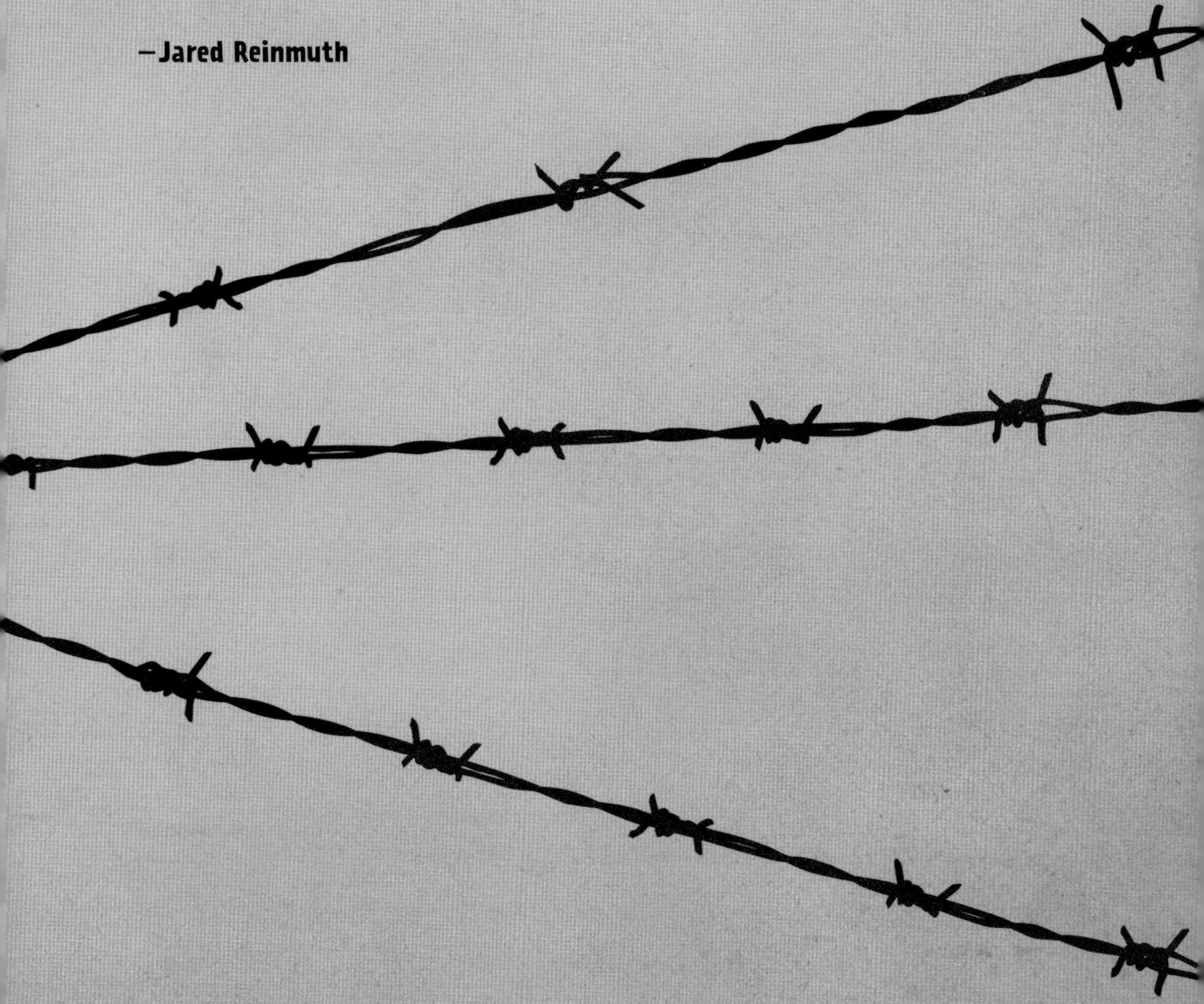

INTRODUCTION

This graphic novel is about real people and events. It is about a courageous, gentle person; a huge man with a booming voice. It is about people who were imprisoned at Attica, the maximum-security penitentiary in upstate New York in 1971. It is about a rebellion for humane treatment. It is about the state's violent repression of an uprising that culminated in a bloody massacre committed by a police force that Dr. Clarence B. Jones (lawyer and former speechwriter for Martin Luther King, Jr., who was present at the prison at the request of the inmates) called "young, tense, and infected with racism." My involvement begins on the day of the uprising with a phone call from the prison to my law office. Here starts a personal and legal commitment that would last three decades.

September 13, 1971 became one of the bloodiest days in modern United States history when N.Y. State Governor Nelson Rockefeller ordered the violent retaking of Attica Prison. Troopers indiscriminately shot two thousand rounds of ammunition at unarmed people trapped within the prison walls, resulting in the deaths of 29 prisoners and 10 guards. After the shooting stopped, police beat and tortured the surviving prisoners. One of the worst atrocities was the sadistic barbarism perpetrated by state police and guards against Frank "Big Black" Smith, the central figure of this book.

To hold the state accountable, in 1974, on behalf of the 1,281 prisoners who were brutalized in D-Yard that morning, I filed a federal class action civil rights damage lawsuit against Governor Nelson Rockefeller and other state officials, seeking compensation for the wrongful deaths and brutalities inflicted against the prisoners. For an incredibly long 26 years, the legal team of five lawyers and innumerable dedicated supporters sought justice in and out of court for the prisoners, who became known as the Attica Brothers.

Following his release from prison, Big Black began working for me and for other lawyers as an investigator for people charged with crimes. He had the ability to make people feel comfortable and forthcoming. He was intelligent, strategic, and charismatic, which made him an ideal investigator.

At Attica, his communication skills and commitment to fair play were displayed as the prisoners' football coach. His stature and character were two of the reasons he was selected by the rebelling inmates to be their chief of security, and he certainly lived up to his reputation. No one was harmed for four days in D-Yard, including state officials, up until the massacre of September 13. As you will see on the pages before you, because of Big Black's role during the uprising, the state tortured him beyond what is imaginable.

After his release from Attica, Big Black also became an early intervention drug counselor for addicted youth. At the time, early intervention, non-punitive treatment was innovative. In Brooklyn, he worked with high school youth in a vocational program sponsored by the United Auto Workers, and had a close relationship with Sam Meyers and other UAW officials.

In his own case, Big Black was a riveting witness. His testimony about enduring sadistic torture and brutality resulted in a unanimous jury verdict. He was awarded compensatory damages in the amount of $4 million, the largest jury verdict for a sole prisoner in the history of the United States. The judgement was wrongfully dismissed, and all other verdicts nullified by an appellate court. In 2000, after 26 years and faced with no credible options, the Attica Brothers Lawsuit settled for the inadequate sum of $12 million to be shared amongst the plaintiffs.

Big Black was so magnetic and respected that the unfavorable trial judge invited him to his and his wife's home for a holiday dinner. Upon hearing of Big Black's declining health, Daniel Callaghan, Former Capt. 19th Special Forces Group, present at Attica and a witness at trial, wrote to Big Black, "...today I am a better human being than I once was, and you made me so."

I have often asked myself how a person could suffer such brutality and remain optimistic and kind. As Big Black's wife Pearl testified at trial, she would often find him underneath their bed, shaking from a PTSD-induced nightmare. But with her loving support, he remained steady and generous. Big Black and Attica Brother Akil Al-Jundi were a driving force in the quest for justice. He remained close to all the surviving Attica Brothers, especially Carlos Roche, until the end of his life in 2004.

With the introduction of the archaic Rockefeller drug laws, and for-profit prisons, mass incarceration has exploded. In 1971, New York State laid claim to 12 prisons and 12,500 prisoners. In 2000, when the case was settled, that number had ballooned to 72 prisons and 72,500 prisoners, ravaging poor communities of color and making the Attica prison uprising a story for today.

This book, with its accuracy and visual depth, is an honest portrayal of those horrifying and tragic events—events which resonate in today's political climate. Frank "Big Black" Smith's story is an inspiration to my family, to Jared, to his siblings and his mom, and it will continue to inspire future generations.

Daniel Meyers, Esq.
Attica Brothers Legal Team, 1974-2000

THE 15 PRACTICAL PROPOSALS
OF REBELLING ATTICA PRISONERS

1. Apply the New York State minimum wage law to all state institutions. STOP SLAVE LABOR.

2. Allow all New York State prisoners to be politically active, without intimidation or reprisals.

3. Give us true religious freedom.

4. End all censorship of newspapers, magazines, letters, and other publications coming from the publisher.

5. Allow all inmates, at their own expense, to communicate with anyone they please.

6. When an inmate reaches conditional release date, give him a full release without parole.

7. Cease administrative resentencing of inmates returned for parole violations.

8. Institute realistic rehabilitation programs for all inmates according to their offense and personal needs.

9. Educate all correctional officers to the needs of the inmates, i.e., understanding rather than punishment.

10. Give us a healthy diet, stop feeding us so much pork, and give us some fresh fruit daily.

11. Modernize the inmate education system.

12. Give us a doctor that will examine and treat all inmates that request treatment.

13. Have an institutional delegation comprised of one inmate from each company authorized to speak to the institution administration concerning grievances (QUARTERLY).

14. Give us less cell time and more recreation with better recreational equipment and facilities.

15. Remove inside walls, making one open yard, and no more segregation or punishment.

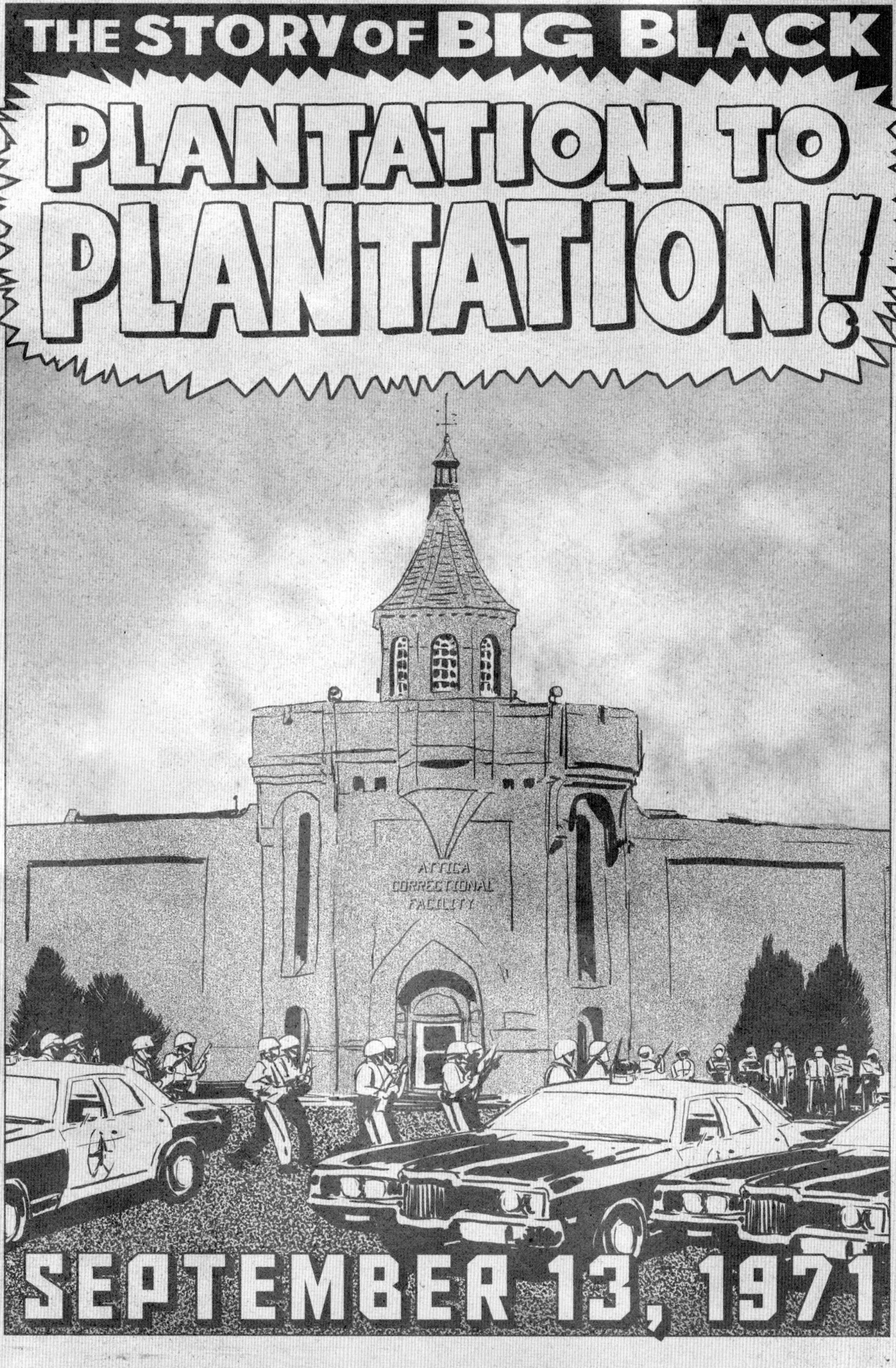
THE STORY OF BIG BLACK
PLANTATION TO PLANTATION!
ATTICA CORRECTIONAL FACILITY
SEPTEMBER 13, 1971

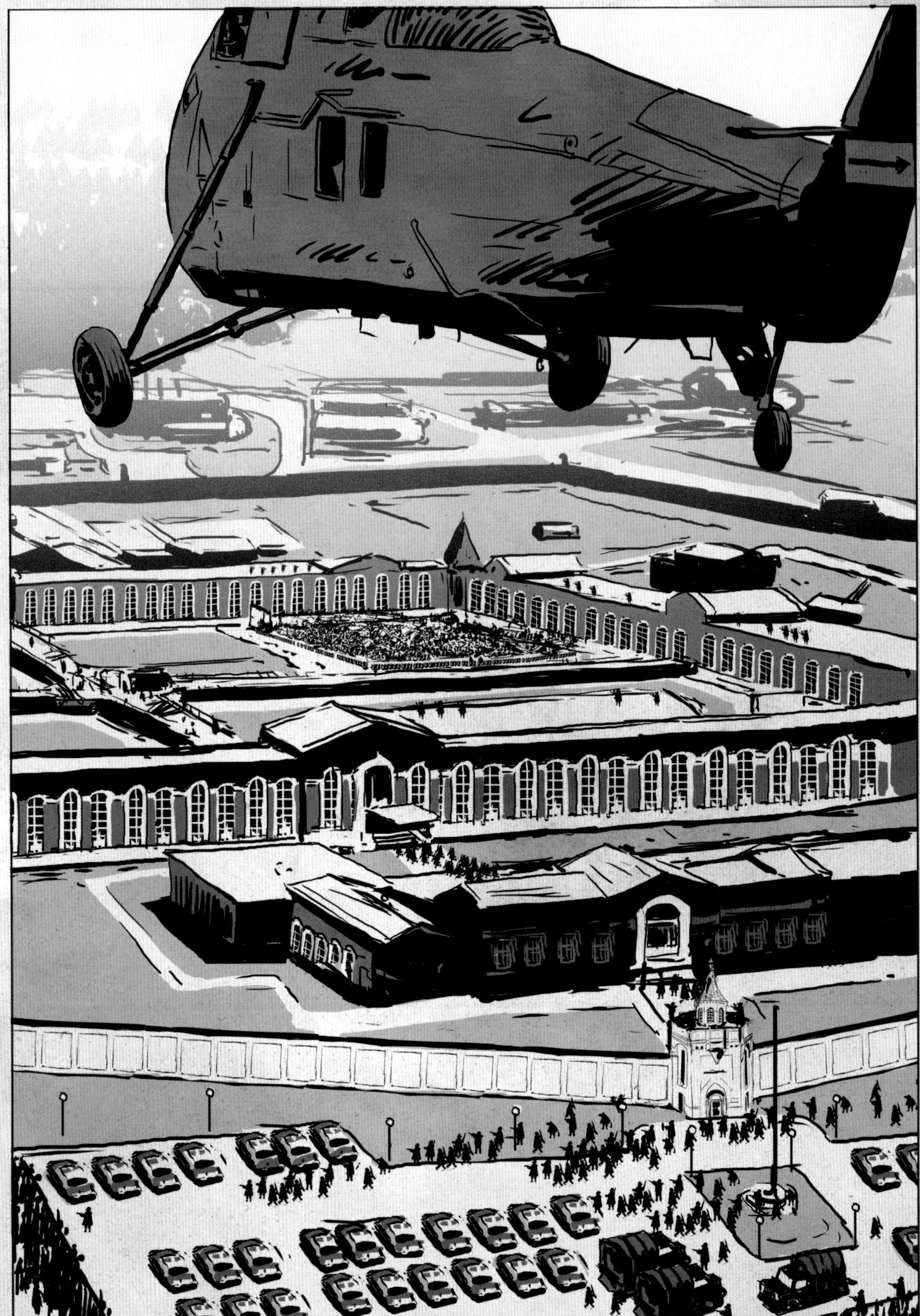

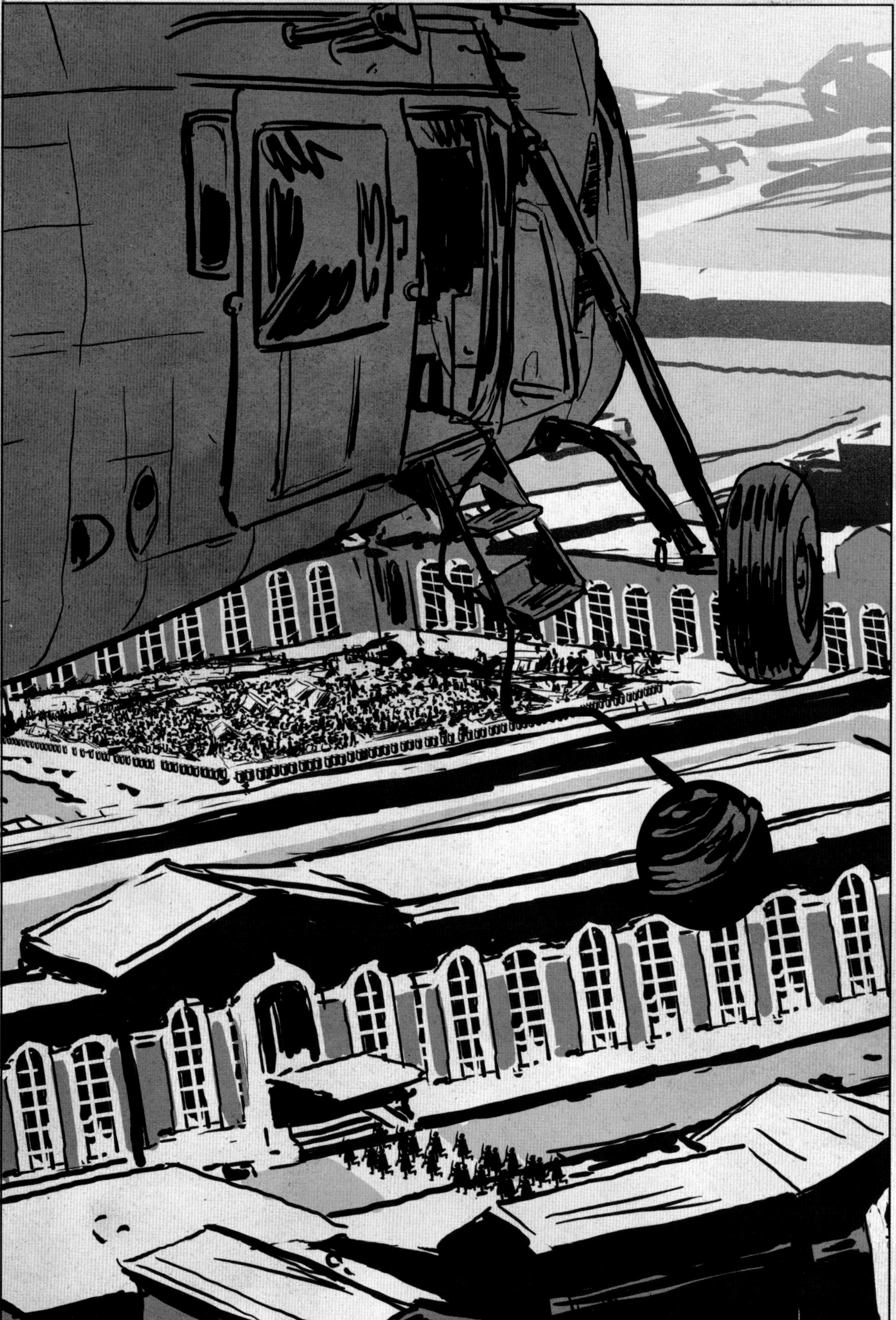

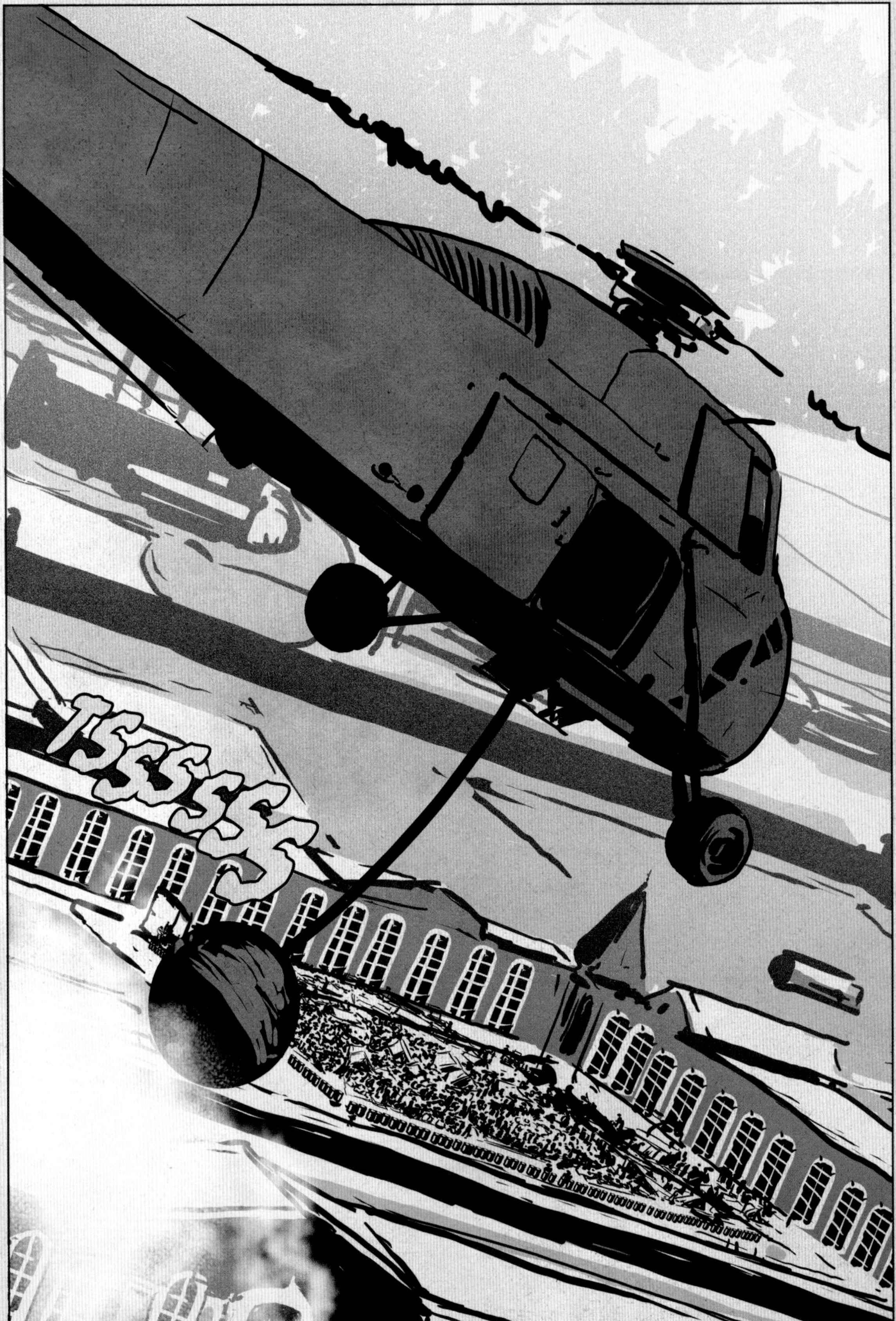
TSSSSS

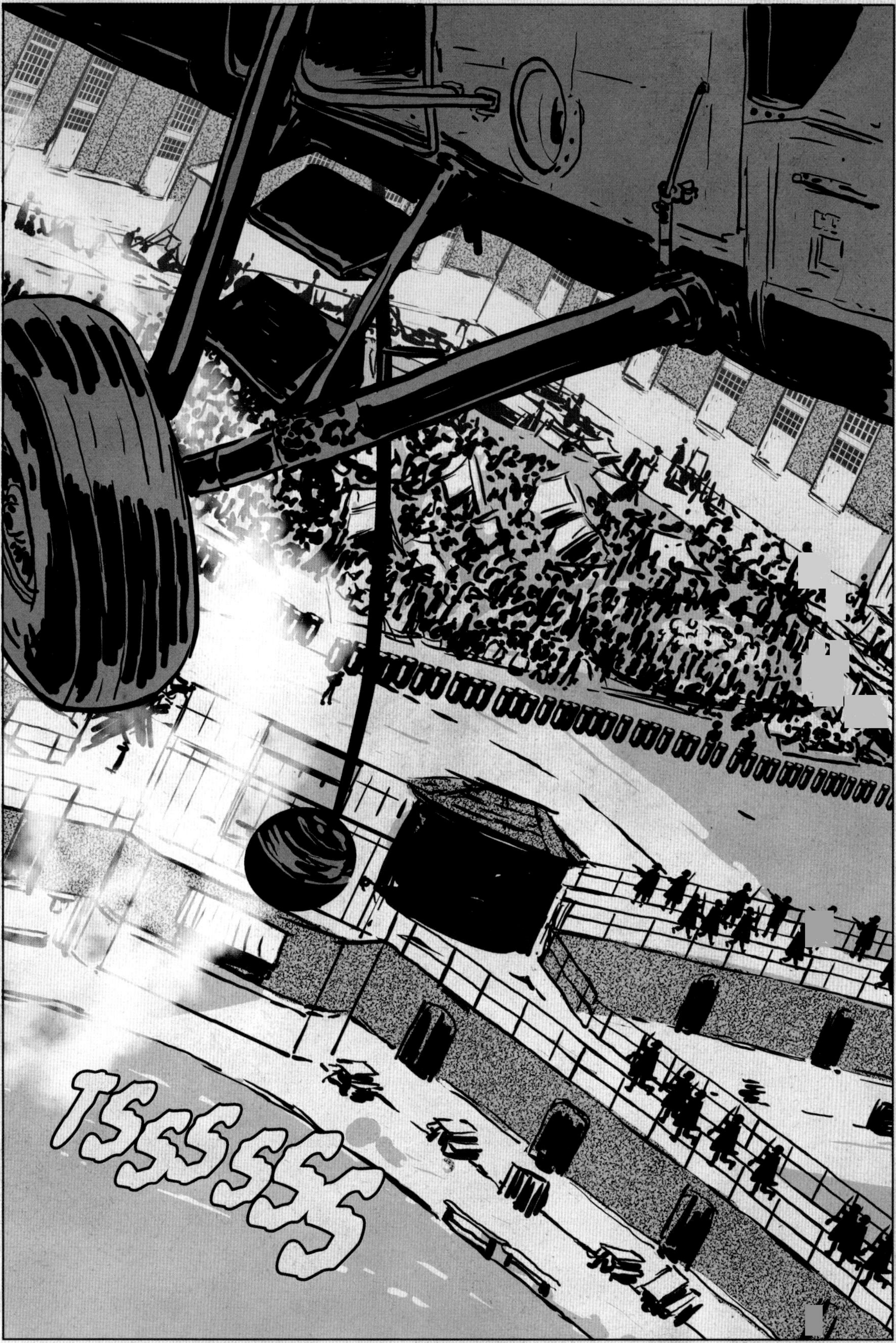
TSSSSSS

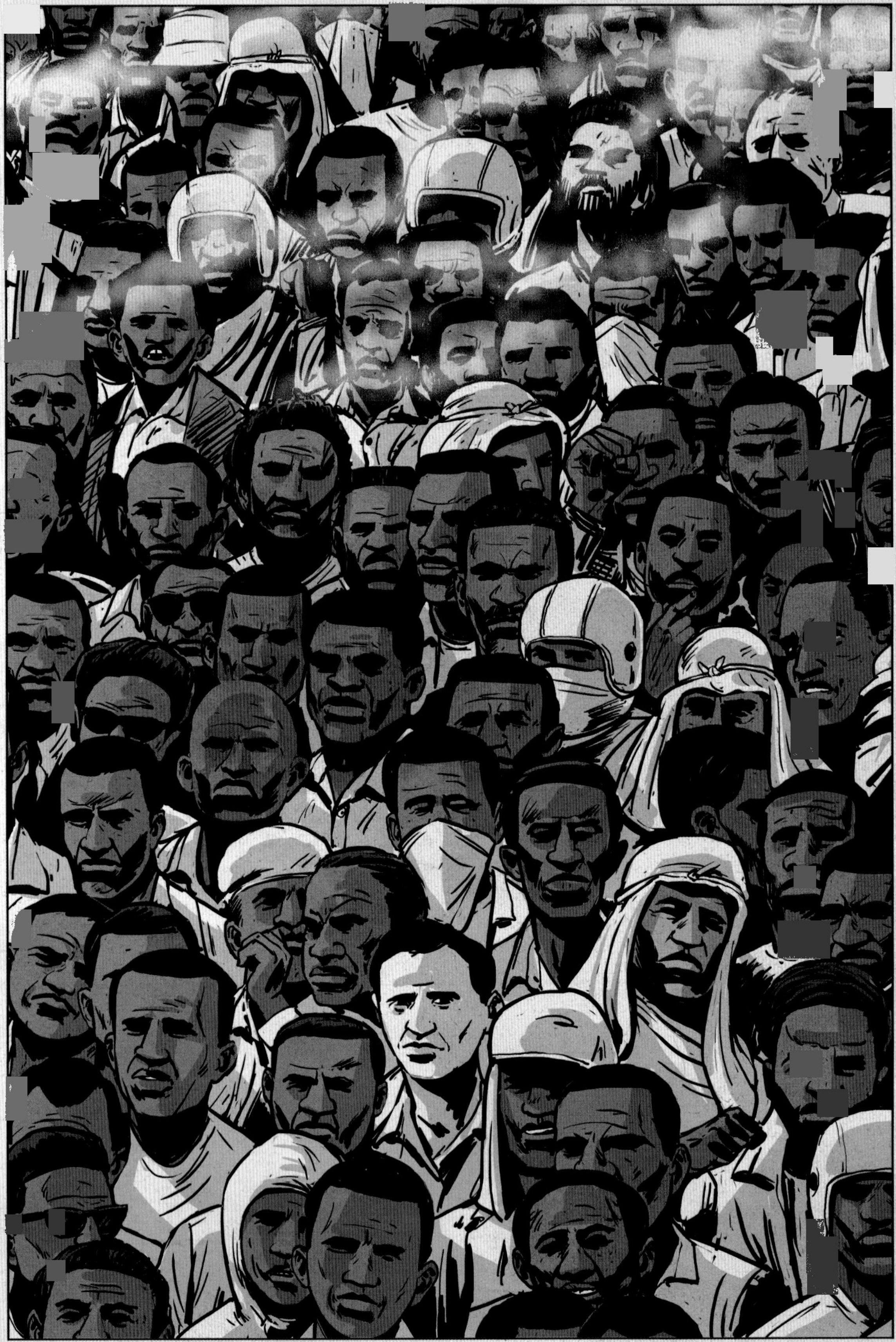

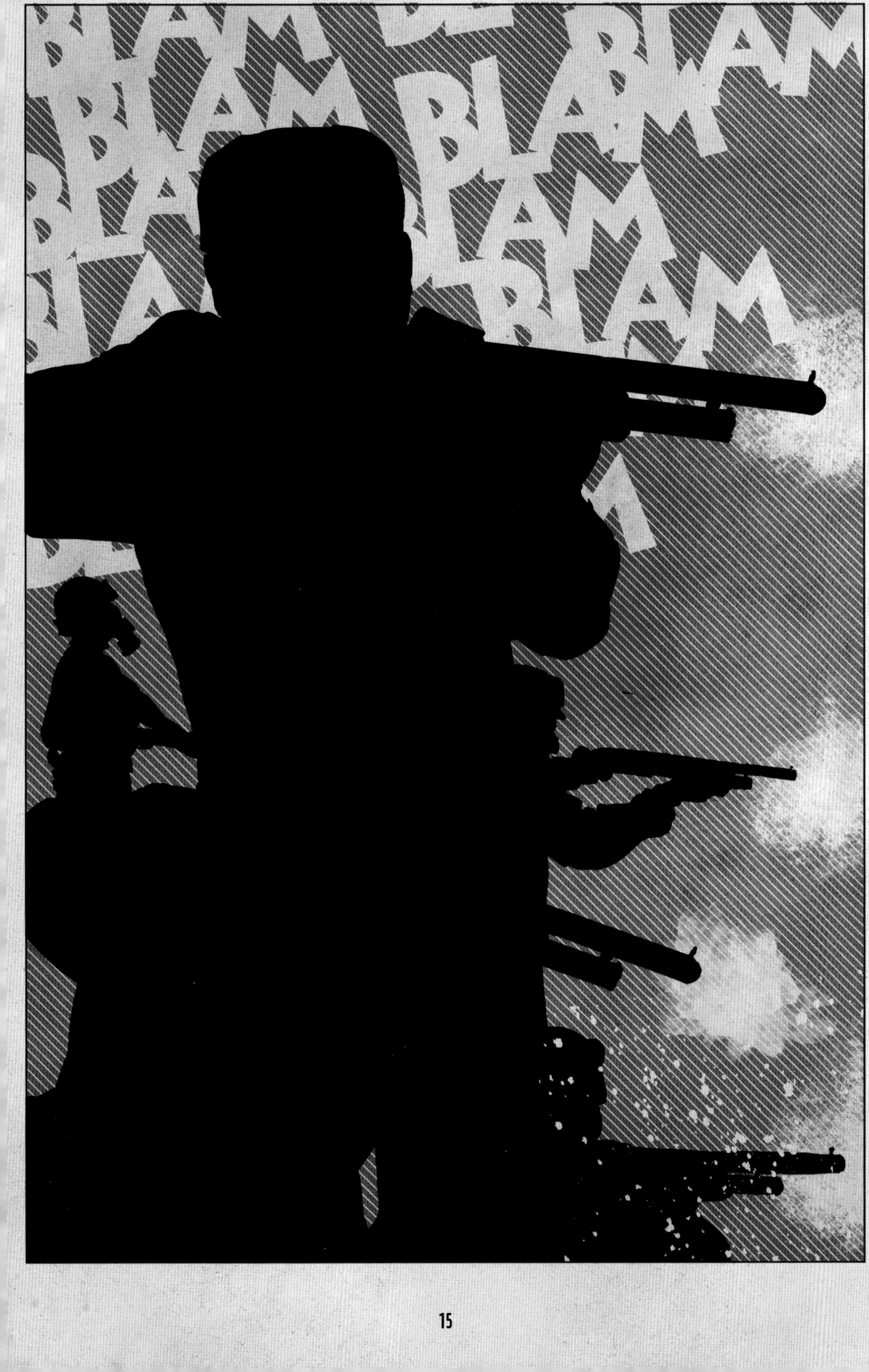
BLAM
BLAM
BLAM
BLAM
BLAM
BLAM
BLAM
BLAM

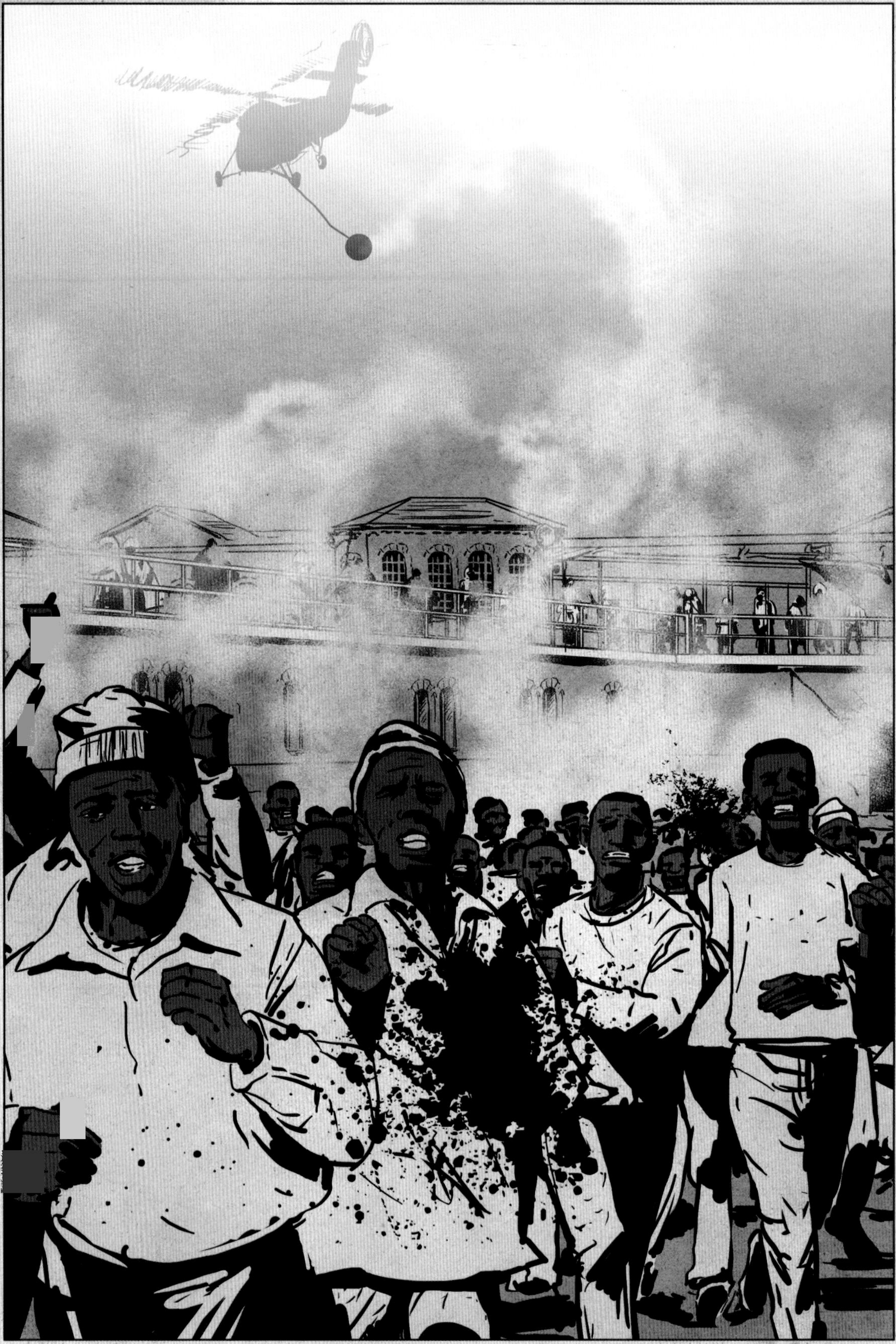

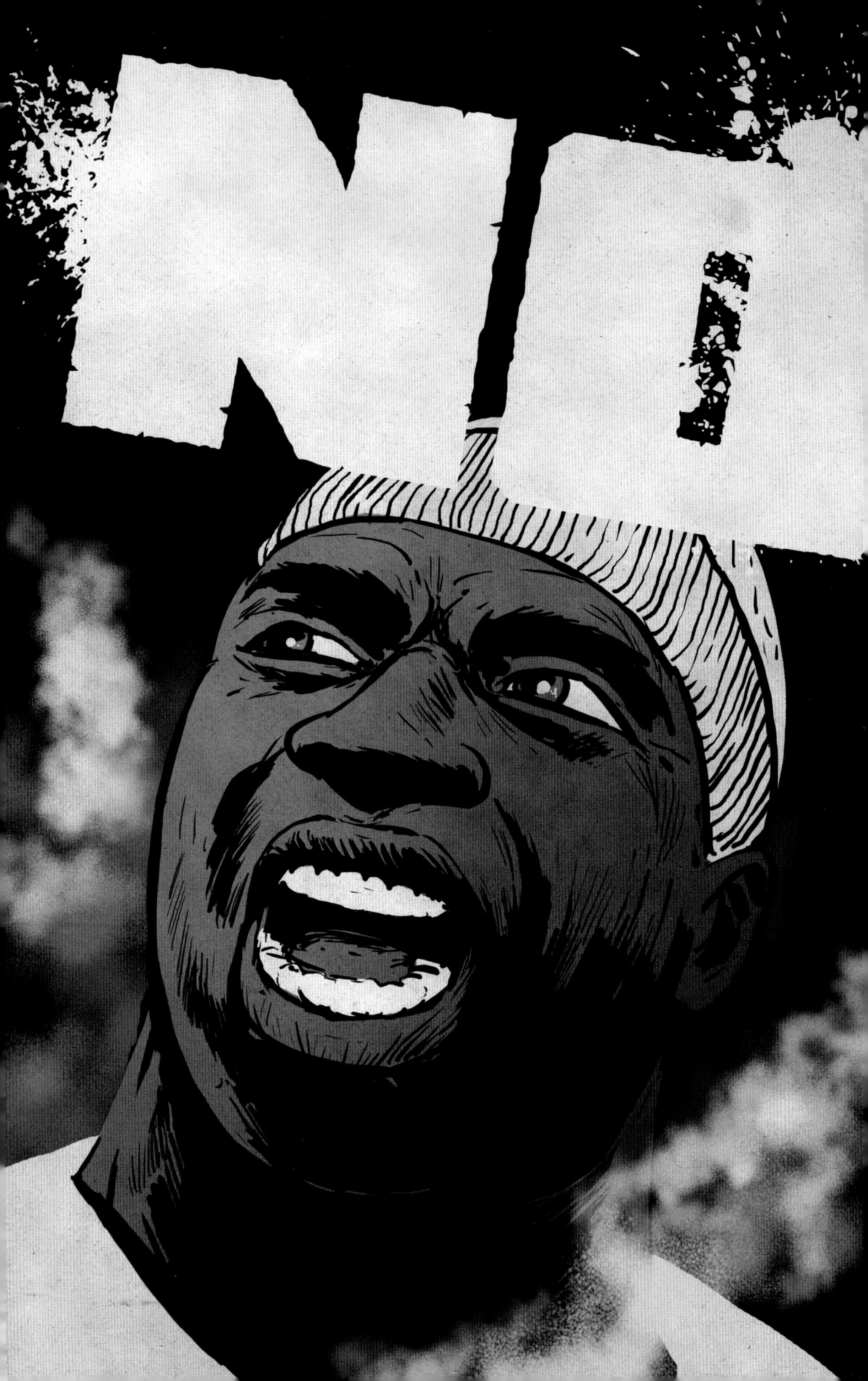
NO

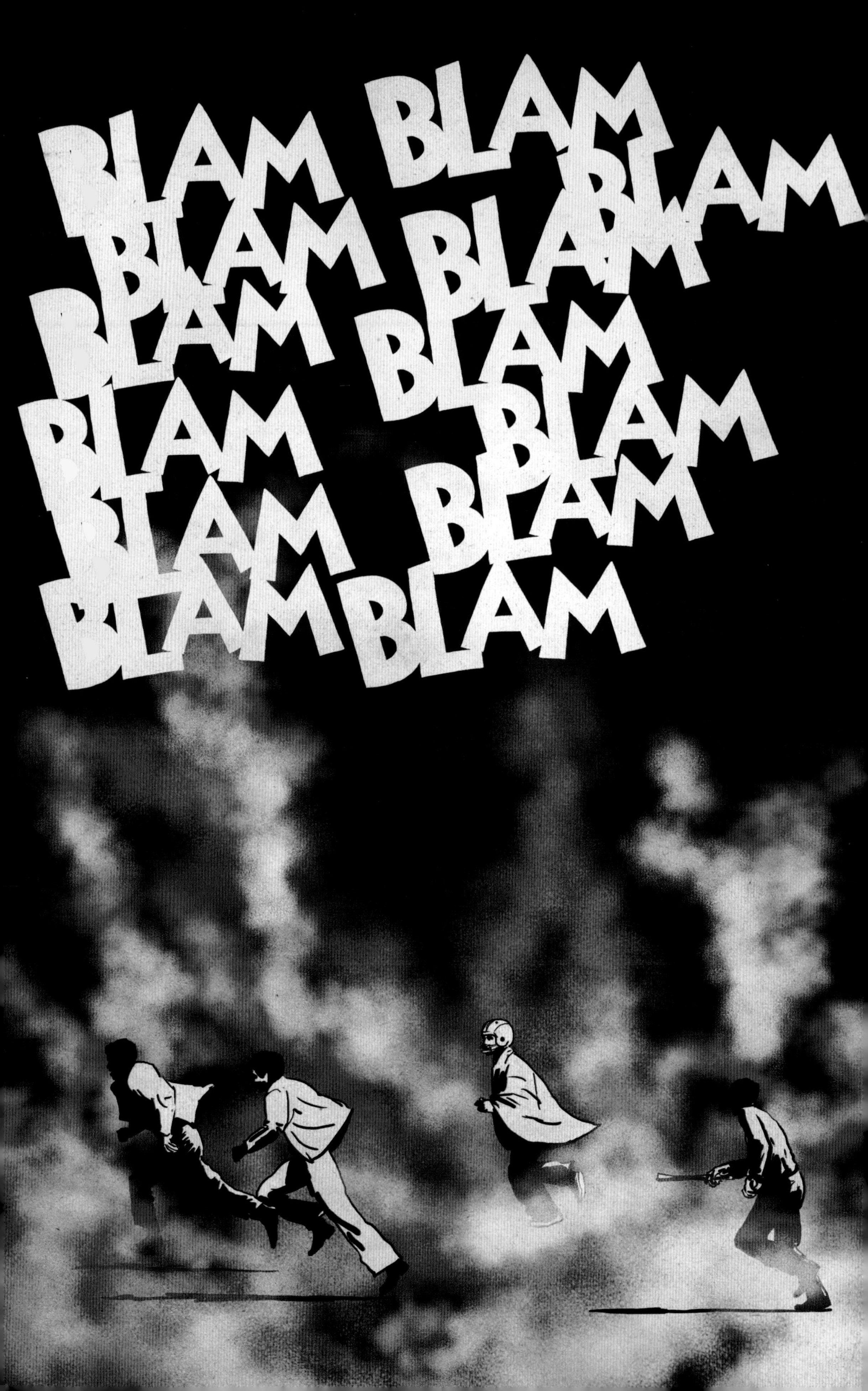
BLAM BLAM BLAM
BLAM BLAM
BLAM BLAM
BLAM BLAM
BLAM BLAM
BLAM BLAM

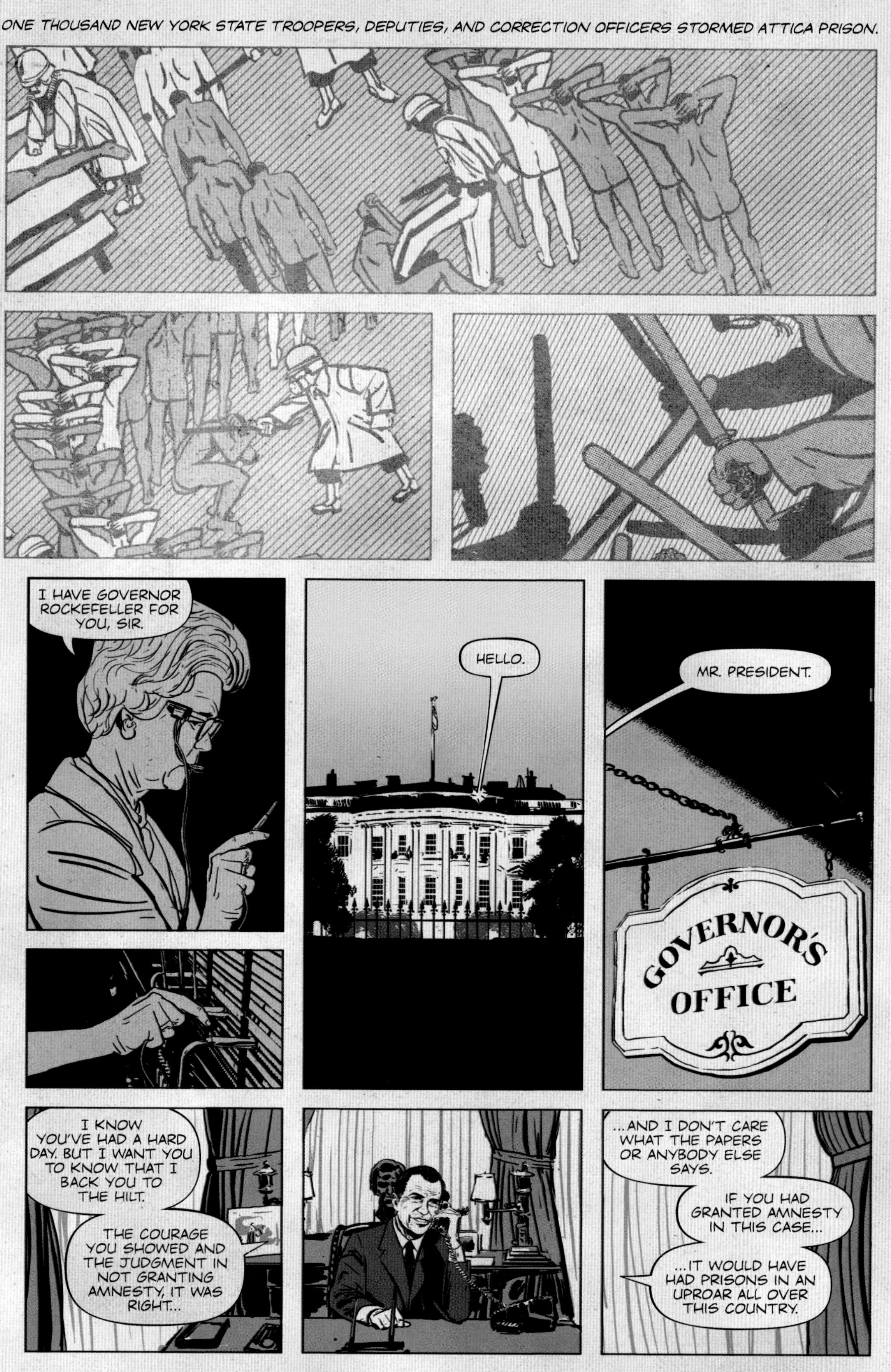
ONE THOUSAND NEW YORK STATE TROOPERS, DEPUTIES, AND CORRECTION OFFICERS STORMED ATTICA PRISON.
I HAVE GOVERNOR ROCKEFELLER FOR YOU, SIR.
HELLO.
MR. PRESIDENT.
GOVERNOR'S OFFICE
I KNOW YOU'VE HAD A HARD DAY. BUT I WANT YOU TO KNOW THAT I BACK YOU TO THE HILT.
THE COURAGE YOU SHOWED AND THE JUDGMENT IN NOT GRANTING AMNESTY, IT WAS RIGHT...
...AND I DON'T CARE WHAT THE PAPERS OR ANYBODY ELSE SAYS.
IF YOU HAD GRANTED AMNESTY IN THIS CASE...
...IT WOULD HAVE HAD PRISONS IN AN UPROAR ALL OVER THIS COUNTRY.

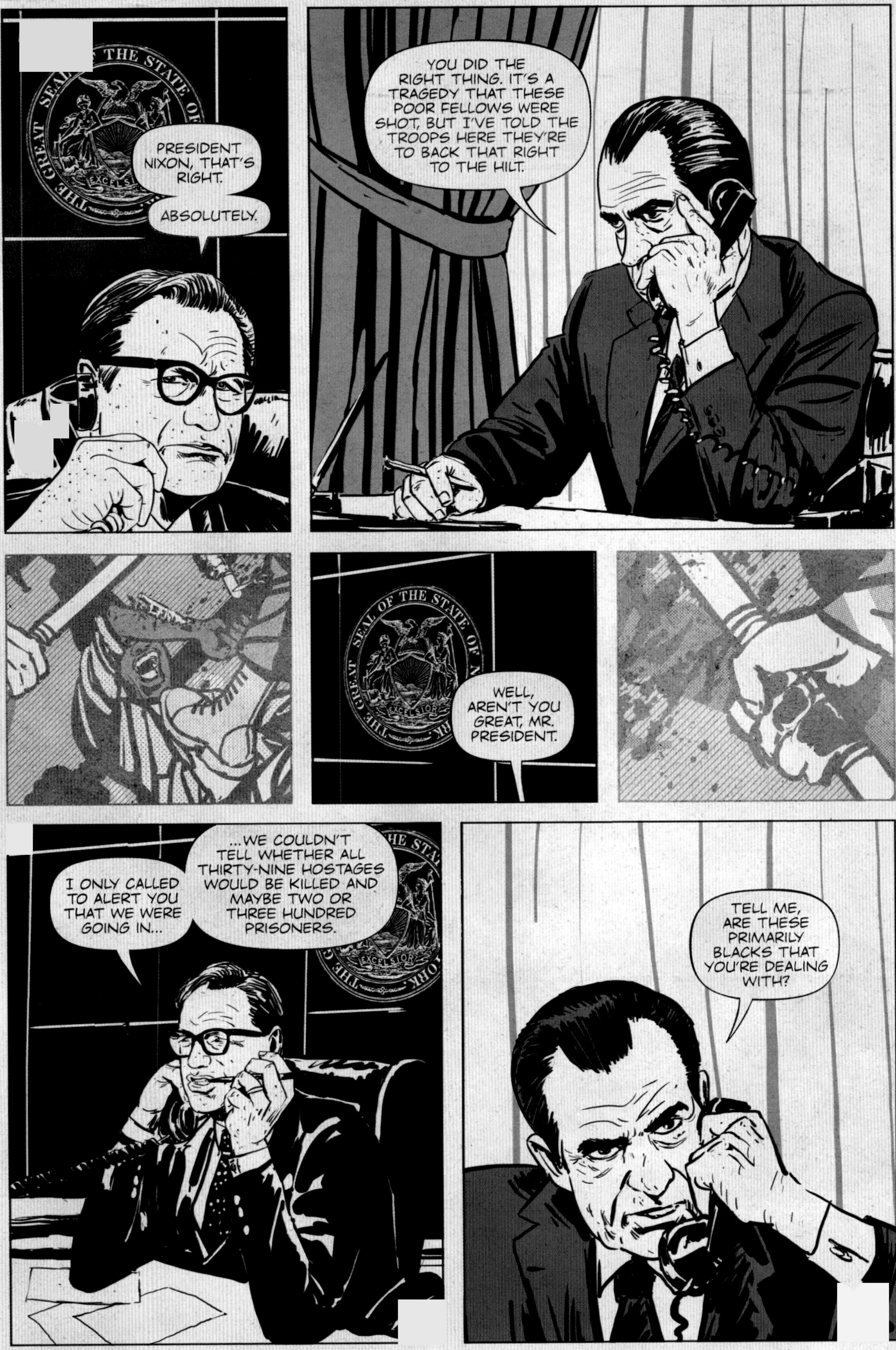
PRESIDENT NIXON, THAT'S RIGHT.
ABSOLUTELY.
YOU DID THE RIGHT THING. IT'S A TRAGEDY THAT THESE POOR FELLOWS WERE SHOT, BUT I'VE TOLD THE TROOPS HERE THEY'RE TO BACK THAT RIGHT TO THE HILT.
WELL, AREN'T YOU GREAT, MR. PRESIDENT.
I ONLY CALLED TO ALERT YOU THAT WE WERE GOING IN...
...WE COULDN'T TELL WHETHER ALL THIRTY-NINE HOSTAGES WOULD BE KILLED AND MAYBE TWO OR THREE HUNDRED PRISONERS.
TELL ME, ARE THESE PRIMARILY BLACKS THAT YOU'RE DEALING WITH?

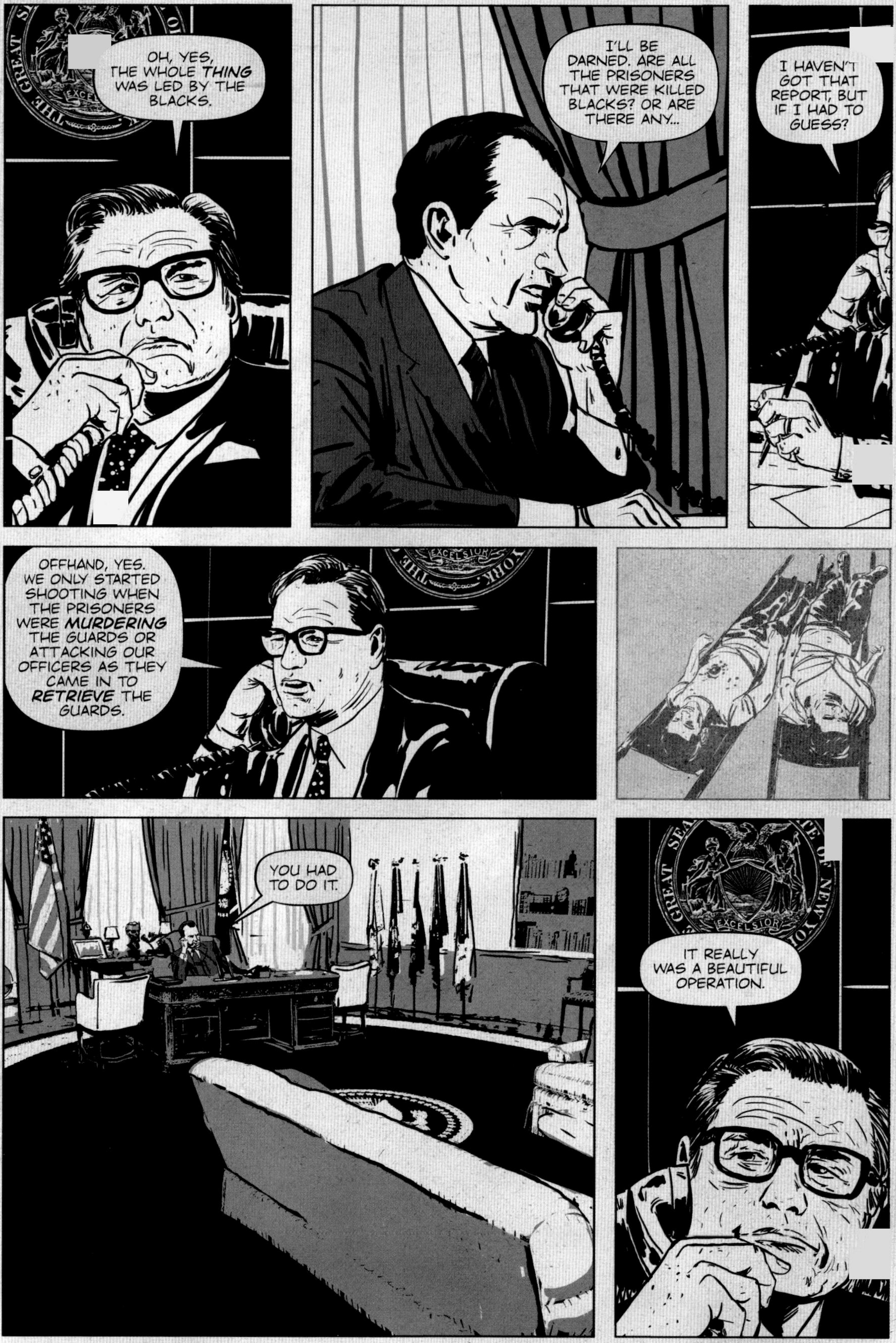
OH, YES, THE WHOLE THING WAS LED BY THE BLACKS.
I'LL BE DARNED. ARE ALL THE PRISONERS THAT WERE KILLED BLACKS? OR ARE THERE ANY...
I HAVEN'T GOT THAT REPORT, BUT IF I HAD TO GUESS?
OFFHAND, YES. WE ONLY STARTED SHOOTING WHEN THE PRISONERS WERE MURDERING THE GUARDS OR ATTACKING OUR OFFICERS AS THEY CAME IN TO RETRIEVE THE GUARDS.
YOU HAD TO DO IT.
IT REALLY WAS A BEAUTIFUL OPERATION.

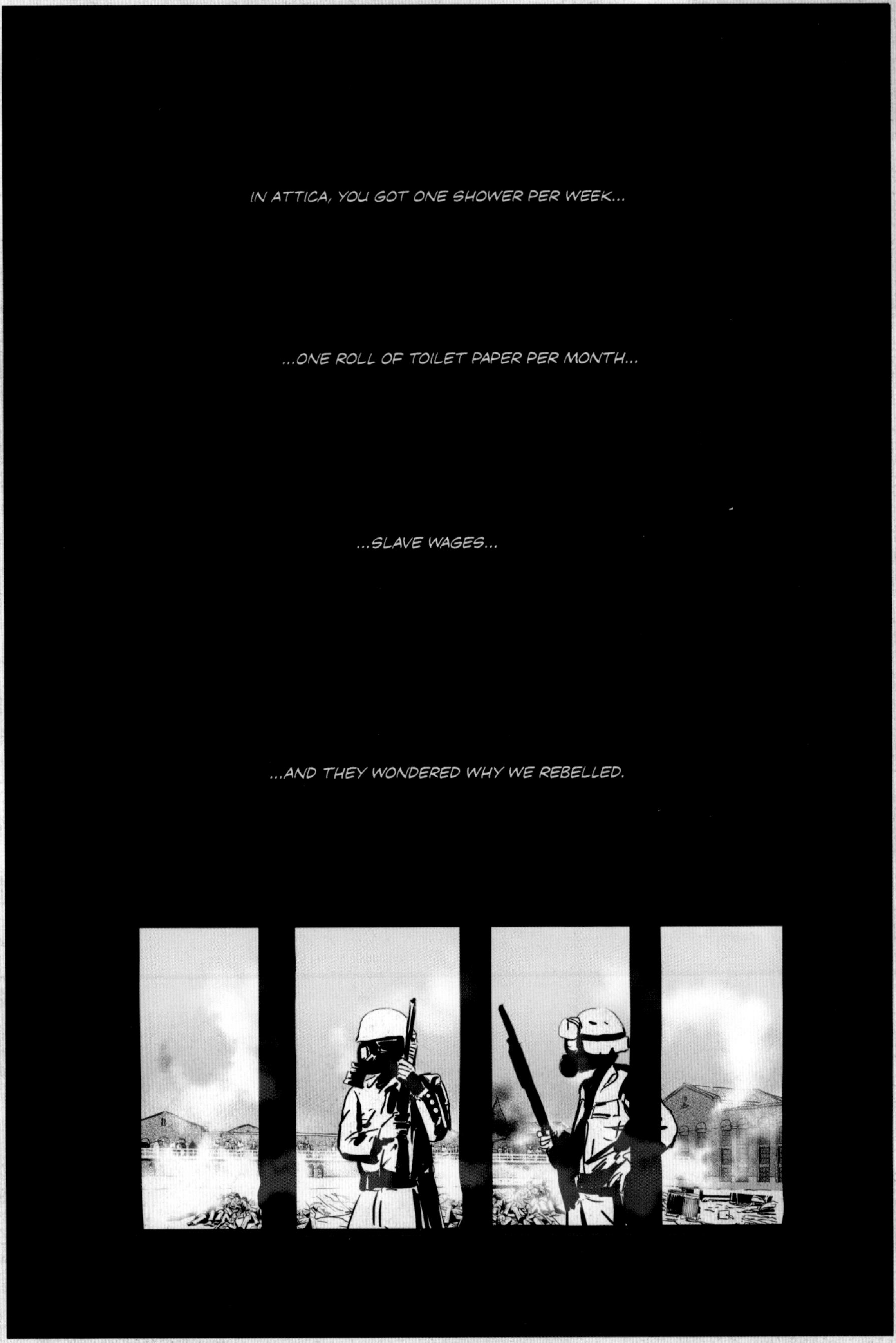
IN ATTICA, YOU GOT ONE SHOWER PER WEEK...
...ONE ROLL OF TOILET PAPER PER MONTH...
...SLAVE WAGES...
...AND THEY WONDERED WHY WE REBELLED.

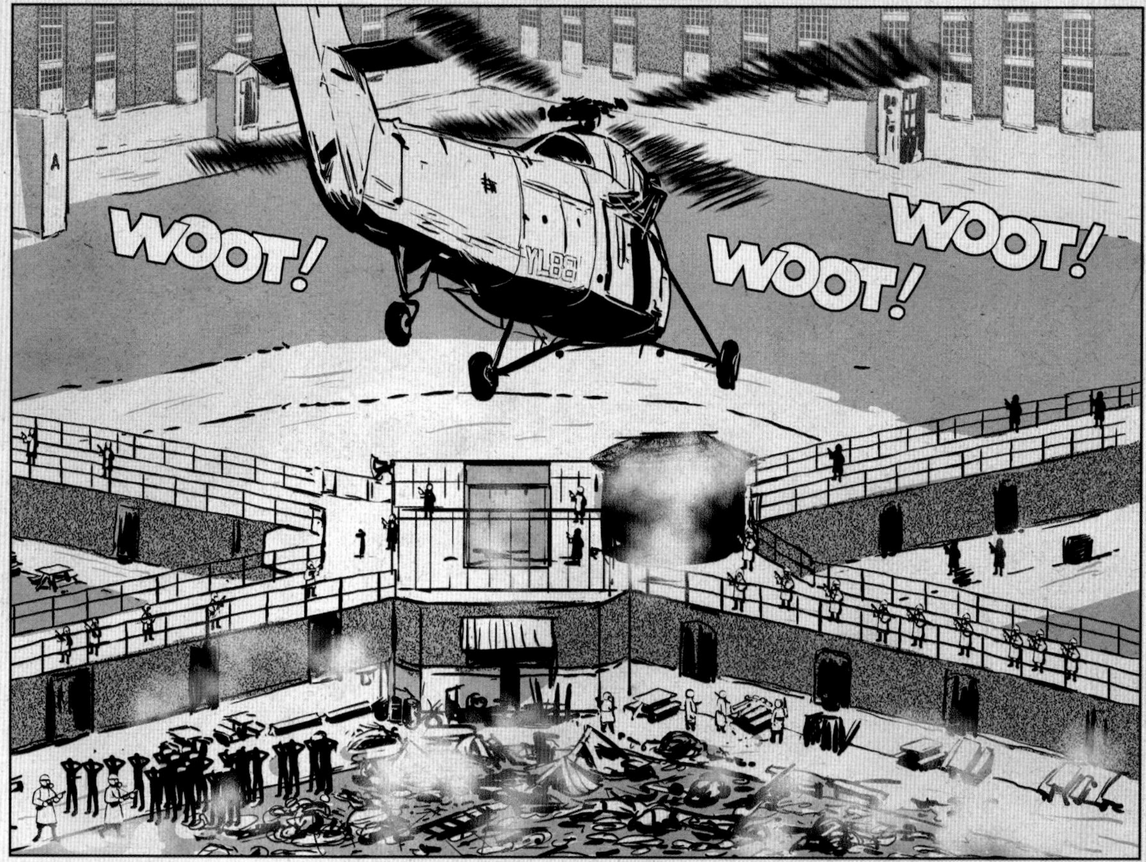
WOOT!
WOOT!
WOOT!

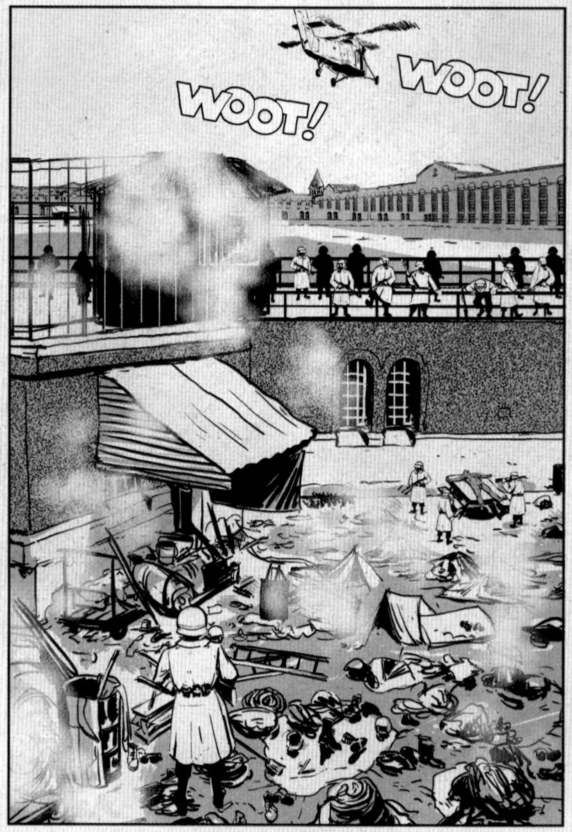
WOOT!
WOOT!

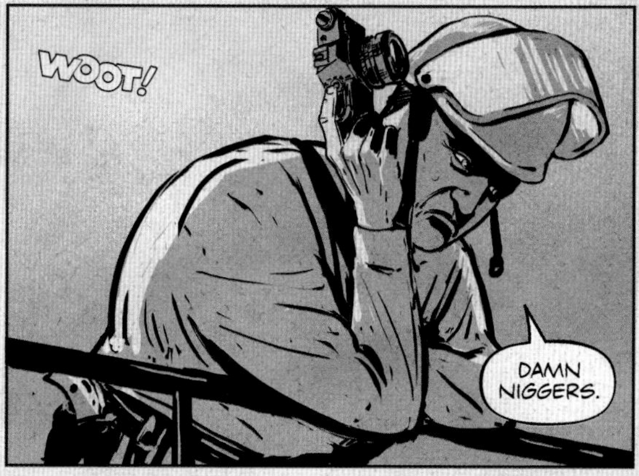
WOOT!
DAMN NIGGERS.

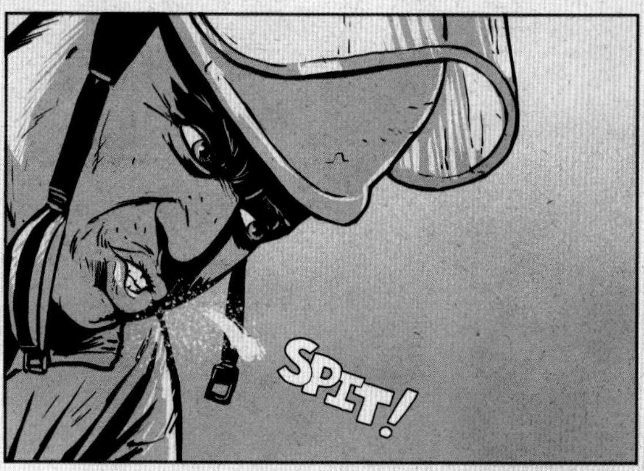
SPIT!

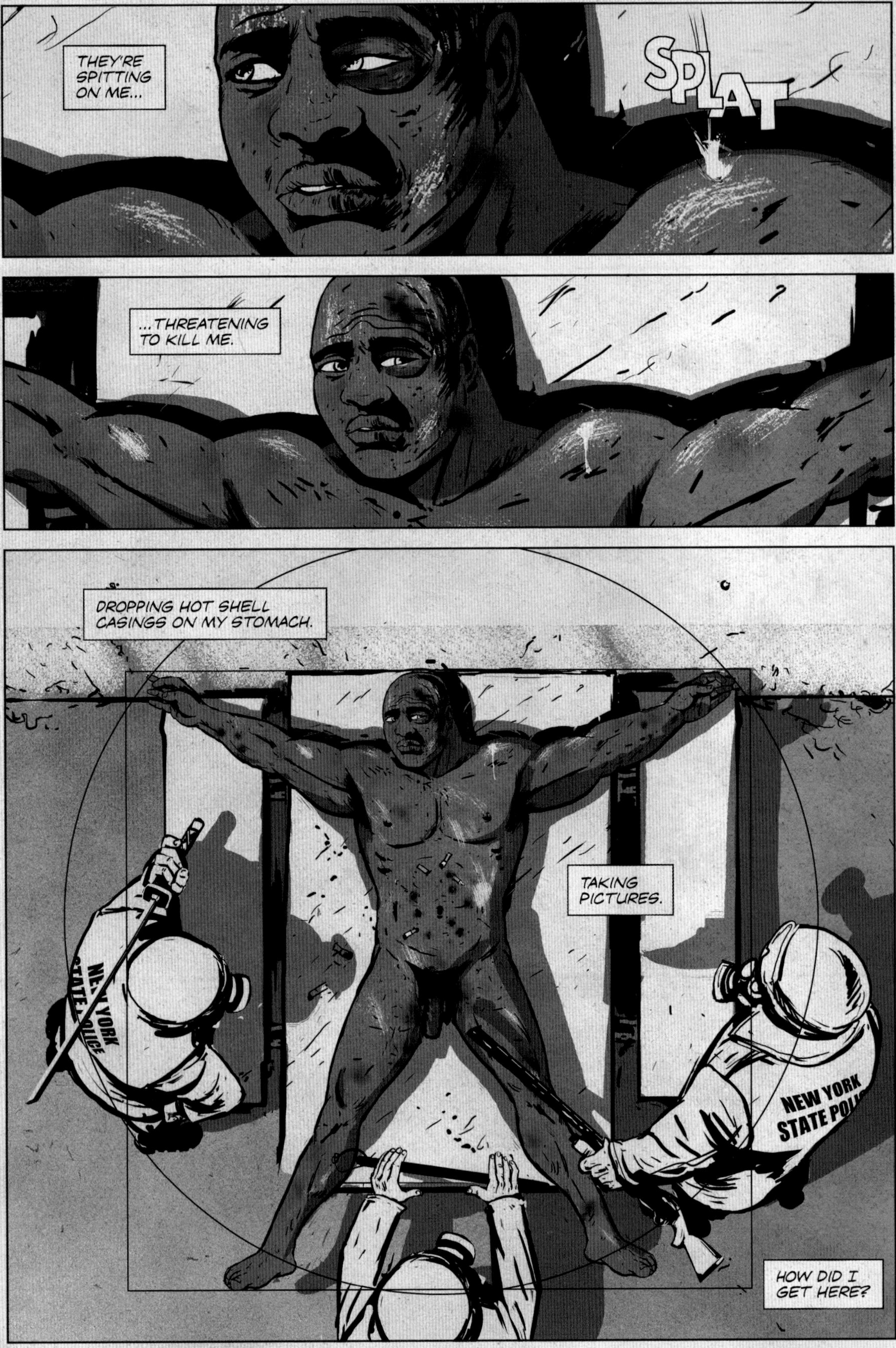
THEY'RE SPITTING ON ME...
SPLAT
...THREATENING TO KILL ME.
DROPPING HOT SHELL CASINGS ON MY STOMACH.
TAKING PICTURES.
NEW YORK STATE POLICE
NEW YORK STATE POLI
HOW DID I GET HERE?

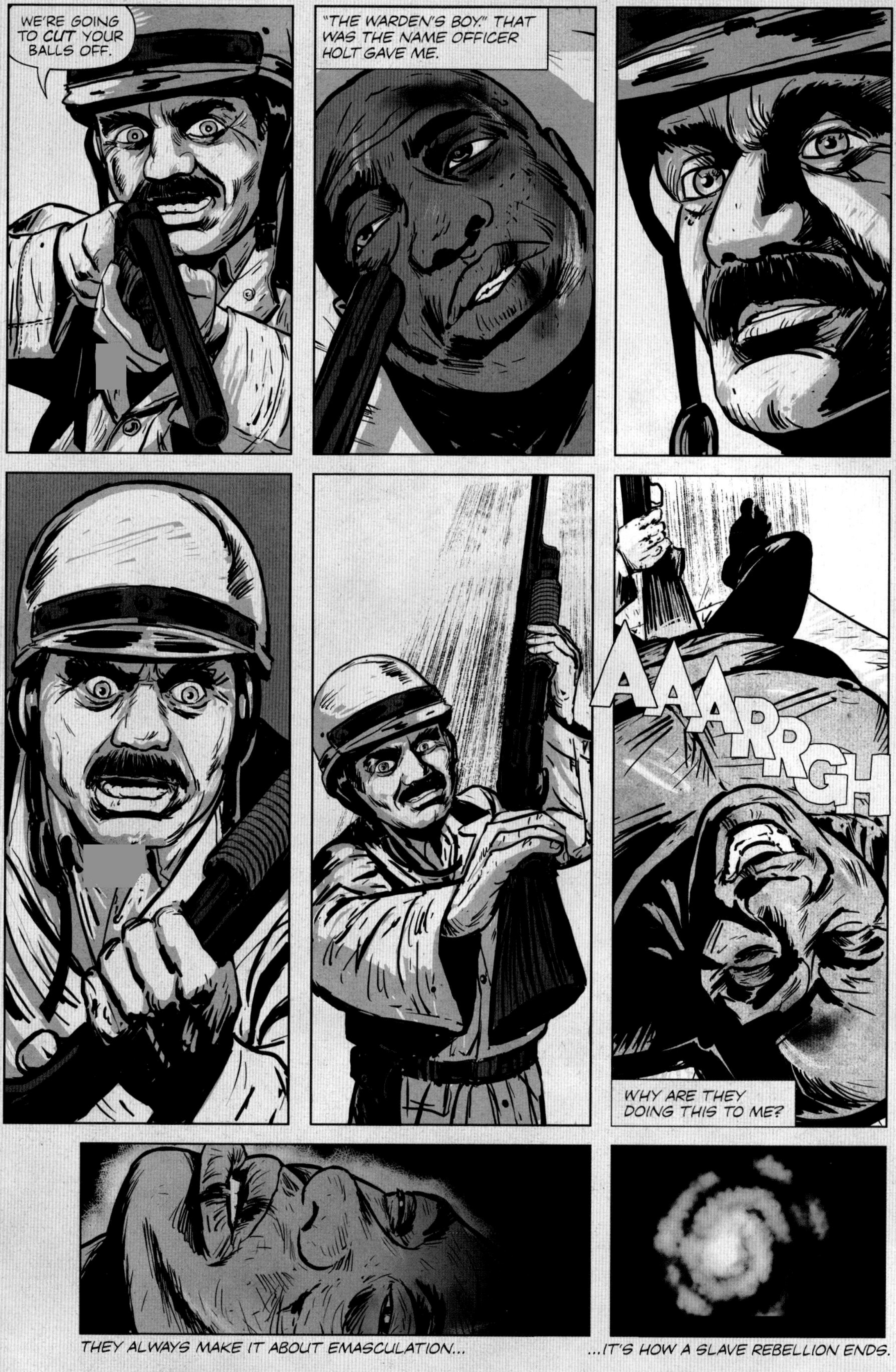
WE'RE GOING TO CUT YOUR BALLS OFF.
"THE WARDEN'S BOY." THAT WAS THE NAME OFFICER HOLT GAVE ME.
AAAARRGH
WHY ARE THEY DOING THIS TO ME?
THEY ALWAYS MAKE IT ABOUT EMASCULATION...
...IT'S HOW A SLAVE REBELLION ENDS.

1997

LEGAL ASSISTANT JOEY LEWIS AND I REVISIT THE PAST.

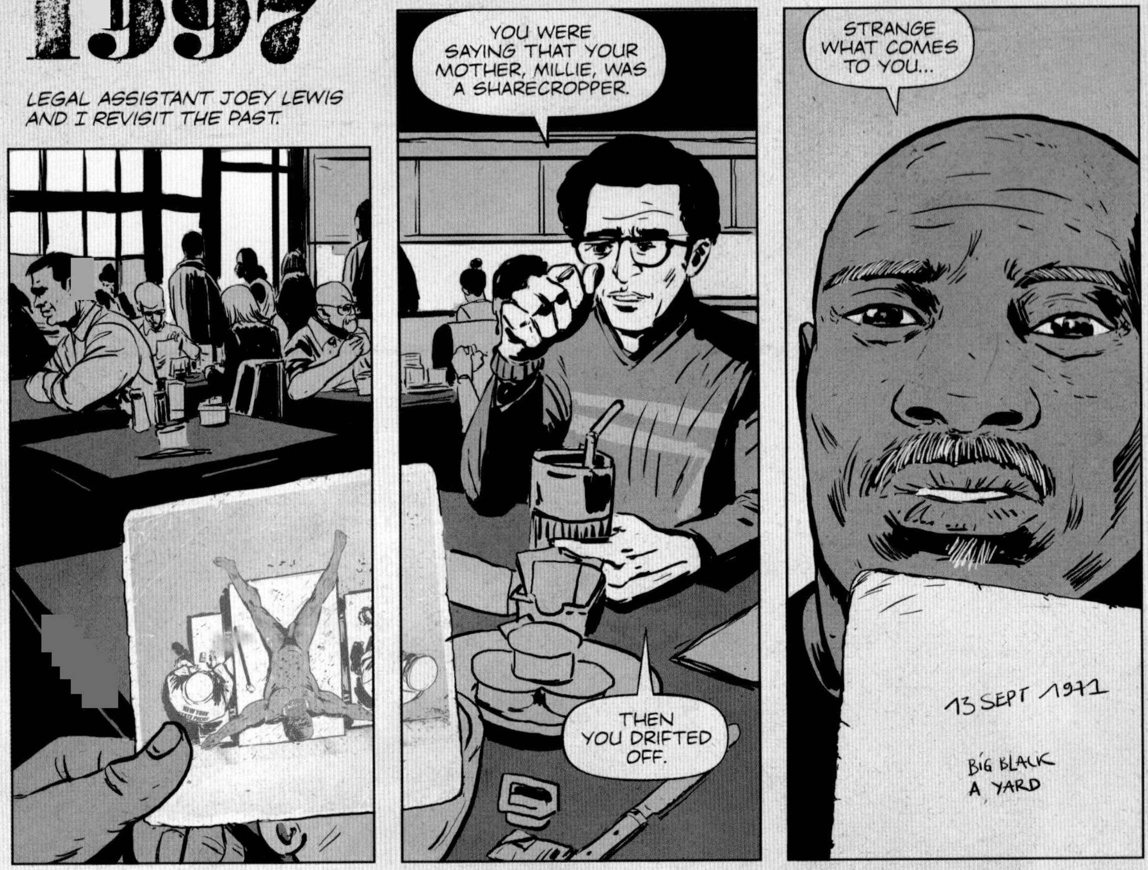
YOU WERE SAYING THAT YOUR MOTHER, MILLIE, WAS A SHARECROPPER.
THEN YOU DRIFTED OFF.
STRANGE WHAT COMES TO YOU...
13 SEPT 1971
BIG BLACK
A YARD

1933

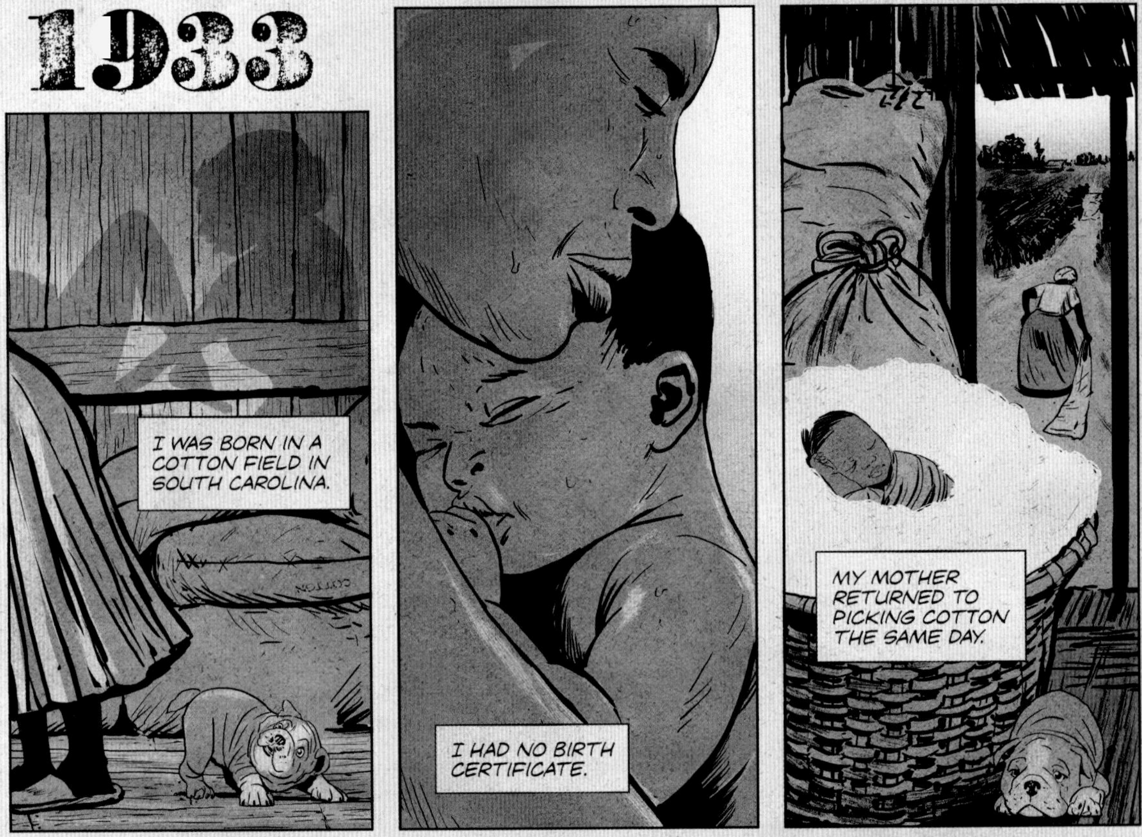
I WAS BORN IN A COTTON FIELD IN SOUTH CAROLINA.
I HAD NO BIRTH CERTIFICATE.
MY MOTHER RETURNED TO PICKING COTTON THE SAME DAY.

1938

WHEN I WAS FIVE YEARS OLD, MY MOTHER PUT ME INTO THE FAMILY WAGON FOR THE MOVE TO NEW YORK CITY.

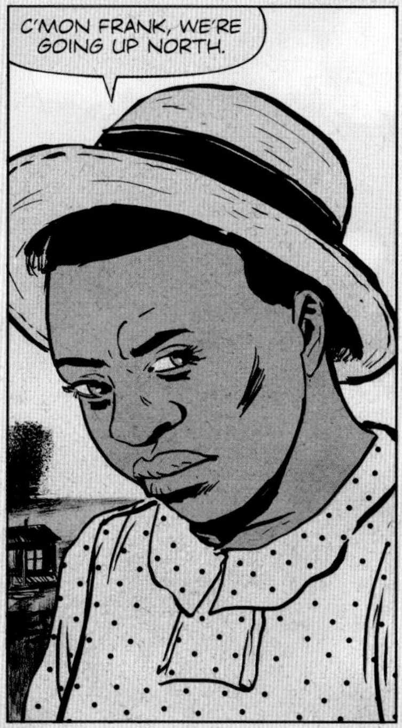
C'MON FRANK, WE'RE GOING UP NORTH.

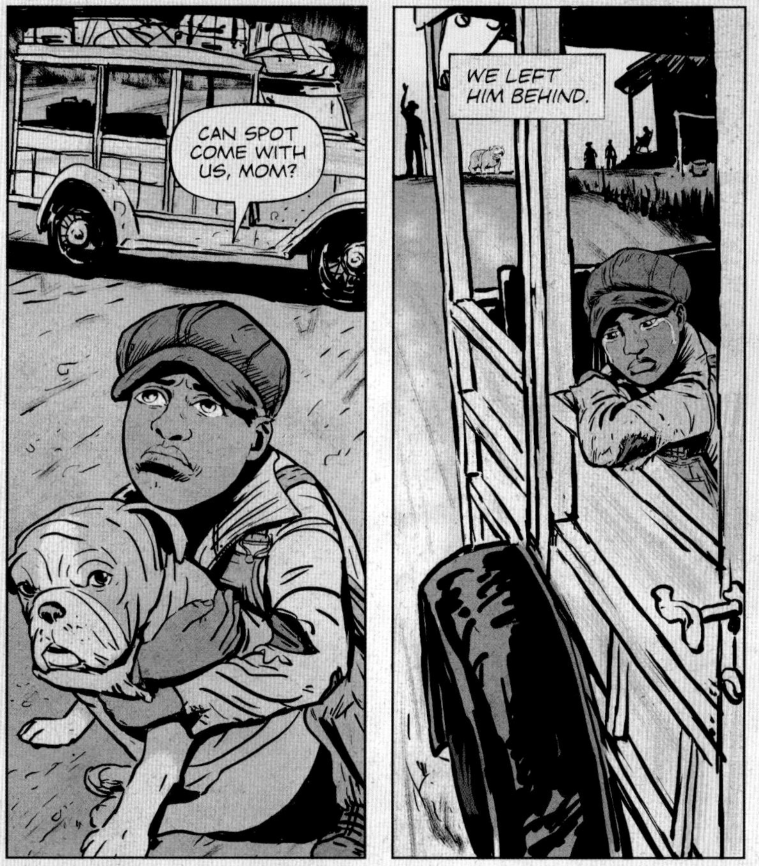
CAN SPOT COME WITH US, MOM?
WE LEFT HIM BEHIND.

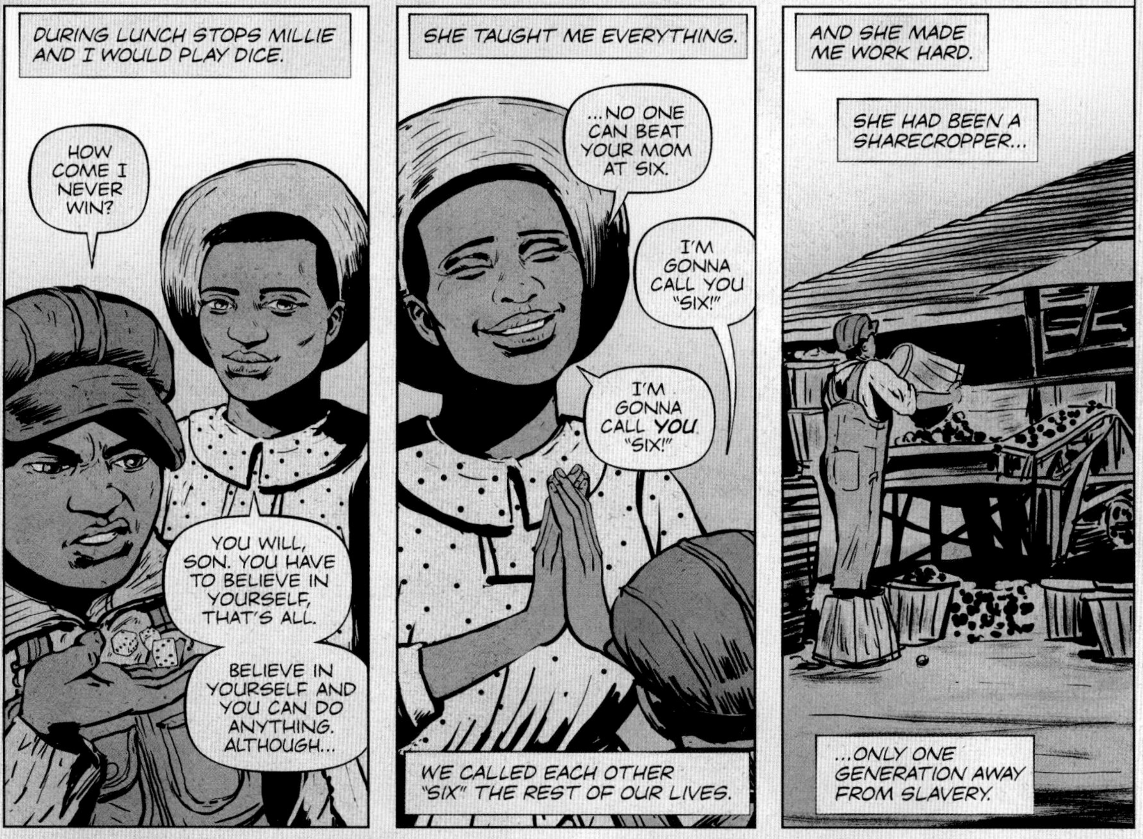
DURING LUNCH STOPS MILLIE AND I WOULD PLAY DICE.
HOW COME I NEVER WIN?
YOU WILL, SON. YOU HAVE TO BELIEVE IN YOURSELF, THAT'S ALL.
BELIEVE IN YOURSELF AND YOU CAN DO ANYTHING. ALTHOUGH...
SHE TAUGHT ME EVERYTHING.
...NO ONE CAN BEAT YOUR MOM AT SIX.
I'M GONNA CALL YOU "SIX!"
I'M GONNA CALL **YOU** "SIX!"
WE CALLED EACH OTHER "SIX" THE REST OF OUR LIVES.
AND SHE MADE ME WORK HARD.
SHE HAD BEEN A SHARECROPPER...
...ONLY ONE GENERATION AWAY FROM SLAVERY.

1950

AS A TEENAGER I WAS A PHYSICAL SPECIMEN, THE LARGEST GUY ON THE FIELD, AND I EXCELLED AT FOOTBALL. MY TEAMMATES HELD CLOSE TO ME.

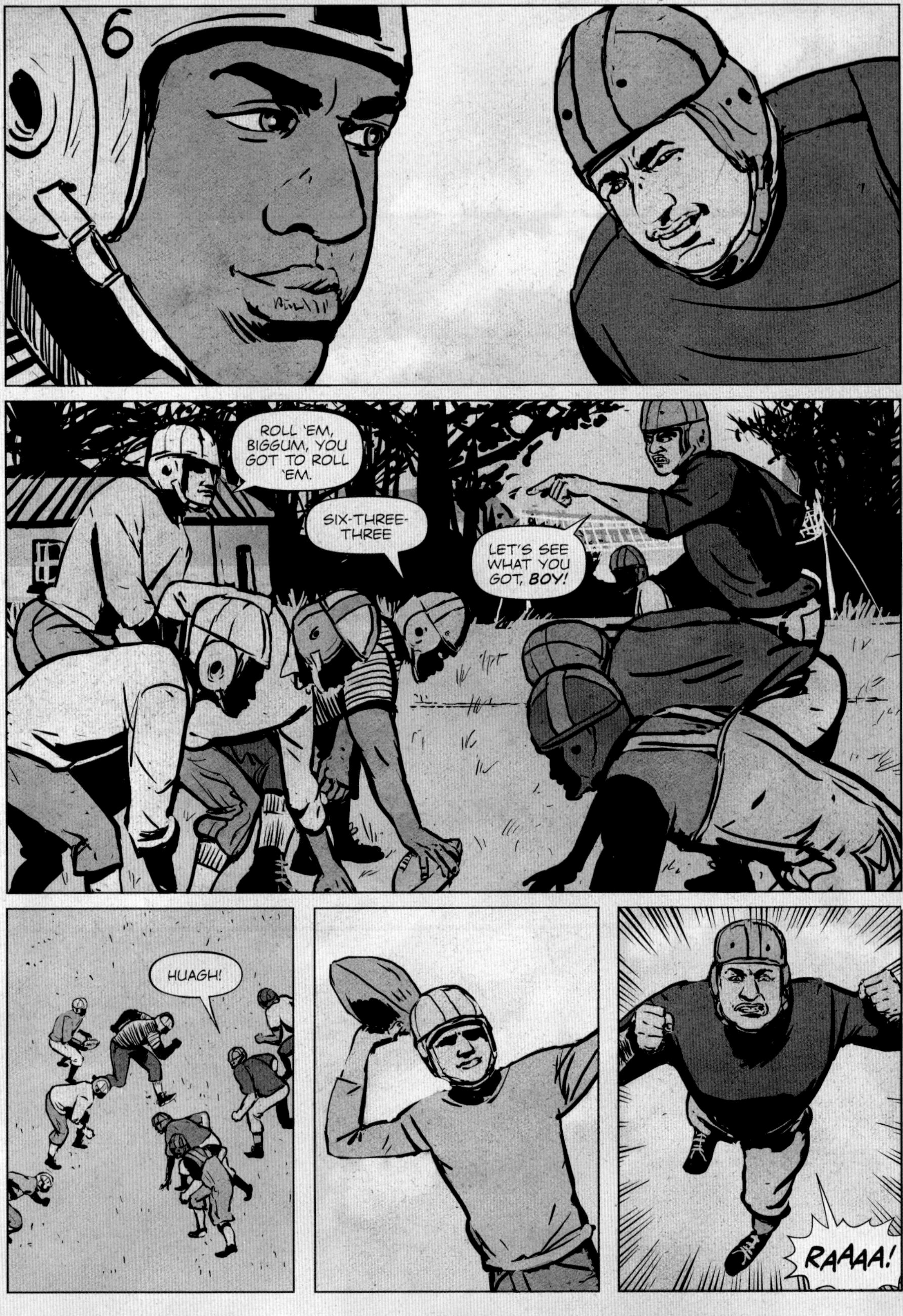

6
ROLL 'EM, BIGGUM, YOU GOT TO ROLL 'EM.
SIX-THREE-THREE
LET'S SEE WHAT YOU GOT, *BOY!*
HUAGH!
RAAAA!

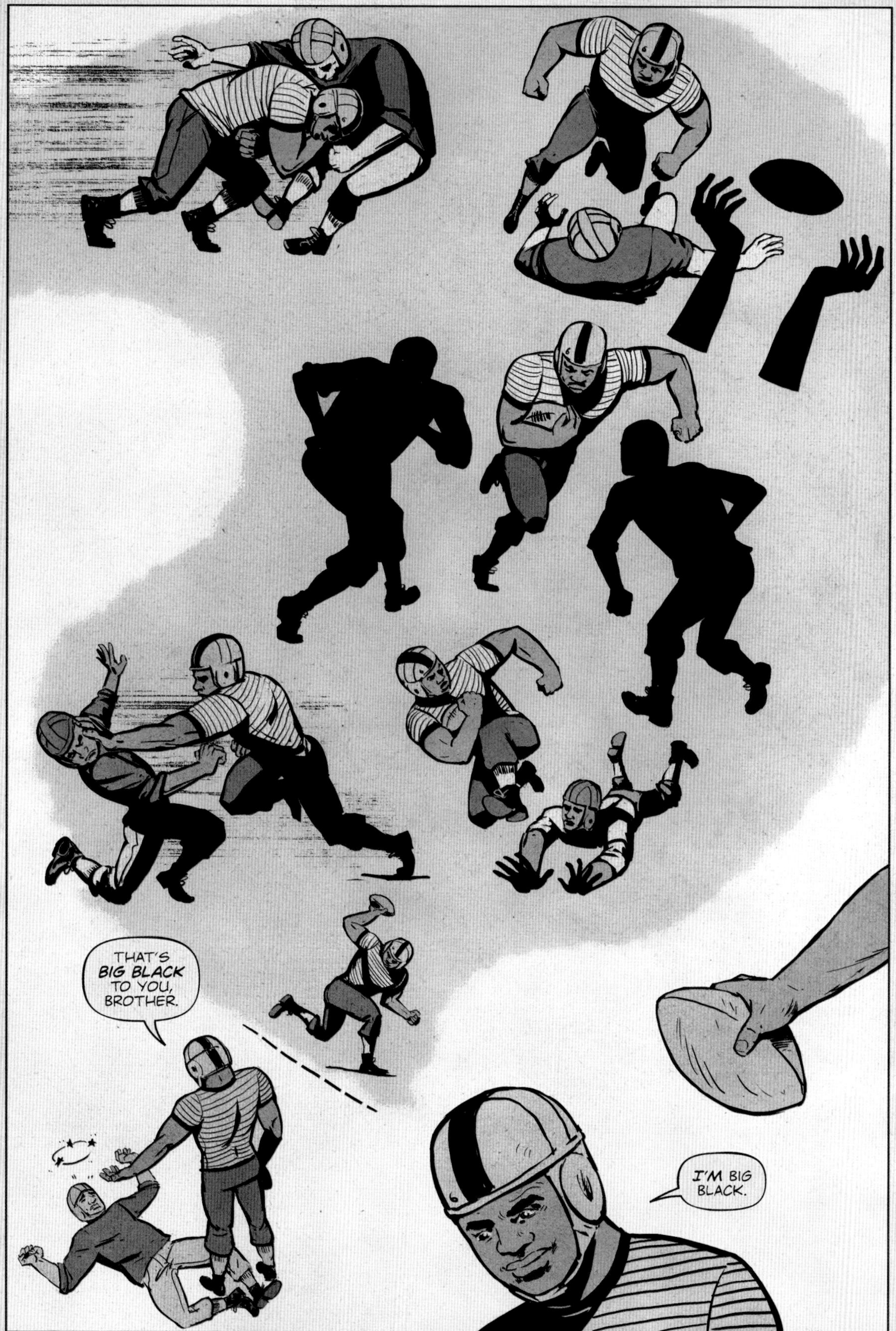
THAT'S BIG BLACK TO YOU, BROTHER.
I'M BIG BLACK.

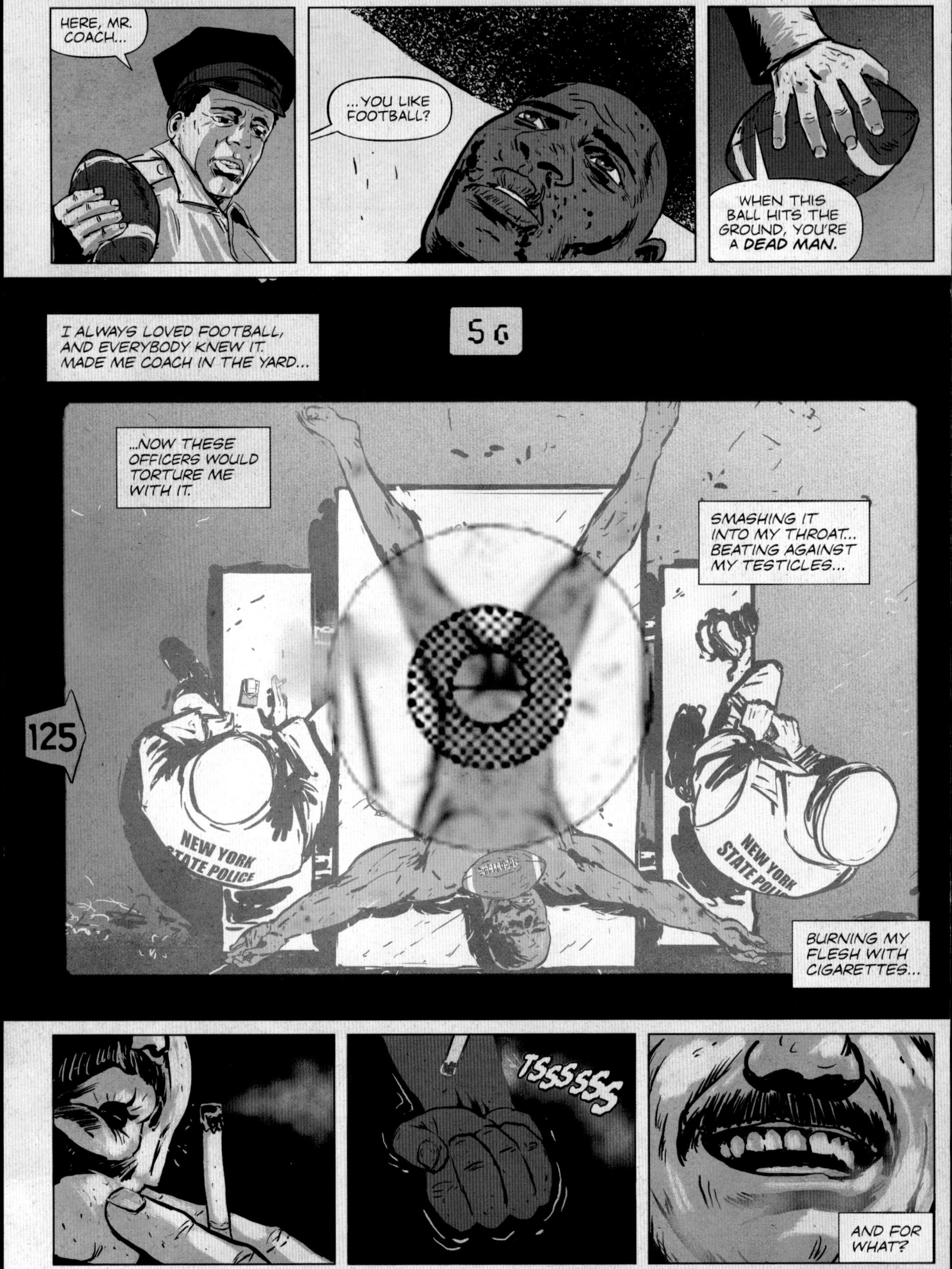
HERE, MR. COACH...
...YOU LIKE FOOTBALL?
WHEN THIS BALL HITS THE GROUND, YOU'RE A DEAD MAN.
I ALWAYS LOVED FOOTBALL, AND EVERYBODY KNEW IT. MADE ME COACH IN THE YARD...
50
...NOW THESE OFFICERS WOULD TORTURE ME WITH IT.
SMASHING IT INTO MY THROAT... BEATING AGAINST MY TESTICLES...
125
NEW YORK STATE POLICE
NEW YORK STATE POLI
BURNING MY FLESH WITH CIGARETTES...
TSSSSSS
AND FOR WHAT?

1965

MY FRIEND IRON HORSE AND I MADE A PLAN.

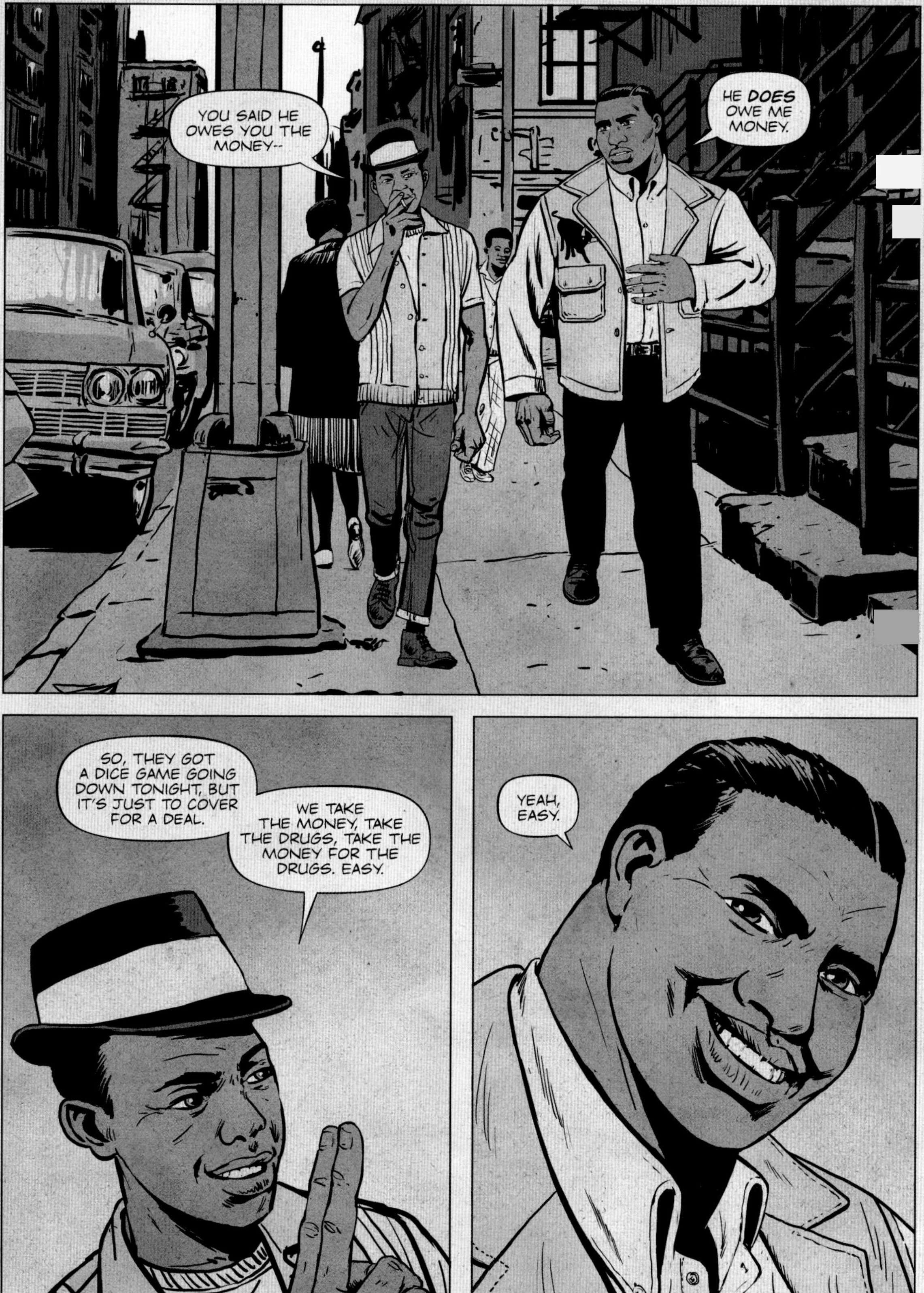

YOU SAID HE OWES YOU THE MONEY--
HE **DOES** OWE ME MONEY.
SO, THEY GOT A DICE GAME GOING DOWN TONIGHT, BUT IT'S JUST TO COVER FOR A DEAL.
WE TAKE THE MONEY, TAKE THE DRUGS, TAKE THE MONEY FOR THE DRUGS. EASY.
YEAH, EASY.

SO ME AND IRON HORSE STUCK UP THE DICE GAME.

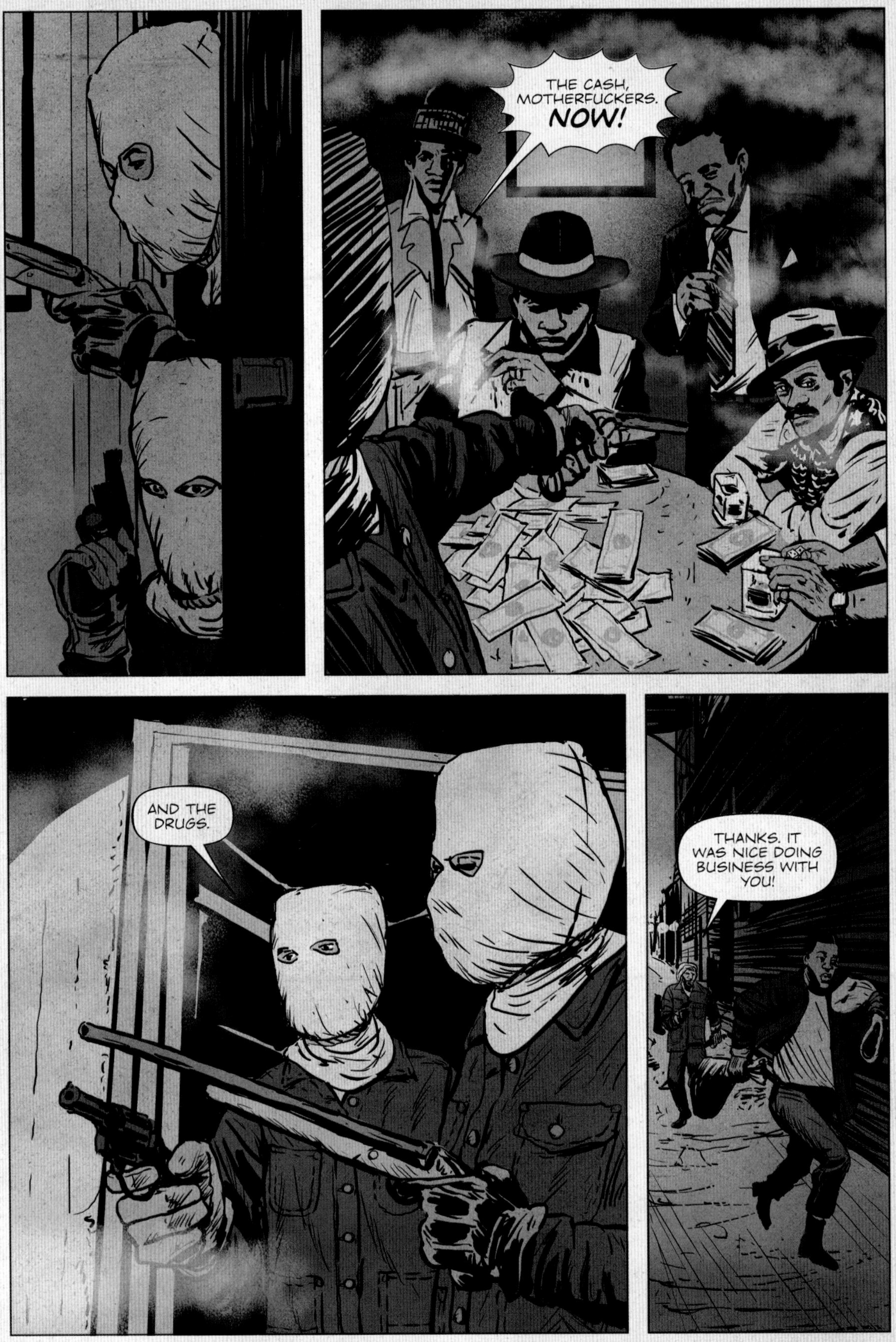
THE CASH, MOTHERFUCKERS. NOW!
AND THE DRUGS.
THANKS. IT WAS NICE DOING BUSINESS WITH YOU!

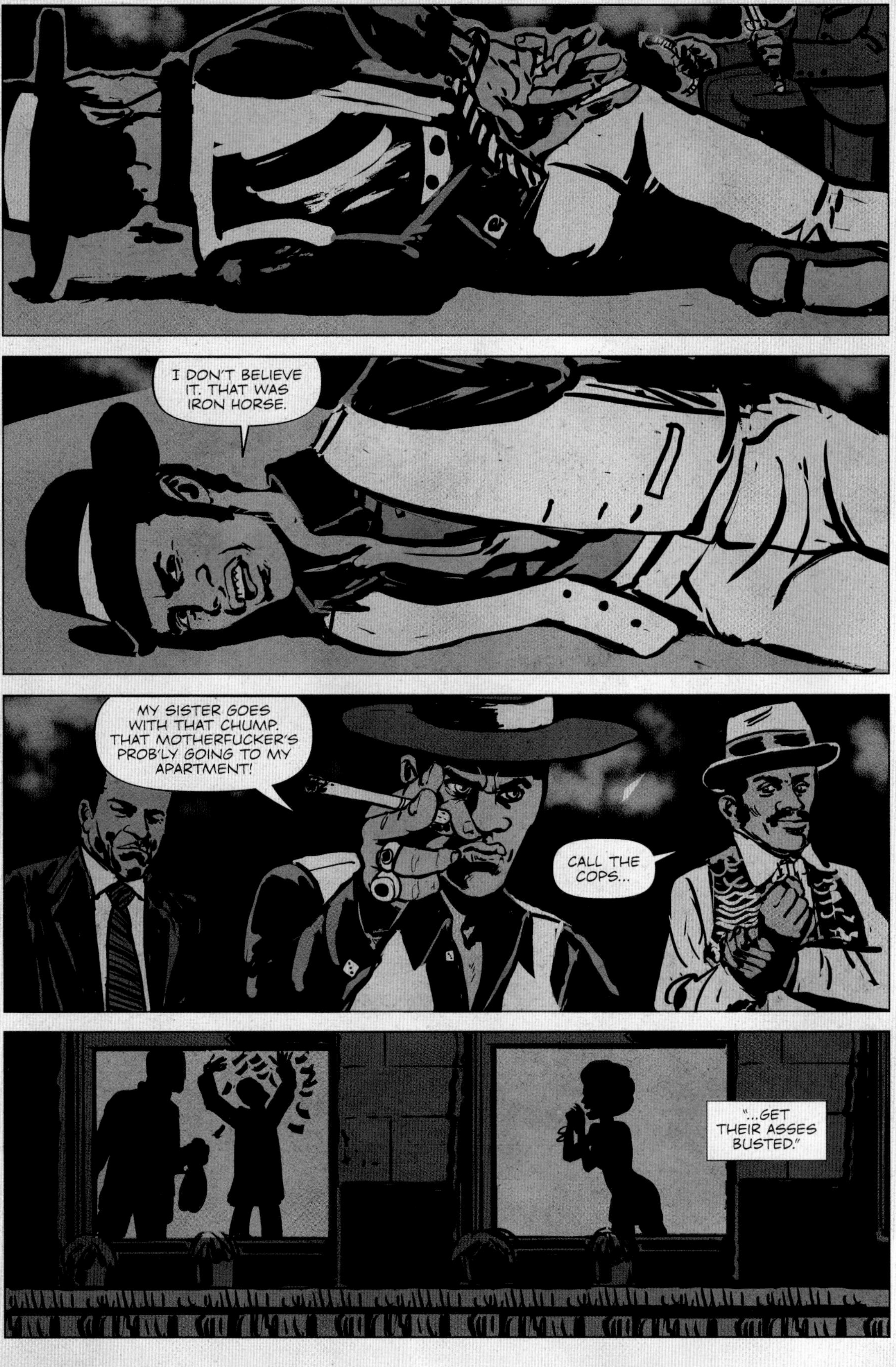
I DON'T BELIEVE IT. THAT WAS IRON HORSE.
MY SISTER GOES WITH THAT CHUMP. THAT MOTHERFUCKER'S PROB'LY GOING TO MY APARTMENT!
CALL THE COPS...
"...GET THEIR ASSES BUSTED."

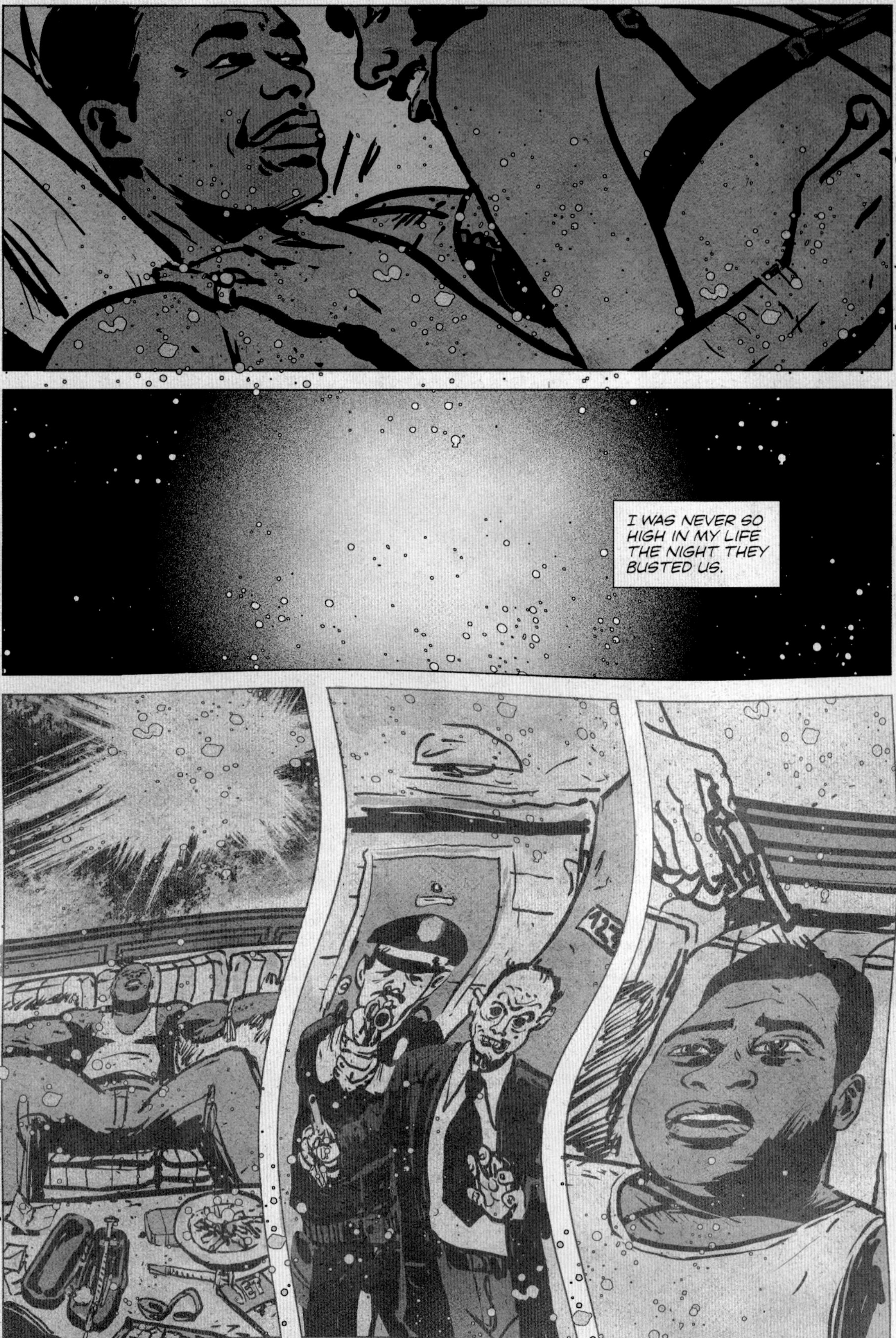
I WAS NEVER SO HIGH IN MY LIFE THE NIGHT THEY BUSTED US.

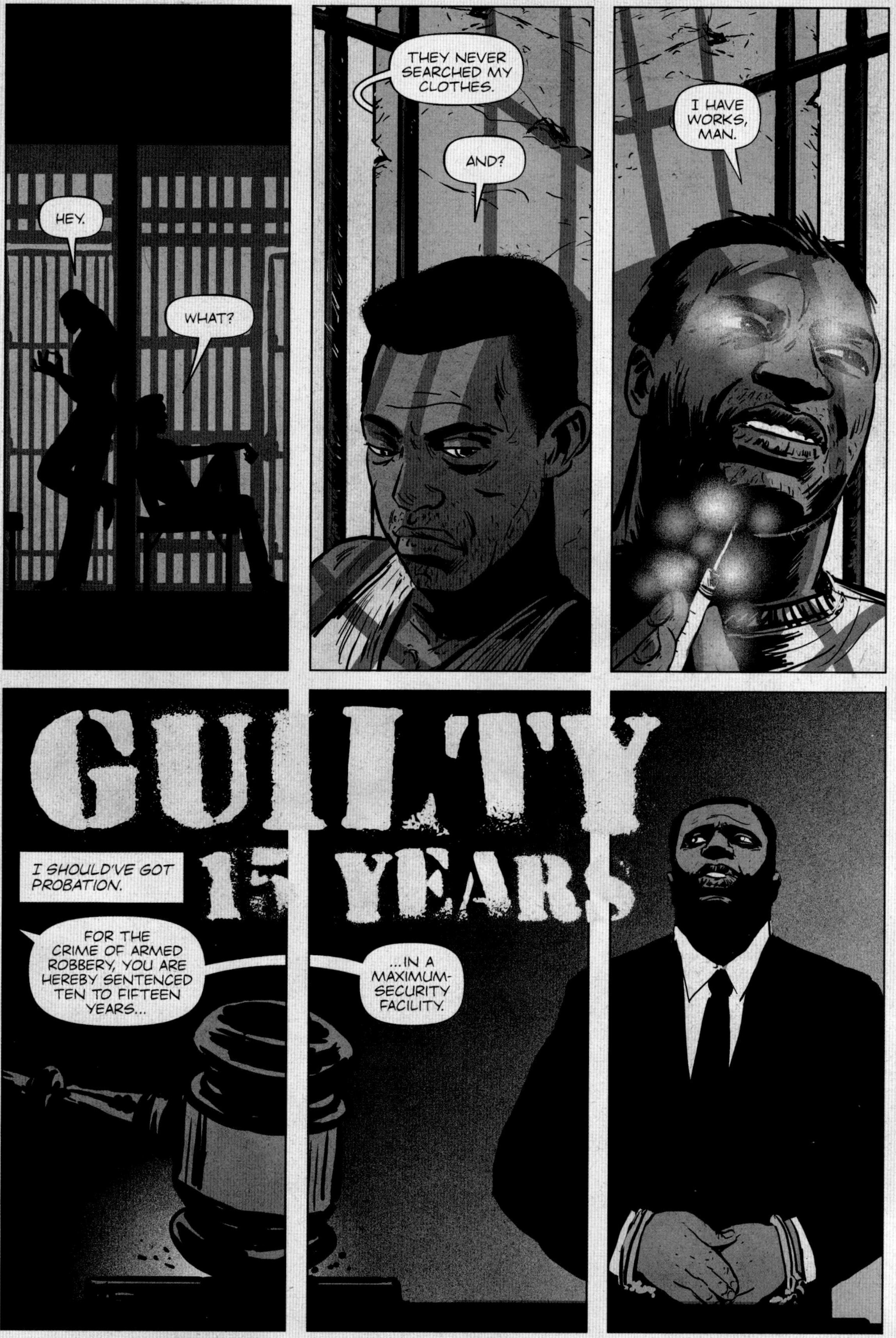
HEY.
WHAT?
THEY NEVER SEARCHED MY CLOTHES.
AND?
I HAVE WORKS, MAN.
GUILTY
15 YEARS
I SHOULD'VE GOT PROBATION.
FOR THE CRIME OF ARMED ROBBERY, YOU ARE HEREBY SENTENCED TEN TO FIFTEEN YEARS...
...IN A MAXIMUM-SECURITY FACILITY.

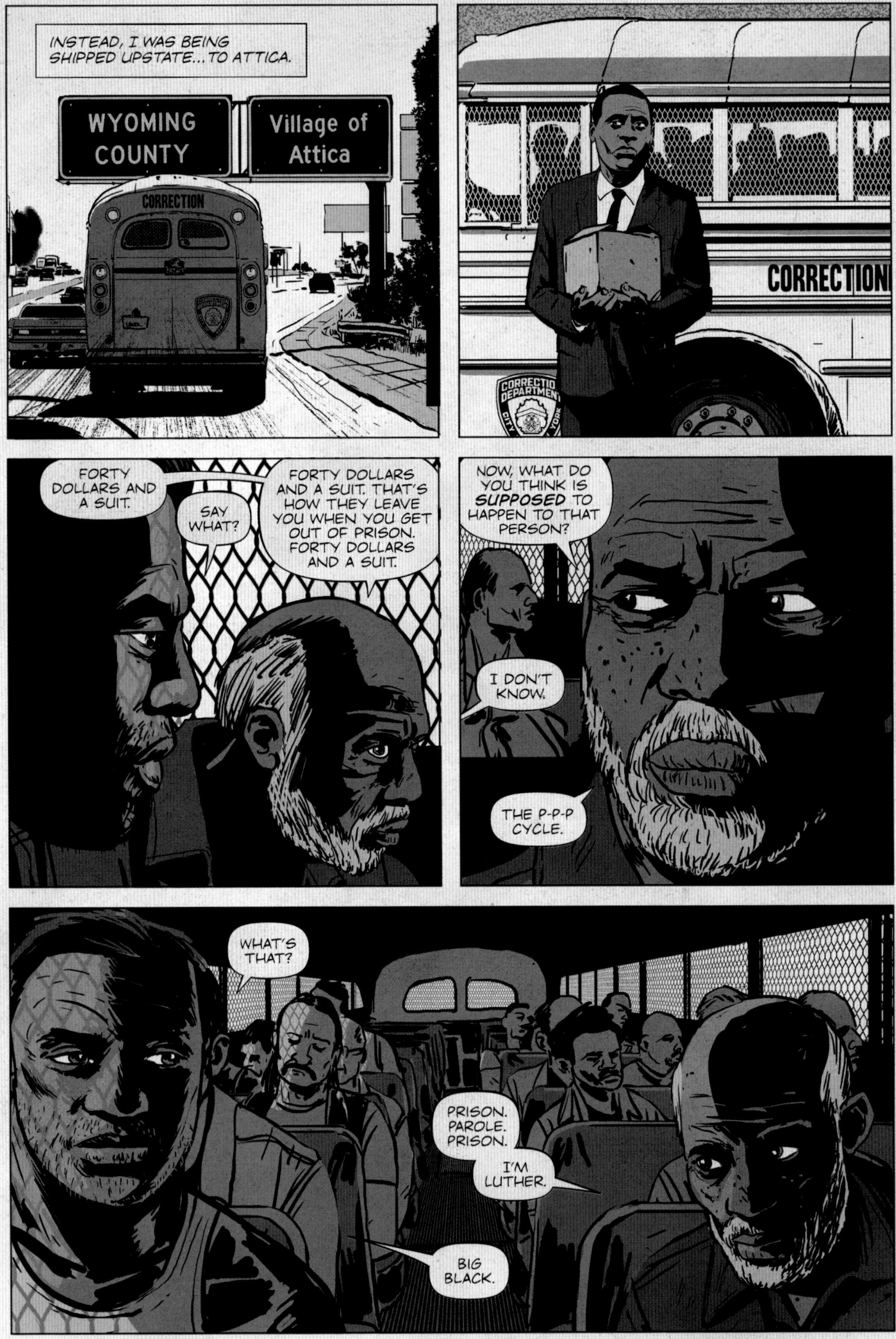
INSTEAD, I WAS BEING SHIPPED UPSTATE... TO ATTICA.
WYOMING COUNTY
Village of Attica
CORRECTION
CORRECTION
FORTY DOLLARS AND A SUIT.
SAY WHAT?
FORTY DOLLARS AND A SUIT. THAT'S HOW THEY LEAVE YOU WHEN YOU GET OUT OF PRISON. FORTY DOLLARS AND A SUIT.
NOW, WHAT DO YOU THINK IS SUPPOSED TO HAPPEN TO THAT PERSON?
I DON'T KNOW.
THE P-P-P CYCLE.
WHAT'S THAT?
PRISON. PAROLE. PRISON.
I'M LUTHER.
BIG BLACK.

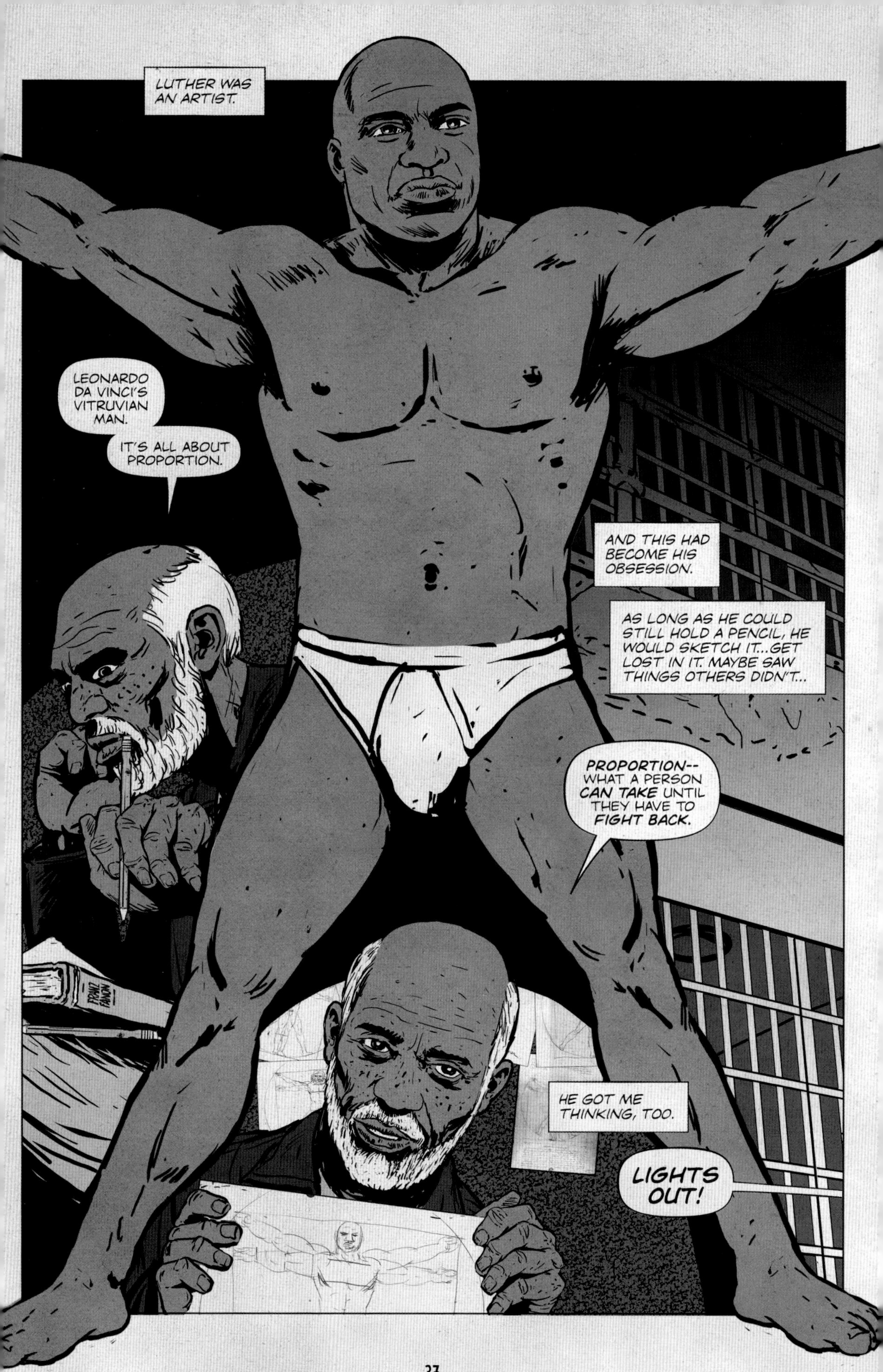
LUTHER WAS AN ARTIST.
LEONARDO DA VINCI'S VITRUVIAN MAN.
IT'S ALL ABOUT PROPORTION.
AND THIS HAD BECOME HIS OBSESSION.
AS LONG AS HE COULD STILL HOLD A PENCIL, HE WOULD SKETCH IT...GET LOST IN IT. MAYBE SAW THINGS OTHERS DIDN'T...
PROPORTION-- WHAT A PERSON CAN TAKE UNTIL THEY HAVE TO FIGHT BACK.
FRANZ FANON
HE GOT ME THINKING, TOO.
LIGHTS OUT!

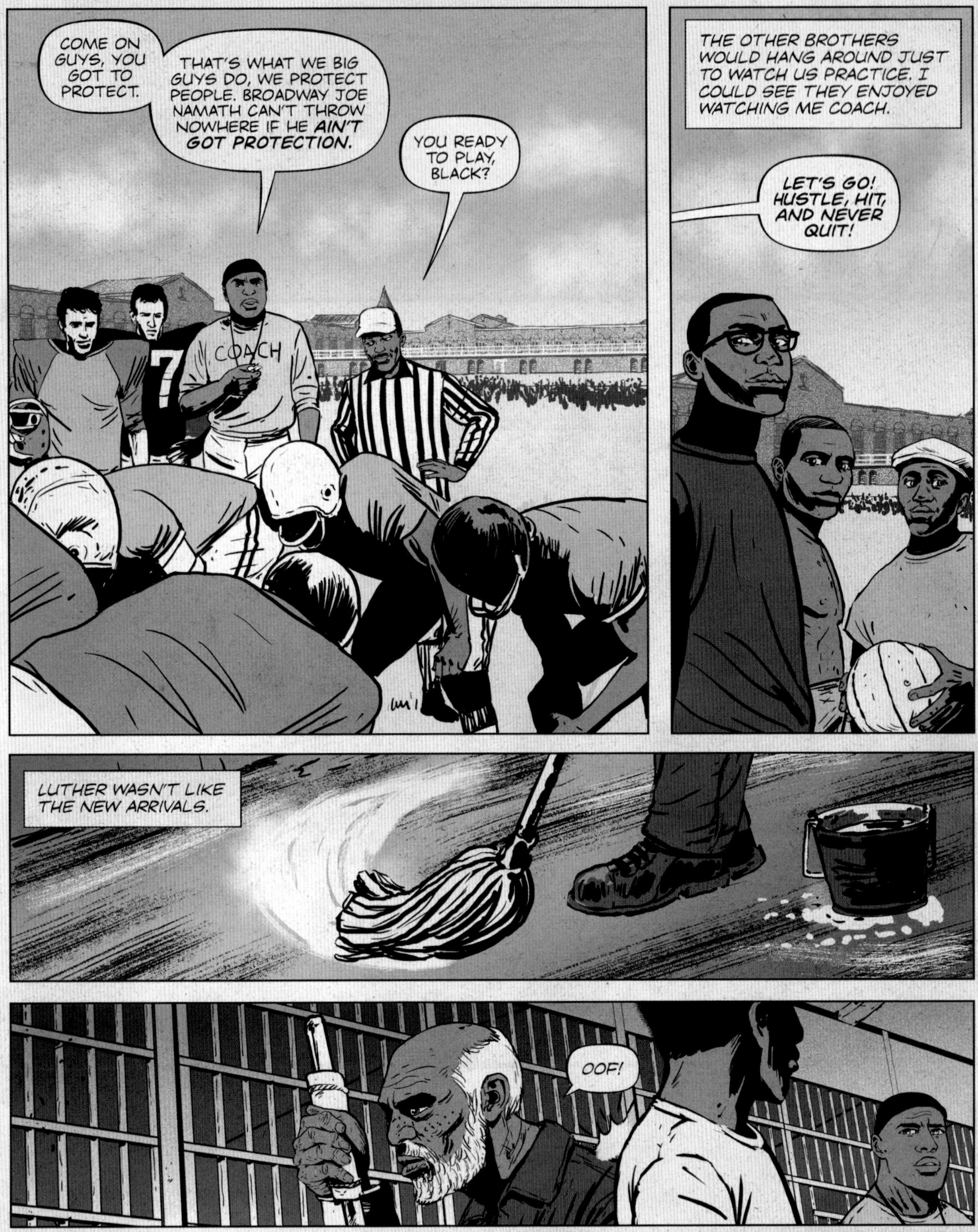
COME ON GUYS, YOU GOT TO PROTECT.
THAT'S WHAT WE BIG GUYS DO, WE PROTECT PEOPLE. BROADWAY JOE NAMATH CAN'T THROW NOWHERE IF HE AIN'T GOT PROTECTION.
YOU READY TO PLAY, BLACK?
COACH
7
THE OTHER BROTHERS WOULD HANG AROUND JUST TO WATCH US PRACTICE. I COULD SEE THEY ENJOYED WATCHING ME COACH.
LET'S GO! HUSTLE, HIT, AND NEVER QUIT!
LUTHER WASN'T LIKE THE NEW ARRIVALS.
OOF!
LAZARUS!

IT WAS AN EPITHET YOUNGER PRISONERS HURLED AT THE OLDER ONES FOR BEING TOO COMPLACENT WITH PRISON LIFE.

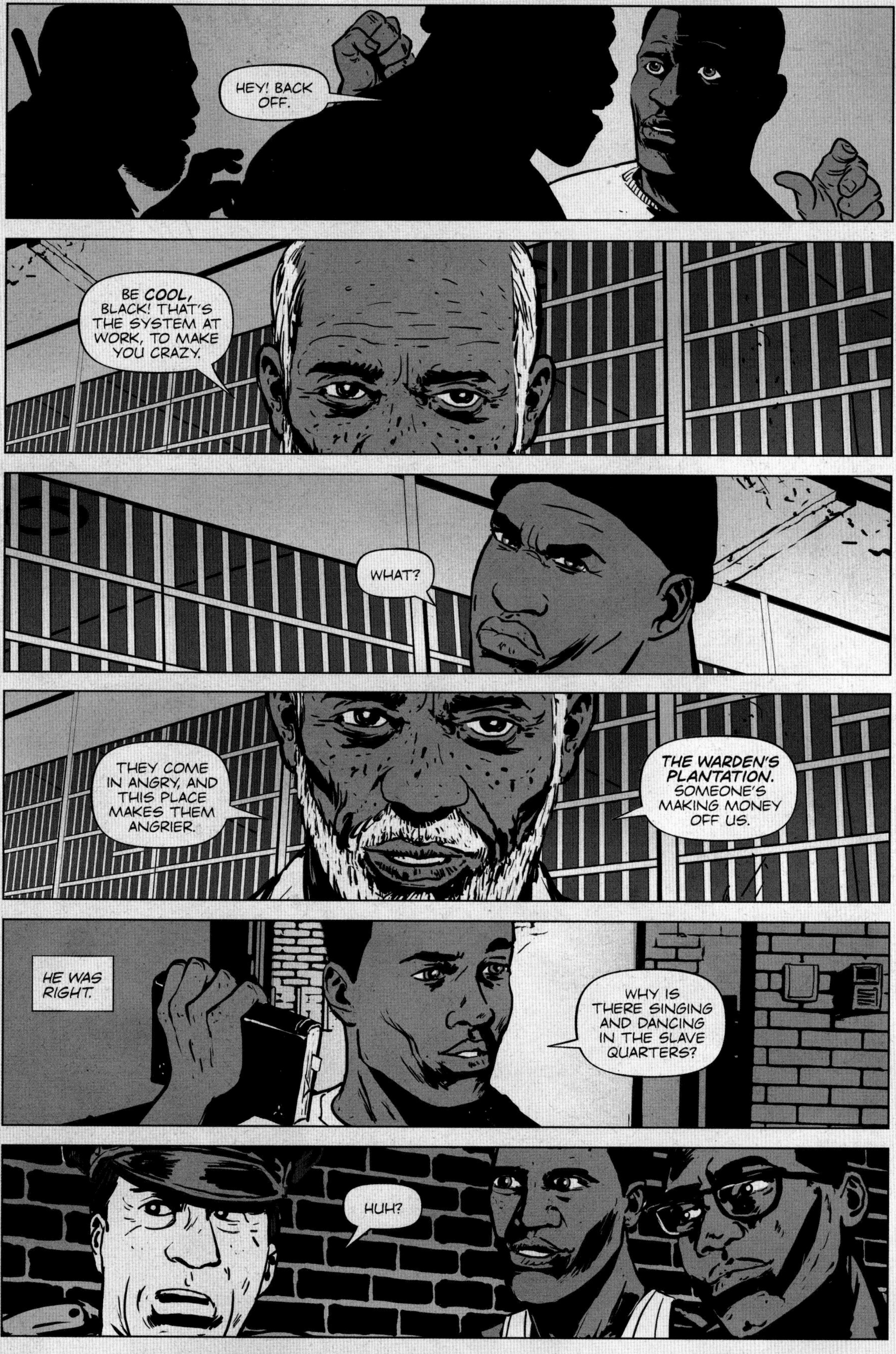
HEY! BACK OFF.
BE COOL, BLACK! THAT'S THE SYSTEM AT WORK, TO MAKE YOU CRAZY.
WHAT?
THEY COME IN ANGRY, AND THIS PLACE MAKES THEM ANGRIER.
THE WARDEN'S PLANTATION. SOMEONE'S MAKING MONEY OFF US.
HE WAS RIGHT.
WHY IS THERE SINGING AND DANCING IN THE SLAVE QUARTERS?
HUH?

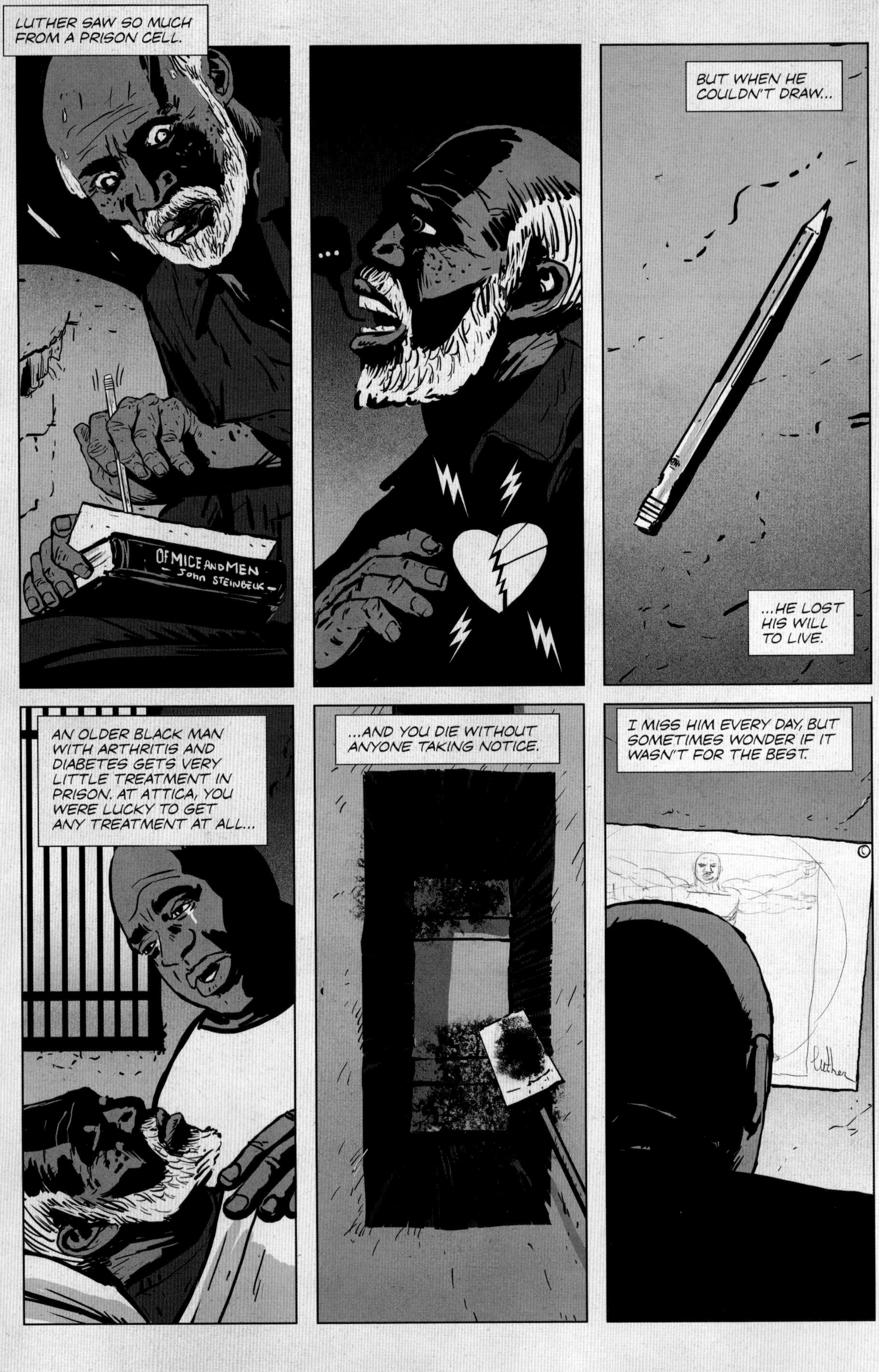
LUTHER SAW SO MUCH FROM A PRISON CELL.
OF MICE AND MEN
John STEINBECK
...
BUT WHEN HE COULDN'T DRAW...
...HE LOST HIS WILL TO LIVE.
AN OLDER BLACK MAN WITH ARTHRITIS AND DIABETES GETS VERY LITTLE TREATMENT IN PRISON. AT ATTICA, YOU WERE LUCKY TO GET ANY TREATMENT AT ALL...
...AND YOU DIE WITHOUT ANYONE TAKING NOTICE.
I MISS HIM EVERY DAY, BUT SOMETIMES WONDER IF IT WASN'T FOR THE BEST.
Luther

1997

GIGI'S RESTAURANT HAD THE BEST SOUL FOOD IN BUFFALO, AND WAS MY FAVORITE PLACE TO EAT DURING THE TRIAL.

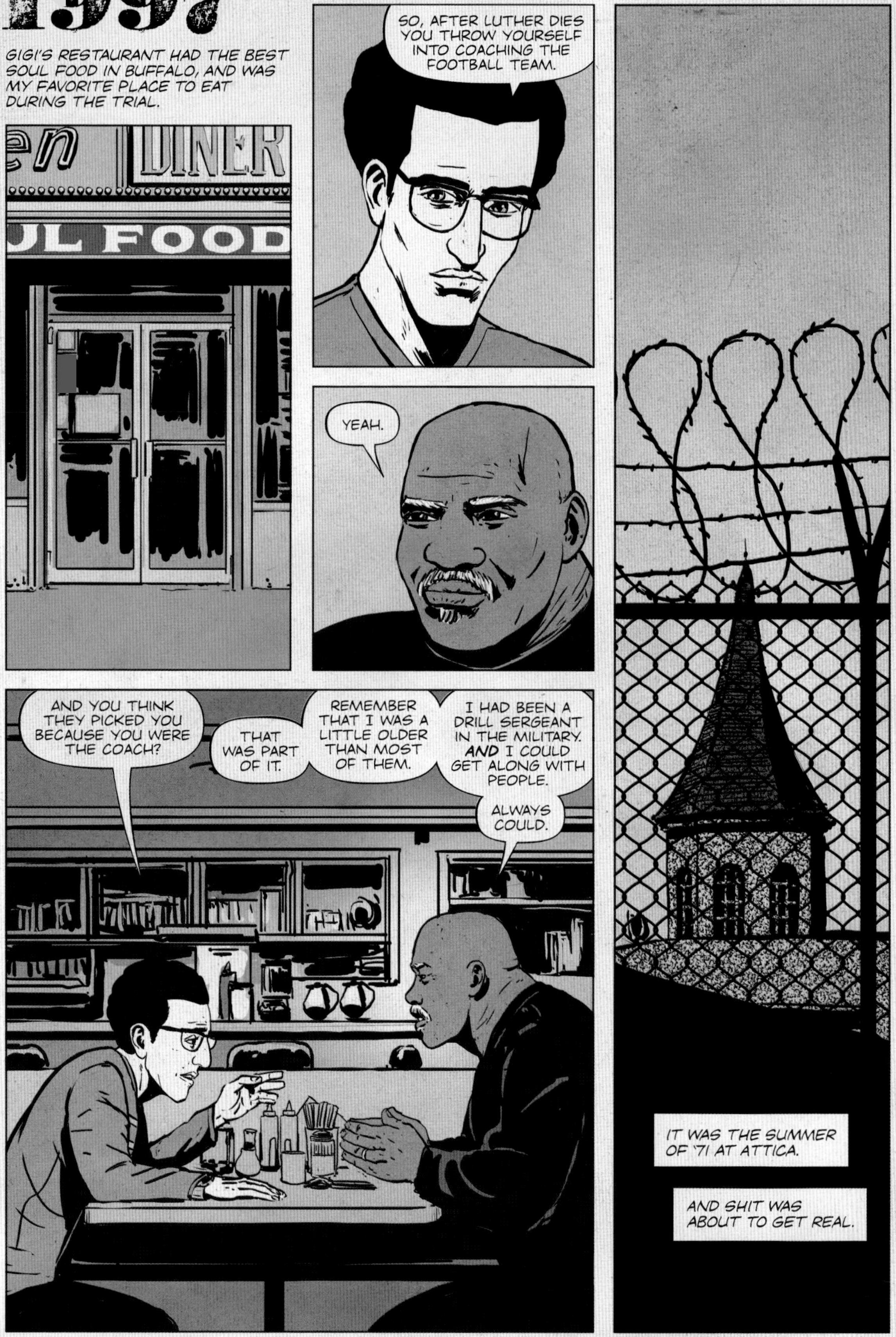

DINER
UL FOOD
SO, AFTER LUTHER DIES YOU THROW YOURSELF INTO COACHING THE FOOTBALL TEAM.
YEAH.
AND YOU THINK THEY PICKED YOU BECAUSE YOU WERE THE COACH?
THAT WAS PART OF IT.
REMEMBER THAT I WAS A LITTLE OLDER THAN MOST OF THEM.
I HAD BEEN A DRILL SERGEANT IN THE MILITARY. AND I COULD GET ALONG WITH PEOPLE.
ALWAYS COULD.
IT WAS THE SUMMER OF '71 AT ATTICA.
AND SHIT WAS ABOUT TO GET REAL.

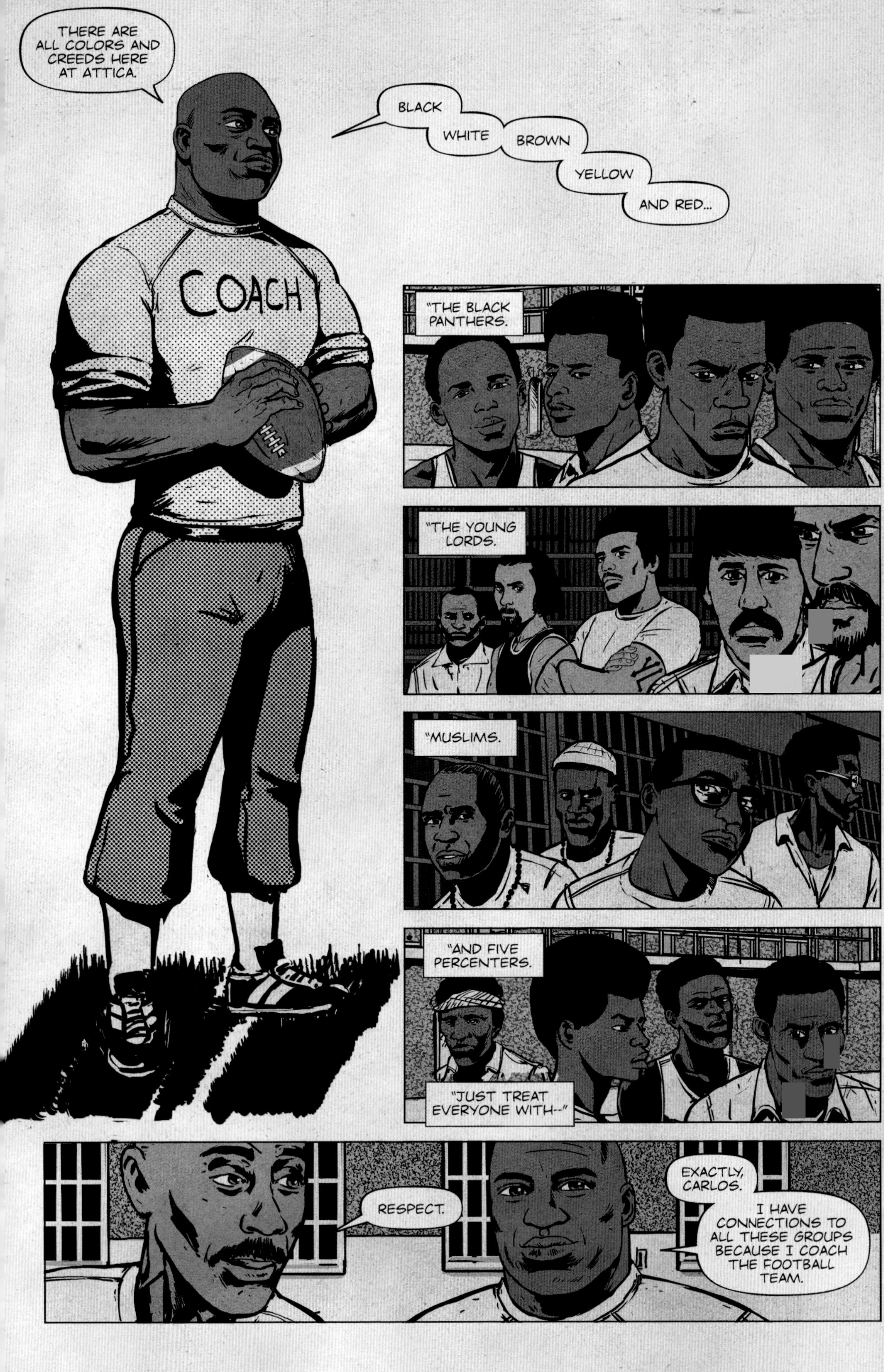

THERE ARE ALL COLORS AND CREEDS HERE AT ATTICA.
BLACK
WHITE
BROWN
YELLOW
AND RED...
COACH
"THE BLACK PANTHERS.
"THE YOUNG LORDS.
"MUSLIMS.
"AND FIVE PERCENTERS.
"JUST TREAT EVERYONE WITH--"
RESPECT.
EXACTLY, CARLOS.
I HAVE CONNECTIONS TO ALL THESE GROUPS BECAUSE I COACH THE FOOTBALL TEAM.

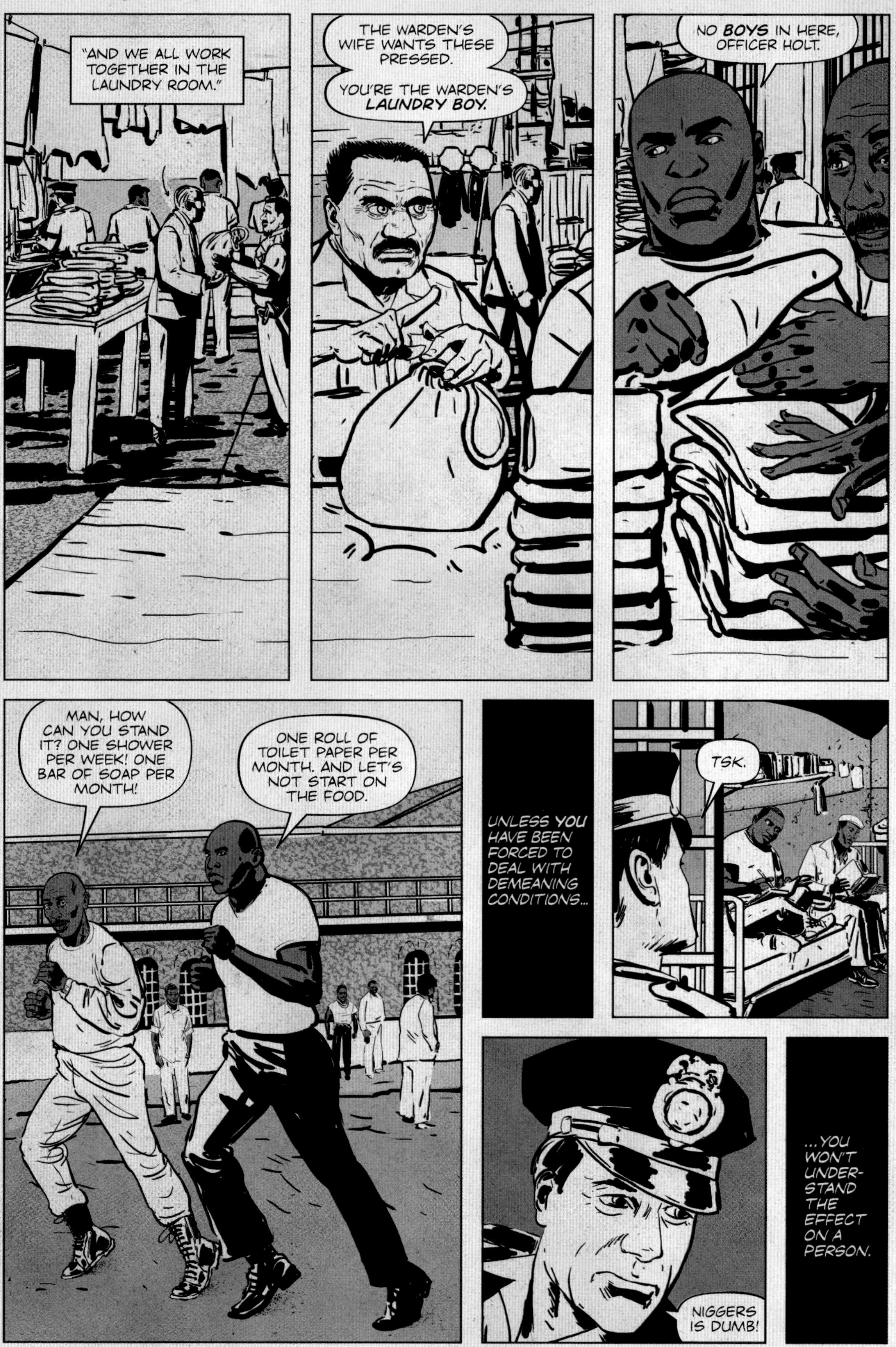
"AND WE ALL WORK TOGETHER IN THE LAUNDRY ROOM."
THE WARDEN'S WIFE WANTS THESE PRESSED.
YOU'RE THE WARDEN'S LAUNDRY BOY.
NO BOYS IN HERE, OFFICER HOLT.
MAN, HOW CAN YOU STAND IT? ONE SHOWER PER WEEK! ONE BAR OF SOAP PER MONTH!
ONE ROLL OF TOILET PAPER PER MONTH. AND LET'S NOT START ON THE FOOD.
UNLESS YOU HAVE BEEN FORCED TO DEAL WITH DEMEANING CONDITIONS...
TSK.
NIGGERS IS DUMB!
...YOU WON'T UNDER-STAND THE EFFECT ON A PERSON.

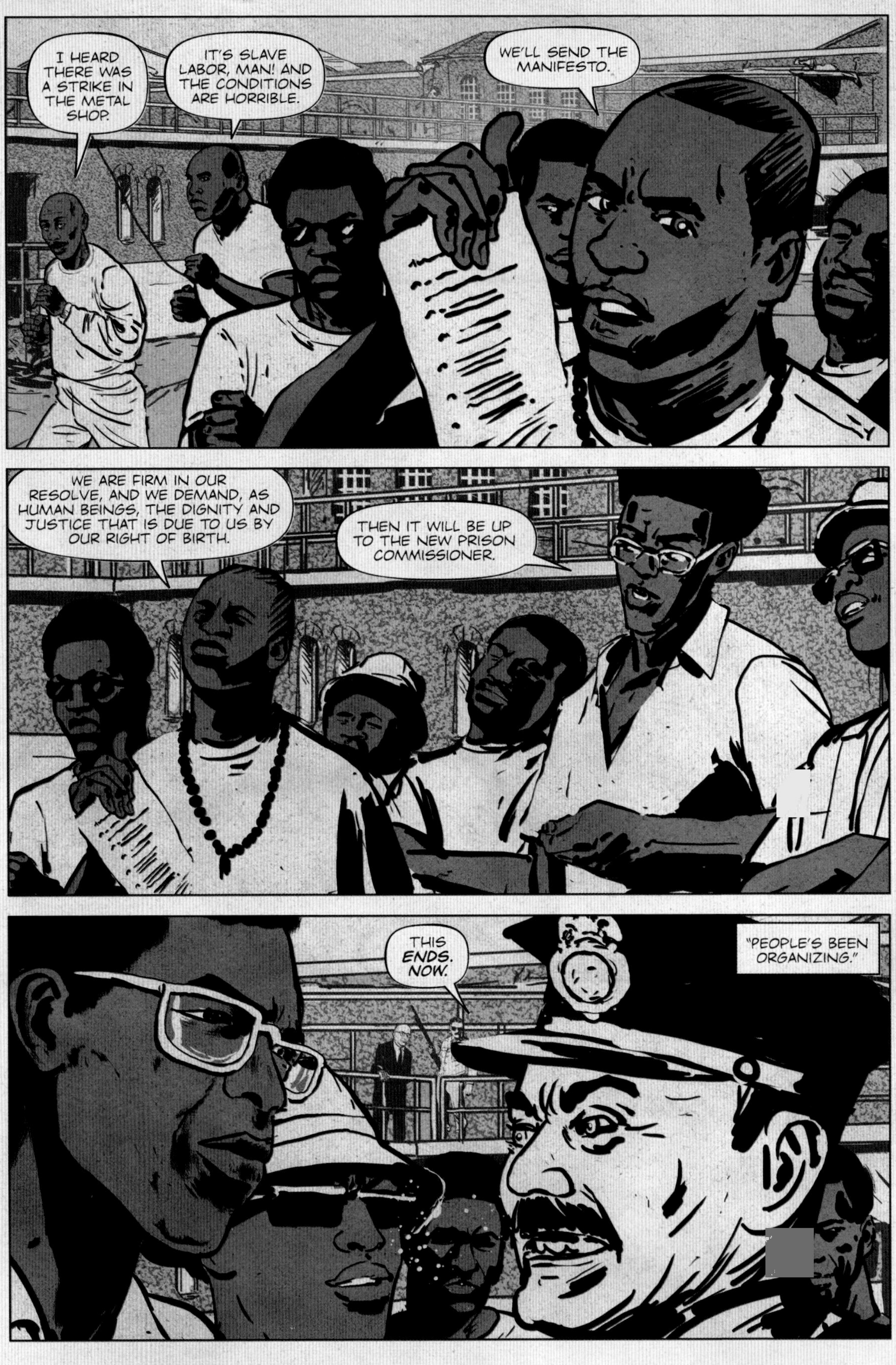
I HEARD THERE WAS A STRIKE IN THE METAL SHOP.
IT'S SLAVE LABOR, MAN! AND THE CONDITIONS ARE HORRIBLE.
WE'LL SEND THE MANIFESTO.
WE ARE FIRM IN OUR RESOLVE, AND WE DEMAND, AS HUMAN BEINGS, THE DIGNITY AND JUSTICE THAT IS DUE TO US BY OUR RIGHT OF BIRTH.
THEN IT WILL BE UP TO THE NEW PRISON COMMISSIONER.
THIS *ENDS. NOW.*
"PEOPLE'S BEEN ORGANIZING."

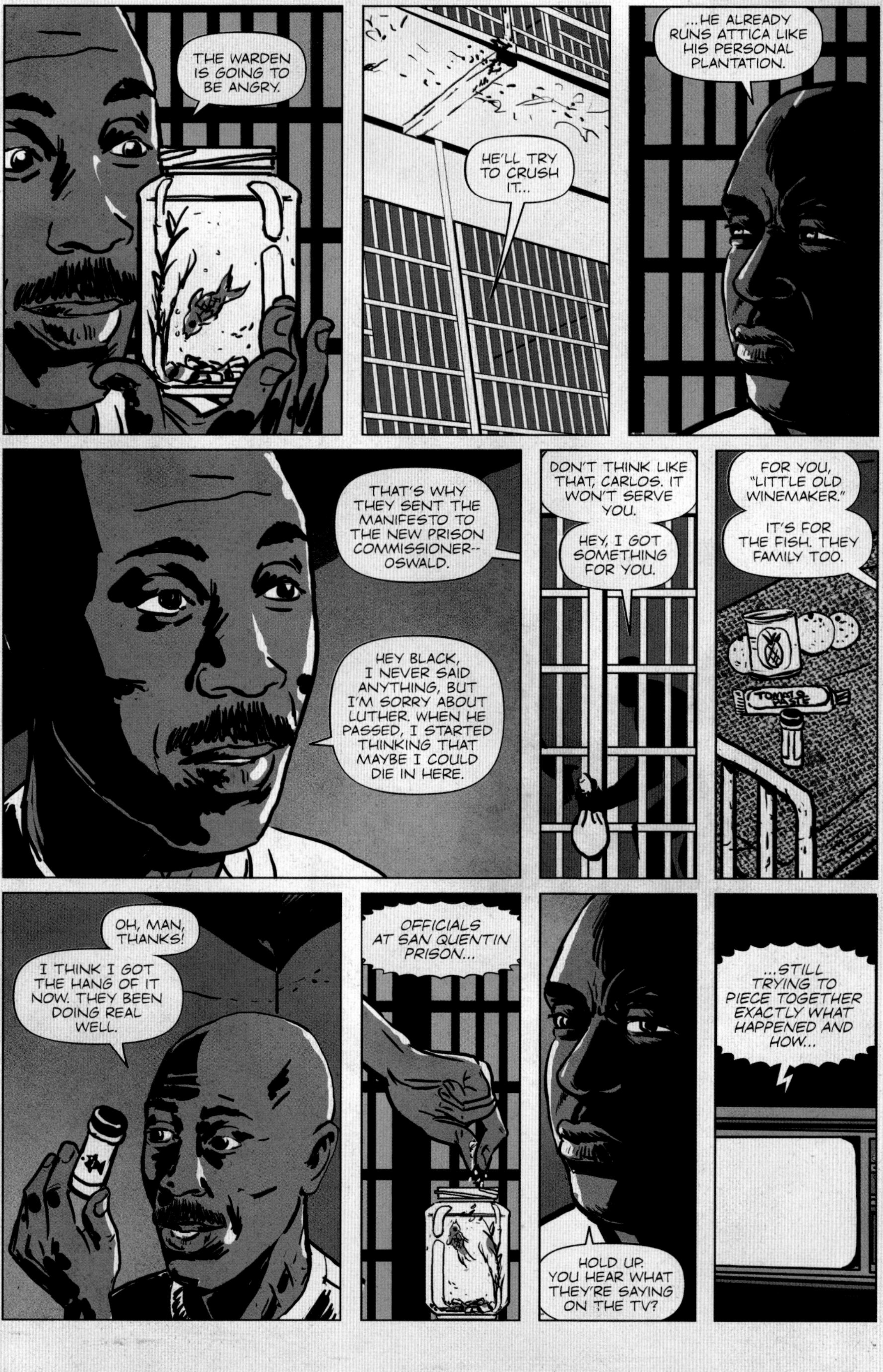
THE WARDEN IS GOING TO BE ANGRY.
HE'LL TRY TO CRUSH IT...
...HE ALREADY RUNS ATTICA LIKE HIS PERSONAL PLANTATION.
THAT'S WHY THEY SENT THE MANIFESTO TO THE NEW PRISON COMMISSIONER--OSWALD.
HEY BLACK, I NEVER SAID ANYTHING, BUT I'M SORRY ABOUT LUTHER. WHEN HE PASSED, I STARTED THINKING THAT MAYBE I COULD DIE IN HERE.
DON'T THINK LIKE THAT, CARLOS. IT WON'T SERVE YOU.
HEY, I GOT SOMETHING FOR YOU.
FOR YOU, "LITTLE OLD WINEMAKER."
IT'S FOR THE FISH. THEY FAMILY TOO.
TOMATO PASTE
OH, MAN, THANKS!
I THINK I GOT THE HANG OF IT NOW. THEY BEEN DOING REAL WELL.
OFFICIALS AT SAN QUENTIN PRISON...
HOLD UP. YOU HEAR WHAT THEY'RE SAYING ON THE TV?
...STILL TRYING TO PIECE TOGETHER EXACTLY WHAT HAPPENED AND HOW...

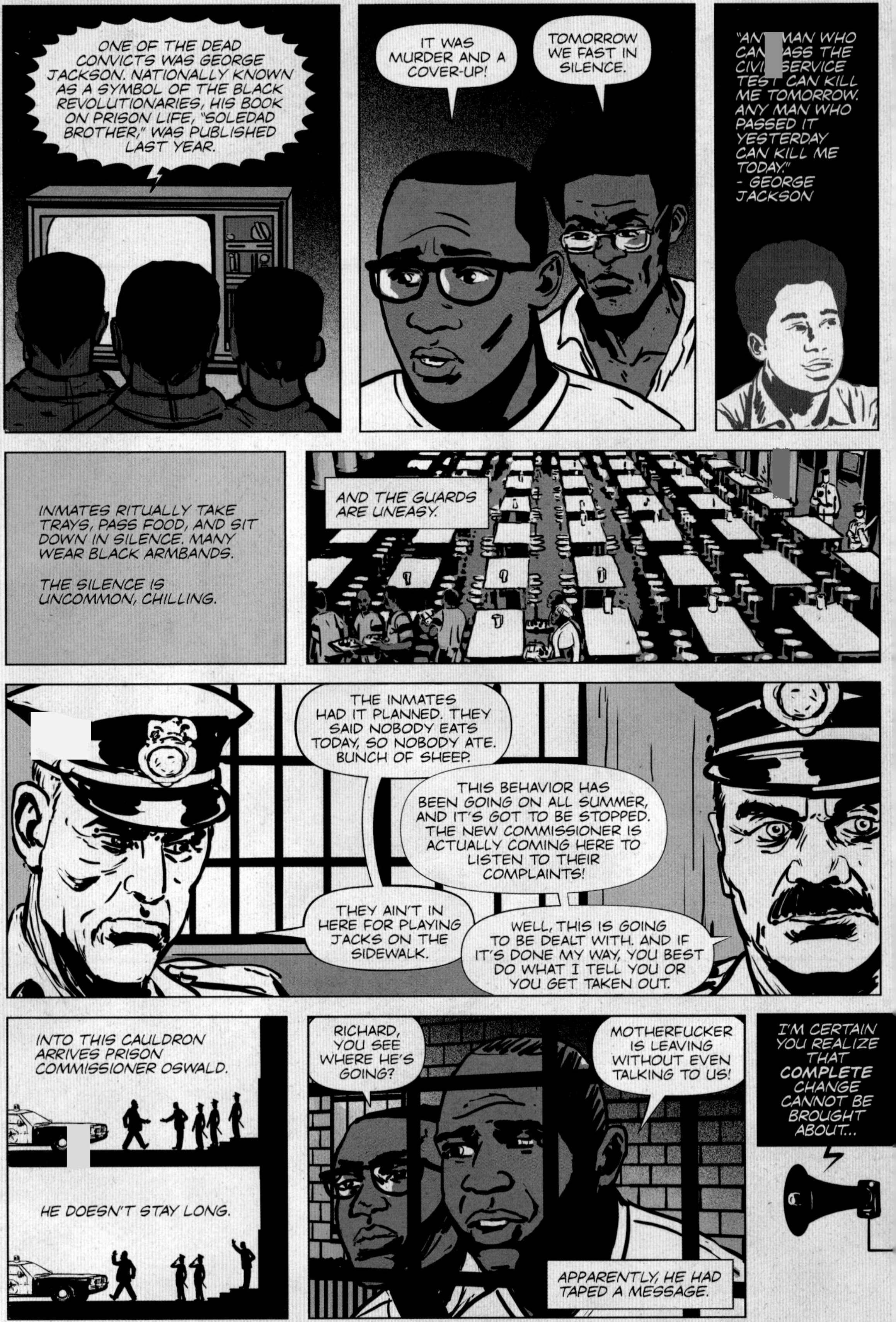
ONE OF THE DEAD CONVICTS WAS GEORGE JACKSON. NATIONALLY KNOWN AS A SYMBOL OF THE BLACK REVOLUTIONARIES, HIS BOOK ON PRISON LIFE, "SOLEDAD BROTHER," WAS PUBLISHED LAST YEAR.
IT WAS MURDER AND A COVER-UP!
TOMORROW WE FAST IN SILENCE.
"AN MAN WHO CAN ASS THE CIVI SERVICE TEST CAN KILL ME TOMORROW. ANY MAN WHO PASSED IT YESTERDAY CAN KILL ME TODAY." - GEORGE JACKSON
INMATES RITUALLY TAKE TRAYS, PASS FOOD, AND SIT DOWN IN SILENCE. MANY WEAR BLACK ARMBANDS.
THE SILENCE IS UNCOMMON, CHILLING.
AND THE GUARDS ARE UNEASY.
THE INMATES HAD IT PLANNED. THEY SAID NOBODY EATS TODAY, SO NOBODY ATE. BUNCH OF SHEEP.
THIS BEHAVIOR HAS BEEN GOING ON ALL SUMMER, AND IT'S GOT TO BE STOPPED. THE NEW COMMISSIONER IS ACTUALLY COMING HERE TO LISTEN TO THEIR COMPLAINTS!
THEY AIN'T IN HERE FOR PLAYING JACKS ON THE SIDEWALK.
WELL, THIS IS GOING TO BE DEALT WITH. AND IF IT'S DONE MY WAY, YOU BEST DO WHAT I TELL YOU OR YOU GET TAKEN OUT.
INTO THIS CAULDRON ARRIVES PRISON COMMISSIONER OSWALD.
HE DOESN'T STAY LONG.
RICHARD, YOU SEE WHERE HE'S GOING?
MOTHERFUCKER IS LEAVING WITHOUT EVEN TALKING TO US!
APPARENTLY, HE HAD TAPED A MESSAGE.
I'M CERTAIN YOU REALIZE THAT COMPLETE CHANGE CANNOT BE BROUGHT ABOUT...

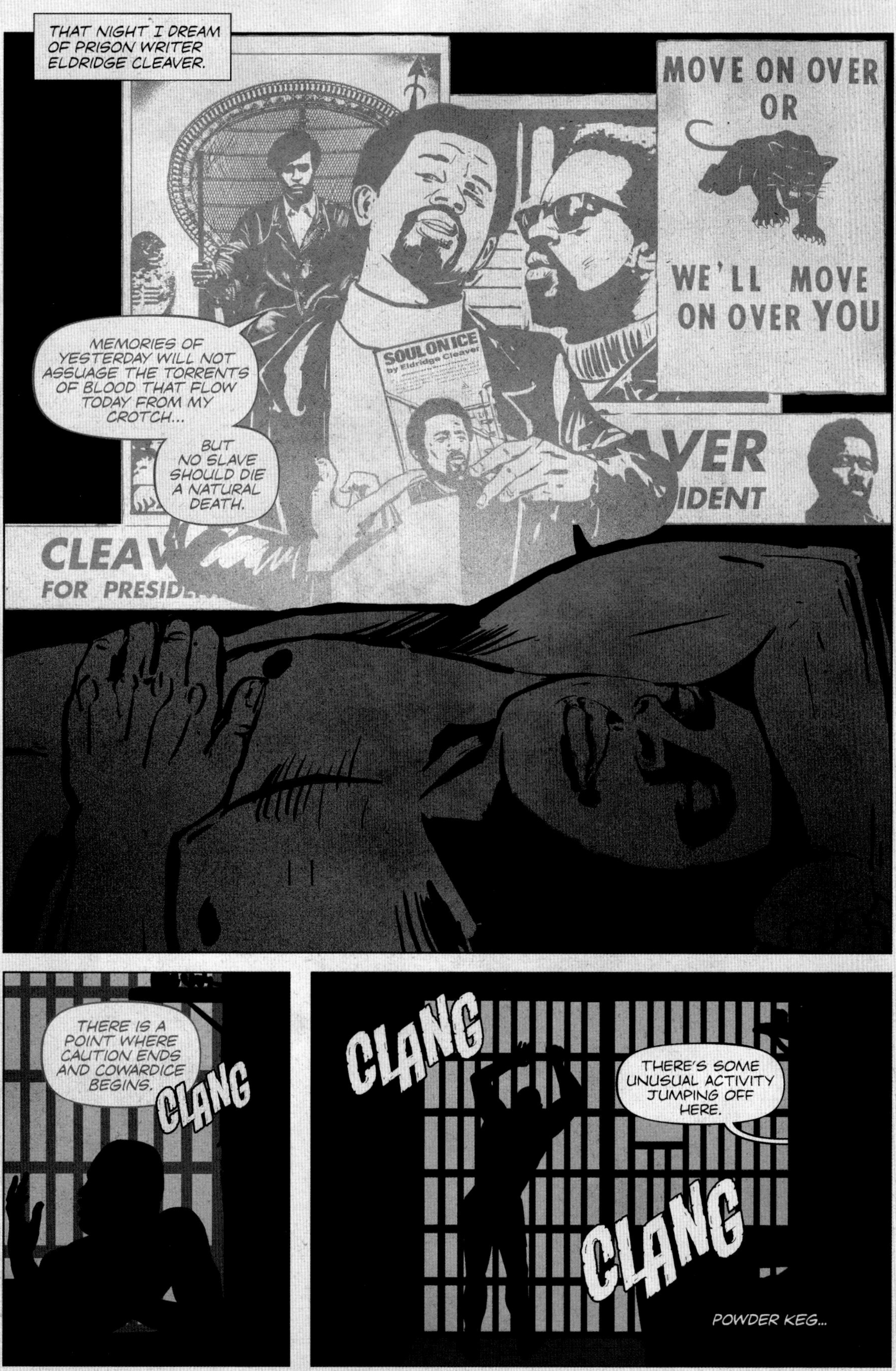
THAT NIGHT I DREAM OF PRISON WRITER ELDRIDGE CLEAVER.
MOVE ON OVER OR WE'LL MOVE ON OVER YOU
SOUL ON ICE by Eldridge Cleaver
MEMORIES OF YESTERDAY WILL NOT ASSUAGE THE TORRENTS OF BLOOD THAT FLOW TODAY FROM MY CROTCH...
BUT NO SLAVE SHOULD DIE A NATURAL DEATH.
VER
IDENT
CLEAV
FOR PRESID
THERE IS A POINT WHERE CAUTION ENDS AND COWARDICE BEGINS.
CLANG
CLANG
THERE'S SOME UNUSUAL ACTIVITY JUMPING OFF HERE.
CLANG
POWDER KEG...

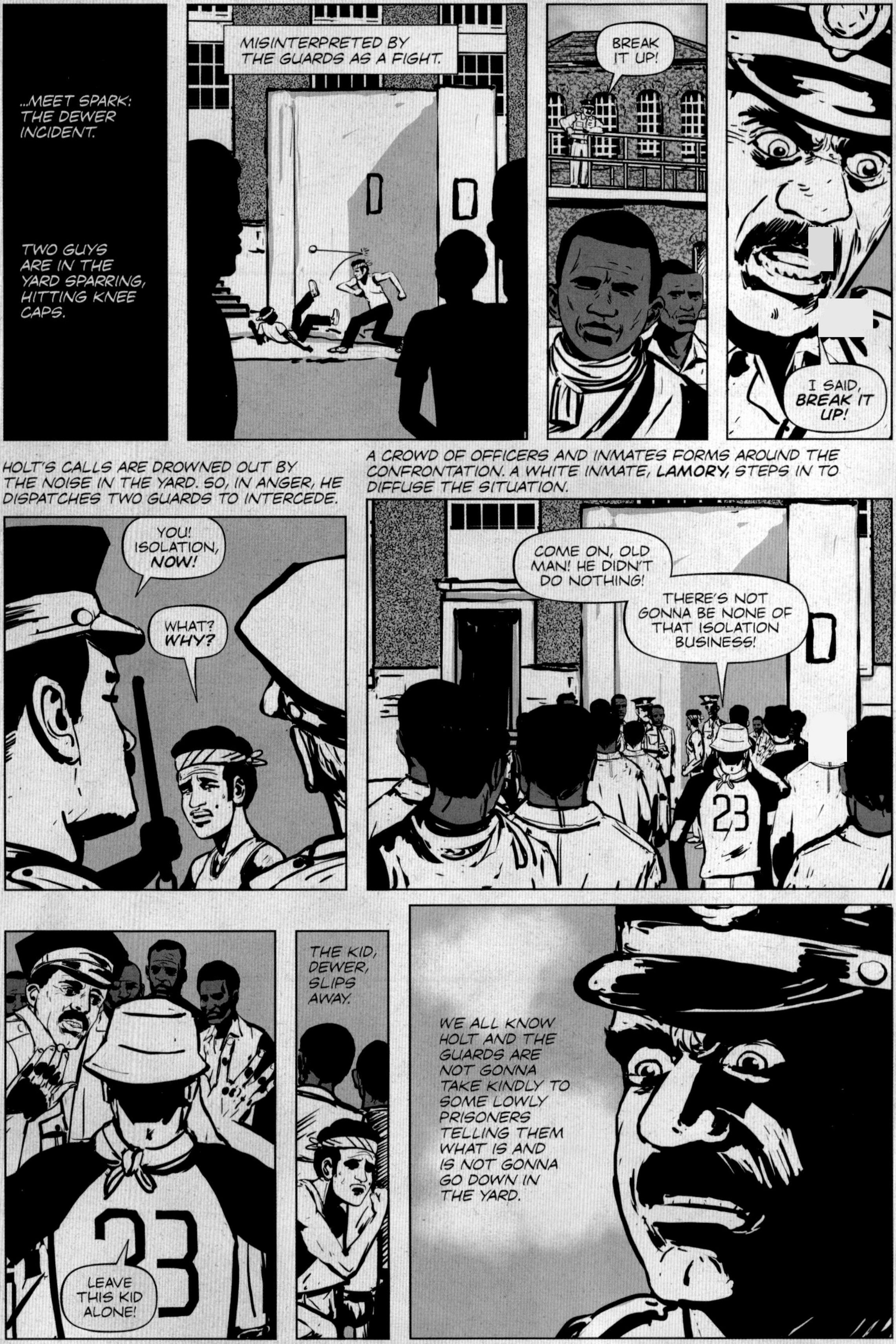
...MEET SPARK: THE DEWER INCIDENT.
TWO GUYS ARE IN THE YARD SPARRING, HITTING KNEE CAPS.
MISINTERPRETED BY THE GUARDS AS A FIGHT.
BREAK IT UP!
I SAID, BREAK IT UP!
HOLT'S CALLS ARE DROWNED OUT BY THE NOISE IN THE YARD. SO, IN ANGER, HE DISPATCHES TWO GUARDS TO INTERCEDE.
YOU! ISOLATION, NOW!
WHAT? WHY?
A CROWD OF OFFICERS AND INMATES FORMS AROUND THE CONFRONTATION. A WHITE INMATE, LAMORY, STEPS IN TO DIFFUSE THE SITUATION.
COME ON, OLD MAN! HE DIDN'T DO NOTHING!
THERE'S NOT GONNA BE NONE OF THAT ISOLATION BUSINESS!
LEAVE THIS KID ALONE!
THE KID, DEWER, SLIPS AWAY.
WE ALL KNOW HOLT AND THE GUARDS ARE NOT GONNA TAKE KINDLY TO SOME LOWLY PRISONERS TELLING THEM WHAT IS AND IS NOT GONNA GO DOWN IN THE YARD.

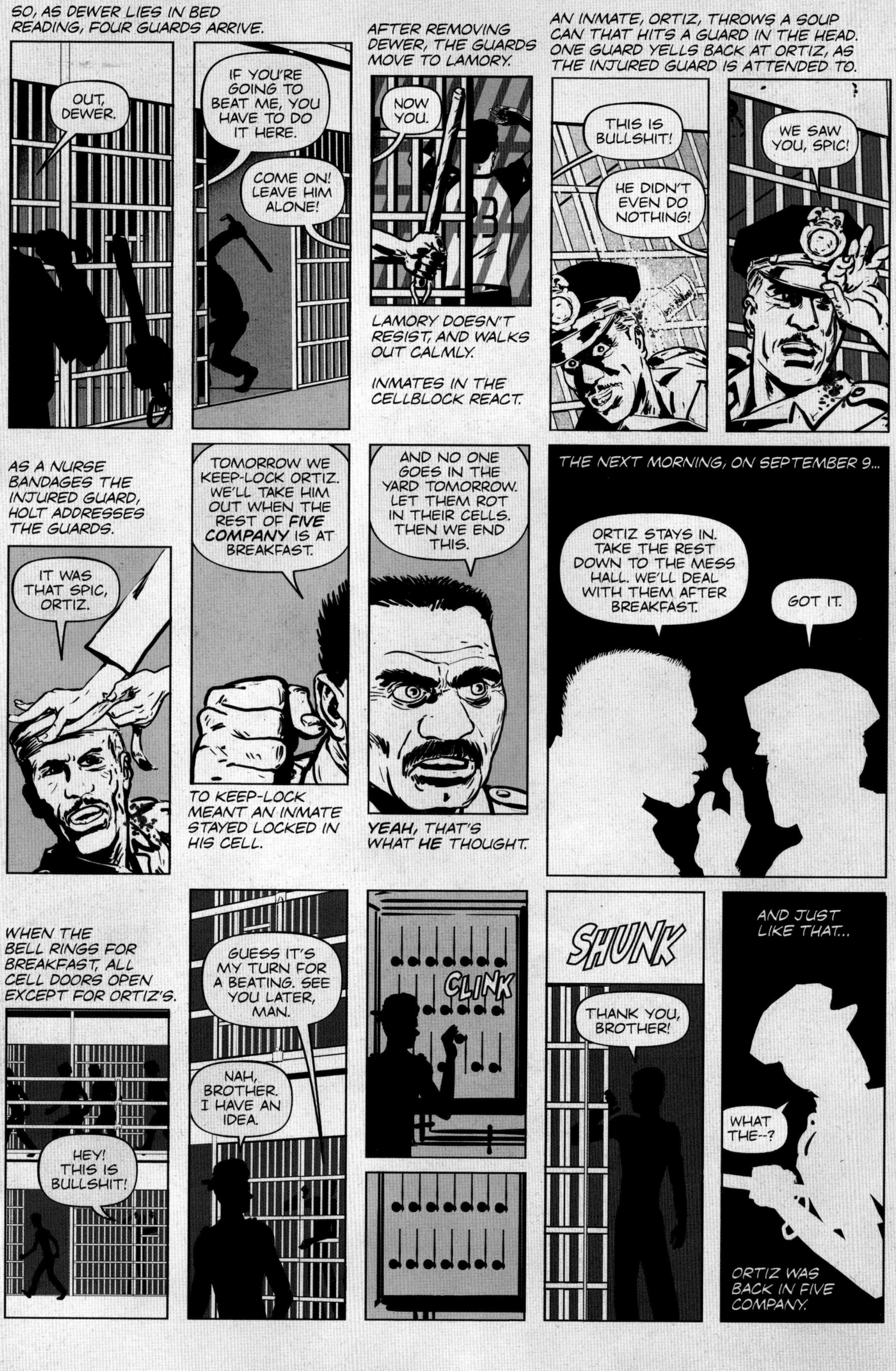
SO, AS DEWER LIES IN BED READING, FOUR GUARDS ARRIVE.
OUT, DEWER.
IF YOU'RE GOING TO BEAT ME, YOU HAVE TO DO IT HERE.
COME ON! LEAVE HIM ALONE!
AFTER REMOVING DEWER, THE GUARDS MOVE TO LAMORY.
NOW YOU.
LAMORY DOESN'T RESIST, AND WALKS OUT CALMLY.
INMATES IN THE CELLBLOCK REACT.
AN INMATE, ORTIZ, THROWS A SOUP CAN THAT HITS A GUARD IN THE HEAD. ONE GUARD YELLS BACK AT ORTIZ, AS THE INJURED GUARD IS ATTENDED TO.
THIS IS BULLSHIT!
HE DIDN'T EVEN DO NOTHING!
WE SAW YOU, SPIC!
AS A NURSE BANDAGES THE INJURED GUARD, HOLT ADDRESSES THE GUARDS.
IT WAS THAT SPIC, ORTIZ.
TOMORROW WE KEEP-LOCK ORTIZ. WE'LL TAKE HIM OUT WHEN THE REST OF FIVE COMPANY IS AT BREAKFAST.
TO KEEP-LOCK MEANT AN INMATE STAYED LOCKED IN HIS CELL.
AND NO ONE GOES IN THE YARD TOMORROW. LET THEM ROT IN THEIR CELLS. THEN WE END THIS.
YEAH, THAT'S WHAT HE THOUGHT.
THE NEXT MORNING, ON SEPTEMBER 9...
ORTIZ STAYS IN. TAKE THE REST DOWN TO THE MESS HALL. WE'LL DEAL WITH THEM AFTER BREAKFAST.
GOT IT.
WHEN THE BELL RINGS FOR BREAKFAST, ALL CELL DOORS OPEN EXCEPT FOR ORTIZ'S.
HEY! THIS IS BULLSHIT!
GUESS IT'S MY TURN FOR A BEATING. SEE YOU LATER, MAN.
NAH, BROTHER. I HAVE AN IDEA.
CLINK
SHUNK
THANK YOU, BROTHER!
AND JUST LIKE THAT...
WHAT THE--?
ORTIZ WAS BACK IN FIVE COMPANY.

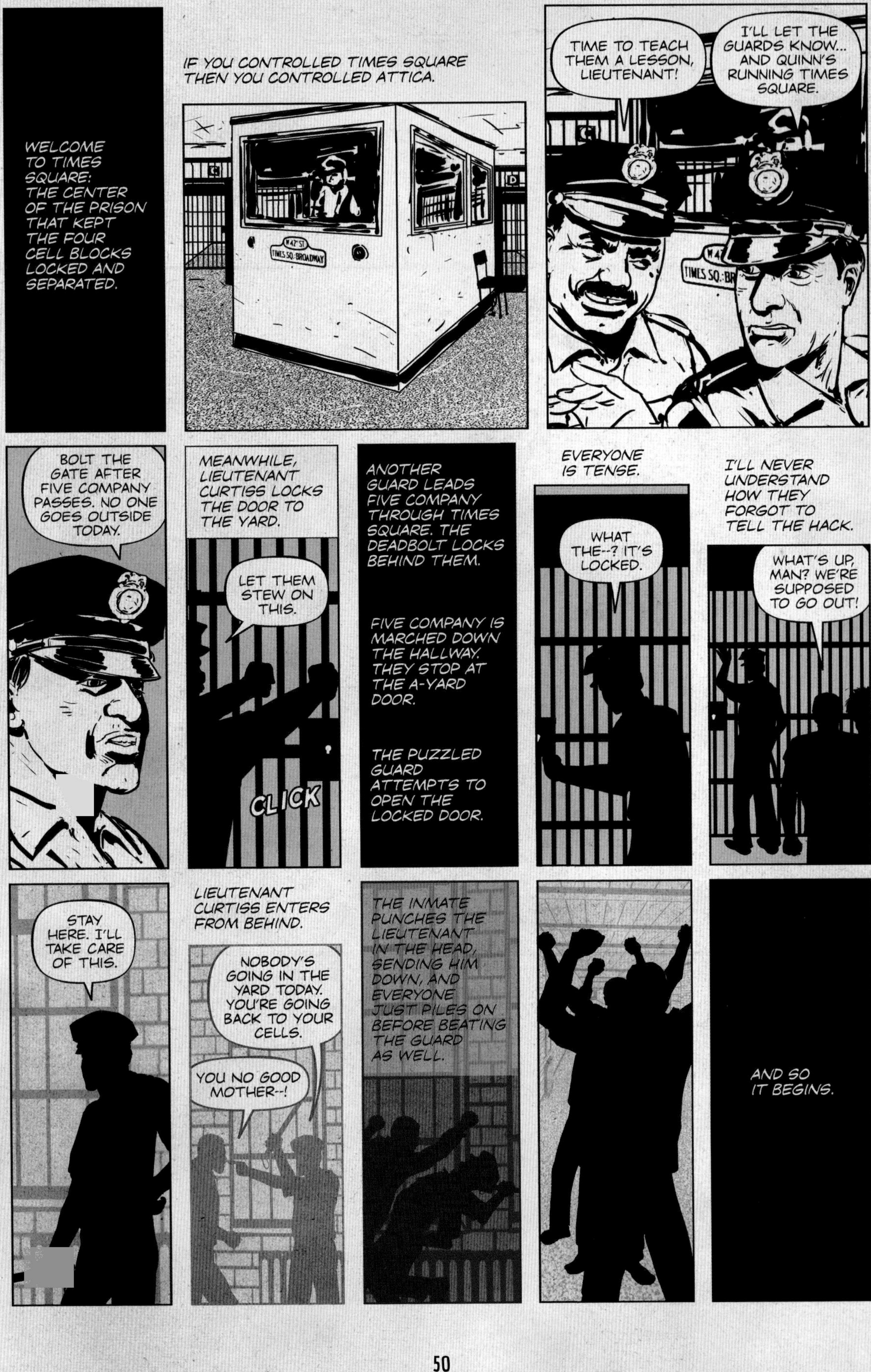
WELCOME TO TIMES SQUARE: THE CENTER OF THE PRISON THAT KEPT THE FOUR CELL BLOCKS LOCKED AND SEPARATED.
IF YOU CONTROLLED TIMES SQUARE THEN YOU CONTROLLED ATTICA.
W 42ND ST
TIMES SQ.-BROADWAY
TIME TO TEACH THEM A LESSON, LIEUTENANT!
I'LL LET THE GUARDS KNOW... AND QUINN'S RUNNING TIMES SQUARE.
BOLT THE GATE AFTER FIVE COMPANY PASSES. NO ONE GOES OUTSIDE TODAY.
MEANWHILE, LIEUTENANT CURTISS LOCKS THE DOOR TO THE YARD.
LET THEM STEW ON THIS.
CLICK
ANOTHER GUARD LEADS FIVE COMPANY THROUGH TIMES SQUARE. THE DEADBOLT LOCKS BEHIND THEM.
FIVE COMPANY IS MARCHED DOWN THE HALLWAY. THEY STOP AT THE A-YARD DOOR.
THE PUZZLED GUARD ATTEMPTS TO OPEN THE LOCKED DOOR.
EVERYONE IS TENSE.
WHAT THE--? IT'S LOCKED.
I'LL NEVER UNDERSTAND HOW THEY FORGOT TO TELL THE HACK.
WHAT'S UP, MAN? WE'RE SUPPOSED TO GO OUT!
STAY HERE. I'LL TAKE CARE OF THIS.
LIEUTENANT CURTISS ENTERS FROM BEHIND.
NOBODY'S GOING IN THE YARD TODAY. YOU'RE GOING BACK TO YOUR CELLS.
YOU NO GOOD MOTHER--!
THE INMATE PUNCHES THE LIEUTENANT IN THE HEAD, SENDING HIM DOWN, AND EVERYONE JUST PILES ON BEFORE BEATING THE GUARD AS WELL.
AND SO IT BEGINS.

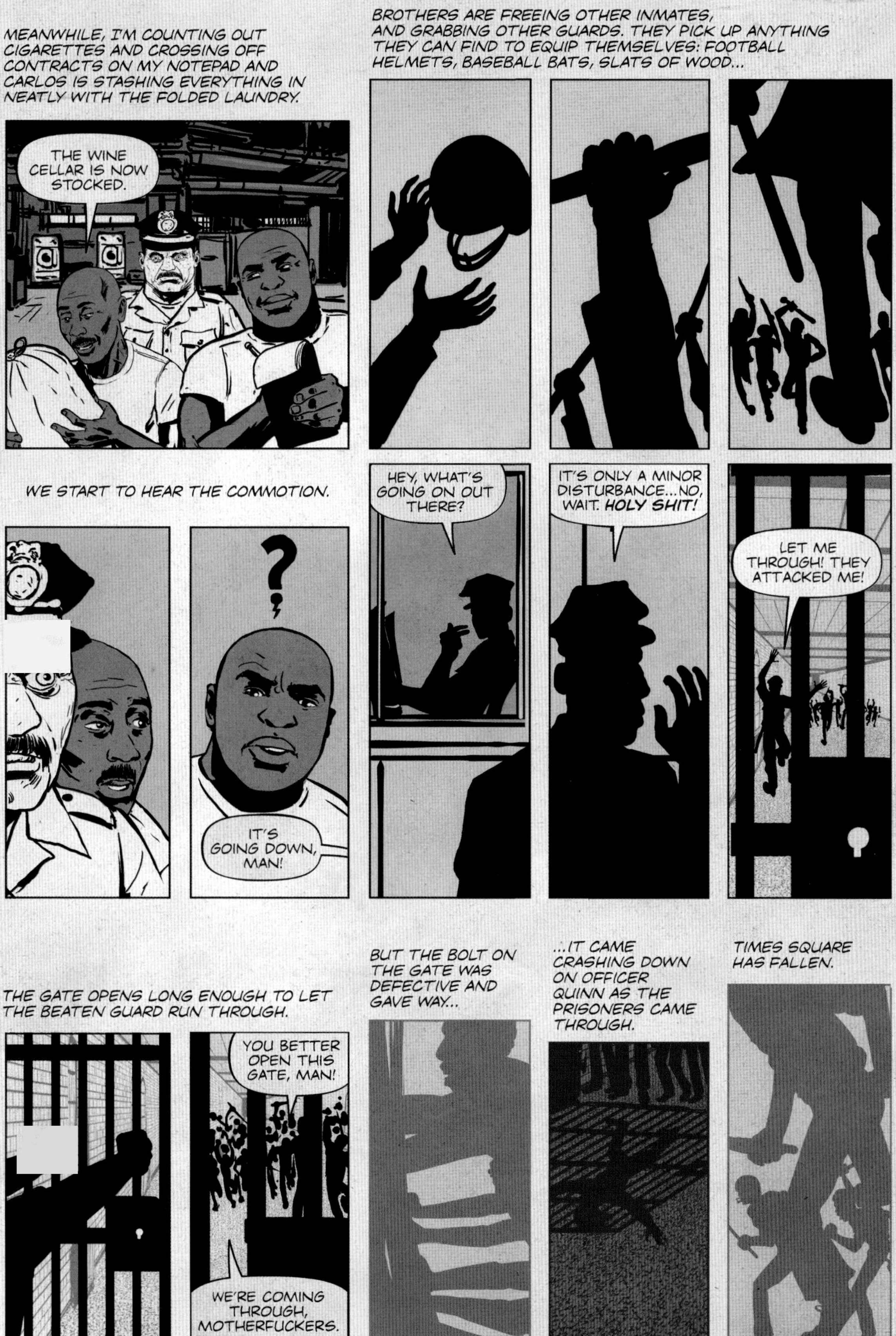

MEANWHILE, I'M COUNTING OUT CIGARETTES AND CROSSING OFF CONTRACTS ON MY NOTEPAD AND CARLOS IS STASHING EVERYTHING IN NEATLY WITH THE FOLDED LAUNDRY.
THE WINE CELLAR IS NOW STOCKED.
BROTHERS ARE FREEING OTHER INMATES, AND GRABBING OTHER GUARDS. THEY PICK UP ANYTHING THEY CAN FIND TO EQUIP THEMSELVES: FOOTBALL HELMETS, BASEBALL BATS, SLATS OF WOOD...
WE START TO HEAR THE COMMOTION.
?
IT'S GOING DOWN, MAN!
HEY, WHAT'S GOING ON OUT THERE?
IT'S ONLY A MINOR DISTURBANCE...NO, WAIT. HOLY SHIT!
LET ME THROUGH! THEY ATTACKED ME!
THE GATE OPENS LONG ENOUGH TO LET THE BEATEN GUARD RUN THROUGH.
YOU BETTER OPEN THIS GATE, MAN!
WE'RE COMING THROUGH, MOTHERFUCKERS.
BUT THE BOLT ON THE GATE WAS DEFECTIVE AND GAVE WAY...
...IT CAME CRASHING DOWN ON OFFICER QUINN AS THE PRISONERS CAME THROUGH.
TIMES SQUARE HAS FALLEN.

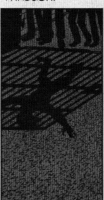

September 9, 1971

The Attica Prison rebellion had begun.

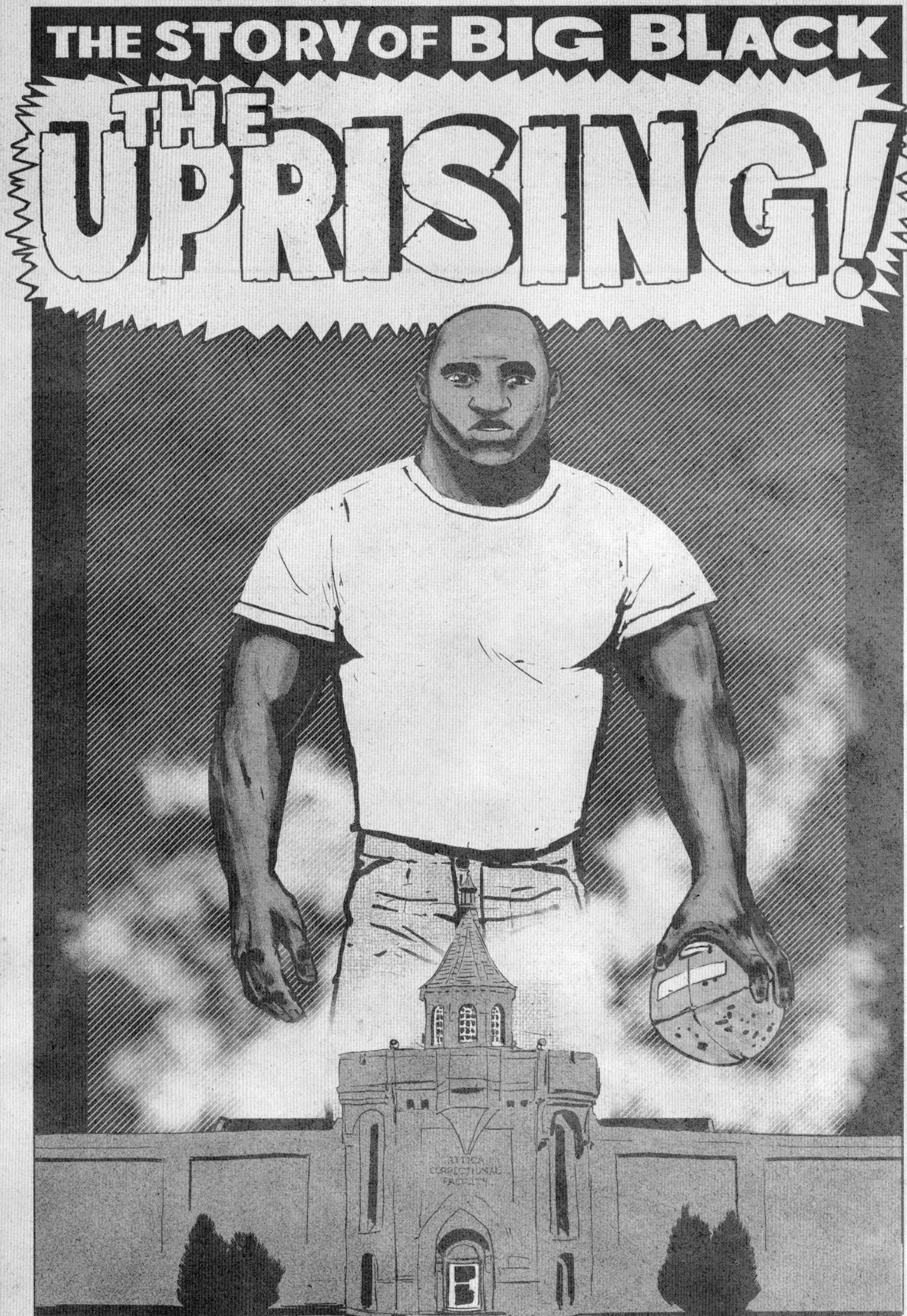
THE STORY OF BIG BLACK
THE UPRISING!
ATTICA CORRECTIONAL FACILITY

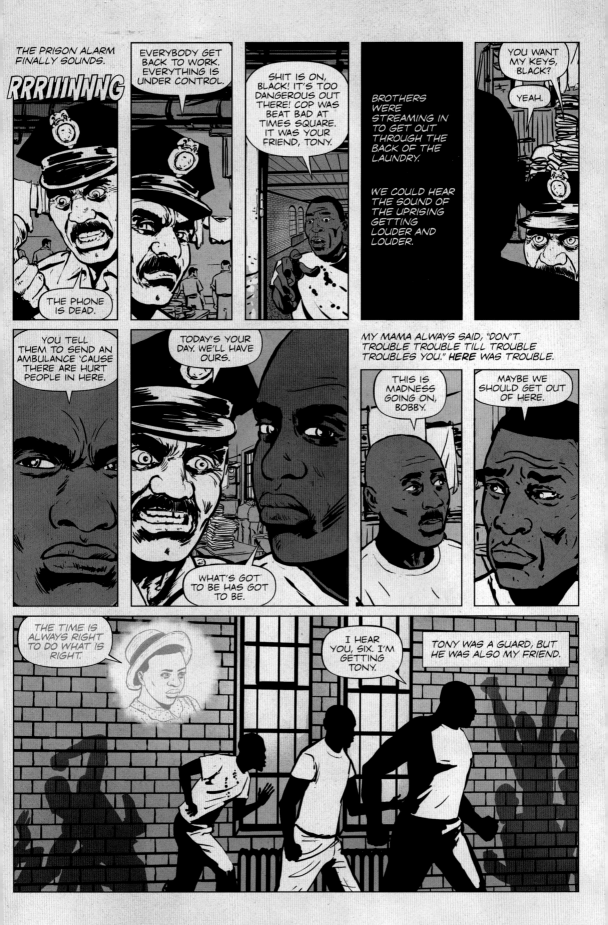

THE PRISON ALARM FINALLY SOUNDS.

RRRIIINNNG

THE PHONE IS DEAD.

EVERYBODY GET BACK TO WORK. EVERYTHING IS UNDER CONTROL.

SHIT IS ON, BLACK! IT'S TOO DANGEROUS OUT THERE! COP WAS BEAT BAD AT TIMES SQUARE. IT WAS YOUR FRIEND, TONY.

BROTHERS WERE STREAMING IN TO GET OUT THROUGH THE BACK OF THE LAUNDRY.

WE COULD HEAR THE SOUND OF THE UPRISING GETTING LOUDER AND LOUDER.

YOU WANT MY KEYS, BLACK?

YEAH.

YOU TELL THEM TO SEND AN AMBULANCE 'CAUSE THERE ARE HURT PEOPLE IN HERE.

TODAY'S YOUR DAY. WE'LL HAVE OURS.

WHAT'S GOT TO BE HAS GOT TO BE.

MY MAMA ALWAYS SAID, "DON'T TROUBLE TROUBLE TILL TROUBLE TROUBLES YOU." *HERE* WAS TROUBLE.

THIS IS MADNESS GOING ON, BOBBY.

MAYBE WE SHOULD GET OUT OF HERE.

THE TIME IS ALWAYS RIGHT TO DO WHAT IS RIGHT.

I HEAR YOU, SIX. I'M GETTING TONY.

TONY WAS A GUARD, BUT HE WAS ALSO MY FRIEND.

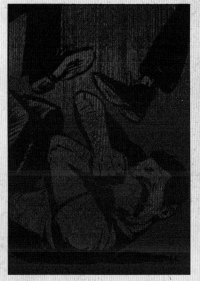

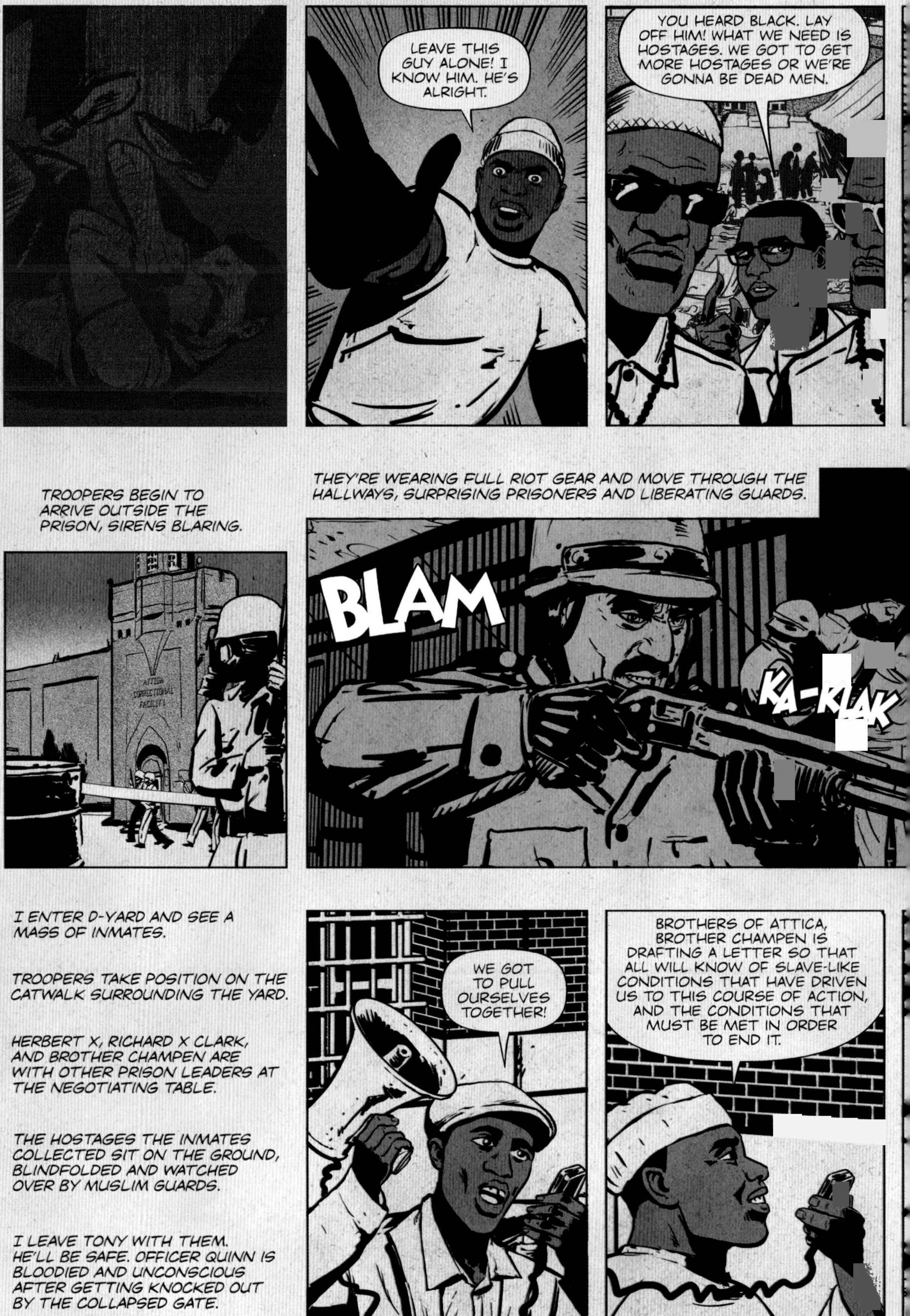
LEAVE THIS GUY ALONE! I KNOW HIM. HE'S ALRIGHT.
YOU HEARD BLACK. LAY OFF HIM! WHAT WE NEED IS HOSTAGES. WE GOT TO GET MORE HOSTAGES OR WE'RE GONNA BE DEAD MEN.
TROOPERS BEGIN TO ARRIVE OUTSIDE THE PRISON, SIRENS BLARING.
THEY'RE WEARING FULL RIOT GEAR AND MOVE THROUGH THE HALLWAYS, SURPRISING PRISONERS AND LIBERATING GUARDS.
BLAM
KA-KLAK
I ENTER D-YARD AND SEE A MASS OF INMATES.
TROOPERS TAKE POSITION ON THE CATWALK SURROUNDING THE YARD.
HERBERT X, RICHARD X CLARK, AND BROTHER CHAMPEN ARE WITH OTHER PRISON LEADERS AT THE NEGOTIATING TABLE.
THE HOSTAGES THE INMATES COLLECTED SIT ON THE GROUND, BLINDFOLDED AND WATCHED OVER BY MUSLIM GUARDS.
I LEAVE TONY WITH THEM. HE'LL BE SAFE. OFFICER QUINN IS BLOODIED AND UNCONSCIOUS AFTER GETTING KNOCKED OUT BY THE COLLAPSED GATE.
WE GOT TO PULL OURSELVES TOGETHER!
BROTHERS OF ATTICA, BROTHER CHAMPEN IS DRAFTING A LETTER SO THAT ALL WILL KNOW OF SLAVE-LIKE CONDITIONS THAT HAVE DRIVEN US TO THIS COURSE OF ACTION, AND THE CONDITIONS THAT MUST BE MET IN ORDER TO END IT.

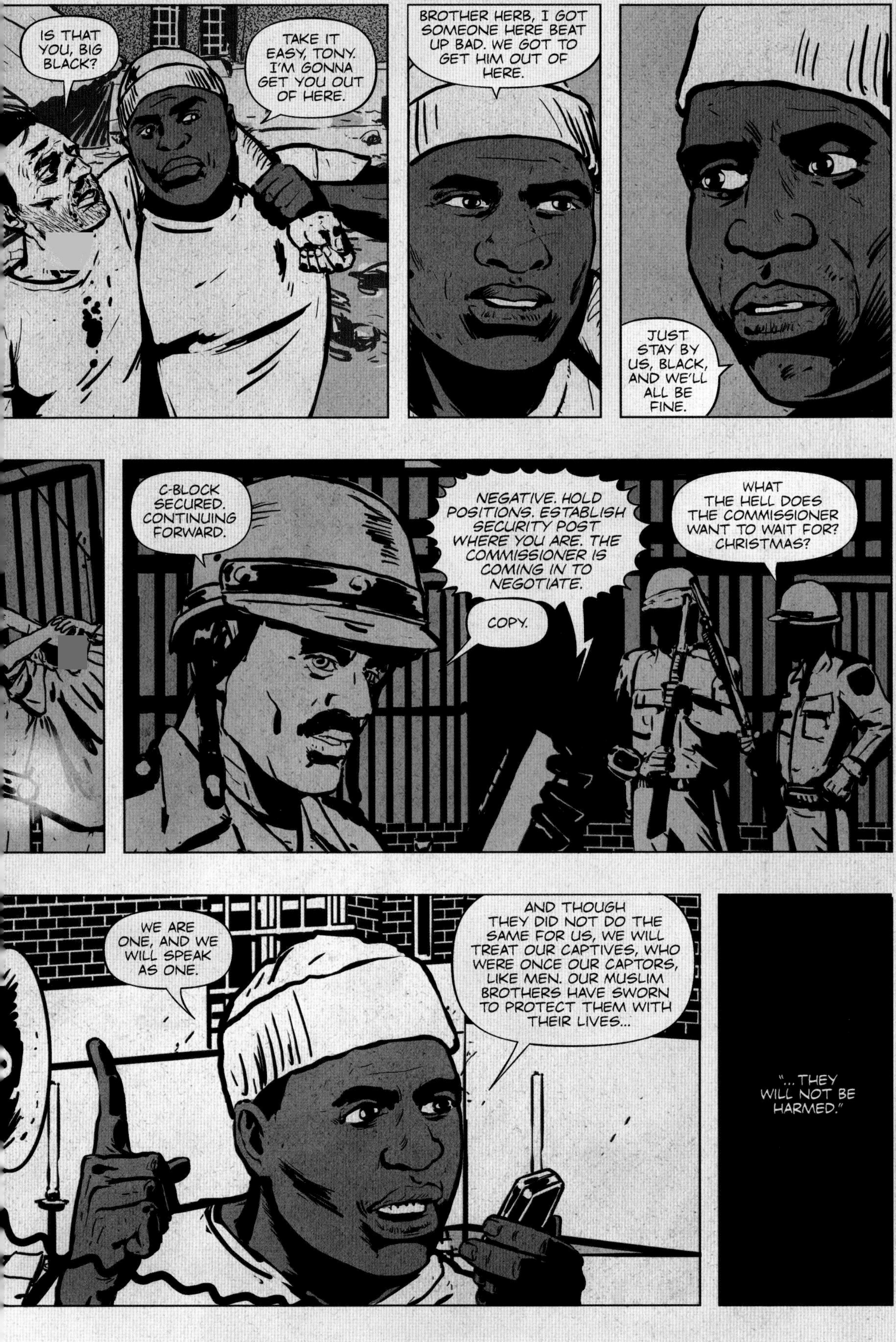
IS THAT YOU, BIG BLACK?
TAKE IT EASY, TONY. I'M GONNA GET YOU OUT OF HERE.
BROTHER HERB, I GOT SOMEONE HERE BEAT UP BAD. WE GOT TO GET HIM OUT OF HERE.
JUST STAY BY US, BLACK, AND WE'LL ALL BE FINE.
C-BLOCK SECURED. CONTINUING FORWARD.
NEGATIVE. HOLD POSITIONS. ESTABLISH SECURITY POST WHERE YOU ARE. THE COMMISSIONER IS COMING IN TO NEGOTIATE.
COPY.
WHAT THE HELL DOES THE COMMISSIONER WANT TO WAIT FOR? CHRISTMAS?
WE ARE ONE, AND WE WILL SPEAK AS ONE.
AND THOUGH THEY DID NOT DO THE SAME FOR US, WE WILL TREAT OUR CAPTIVES, WHO WERE ONCE OUR CAPTORS, LIKE MEN. OUR MUSLIM BROTHERS HAVE SWORN TO PROTECT THEM WITH THEIR LIVES...
"...THEY WILL NOT BE HARMED."

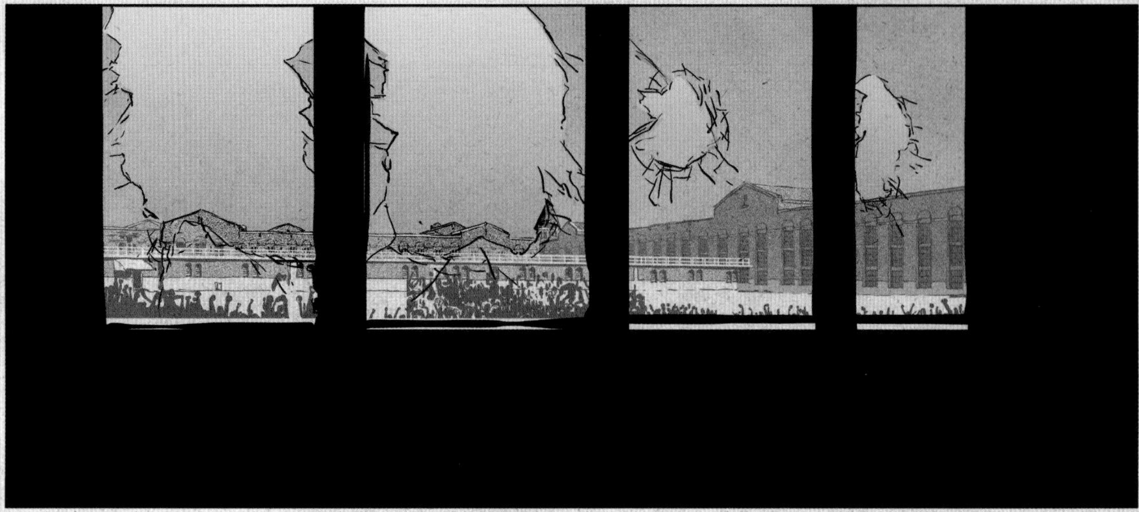

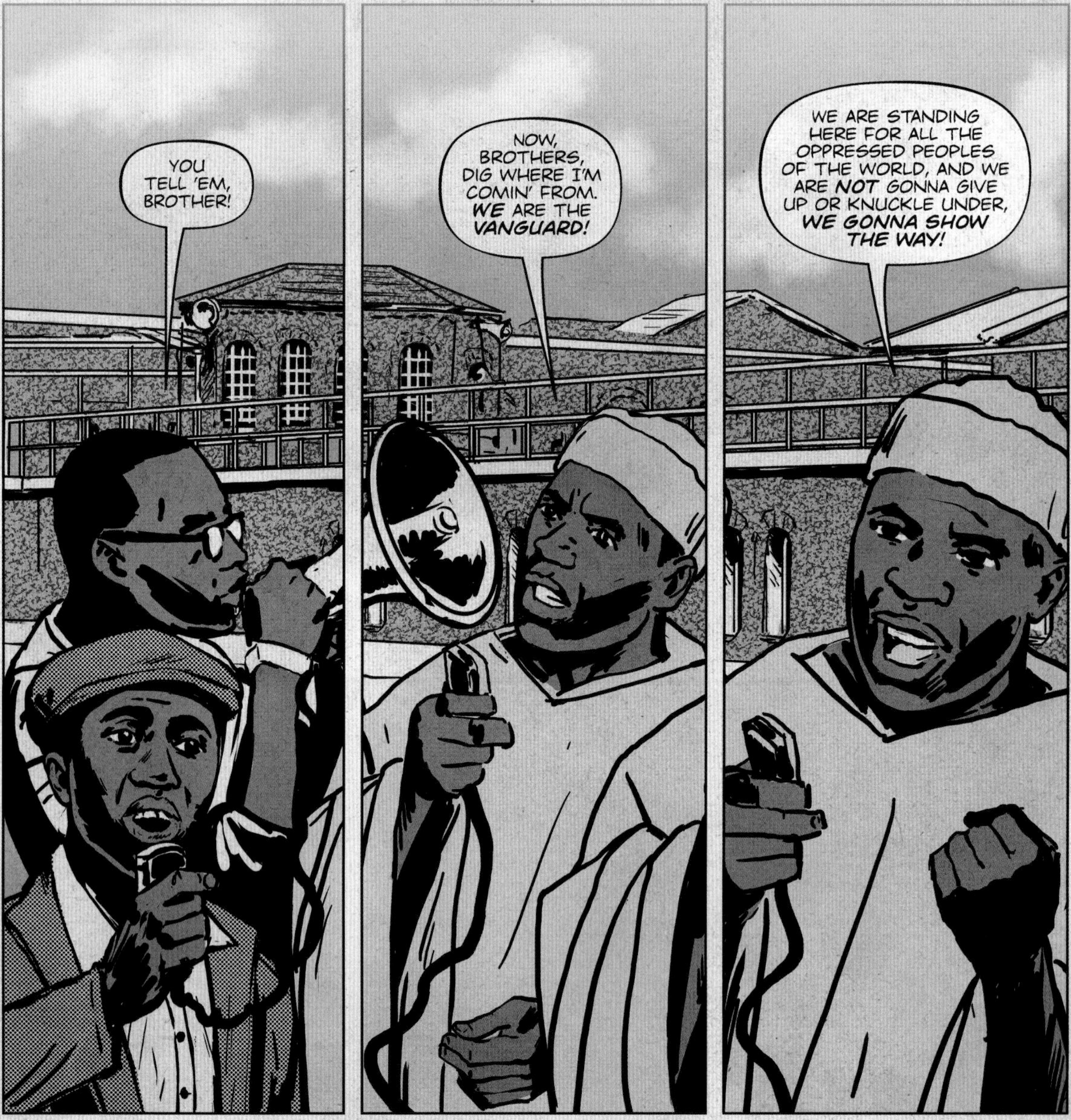
YOU TELL 'EM, BROTHER!
NOW, BROTHERS, DIG WHERE I'M COMIN' FROM. **WE** ARE THE **VANGUARD!**
WE ARE STANDING HERE FOR ALL THE OPPRESSED PEOPLES OF THE WORLD, AND WE ARE **NOT** GONNA GIVE UP OR KNUCKLE UNDER, **WE GONNA SHOW THE WAY!**

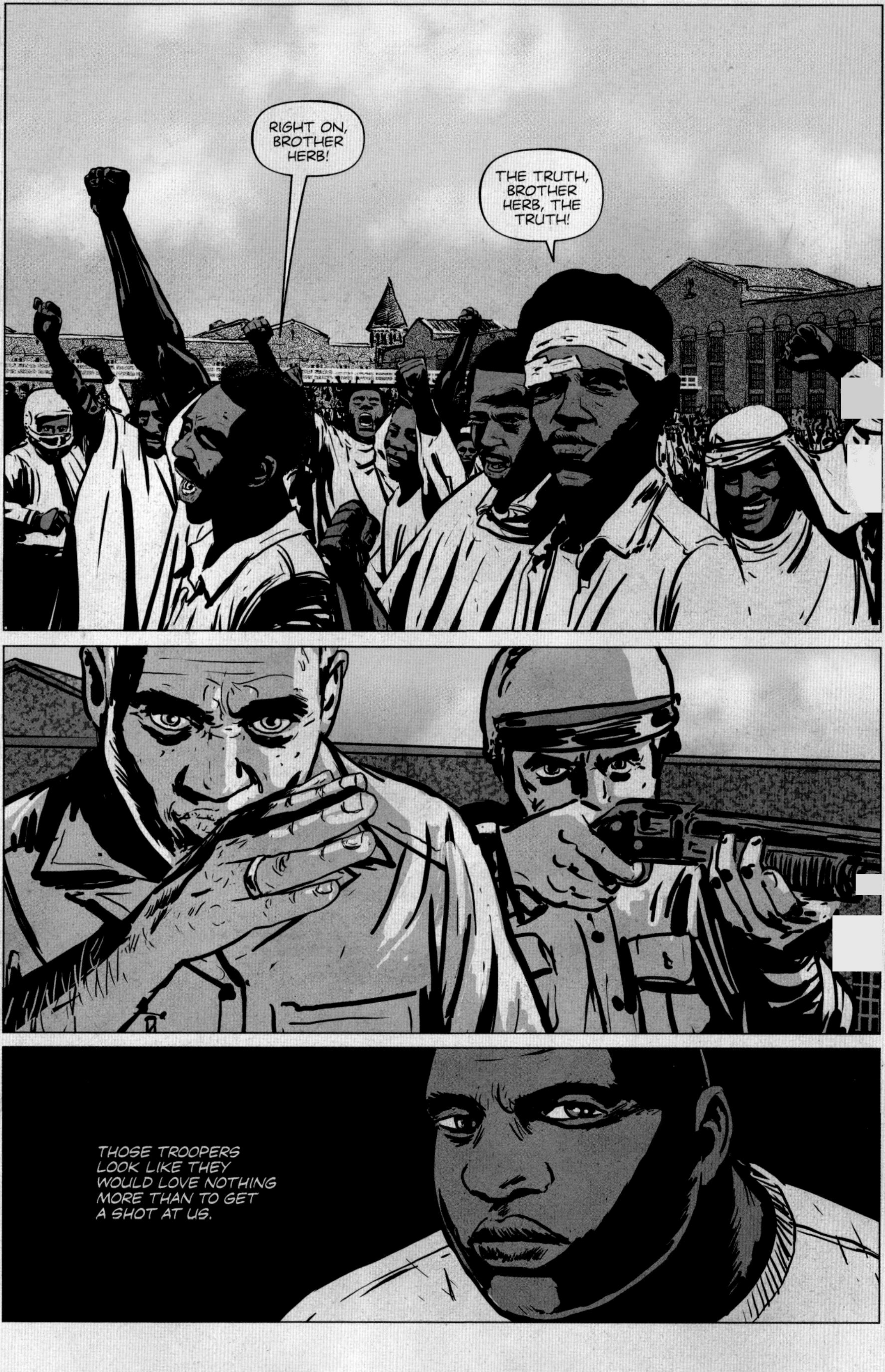
RIGHT ON, BROTHER HERB!
THE TRUTH, BROTHER HERB, THE TRUTH!
THOSE TROOPERS LOOK LIKE THEY WOULD LOVE NOTHING MORE THAN TO GET A SHOT AT US.

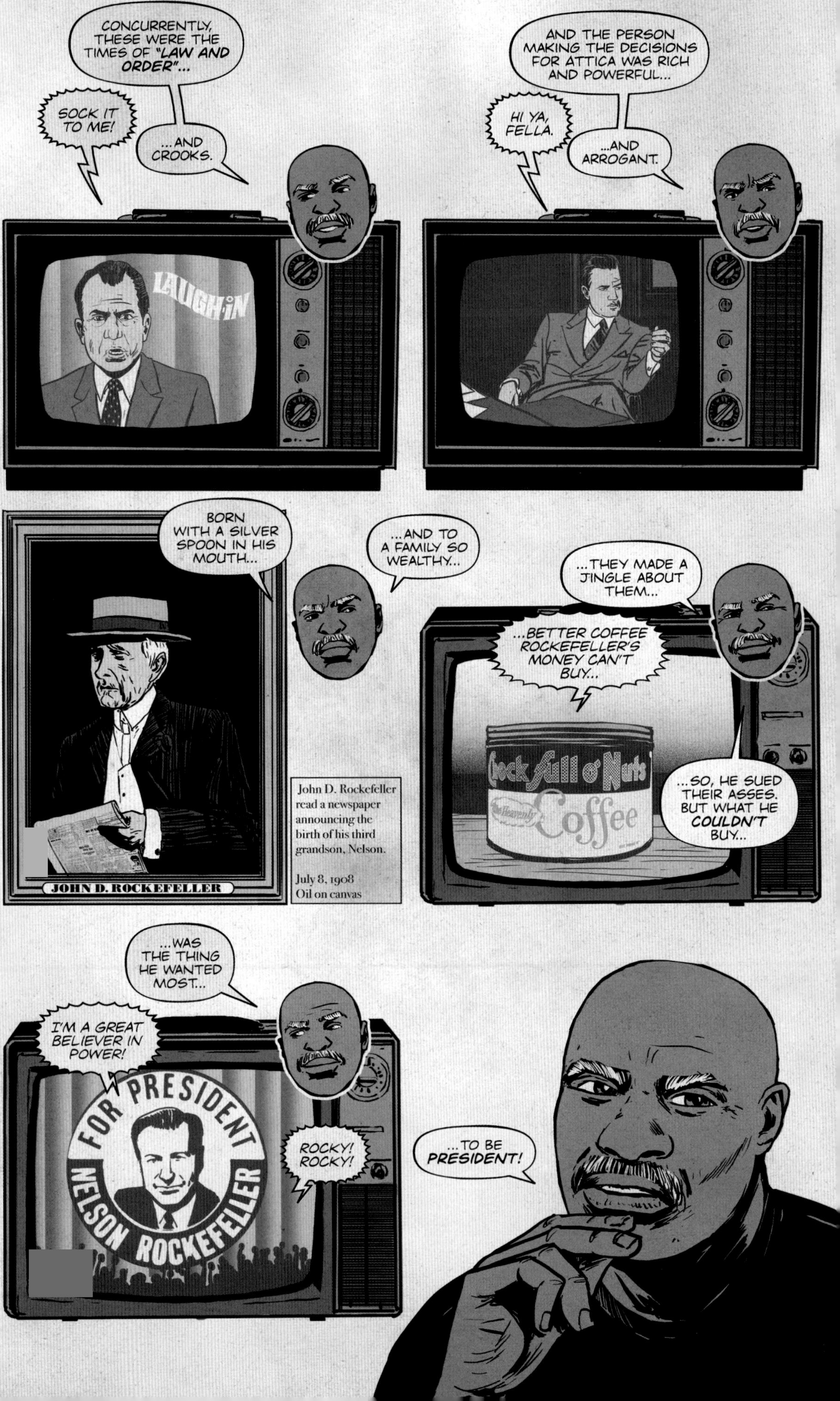
CONCURRENTLY, THESE WERE THE TIMES OF "LAW AND ORDER"...
SOCK IT TO ME!
...AND CROOKS.
LAUGH-IN
AND THE PERSON MAKING THE DECISIONS FOR ATTICA WAS RICH AND POWERFUL...
HI YA, FELLA.
...AND ARROGANT.
BORN WITH A SILVER SPOON IN HIS MOUTH...
JOHN D. ROCKEFELLER
John D. Rockefeller read a newspaper announcing the birth of his third grandson, Nelson.
July 8, 1908
Oil on canvas
...AND TO A FAMILY SO WEALTHY...
...THEY MADE A JINGLE ABOUT THEM...
...BETTER COFFEE ROCKEFELLER'S MONEY CAN'T BUY...
Chock full o' Nuts
The Heavenly Coffee
...SO, HE SUED THEIR ASSES. BUT WHAT HE COULDN'T BUY...
...WAS THE THING HE WANTED MOST...
I'M A GREAT BELIEVER IN POWER!
FOR PRESIDENT
NELSON ROCKEFELLER
ROCKY! ROCKY!
...TO BE PRESIDENT!

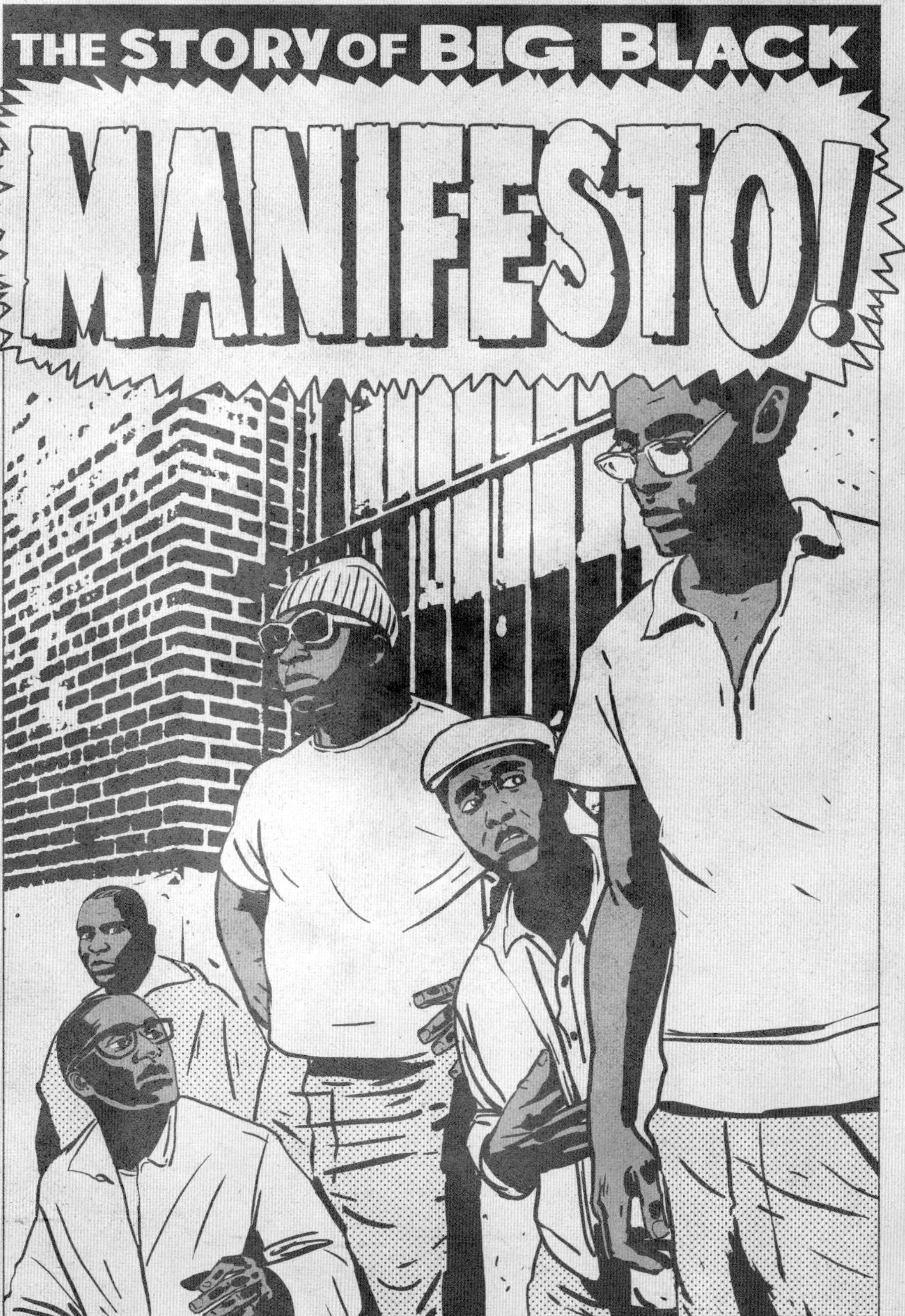
THE STORY OF BIG BLACK
MANIFESTO!

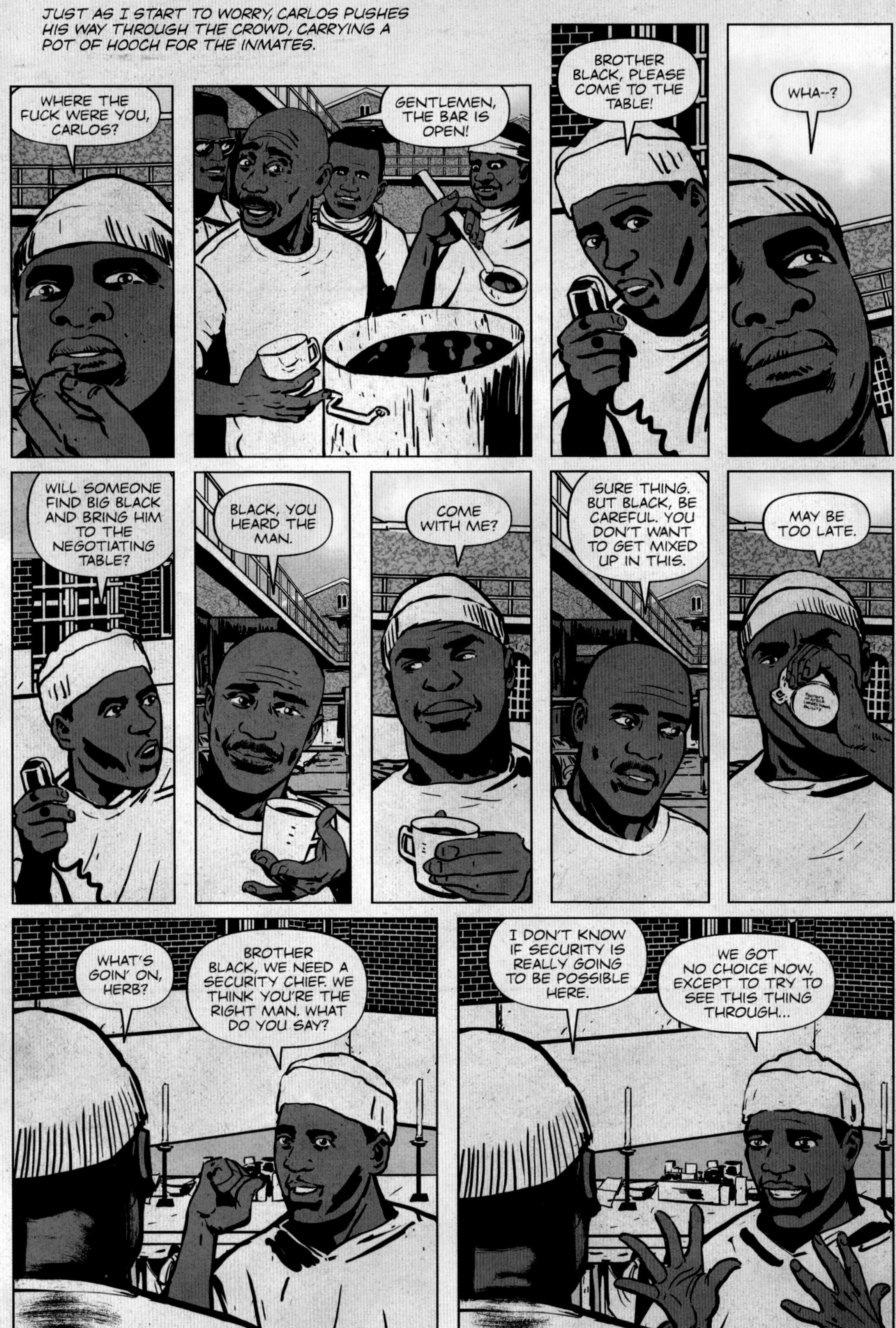
JUST AS I START TO WORRY, CARLOS PUSHES HIS WAY THROUGH THE CROWD, CARRYING A POT OF HOOCH FOR THE INMATES.
WHERE THE FUCK WERE YOU, CARLOS?
GENTLEMEN, THE BAR IS OPEN!
BROTHER BLACK, PLEASE COME TO THE TABLE!
WHA--?
WILL SOMEONE FIND BIG BLACK AND BRING HIM TO THE NEGOTIATING TABLE?
BLACK, YOU HEARD THE MAN.
COME WITH ME?
SURE THING. BUT BLACK, BE CAREFUL. YOU DON'T WANT TO GET MIXED UP IN THIS.
MAY BE TOO LATE.
WHAT'S GOIN' ON, HERB?
BROTHER BLACK, WE NEED A SECURITY CHIEF. WE THINK YOU'RE THE RIGHT MAN. WHAT DO YOU SAY?
I DON'T KNOW IF SECURITY IS REALLY GOING TO BE POSSIBLE HERE.
WE GOT NO CHOICE NOW, EXCEPT TO TRY TO SEE THIS THING THROUGH...

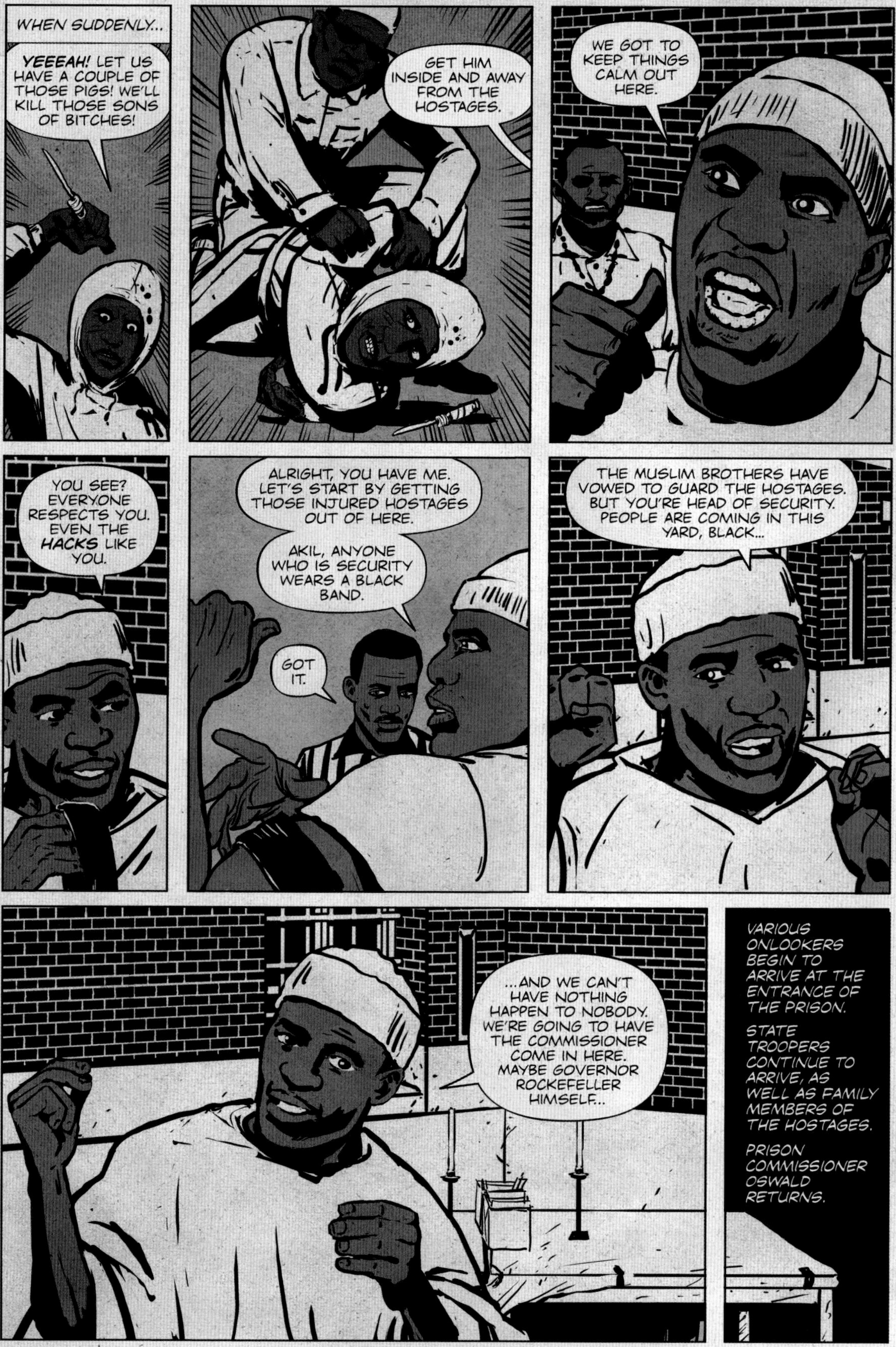
WHEN SUDDENLY...
YEEEAH! LET US HAVE A COUPLE OF THOSE PIGS! WE'LL KILL THOSE SONS OF BITCHES!
GET HIM INSIDE AND AWAY FROM THE HOSTAGES.
WE GOT TO KEEP THINGS CALM OUT HERE.
YOU SEE? EVERYONE RESPECTS YOU. EVEN THE HACKS LIKE YOU.
ALRIGHT, YOU HAVE ME. LET'S START BY GETTING THOSE INJURED HOSTAGES OUT OF HERE.
AKIL, ANYONE WHO IS SECURITY WEARS A BLACK BAND.
GOT IT.
THE MUSLIM BROTHERS HAVE VOWED TO GUARD THE HOSTAGES. BUT YOU'RE HEAD OF SECURITY. PEOPLE ARE COMING IN THIS YARD, BLACK...
...AND WE CAN'T HAVE NOTHING HAPPEN TO NOBODY. WE'RE GOING TO HAVE THE COMMISSIONER COME IN HERE. MAYBE GOVERNOR ROCKEFELLER HIMSELF...
VARIOUS ONLOOKERS BEGIN TO ARRIVE AT THE ENTRANCE OF THE PRISON.
STATE TROOPERS CONTINUE TO ARRIVE, AS WELL AS FAMILY MEMBERS OF THE HOSTAGES.
PRISON COMMISSIONER OSWALD RETURNS.

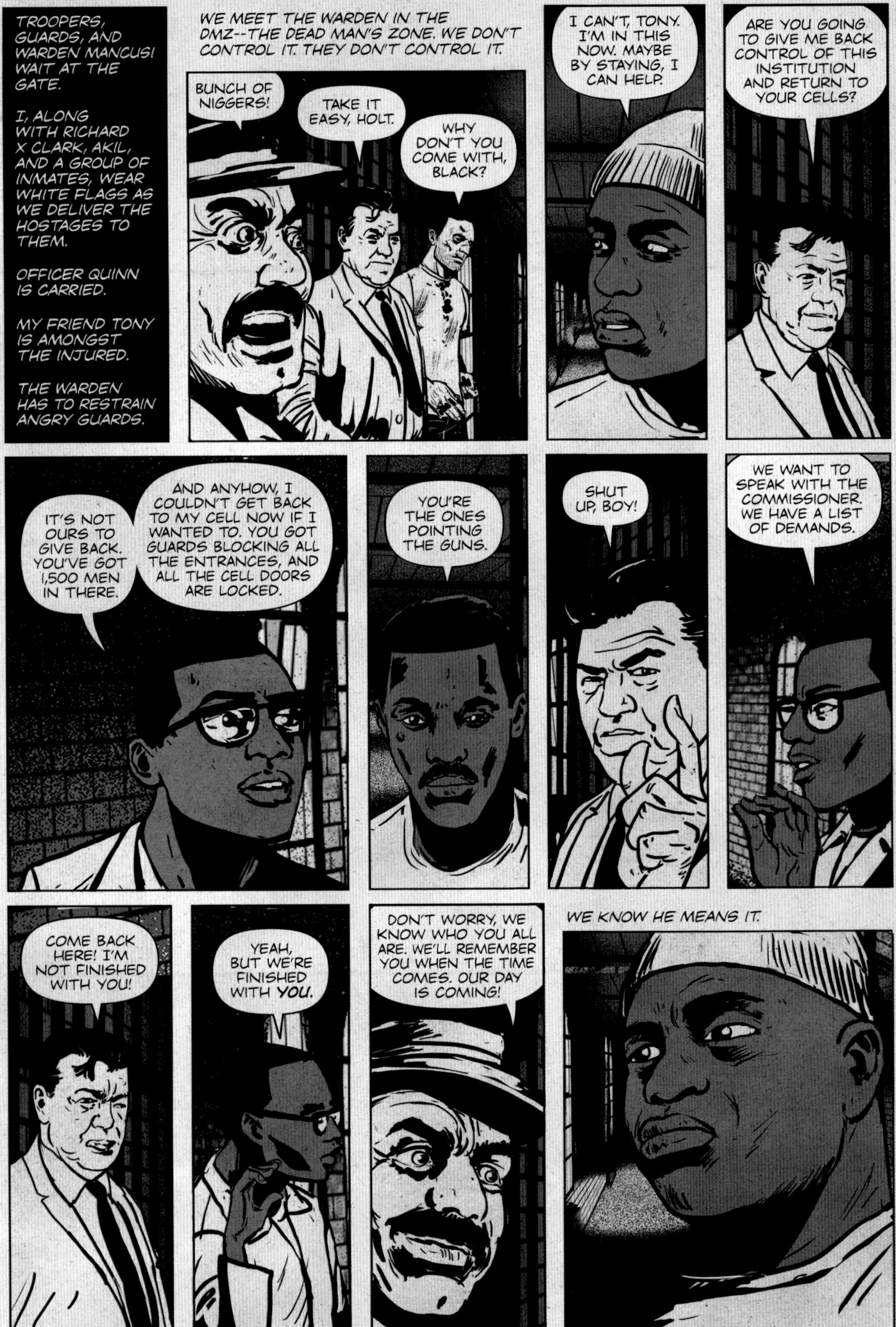

TROOPERS, GUARDS, AND WARDEN MANCUSI WAIT AT THE GATE.
I, ALONG WITH RICHARD X CLARK, AKIL, AND A GROUP OF INMATES, WEAR WHITE FLAGS AS WE DELIVER THE HOSTAGES TO THEM.
OFFICER QUINN IS CARRIED.
MY FRIEND TONY IS AMONGST THE INJURED.
THE WARDEN HAS TO RESTRAIN ANGRY GUARDS.
WE MEET THE WARDEN IN THE DMZ--THE DEAD MAN'S ZONE. WE DON'T CONTROL IT. THEY DON'T CONTROL IT.
BUNCH OF NIGGERS!
TAKE IT EASY, HOLT.
WHY DON'T YOU COME WITH, BLACK?
I CAN'T, TONY. I'M IN THIS NOW. MAYBE BY STAYING, I CAN HELP.
ARE YOU GOING TO GIVE ME BACK CONTROL OF THIS INSTITUTION AND RETURN TO YOUR CELLS?
IT'S NOT OURS TO GIVE BACK. YOU'VE GOT 1,500 MEN IN THERE.
AND ANYHOW, I COULDN'T GET BACK TO MY CELL NOW IF I WANTED TO. YOU GOT GUARDS BLOCKING ALL THE ENTRANCES, AND ALL THE CELL DOORS ARE LOCKED.
YOU'RE THE ONES POINTING THE GUNS.
SHUT UP, BOY!
WE WANT TO SPEAK WITH THE COMMISSIONER. WE HAVE A LIST OF DEMANDS.
COME BACK HERE! I'M NOT FINISHED WITH YOU!
YEAH, BUT WE'RE FINISHED WITH *YOU*.
DON'T WORRY, WE KNOW WHO YOU ALL ARE. WE'LL REMEMBER YOU WHEN THE TIME COMES. OUR DAY IS COMING!
WE KNOW HE MEANS IT.

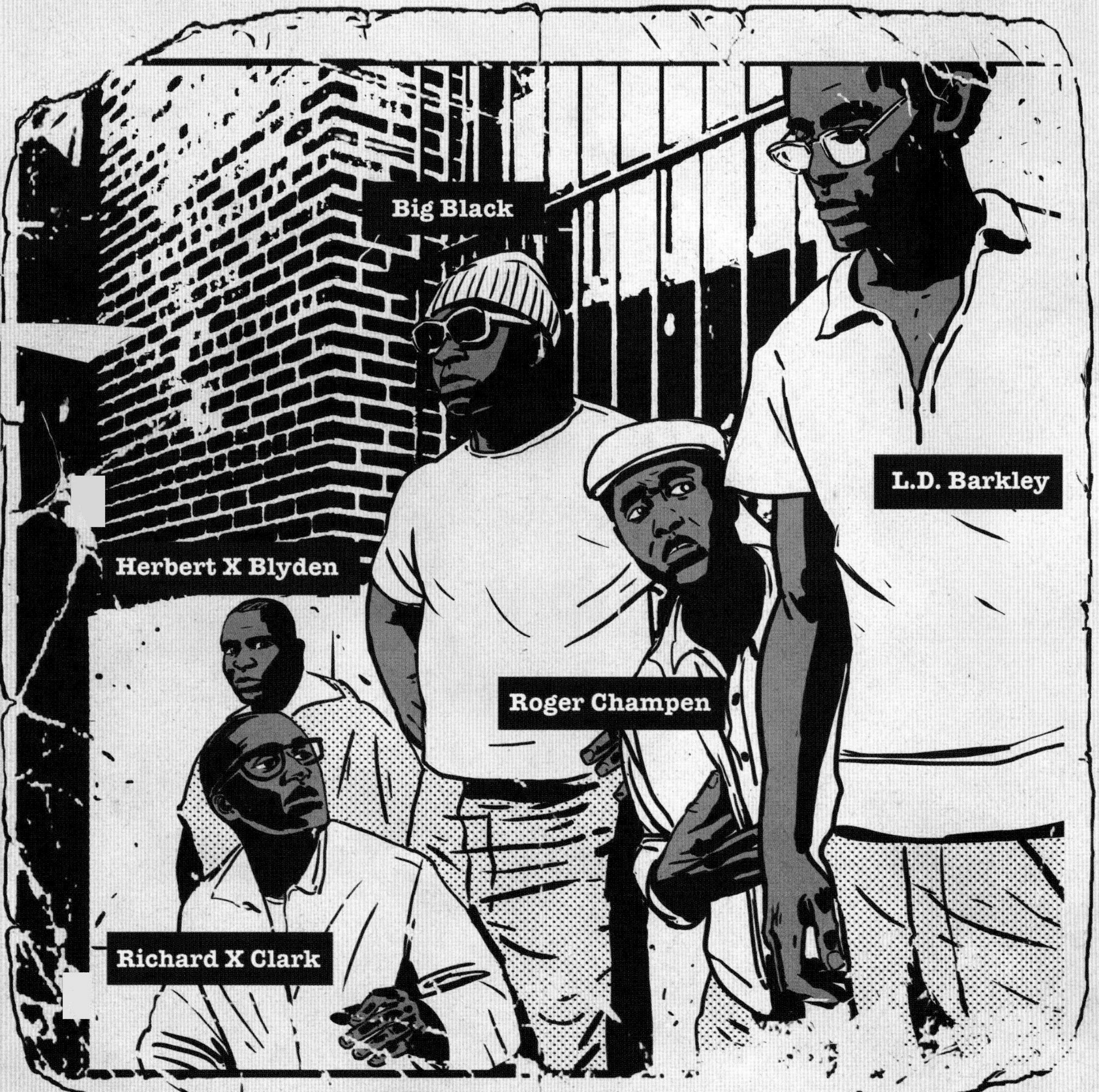
Big Black
L.D. Barkley
Herbert X Blyden
Roger Champen
Richard X Clark

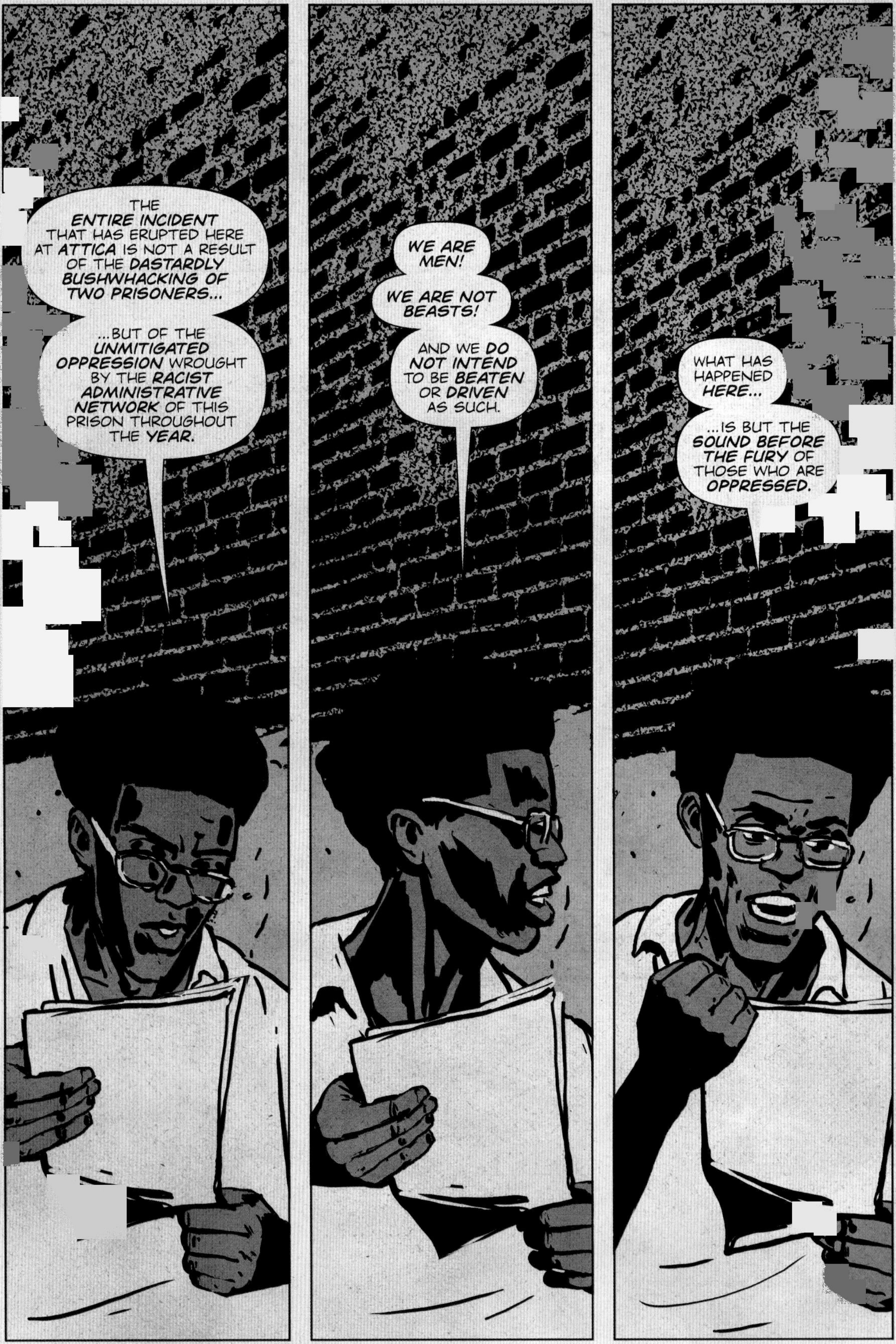
THE ENTIRE INCIDENT THAT HAS ERUPTED HERE AT ATTICA IS NOT A RESULT OF THE DASTARDLY BUSHWHACKING OF TWO PRISONERS...
...BUT OF THE UNMITIGATED OPPRESSION WROUGHT BY THE RACIST ADMINISTRATIVE NETWORK OF THIS PRISON THROUGHOUT THE YEAR.
WE ARE MEN!
WE ARE NOT BEASTS!
AND WE DO NOT INTEND TO BE BEATEN OR DRIVEN AS SUCH.
WHAT HAS HAPPENED HERE...
...IS BUT THE SOUND BEFORE THE FURY OF THOSE WHO ARE OPPRESSED.

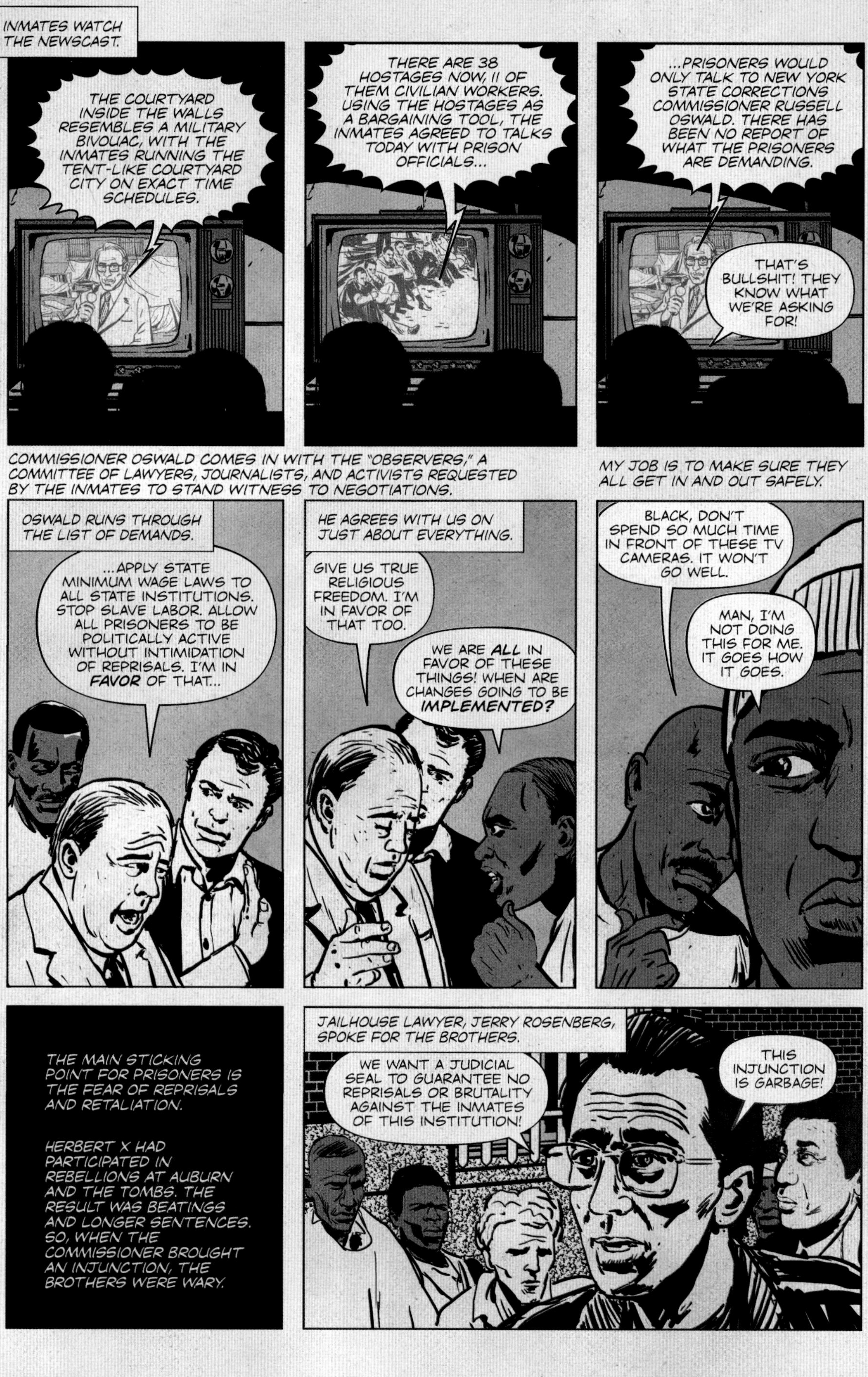

INMATES WATCH THE NEWSCAST.
THE COURTYARD INSIDE THE WALLS RESEMBLES A MILITARY BIVOUAC, WITH THE INMATES RUNNING THE TENT-LIKE COURTYARD CITY ON EXACT TIME SCHEDULES.
THERE ARE 38 HOSTAGES NOW, 11 OF THEM CIVILIAN WORKERS. USING THE HOSTAGES AS A BARGAINING TOOL, THE INMATES AGREED TO TALKS TODAY WITH PRISON OFFICIALS...
...PRISONERS WOULD ONLY TALK TO NEW YORK STATE CORRECTIONS COMMISSIONER RUSSELL OSWALD. THERE HAS BEEN NO REPORT OF WHAT THE PRISONERS ARE DEMANDING.
THAT'S BULLSHIT! THEY KNOW WHAT WE'RE ASKING FOR!
COMMISSIONER OSWALD COMES IN WITH THE "OBSERVERS," A COMMITTEE OF LAWYERS, JOURNALISTS, AND ACTIVISTS REQUESTED BY THE INMATES TO STAND WITNESS TO NEGOTIATIONS.
MY JOB IS TO MAKE SURE THEY ALL GET IN AND OUT SAFELY.
OSWALD RUNS THROUGH THE LIST OF DEMANDS.
...APPLY STATE MINIMUM WAGE LAWS TO ALL STATE INSTITUTIONS. STOP SLAVE LABOR. ALLOW ALL PRISONERS TO BE POLITICALLY ACTIVE WITHOUT INTIMIDATION OF REPRISALS. I'M IN **FAVOR** OF THAT...
HE AGREES WITH US ON JUST ABOUT EVERYTHING.
GIVE US TRUE RELIGIOUS FREEDOM. I'M IN FAVOR OF THAT TOO.
WE ARE **ALL** IN FAVOR OF THESE THINGS! WHEN ARE CHANGES GOING TO BE **IMPLEMENTED?**
BLACK, DON'T SPEND SO MUCH TIME IN FRONT OF THESE TV CAMERAS. IT WON'T GO WELL.
MAN, I'M NOT DOING THIS FOR ME. IT GOES HOW IT GOES.
THE MAIN STICKING POINT FOR PRISONERS IS THE FEAR OF REPRISALS AND RETALIATION.
HERBERT X HAD PARTICIPATED IN REBELLIONS AT AUBURN AND THE TOMBS. THE RESULT WAS BEATINGS AND LONGER SENTENCES. SO, WHEN THE COMMISSIONER BROUGHT AN INJUNCTION, THE BROTHERS WERE WARY.
JAILHOUSE LAWYER, JERRY ROSENBERG, SPOKE FOR THE BROTHERS.
WE WANT A JUDICIAL SEAL TO GUARANTEE NO REPRISALS OR BRUTALITY AGAINST THE INMATES OF THIS INSTITUTION!
THIS INJUNCTION IS GARBAGE!

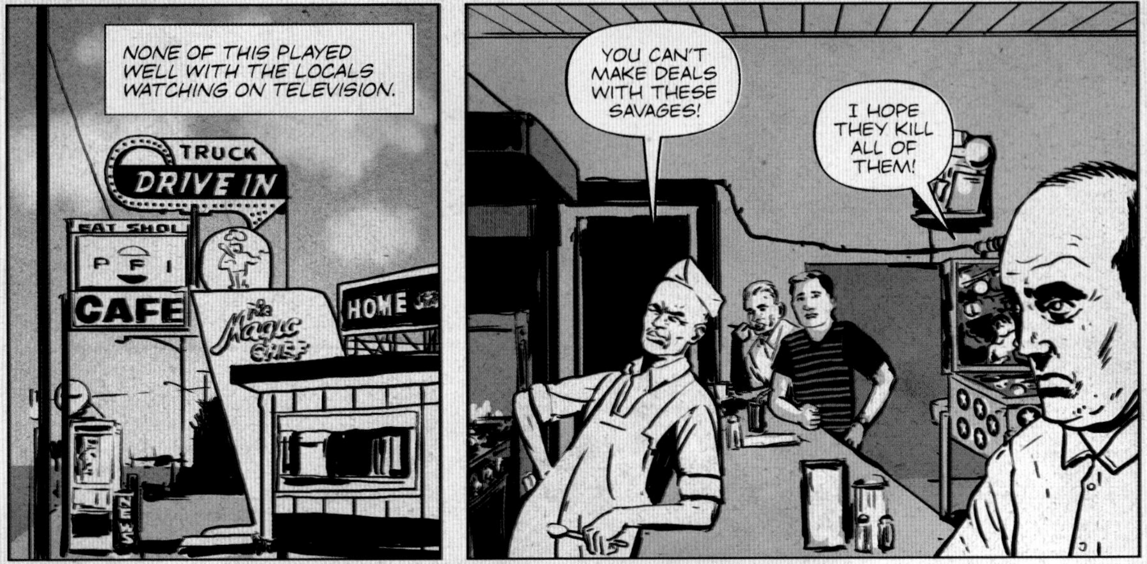
NONE OF THIS PLAYED WELL WITH THE LOCALS WATCHING ON TELEVISION.
TRUCK
DRIVE IN
CAFE
HOME
Magic Chef
NEWS
YOU CAN'T MAKE DEALS WITH THESE SAVAGES!
I HOPE THEY KILL ALL OF THEM!

TENSIONS ARE HIGH, IT FEELS LIKE IT'S ABOUT TO JUMP OFF AGAIN.

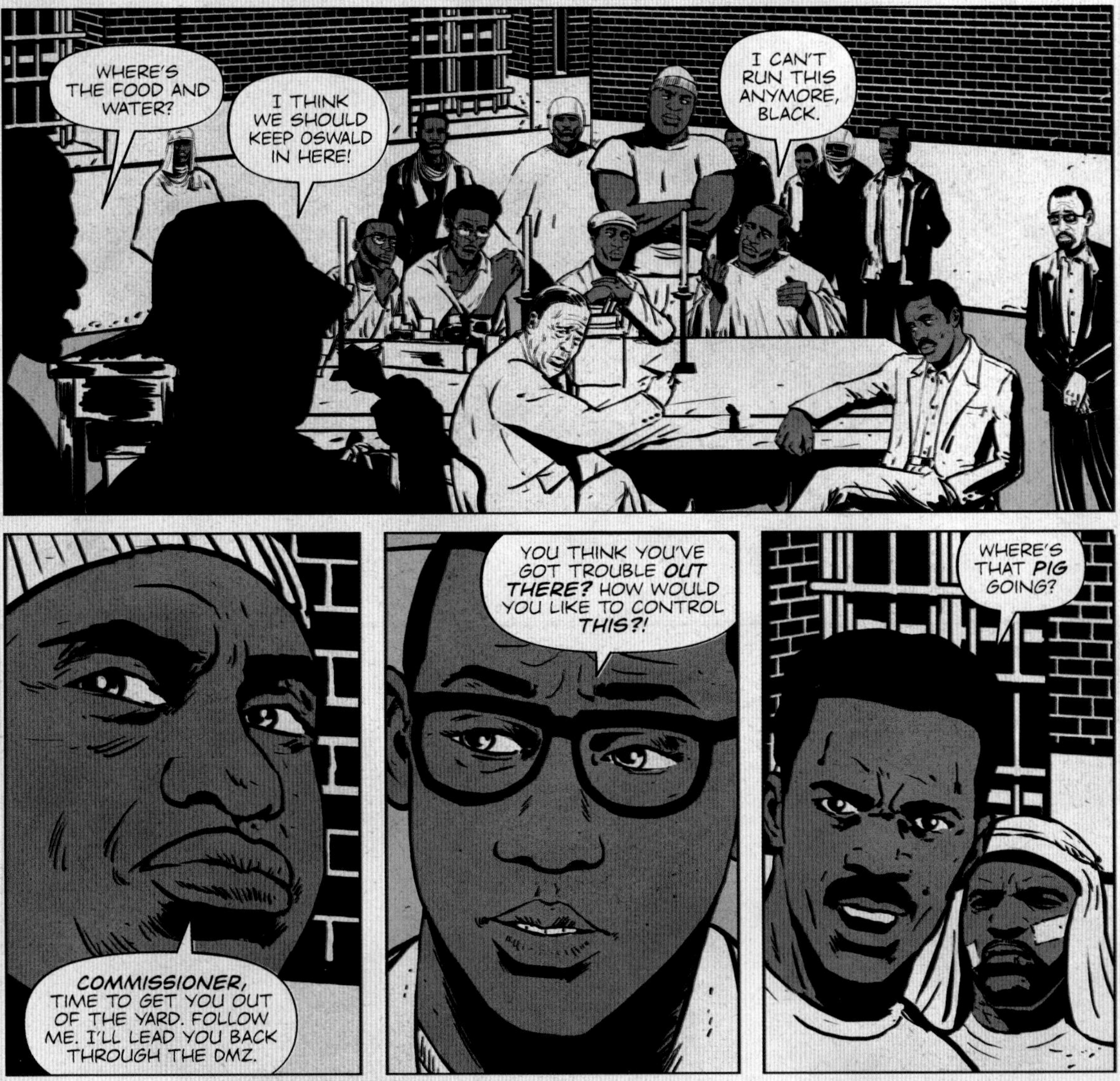
WHERE'S THE FOOD AND WATER?
I THINK WE SHOULD KEEP OSWALD IN HERE!
I CAN'T RUN THIS ANYMORE, BLACK.
COMMISSIONER, TIME TO GET YOU OUT OF THE YARD. FOLLOW ME. I'LL LEAD YOU BACK THROUGH THE DMZ.
YOU THINK YOU'VE GOT TROUBLE ***OUT THERE?*** HOW WOULD YOU LIKE TO CONTROL ***THIS?!***
WHERE'S THAT ***PIG*** GOING?

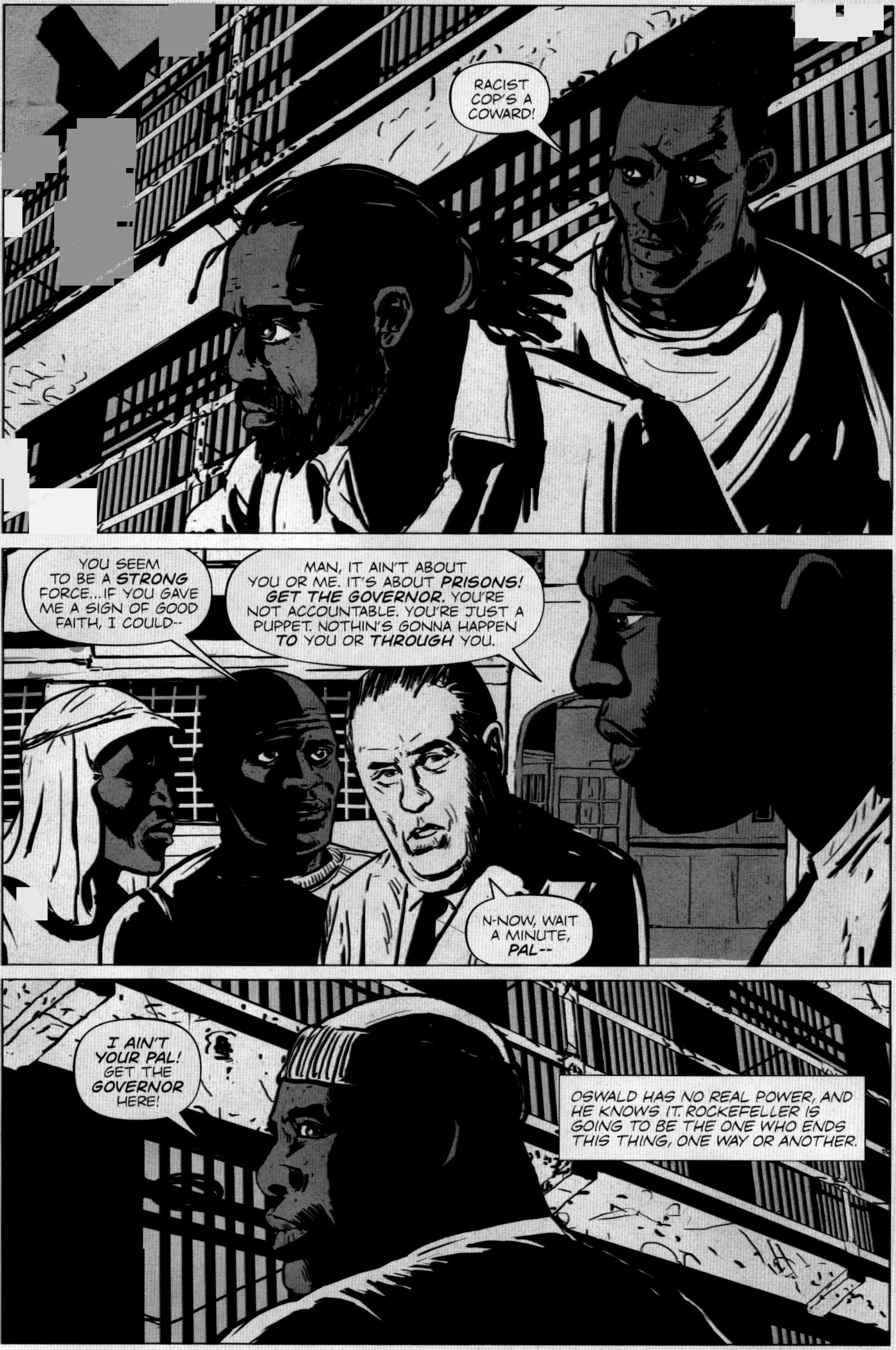
RACIST COP'S A COWARD!
YOU SEEM TO BE A STRONG FORCE...IF YOU GAVE ME A SIGN OF GOOD FAITH, I COULD--
MAN, IT AIN'T ABOUT YOU OR ME. IT'S ABOUT PRISONS! GET THE GOVERNOR. YOU'RE NOT ACCOUNTABLE. YOU'RE JUST A PUPPET. NOTHIN'S GONNA HAPPEN TO YOU OR THROUGH YOU.
N-NOW, WAIT A MINUTE, PAL--
I AIN'T YOUR PAL! GET THE GOVERNOR HERE!
OSWALD HAS NO REAL POWER, AND HE KNOWS IT. ROCKEFELLER IS GOING TO BE THE ONE WHO ENDS THIS THING, ONE WAY OR ANOTHER.

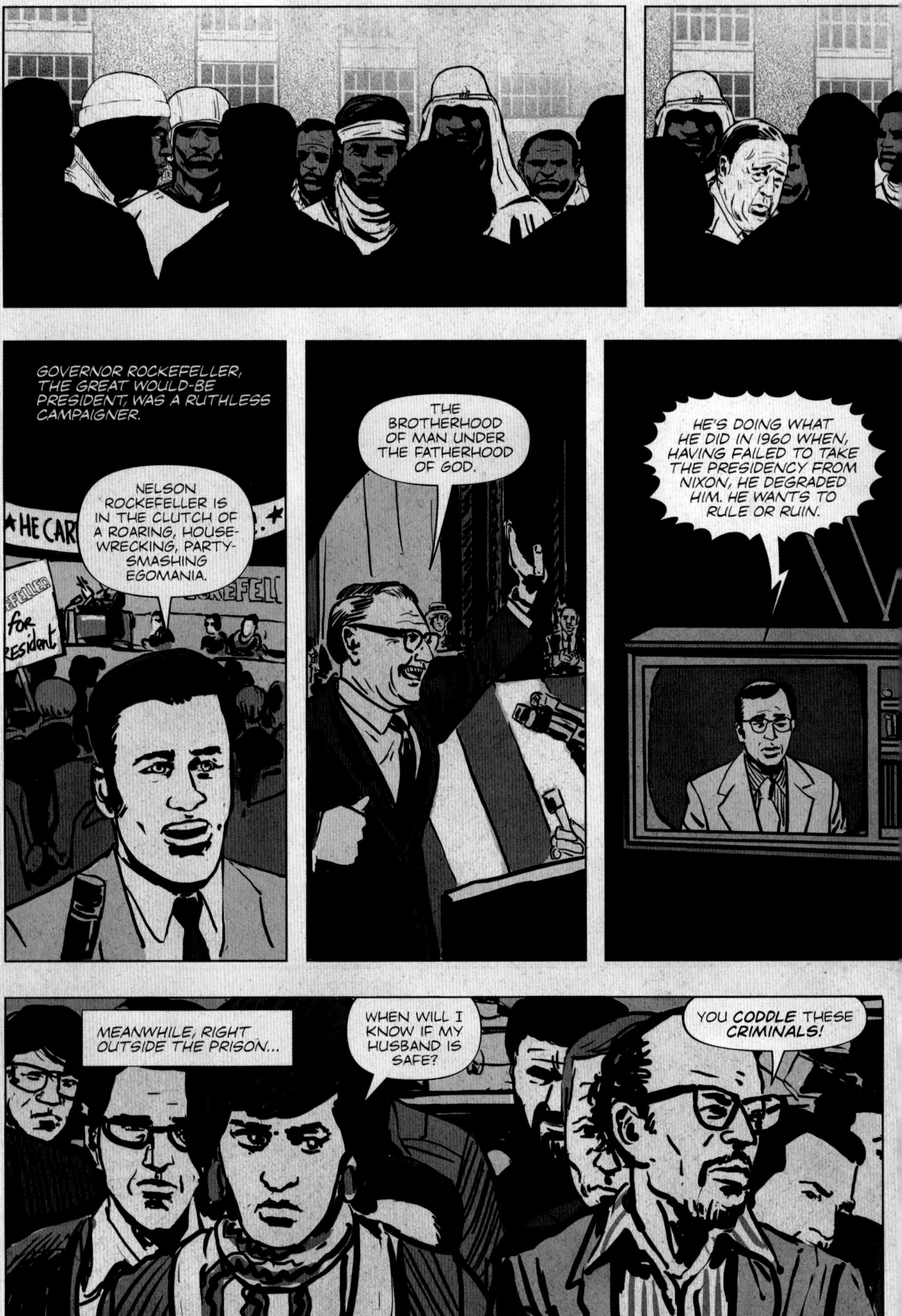

GOVERNOR ROCKEFELLER, THE GREAT WOULD-BE PRESIDENT, WAS A RUTHLESS CAMPAIGNER.
NELSON ROCKEFELLER IS IN THE CLUTCH OF A ROARING, HOUSE-WRECKING, PARTY-SMASHING EGOMANIA.
THE BROTHERHOOD OF MAN UNDER THE FATHERHOOD OF GOD.
HE'S DOING WHAT HE DID IN 1960 WHEN, HAVING FAILED TO TAKE THE PRESIDENCY FROM NIXON, HE DEGRADED HIM. HE WANTS TO RULE OR RUIN.
MEANWHILE, RIGHT OUTSIDE THE PRISON...
WHEN WILL I KNOW IF MY HUSBAND IS SAFE?
YOU **CODDLE** THESE **CRIMINALS!**

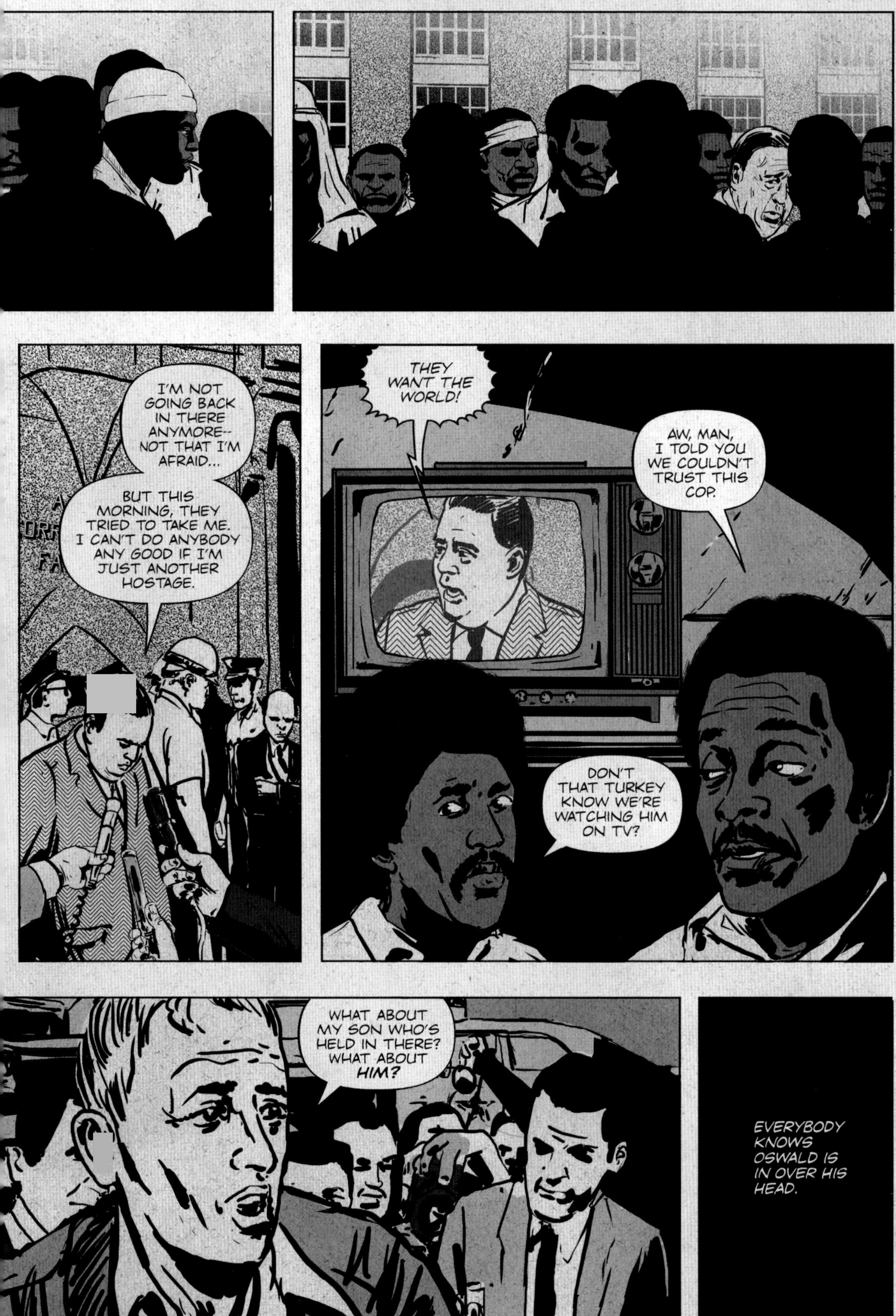
I'M NOT GOING BACK IN THERE ANYMORE-- NOT THAT I'M AFRAID...
BUT THIS MORNING, THEY TRIED TO TAKE ME. I CAN'T DO ANYBODY ANY GOOD IF I'M JUST ANOTHER HOSTAGE.
THEY WANT THE WORLD!
AW, MAN, I TOLD YOU WE COULDN'T TRUST THIS COP.
DON'T THAT TURKEY KNOW WE'RE WATCHING HIM ON TV?
WHAT ABOUT MY SON WHO'S HELD IN THERE? WHAT ABOUT HIM?
EVERYBODY KNOWS OSWALD IS IN OVER HIS HEAD.

IN D-YARD, TWO INMATES ARE BROUGHT BEFORE ME, ACCUSED BY THE OTHER INMATES OF BREAKING RULES.

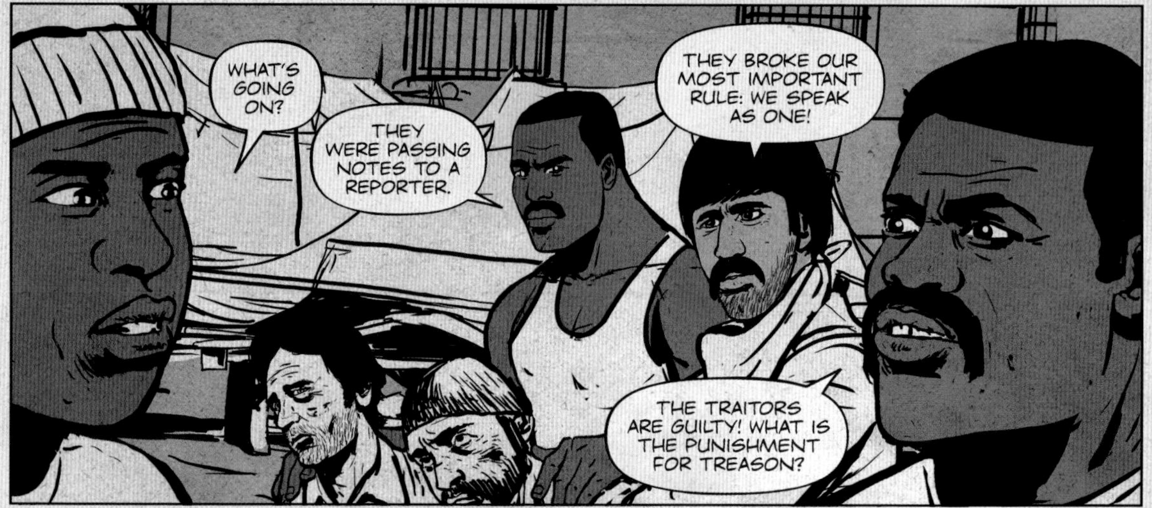
WHAT'S GOING ON?
THEY WERE PASSING NOTES TO A REPORTER.
THEY BROKE OUR MOST IMPORTANT RULE: WE SPEAK AS ONE!
THE TRAITORS ARE GUILTY! WHAT IS THE PUNISHMENT FOR TREASON?

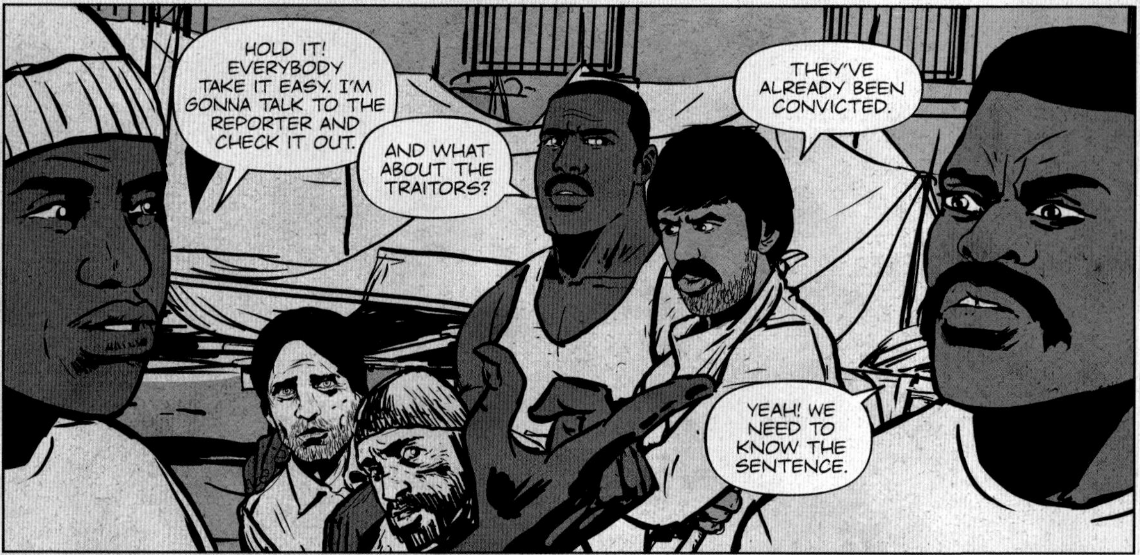
HOLD IT! EVERYBODY TAKE IT EASY. I'M GONNA TALK TO THE REPORTER AND CHECK IT OUT.
AND WHAT ABOUT THE TRAITORS?
THEY'VE ALREADY BEEN CONVICTED.
YEAH! WE NEED TO KNOW THE SENTENCE.

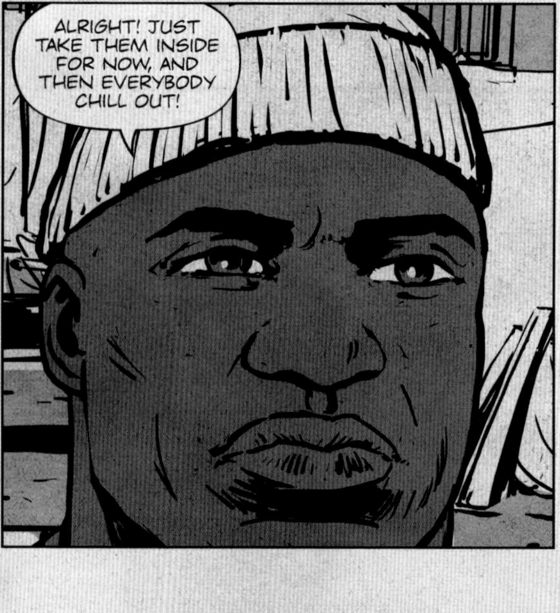
ALRIGHT! JUST TAKE THEM INSIDE FOR NOW, AND THEN EVERYBODY CHILL OUT!

PEOPLE ARE GETTING RATTLED. LOSING THEIR COOL.

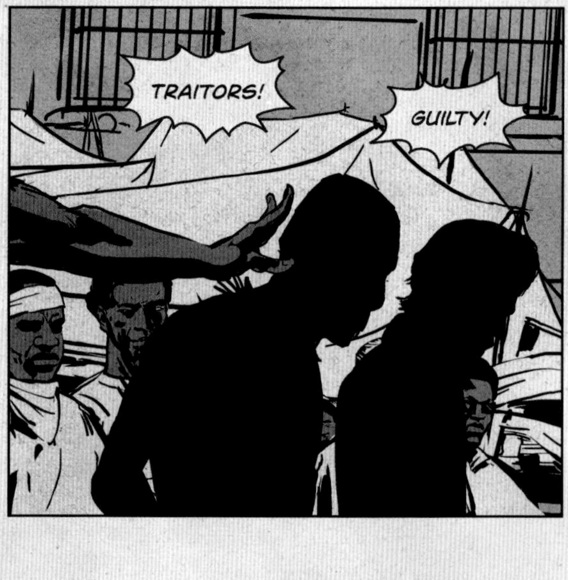
TRAITORS!
GUILTY!

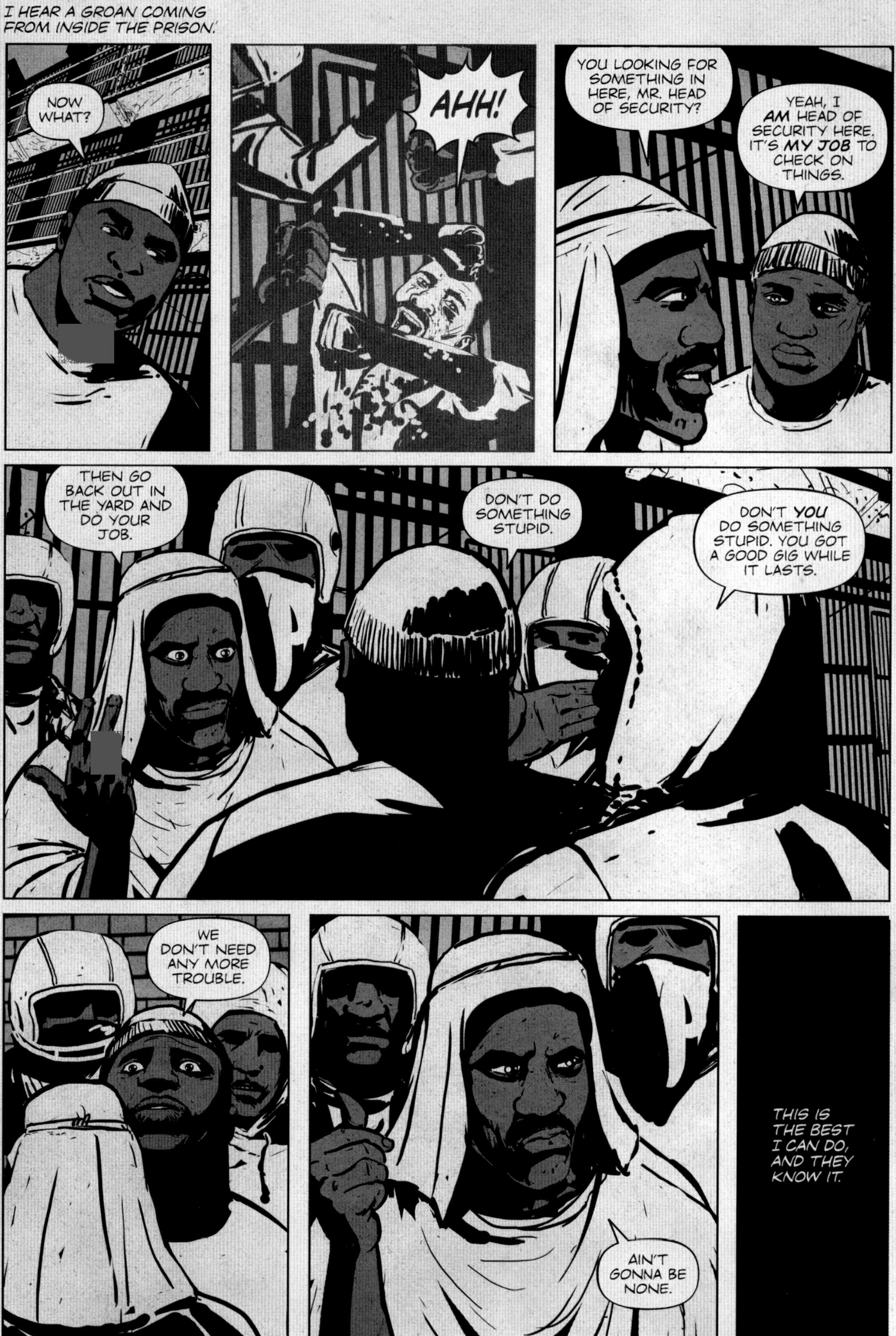
I HEAR A GROAN COMING FROM INSIDE THE PRISON.
NOW WHAT?
AHH!
YOU LOOKING FOR SOMETHING IN HERE, MR. HEAD OF SECURITY?
YEAH, I **AM** HEAD OF SECURITY HERE. IT'S **MY JOB** TO CHECK ON THINGS.
THEN GO BACK OUT IN THE YARD AND DO YOUR JOB.
DON'T DO SOMETHING STUPID.
DON'T **YOU** DO SOMETHING STUPID. YOU GOT A GOOD GIG WHILE IT LASTS.
WE DON'T NEED ANY MORE TROUBLE.
AIN'T GONNA BE NONE.
THIS IS THE BEST I CAN DO, AND THEY KNOW IT.

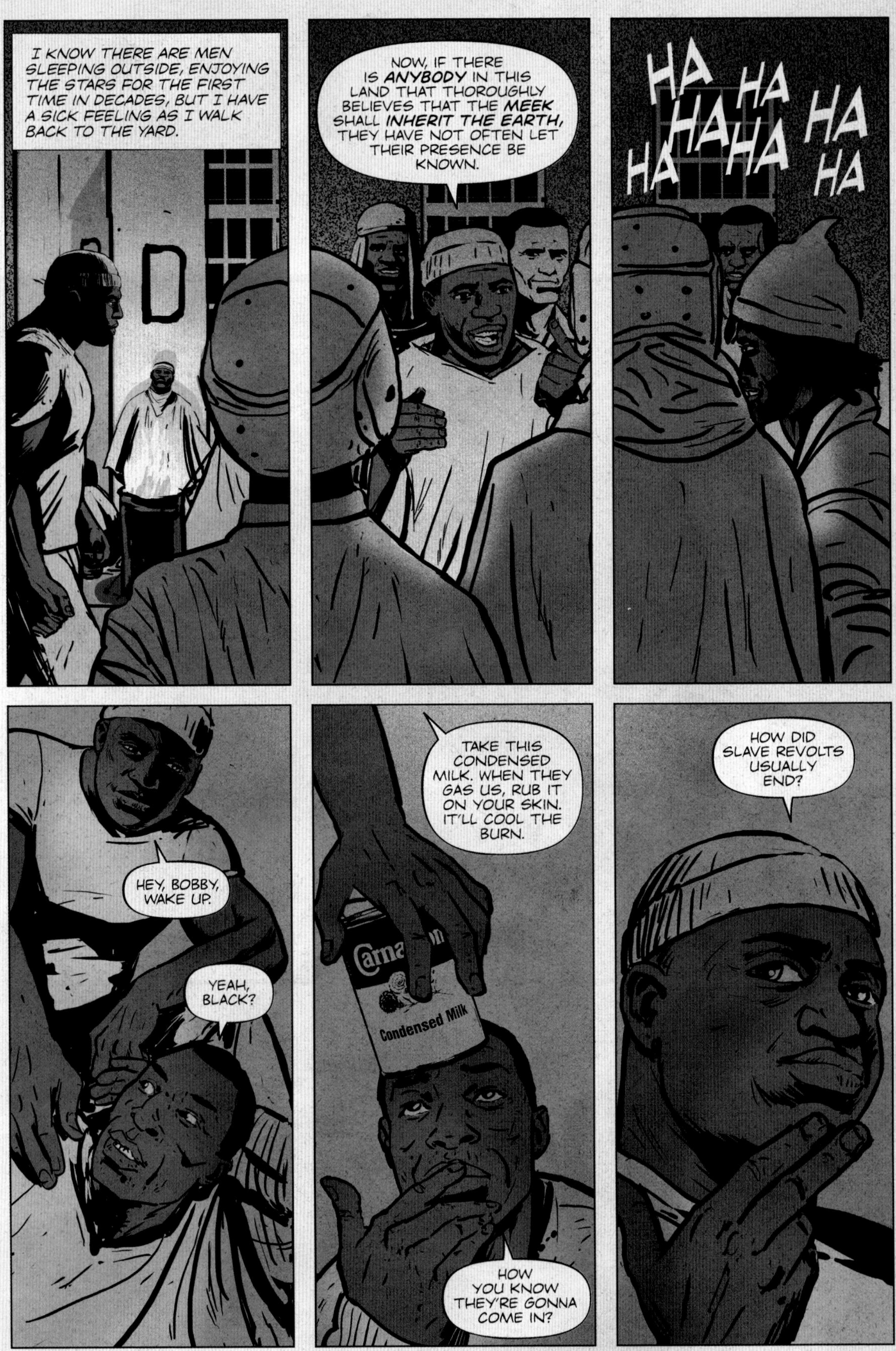
I KNOW THERE ARE MEN SLEEPING OUTSIDE, ENJOYING THE STARS FOR THE FIRST TIME IN DECADES, BUT I HAVE A SICK FEELING AS I WALK BACK TO THE YARD.
D
NOW, IF THERE IS **ANYBODY** IN THIS LAND THAT THOROUGHLY BELIEVES THAT THE **MEEK** SHALL **INHERIT THE EARTH,** THEY HAVE NOT OFTEN LET THEIR PRESENCE BE KNOWN.
HA HA HA HA HA HA HA HA HA
HEY, BOBBY, WAKE UP.
YEAH, BLACK?
TAKE THIS CONDENSED MILK. WHEN THEY GAS US, RUB IT ON YOUR SKIN. IT'LL COOL THE BURN.
Condensed Milk
HOW YOU KNOW THEY'RE GONNA COME IN?
HOW DID SLAVE REVOLTS USUALLY END?

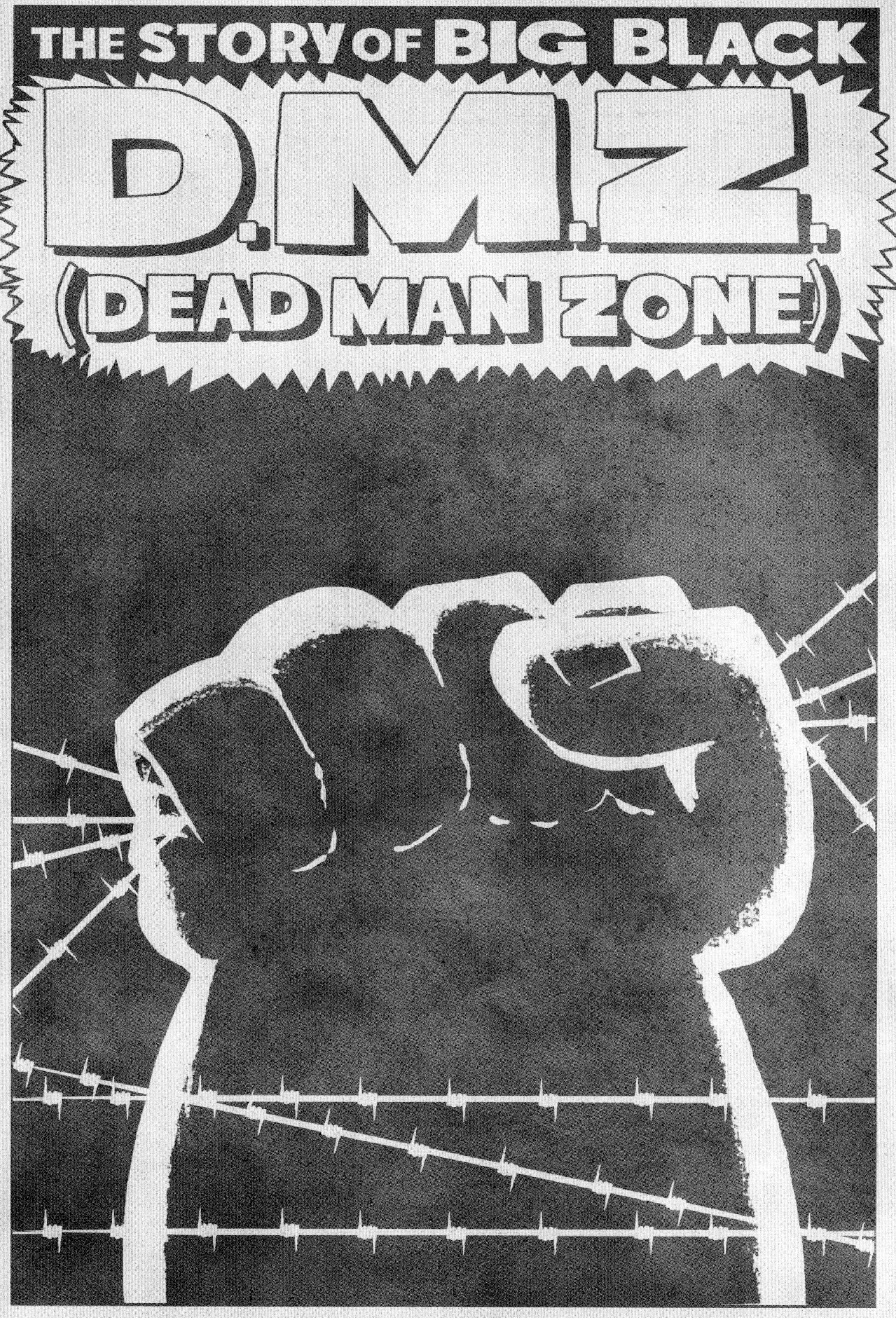
THE STORY OF BIG BLACK
D.M.Z.
(DEAD MAN ZONE)

September 11, 1971

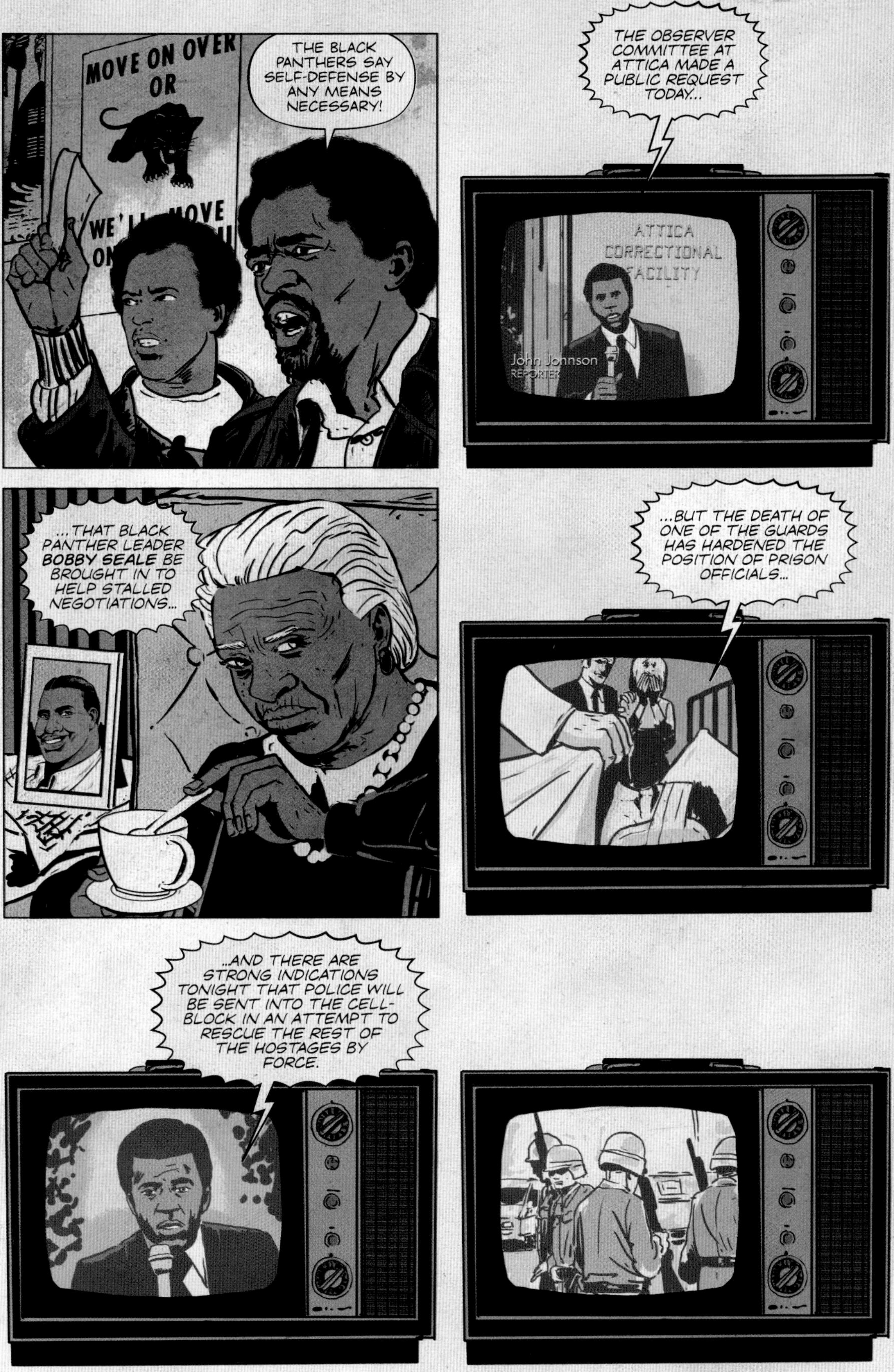
MOVE ON OVER OR
WE'LL MOVE
THE BLACK PANTHERS SAY SELF-DEFENSE BY ANY MEANS NECESSARY!
THE OBSERVER COMMITTEE AT ATTICA MADE A PUBLIC REQUEST TODAY...
ATTICA CORRECTIONAL FACILITY
John Johnson
REPORTER
...THAT BLACK PANTHER LEADER BOBBY SEALE BE BROUGHT IN TO HELP STALLED NEGOTIATIONS...
...BUT THE DEATH OF ONE OF THE GUARDS HAS HARDENED THE POSITION OF PRISON OFFICIALS...
...AND THERE ARE STRONG INDICATIONS TONIGHT THAT POLICE WILL BE SENT INTO THE CELL-BLOCK IN AN ATTEMPT TO RESCUE THE REST OF THE HOSTAGES BY FORCE.

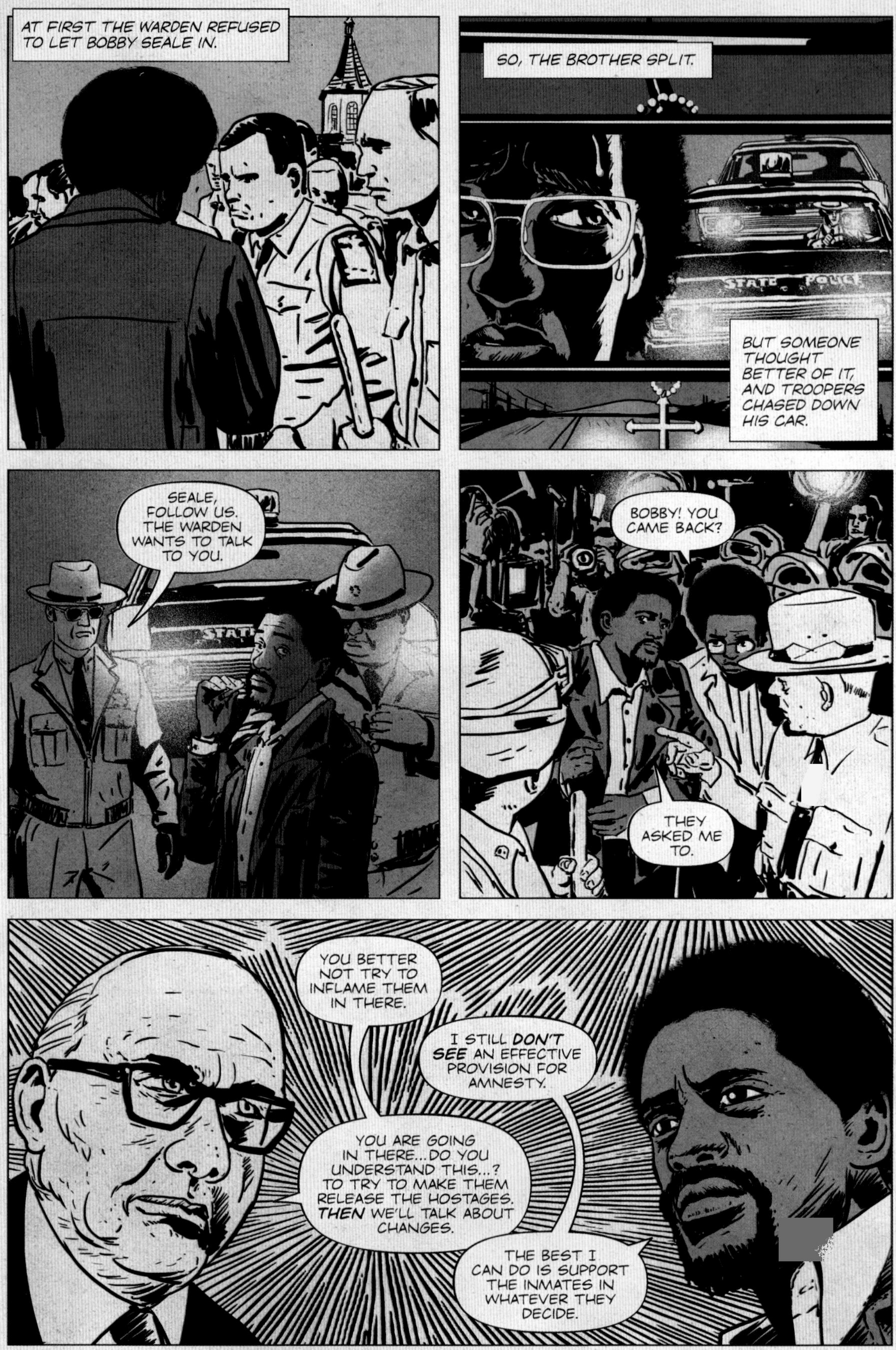
AT FIRST THE WARDEN REFUSED TO LET BOBBY SEALE IN.
SO, THE BROTHER SPLIT.
STATE POLICE
BUT SOMEONE THOUGHT BETTER OF IT, AND TROOPERS CHASED DOWN HIS CAR.
SEALE, FOLLOW US. THE WARDEN WANTS TO TALK TO YOU.
BOBBY! YOU CAME BACK?
THEY ASKED ME TO.
YOU BETTER NOT TRY TO INFLAME THEM IN THERE.
I STILL **DON'T SEE** AN EFFECTIVE PROVISION FOR AMNESTY.
YOU ARE GOING IN THERE...DO YOU UNDERSTAND THIS...? TO TRY TO MAKE THEM RELEASE THE HOSTAGES. **THEN** WE'LL TALK ABOUT CHANGES.
THE BEST I CAN DO IS SUPPORT THE INMATES IN WHATEVER THEY DECIDE.

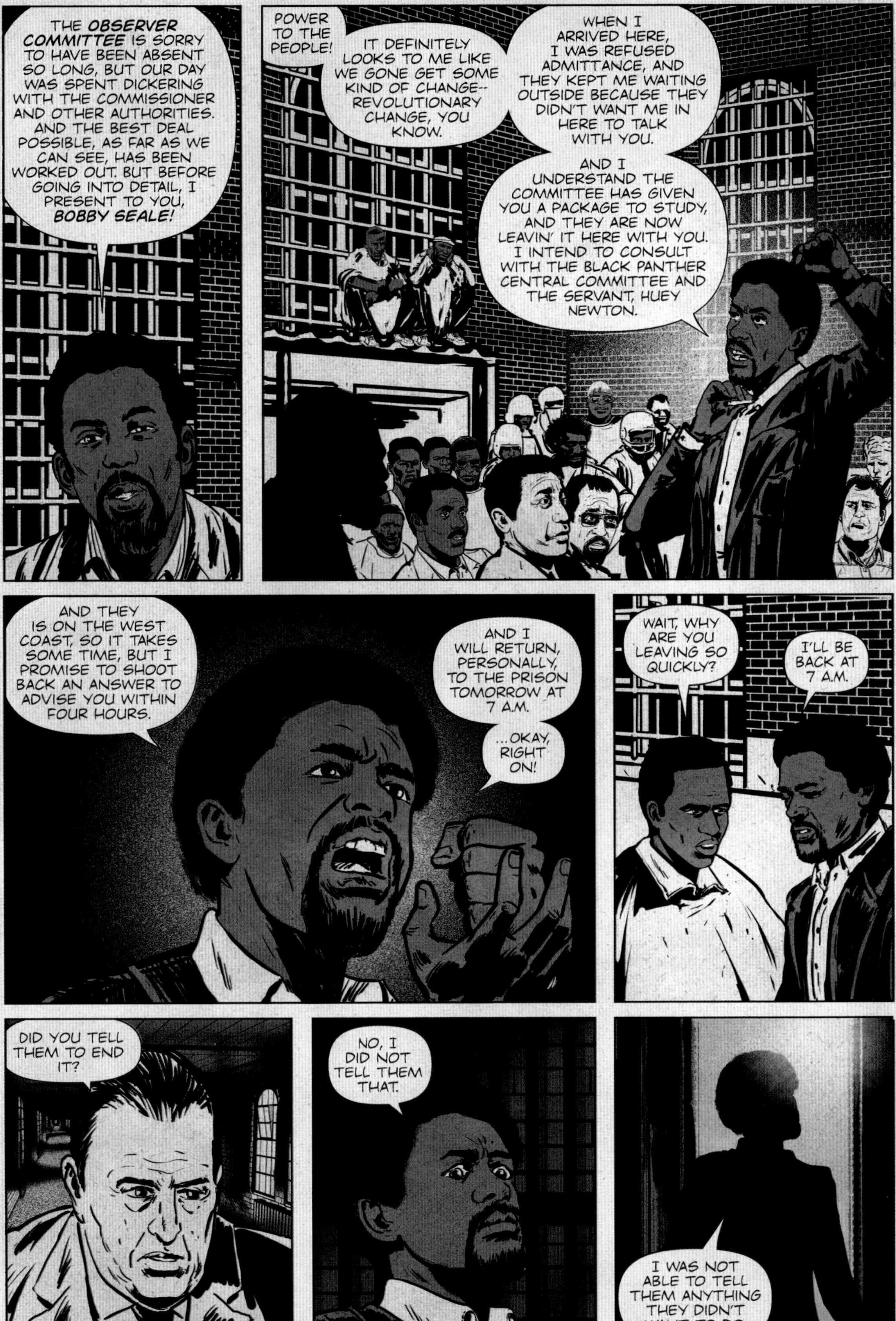
THE OBSERVER COMMITTEE IS SORRY TO HAVE BEEN ABSENT SO LONG, BUT OUR DAY WAS SPENT DICKERING WITH THE COMMISSIONER AND OTHER AUTHORITIES. AND THE BEST DEAL POSSIBLE, AS FAR AS WE CAN SEE, HAS BEEN WORKED OUT. BUT BEFORE GOING INTO DETAIL, I PRESENT TO YOU, BOBBY SEALE!
POWER TO THE PEOPLE!
IT DEFINITELY LOOKS TO ME LIKE WE GONE GET SOME KIND OF CHANGE-- REVOLUTIONARY CHANGE, YOU KNOW.
WHEN I ARRIVED HERE, I WAS REFUSED ADMITTANCE, AND THEY KEPT ME WAITING OUTSIDE BECAUSE THEY DIDN'T WANT ME IN HERE TO TALK WITH YOU.
AND I UNDERSTAND THE COMMITTEE HAS GIVEN YOU A PACKAGE TO STUDY, AND THEY ARE NOW LEAVIN' IT HERE WITH YOU. I INTEND TO CONSULT WITH THE BLACK PANTHER CENTRAL COMMITTEE AND THE SERVANT, HUEY NEWTON.
AND THEY IS ON THE WEST COAST, SO IT TAKES SOME TIME, BUT I PROMISE TO SHOOT BACK AN ANSWER TO ADVISE YOU WITHIN FOUR HOURS.
AND I WILL RETURN, PERSONALLY, TO THE PRISON TOMORROW AT 7 A.M.
...OKAY, RIGHT ON!
WAIT, WHY ARE YOU LEAVING SO QUICKLY?
I'LL BE BACK AT 7 A.M.
DID YOU TELL THEM TO END IT?
NO, I DID NOT TELL THEM THAT.
I WAS NOT ABLE TO TELL THEM ANYTHING THEY DIDN'T WANT TO DO.

September 12, 1971

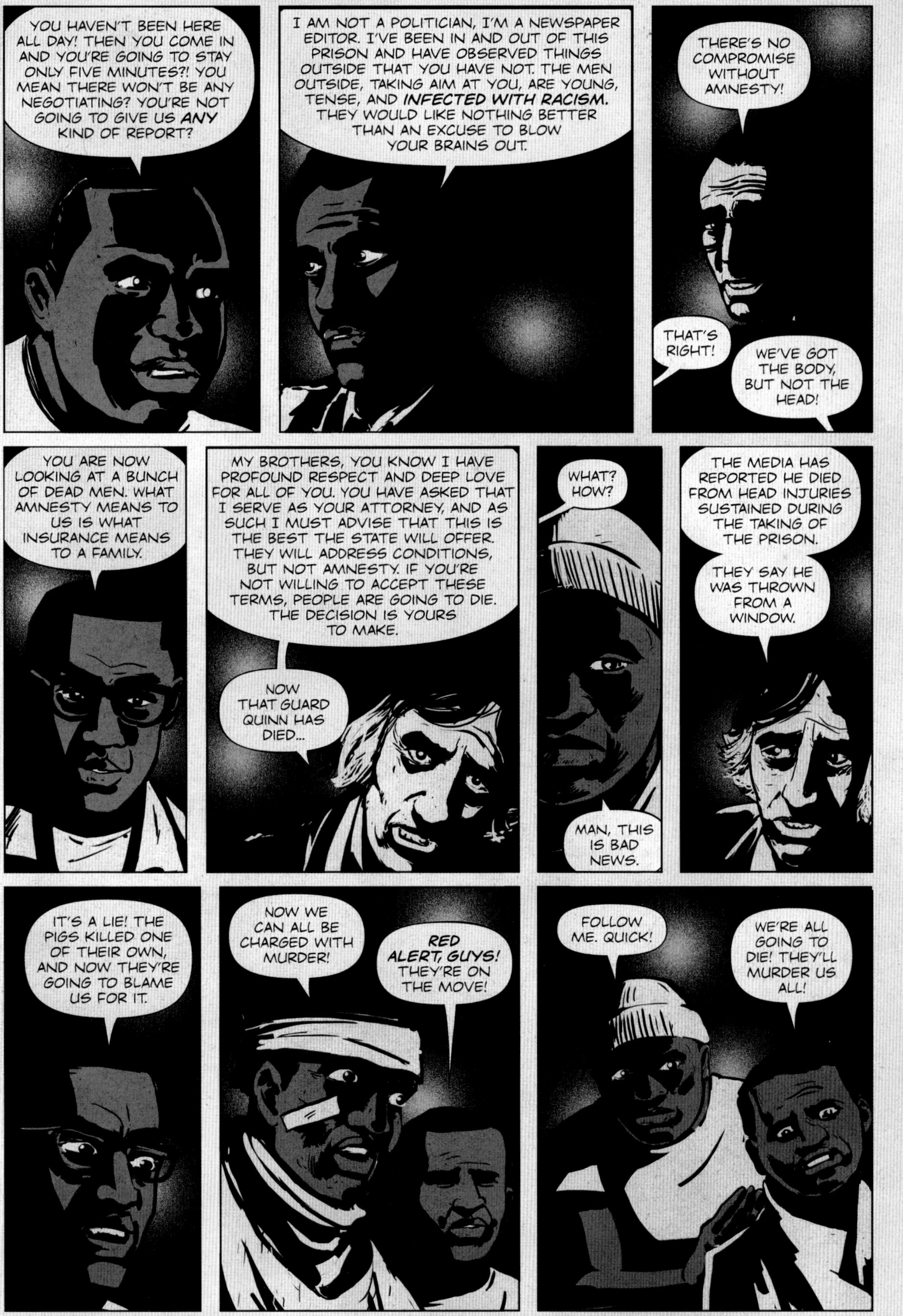
YOU HAVEN'T BEEN HERE ALL DAY! THEN YOU COME IN AND YOU'RE GOING TO STAY ONLY FIVE MINUTES?! YOU MEAN THERE WON'T BE ANY NEGOTIATING? YOU'RE NOT GOING TO GIVE US ANY KIND OF REPORT?
I AM NOT A POLITICIAN, I'M A NEWSPAPER EDITOR. I'VE BEEN IN AND OUT OF THIS PRISON AND HAVE OBSERVED THINGS OUTSIDE THAT YOU HAVE NOT. THE MEN OUTSIDE, TAKING AIM AT YOU, ARE YOUNG, TENSE, AND INFECTED WITH RACISM. THEY WOULD LIKE NOTHING BETTER THAN AN EXCUSE TO BLOW YOUR BRAINS OUT.
THERE'S NO COMPROMISE WITHOUT AMNESTY!
THAT'S RIGHT!
WE'VE GOT THE BODY, BUT NOT THE HEAD!
YOU ARE NOW LOOKING AT A BUNCH OF DEAD MEN. WHAT AMNESTY MEANS TO US IS WHAT INSURANCE MEANS TO A FAMILY.
MY BROTHERS, YOU KNOW I HAVE PROFOUND RESPECT AND DEEP LOVE FOR ALL OF YOU. YOU HAVE ASKED THAT I SERVE AS YOUR ATTORNEY, AND AS SUCH I MUST ADVISE THAT THIS IS THE BEST THE STATE WILL OFFER. THEY WILL ADDRESS CONDITIONS, BUT NOT AMNESTY. IF YOU'RE NOT WILLING TO ACCEPT THESE TERMS, PEOPLE ARE GOING TO DIE. THE DECISION IS YOURS TO MAKE.
NOW THAT GUARD QUINN HAS DIED...
WHAT? HOW?
MAN, THIS IS BAD NEWS.
THE MEDIA HAS REPORTED HE DIED FROM HEAD INJURIES SUSTAINED DURING THE TAKING OF THE PRISON.
THEY SAY HE WAS THROWN FROM A WINDOW.
IT'S A LIE! THE PIGS KILLED ONE OF THEIR OWN, AND NOW THEY'RE GOING TO BLAME US FOR IT.
NOW WE CAN ALL BE CHARGED WITH MURDER!
RED ALERT, GUYS! THEY'RE ON THE MOVE!
FOLLOW ME. QUICK!
WE'RE ALL GOING TO DIE! THEY'LL MURDER US ALL!

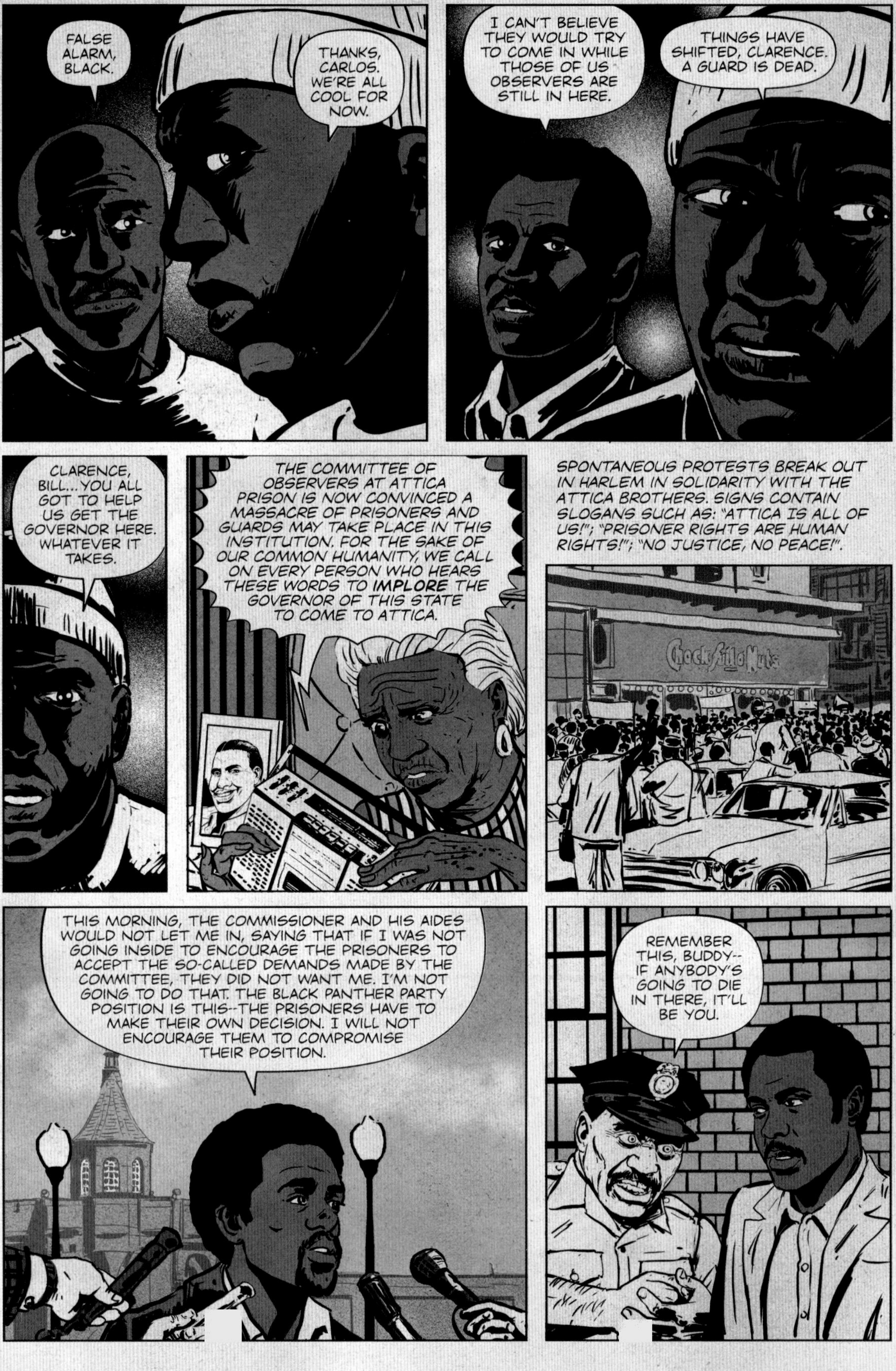
FALSE ALARM, BLACK.
THANKS, CARLOS. WE'RE ALL COOL FOR NOW.
I CAN'T BELIEVE THEY WOULD TRY TO COME IN WHILE THOSE OF US OBSERVERS ARE STILL IN HERE.
THINGS HAVE SHIFTED, CLARENCE. A GUARD IS DEAD.
CLARENCE, BILL...YOU ALL GOT TO HELP US GET THE GOVERNOR HERE. WHATEVER IT TAKES.
THE COMMITTEE OF OBSERVERS AT ATTICA PRISON IS NOW CONVINCED A MASSACRE OF PRISONERS AND GUARDS MAY TAKE PLACE IN THIS INSTITUTION. FOR THE SAKE OF OUR COMMON HUMANITY, WE CALL ON EVERY PERSON WHO HEARS THESE WORDS TO IMPLORE THE GOVERNOR OF THIS STATE TO COME TO ATTICA.
SPONTANEOUS PROTESTS BREAK OUT IN HARLEM IN SOLIDARITY WITH THE ATTICA BROTHERS. SIGNS CONTAIN SLOGANS SUCH AS: "ATTICA IS ALL OF US!"; "PRISONER RIGHTS ARE HUMAN RIGHTS!"; "NO JUSTICE, NO PEACE!".
THIS MORNING, THE COMMISSIONER AND HIS AIDES WOULD NOT LET ME IN, SAYING THAT IF I WAS NOT GOING INSIDE TO ENCOURAGE THE PRISONERS TO ACCEPT THE SO-CALLED DEMANDS MADE BY THE COMMITTEE, THEY DID NOT WANT ME. I'M NOT GOING TO DO THAT. THE BLACK PANTHER PARTY POSITION IS THIS--THE PRISONERS HAVE TO MAKE THEIR OWN DECISION. I WILL NOT ENCOURAGE THEM TO COMPROMISE THEIR POSITION.
REMEMBER THIS, BUDDY-- IF ANYBODY'S GOING TO DIE IN THERE, IT'LL BE YOU.

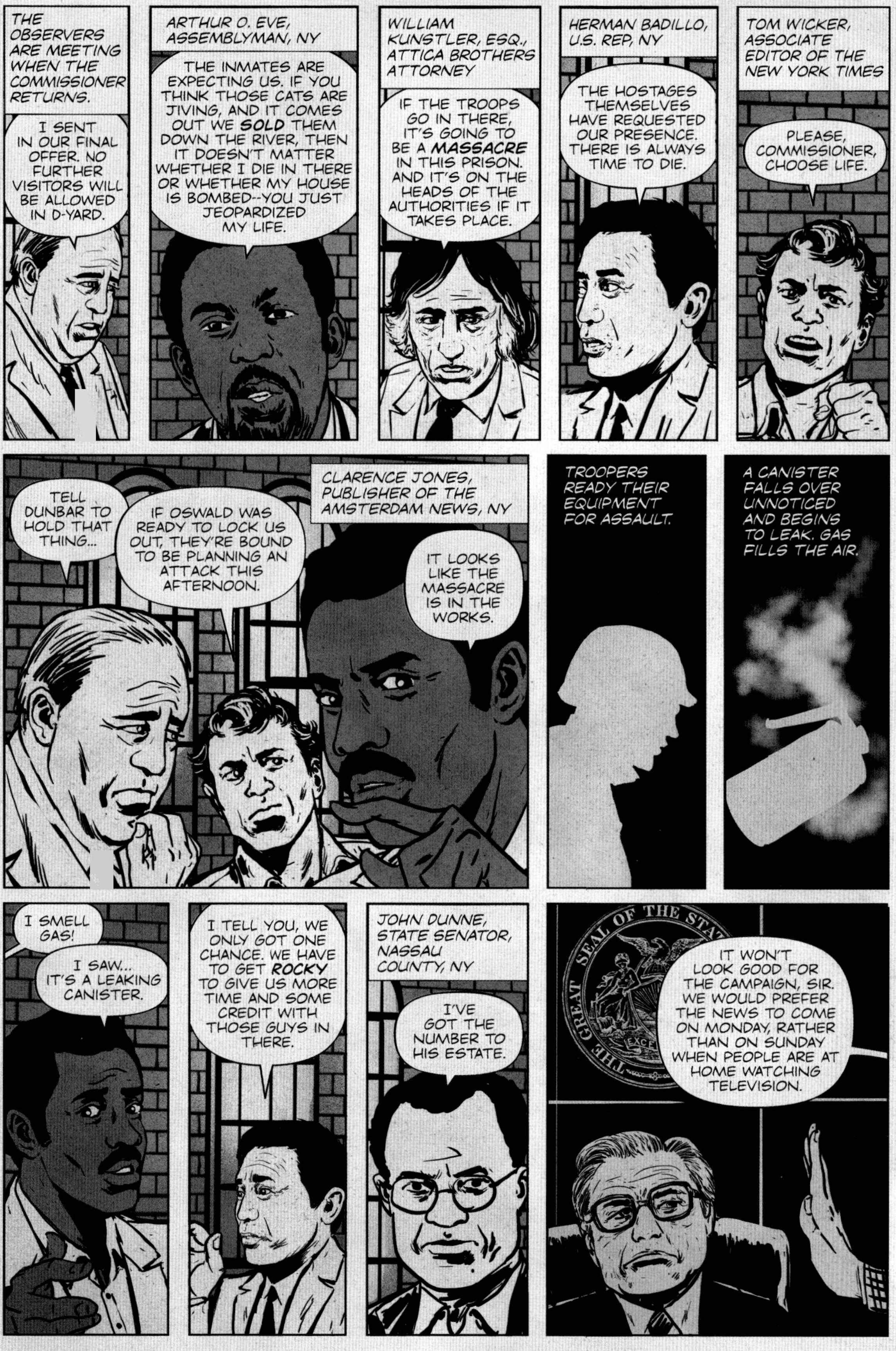
THE OBSERVERS ARE MEETING WHEN THE COMMISSIONER RETURNS.
I SENT IN OUR FINAL OFFER. NO FURTHER VISITORS WILL BE ALLOWED IN D-YARD.
ARTHUR O. EVE, ASSEMBLYMAN, NY
THE INMATES ARE EXPECTING US. IF YOU THINK THOSE CATS ARE JIVING, AND IT COMES OUT WE SOLD THEM DOWN THE RIVER, THEN IT DOESN'T MATTER WHETHER I DIE IN THERE OR WHETHER MY HOUSE IS BOMBED--YOU JUST JEOPARDIZED MY LIFE.
WILLIAM KUNSTLER, ESQ., ATTICA BROTHERS ATTORNEY
IF THE TROOPS GO IN THERE, IT'S GOING TO BE A MASSACRE IN THIS PRISON. AND IT'S ON THE HEADS OF THE AUTHORITIES IF IT TAKES PLACE.
HERMAN BADILLO, U.S. REP, NY
THE HOSTAGES THEMSELVES HAVE REQUESTED OUR PRESENCE. THERE IS ALWAYS TIME TO DIE.
TOM WICKER, ASSOCIATE EDITOR OF THE NEW YORK TIMES
PLEASE, COMMISSIONER, CHOOSE LIFE.
TELL DUNBAR TO HOLD THAT THING...
IF OSWALD WAS READY TO LOCK US OUT, THEY'RE BOUND TO BE PLANNING AN ATTACK THIS AFTERNOON.
CLARENCE JONES, PUBLISHER OF THE AMSTERDAM NEWS, NY
IT LOOKS LIKE THE MASSACRE IS IN THE WORKS.
TROOPERS READY THEIR EQUIPMENT FOR ASSAULT.
A CANISTER FALLS OVER UNNOTICED AND BEGINS TO LEAK. GAS FILLS THE AIR.
I SMELL GAS!
I SAW... IT'S A LEAKING CANISTER.
I TELL YOU, WE ONLY GOT ONE CHANCE. WE HAVE TO GET ROCKY TO GIVE US MORE TIME AND SOME CREDIT WITH THOSE GUYS IN THERE.
JOHN DUNNE, STATE SENATOR, NASSAU COUNTY, NY
I'VE GOT THE NUMBER TO HIS ESTATE.
THE GREAT SEAL OF THE STATE
IT WON'T LOOK GOOD FOR THE CAMPAIGN, SIR. WE WOULD PREFER THE NEWS TO COME ON MONDAY, RATHER THAN ON SUNDAY WHEN PEOPLE ARE AT HOME WATCHING TELEVISION.

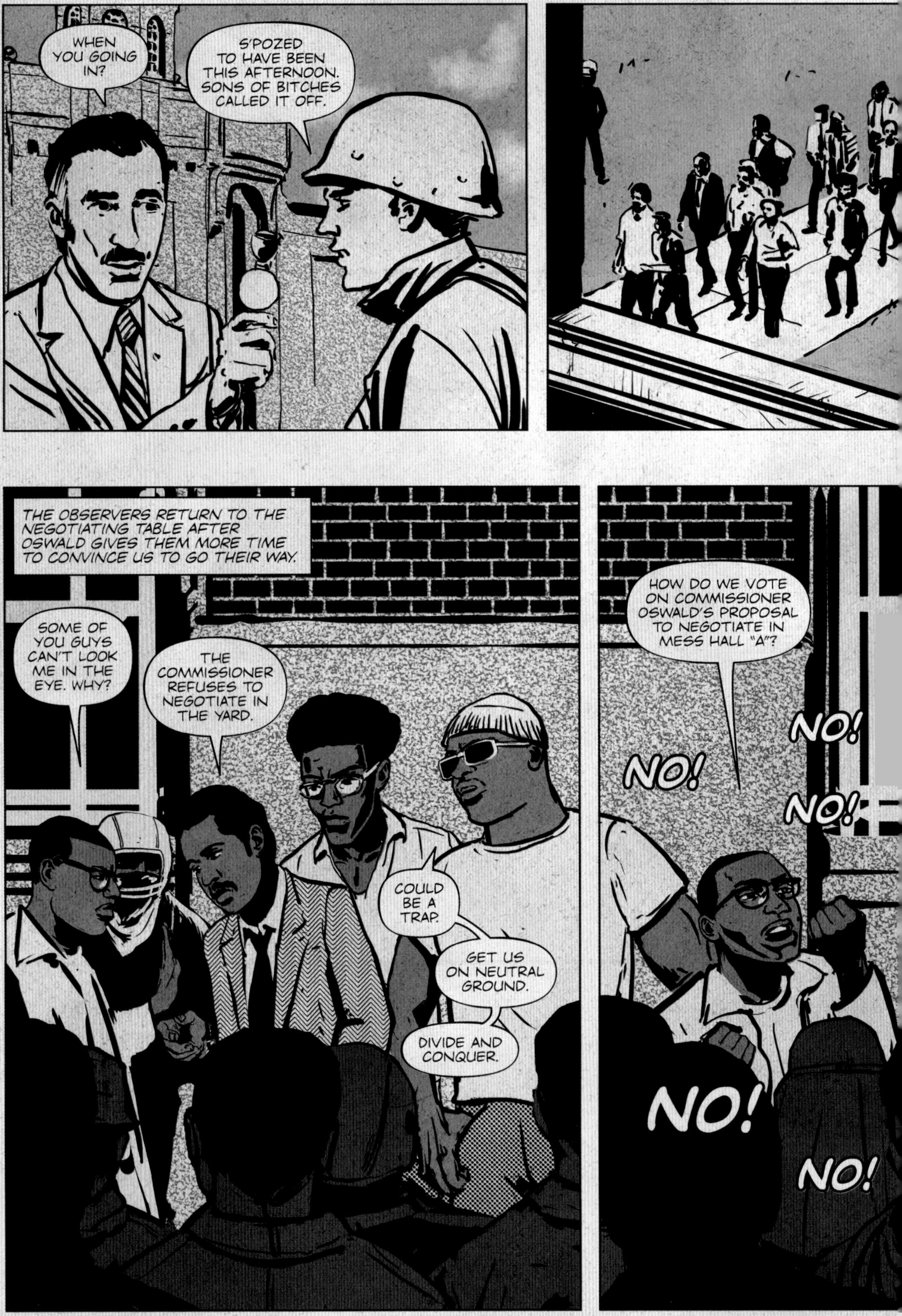
WHEN YOU GOING IN?
S'POZED TO HAVE BEEN THIS AFTERNOON. SONS OF BITCHES CALLED IT OFF.
THE OBSERVERS RETURN TO THE NEGOTIATING TABLE AFTER OSWALD GIVES THEM MORE TIME TO CONVINCE US TO GO THEIR WAY.
SOME OF YOU GUYS CAN'T LOOK ME IN THE EYE. WHY?
THE COMMISSIONER REFUSES TO NEGOTIATE IN THE YARD.
COULD BE A TRAP.
GET US ON NEUTRAL GROUND.
DIVIDE AND CONQUER.
HOW DO WE VOTE ON COMMISSIONER OSWALD'S PROPOSAL TO NEGOTIATE IN MESS HALL "A"?
NO!
NO!
NO!
NO!
NO!

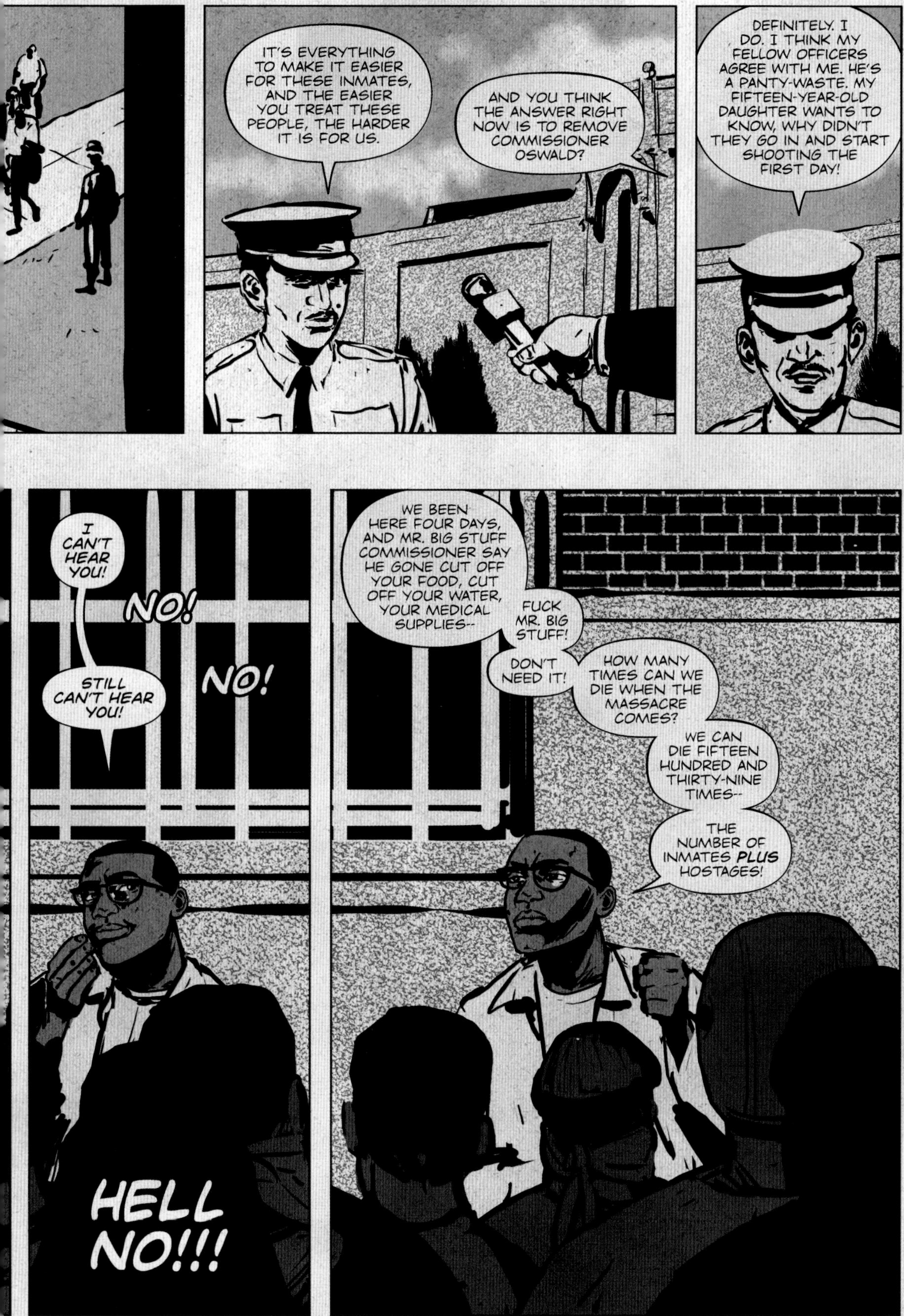
IT'S EVERYTHING TO MAKE IT EASIER FOR THESE INMATES, AND THE EASIER YOU TREAT THESE PEOPLE, THE HARDER IT IS FOR US.
AND YOU THINK THE ANSWER RIGHT NOW IS TO REMOVE COMMISSIONER OSWALD?
DEFINITELY. I DO. I THINK MY FELLOW OFFICERS AGREE WITH ME. HE'S A PANTY-WASTE. MY FIFTEEN-YEAR-OLD DAUGHTER WANTS TO KNOW, WHY DIDN'T THEY GO IN AND START SHOOTING THE FIRST DAY!
I CAN'T HEAR YOU!
NO!
STILL CAN'T HEAR YOU!
NO!
HELL NO!!!
WE BEEN HERE FOUR DAYS, AND MR. BIG STUFF COMMISSIONER SAY HE GONE CUT OFF YOUR FOOD, CUT OFF YOUR WATER, YOUR MEDICAL SUPPLIES--
FUCK MR. BIG STUFF!
DON'T NEED IT!
HOW MANY TIMES CAN WE DIE WHEN THE MASSACRE COMES?
WE CAN DIE FIFTEEN HUNDRED AND THIRTY-NINE TIMES--
THE NUMBER OF INMATES **PLUS** HOSTAGES!

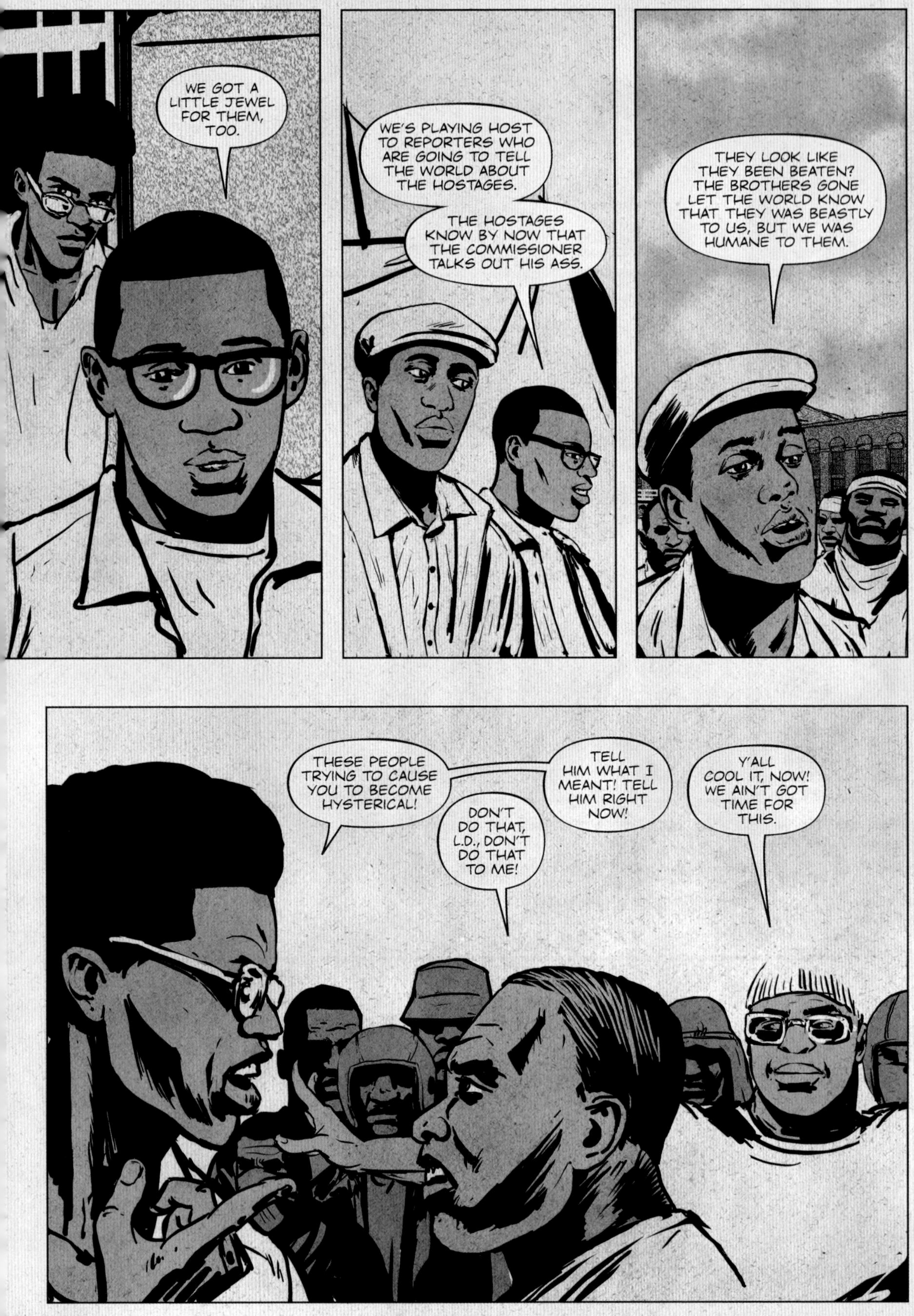
WE GOT A LITTLE JEWEL FOR THEM, TOO.
WE'S PLAYING HOST TO REPORTERS WHO ARE GOING TO TELL THE WORLD ABOUT THE HOSTAGES.
THE HOSTAGES KNOW BY NOW THAT THE COMMISSIONER TALKS OUT HIS ASS.
THEY LOOK LIKE THEY BEEN BEATEN? THE BROTHERS GONE LET THE WORLD KNOW THAT THEY WAS BEASTLY TO US, BUT WE WAS HUMANE TO THEM.
THESE PEOPLE TRYING TO CAUSE YOU TO BECOME HYSTERICAL!
TELL HIM WHAT I MEANT! TELL HIM RIGHT NOW!
DON'T DO THAT, L.D., DON'T DO THAT TO ME!
Y'ALL COOL IT, NOW! WE AIN'T GOT TIME FOR THIS.

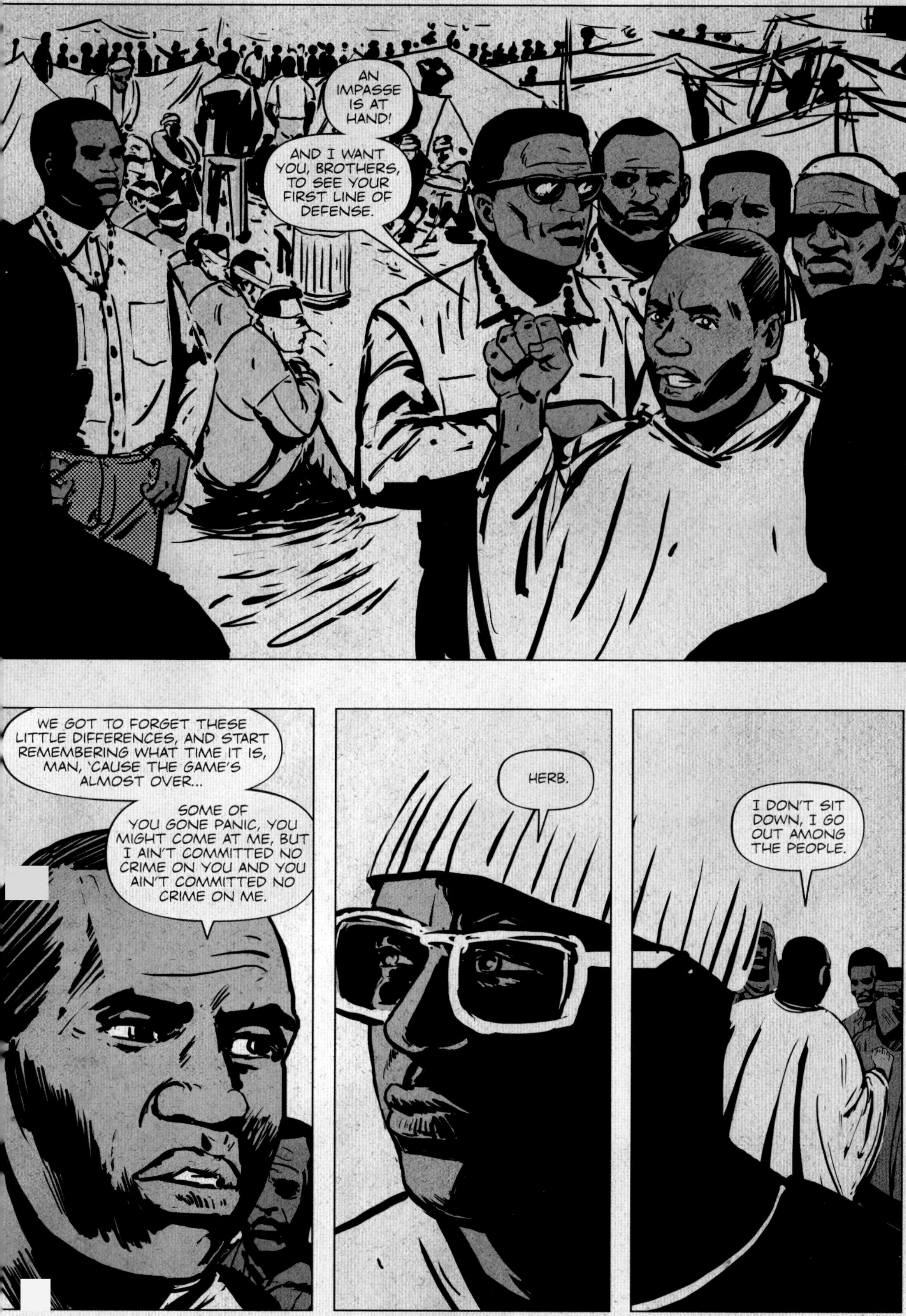
AN IMPASSE IS AT HAND!
AND I WANT YOU, BROTHERS, TO SEE YOUR FIRST LINE OF DEFENSE.
WE GOT TO FORGET THESE LITTLE DIFFERENCES, AND START REMEMBERING WHAT TIME IT IS, MAN, 'CAUSE THE GAME'S ALMOST OVER...
SOME OF YOU GONE PANIC, YOU MIGHT COME AT ME, BUT I AIN'T COMMITTED NO CRIME ON YOU AND YOU AIN'T COMMITTED NO CRIME ON ME.
HERB.
I DON'T SIT DOWN, I GO OUT AMONG THE PEOPLE.

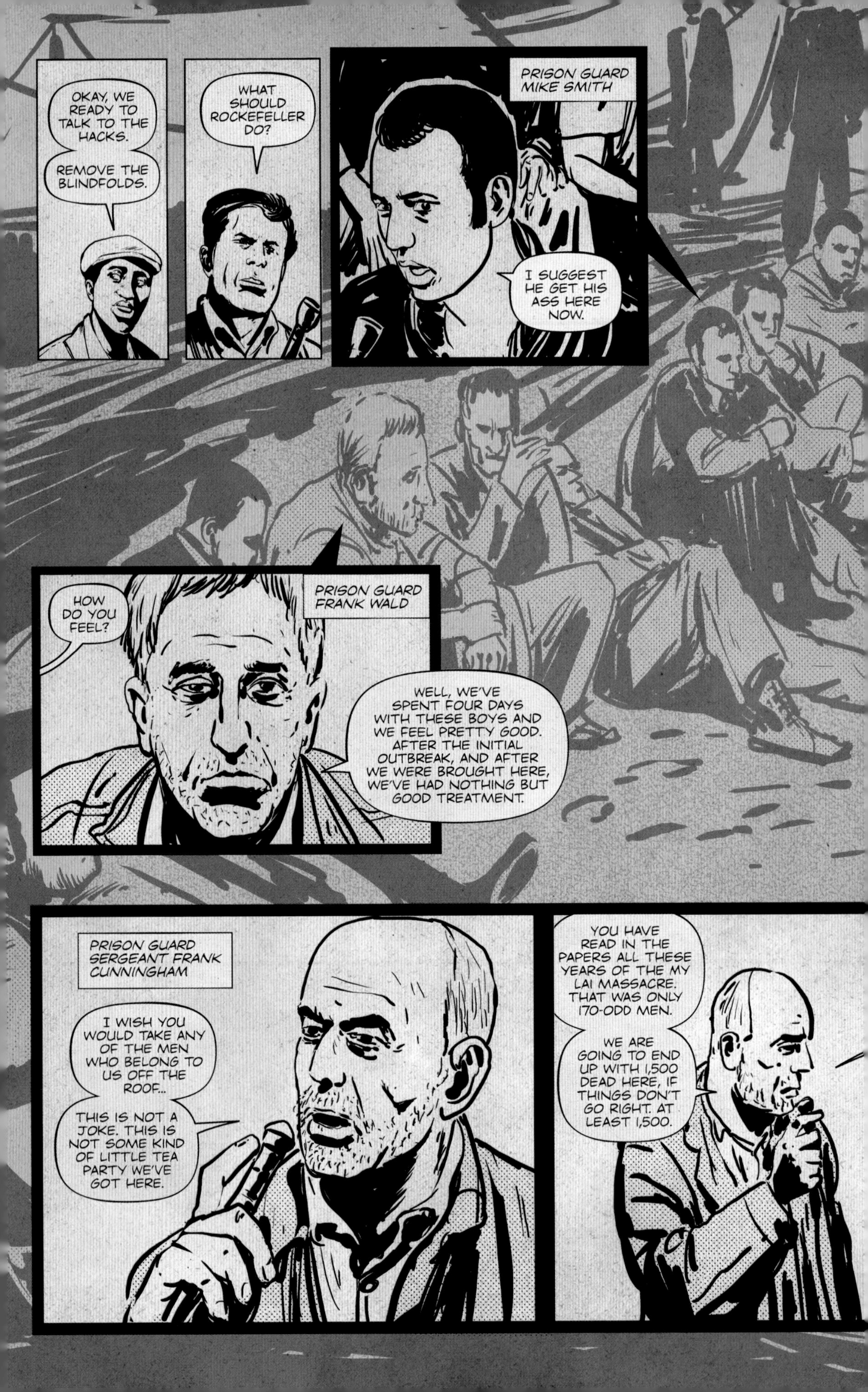
OKAY, WE READY TO TALK TO THE HACKS.
REMOVE THE BLINDFOLDS.
WHAT SHOULD ROCKEFELLER DO?
PRISON GUARD MIKE SMITH
I SUGGEST HE GET HIS ASS HERE NOW.
HOW DO YOU FEEL?
PRISON GUARD FRANK WALD
WELL, WE'VE SPENT FOUR DAYS WITH THESE BOYS AND WE FEEL PRETTY GOOD. AFTER THE INITIAL OUTBREAK, AND AFTER WE WERE BROUGHT HERE, WE'VE HAD NOTHING BUT GOOD TREATMENT.
PRISON GUARD SERGEANT FRANK CUNNINGHAM
I WISH YOU WOULD TAKE ANY OF THE MEN WHO BELONG TO US OFF THE ROOF...
THIS IS NOT A JOKE. THIS IS NOT SOME KIND OF LITTLE TEA PARTY WE'VE GOT HERE.
YOU HAVE READ IN THE PAPERS ALL THESE YEARS OF THE MY LAI MASSACRE. THAT WAS ONLY 170-ODD MEN.
WE ARE GOING TO END UP WITH 1,500 DEAD HERE, IF THINGS DON'T GO RIGHT. AT LEAST 1,500.

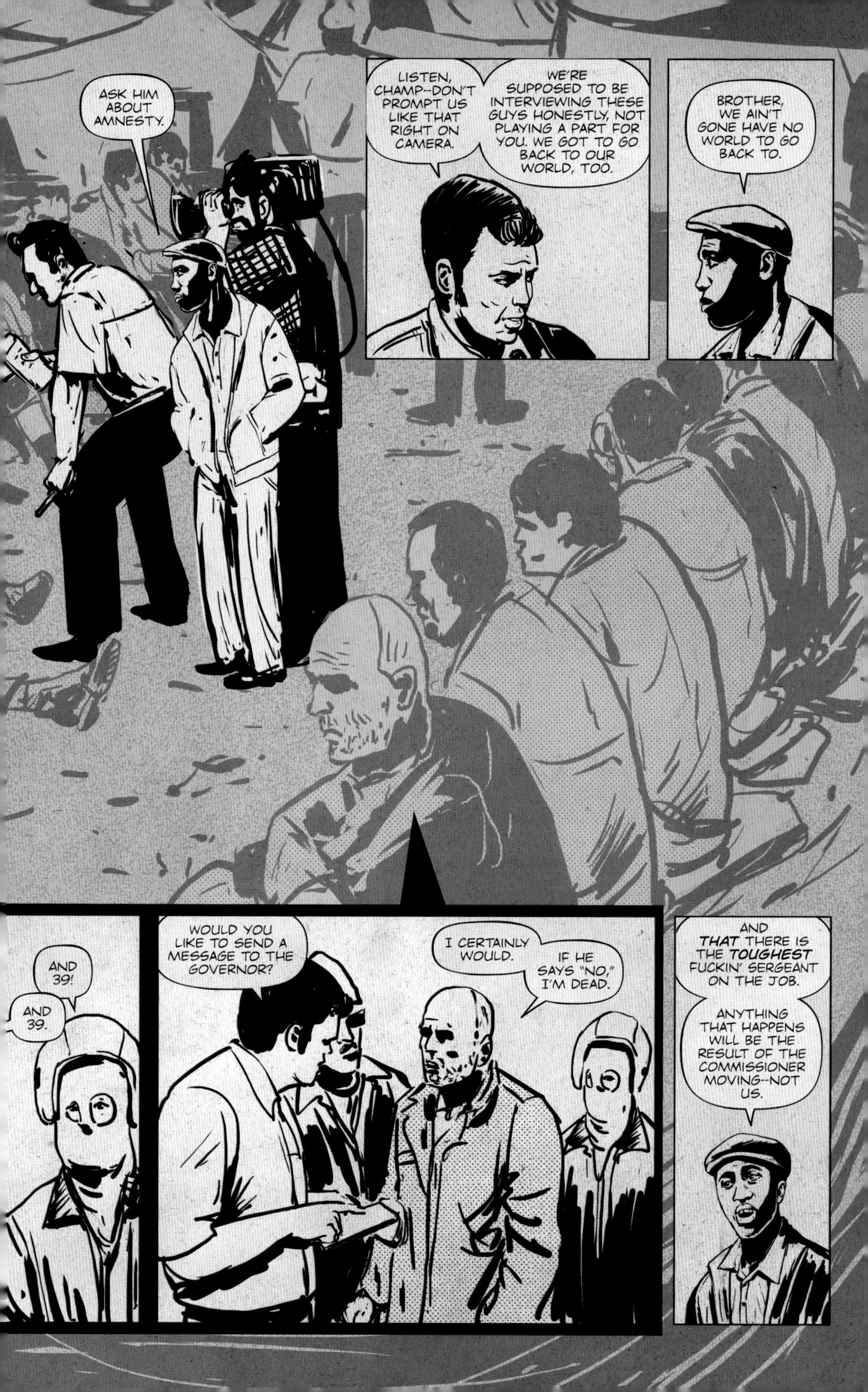
ASK HIM ABOUT AMNESTY.
LISTEN, CHAMP--DON'T PROMPT US LIKE THAT RIGHT ON CAMERA.
WE'RE SUPPOSED TO BE INTERVIEWING THESE GUYS HONESTLY, NOT PLAYING A PART FOR YOU. WE GOT TO GO BACK TO OUR WORLD, TOO.
BROTHER, WE AIN'T GONE HAVE NO WORLD TO GO BACK TO.
AND 39!
AND 39.
WOULD YOU LIKE TO SEND A MESSAGE TO THE GOVERNOR?
I CERTAINLY WOULD.
IF HE SAYS "NO," I'M DEAD.
AND *THAT* THERE IS THE ***TOUGHEST*** FUCKIN' SERGEANT ON THE JOB.
ANYTHING THAT HAPPENS WILL BE THE RESULT OF THE COMMISSIONER MOVING--NOT US.

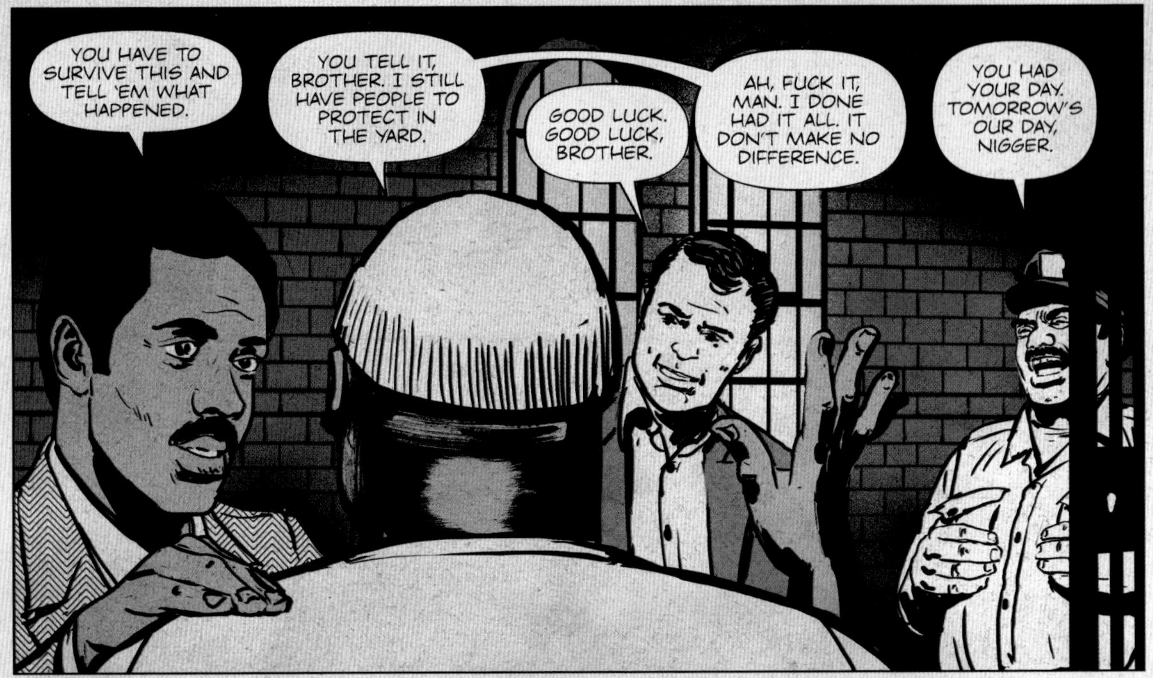
YOU HAVE TO SURVIVE THIS AND TELL 'EM WHAT HAPPENED.
YOU TELL IT, BROTHER. I STILL HAVE PEOPLE TO PROTECT IN THE YARD.
GOOD LUCK. GOOD LUCK, BROTHER.
AH, FUCK IT, MAN. I DONE HAD IT ALL. IT DON'T MAKE NO DIFFERENCE.
YOU HAD YOUR DAY. TOMORROW'S OUR DAY, NIGGER.

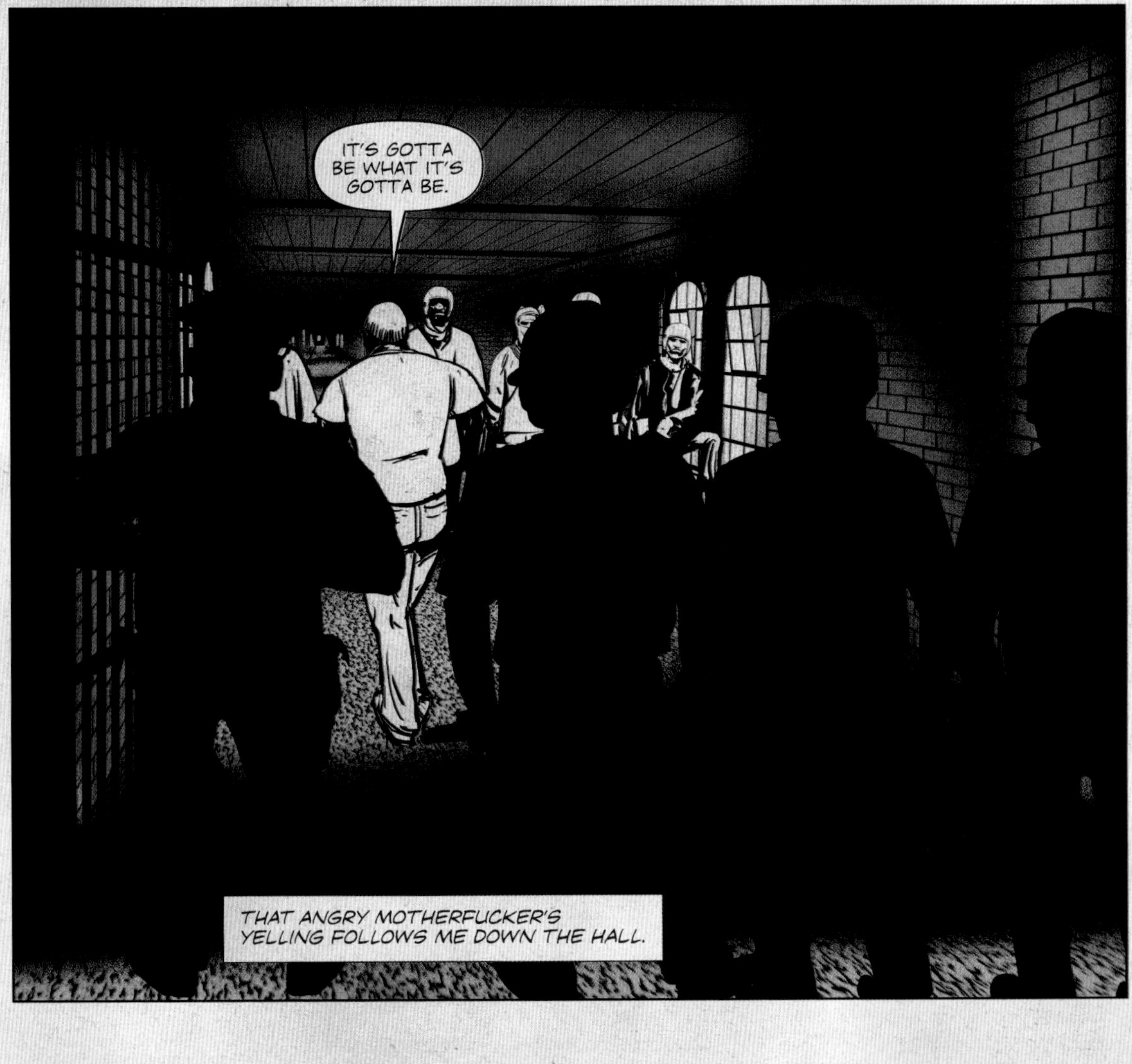
IT'S GOTTA BE WHAT IT'S GOTTA BE.
THAT ANGRY MOTHERFUCKER'S YELLING FOLLOWS ME DOWN THE HALL.

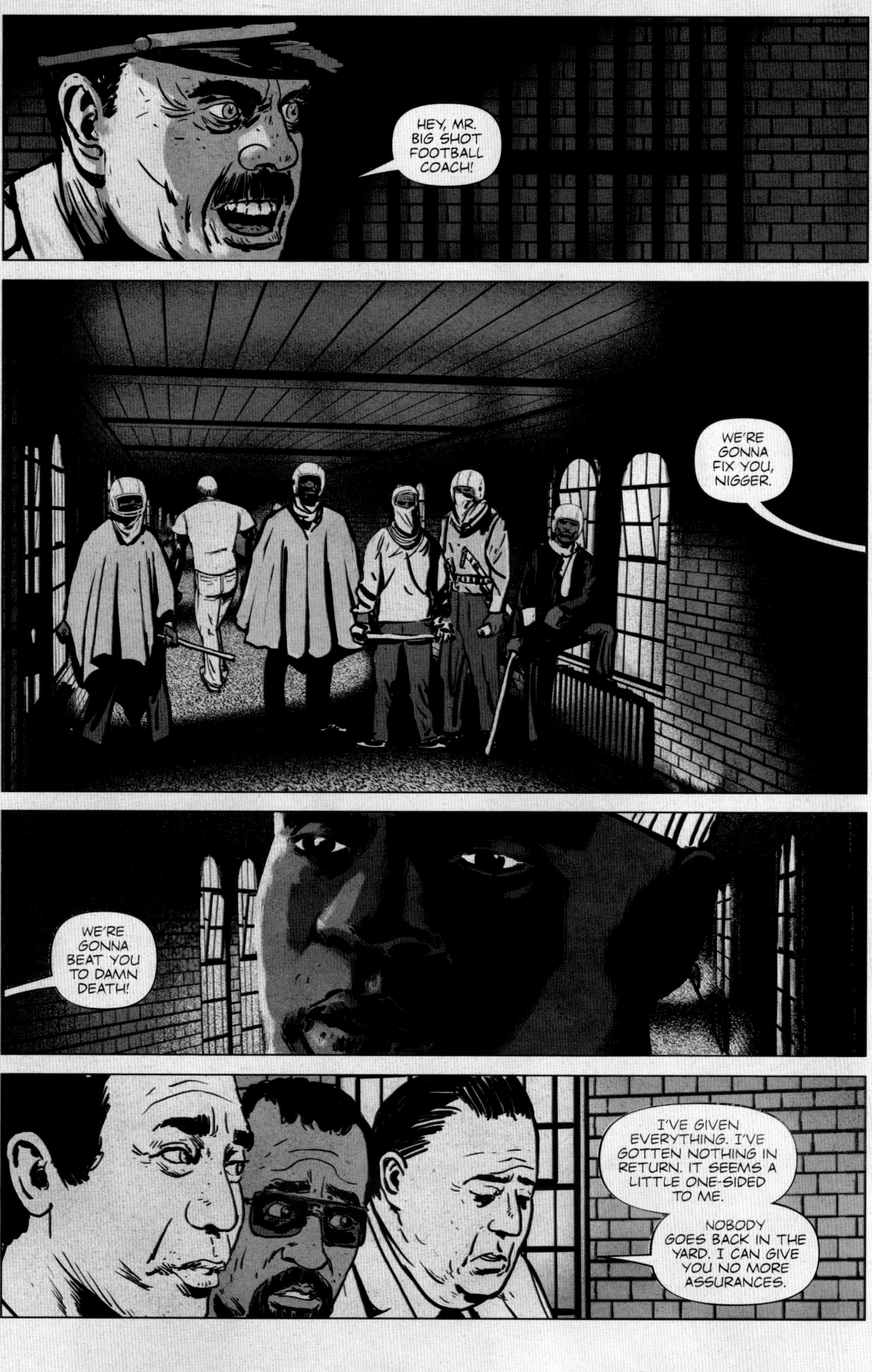
HEY, MR. BIG SHOT FOOTBALL COACH!
WE'RE GONNA FIX YOU, NIGGER.
WE'RE GONNA BEAT YOU TO DAMN DEATH!
I'VE GIVEN EVERYTHING. I'VE GOTTEN NOTHING IN RETURN. IT SEEMS A LITTLE ONE-SIDED TO ME.
NOBODY GOES BACK IN THE YARD. I CAN GIVE YOU NO MORE ASSURANCES.

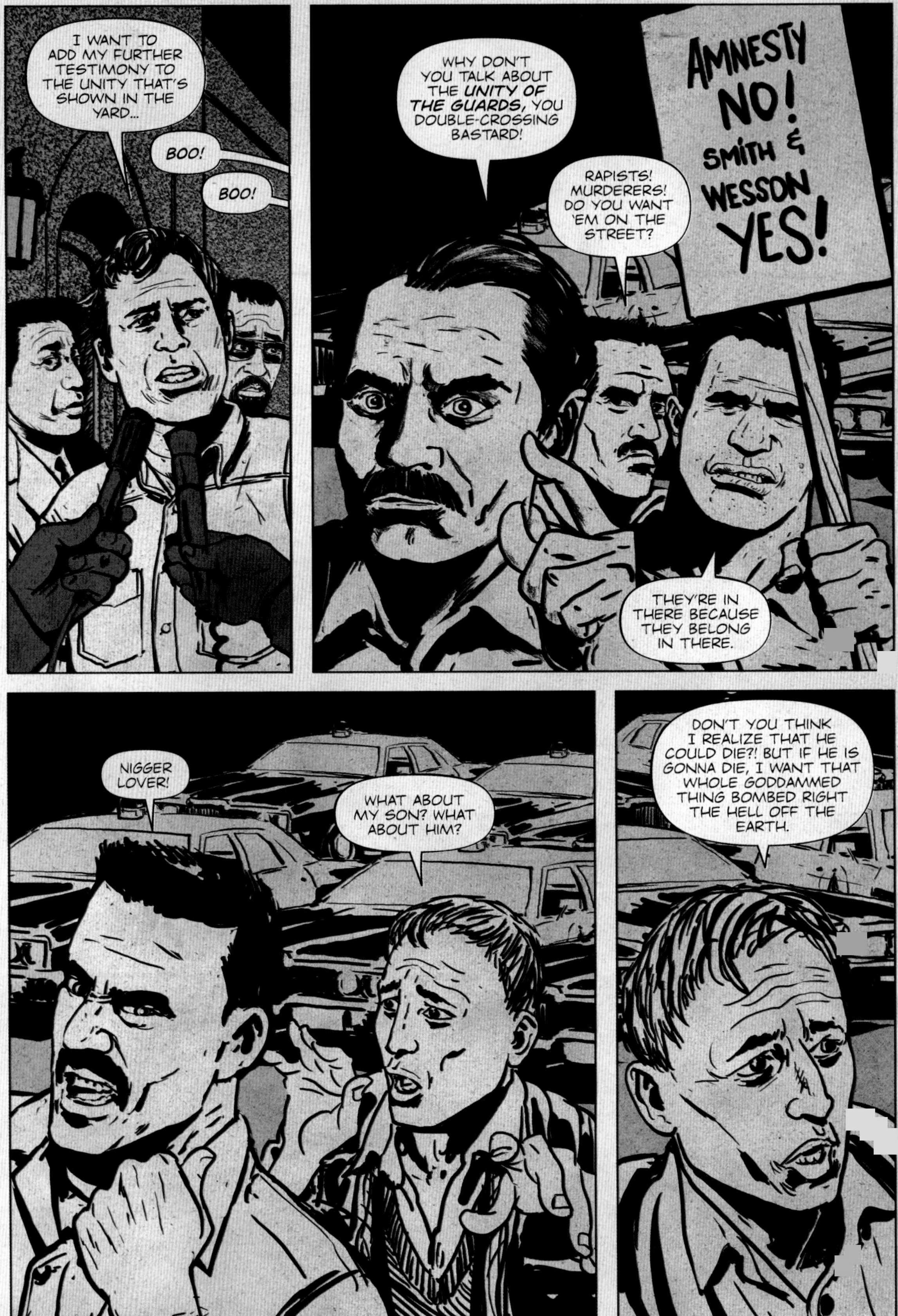
I WANT TO ADD MY FURTHER TESTIMONY TO THE UNITY THAT'S SHOWN IN THE YARD...
BOO!
BOO!
WHY DON'T YOU TALK ABOUT THE *UNITY OF THE GUARDS,* YOU DOUBLE-CROSSING BASTARD!
AMNESTY NO! SMITH & WESSON YES!
RAPISTS! MURDERERS! DO YOU WANT 'EM ON THE STREET?
THEY'RE IN THERE BECAUSE THEY BELONG IN THERE.
NIGGER LOVER!
WHAT ABOUT MY SON? WHAT ABOUT HIM?
DON'T YOU THINK I REALIZE THAT HE COULD DIE?! BUT IF HE IS GONNA DIE, I WANT THAT WHOLE GODDAMMED THING BOMBED RIGHT THE HELL OFF THE EARTH.

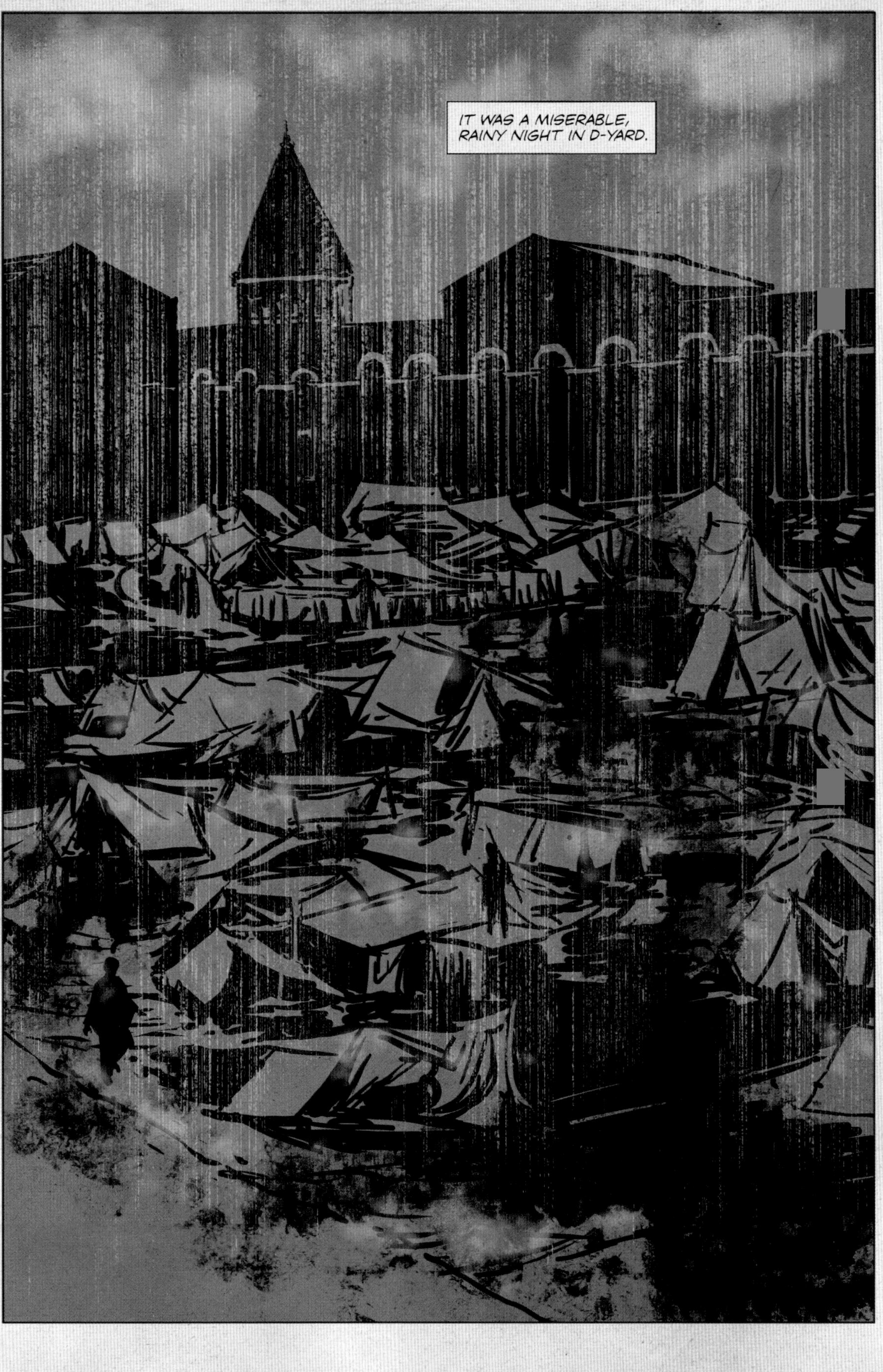
IT WAS A MISERABLE,
RAINY NIGHT IN D-YARD.

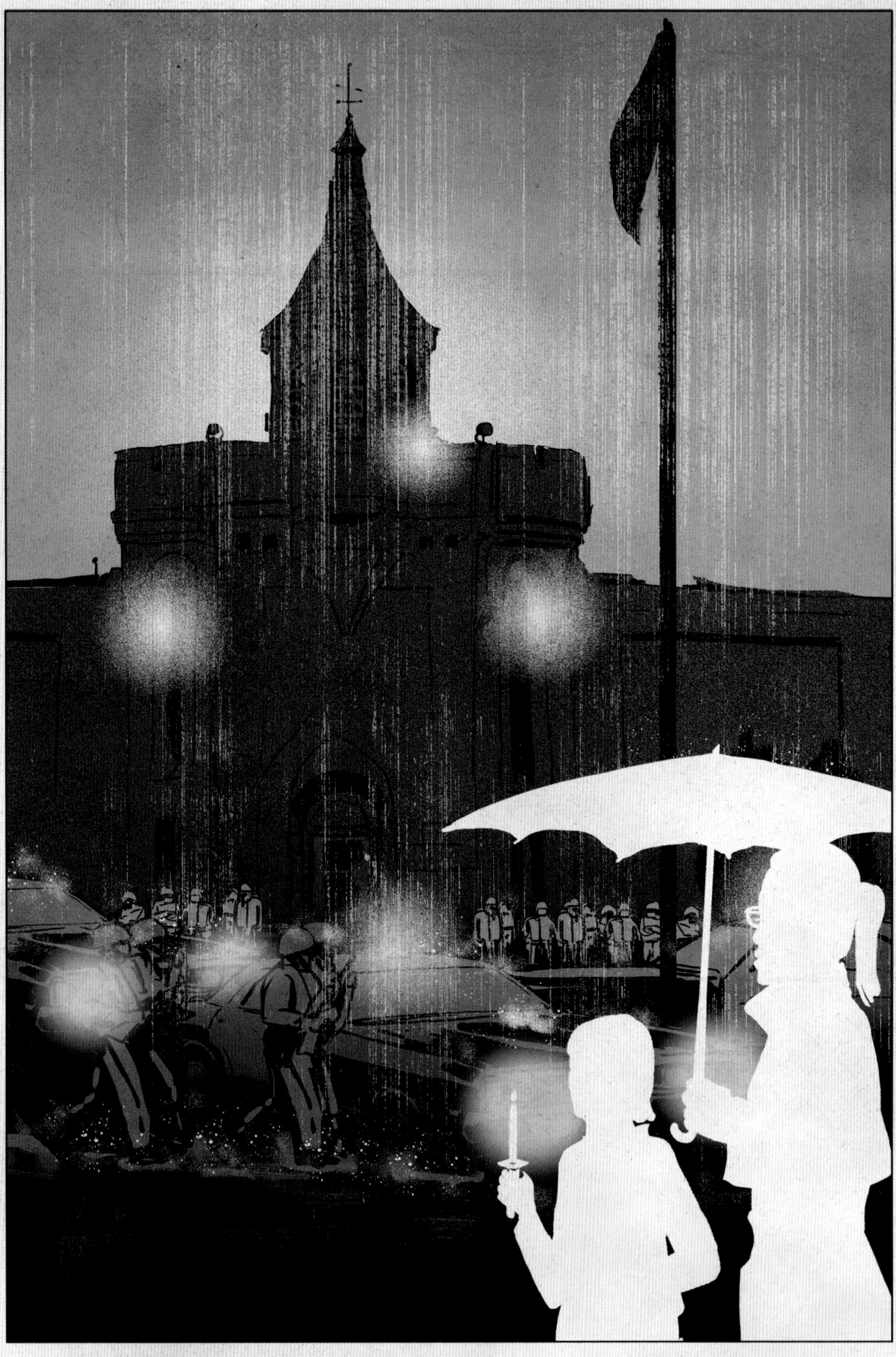

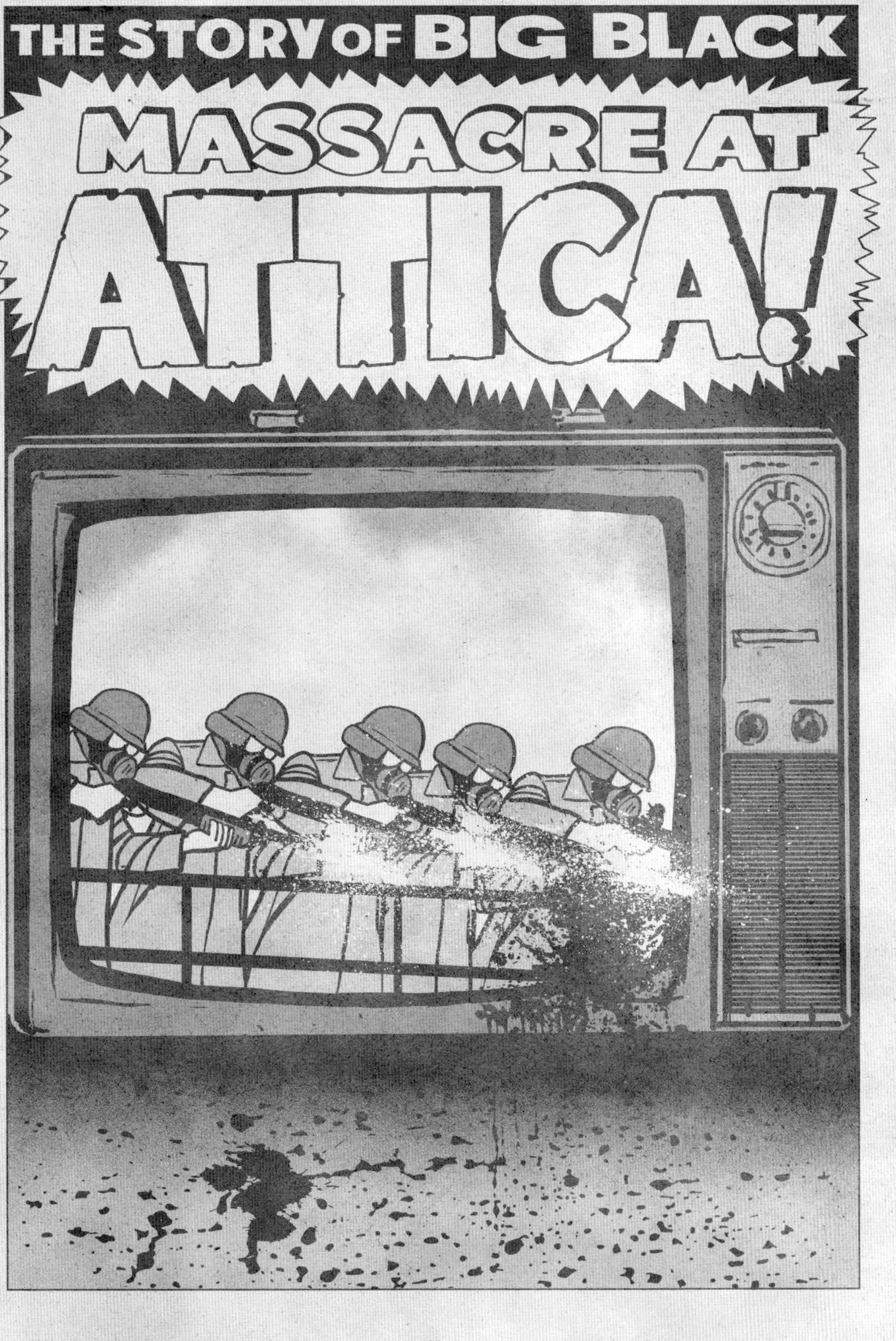
THE STORY OF BIG BLACK
MASSACRE AT
ATTICA!

September 13, 1971.

GOVERNOR ROCKEFELLER ADDRESSES HIS STAFF IN THE LIBRARY OF HIS POCANTICO HILLS ESTATE.

HE'S IN A JOVIAL MOOD AS HE SHOWS OFF A NEW RAINCOAT TO THE ASSEMBLED GROUP.

HOW YA LIKE THE NEW SLICKER?

I'VE MADE A DECISION ABOUT ATTICA. IT'S A MATTER OF PRINCIPLE. WE'RE DEALING WITH REVOLUTIONARIES HERE, AN INTERNATIONAL CONSPIRACY, AND IF THEY THINK THEY CAN FORCE ME TO NEGOTIATE--THIS THING WILL SPREAD LIKE WILDFIRE. I WON'T BE SEEN AS KNUCKLING UNDER...NOT IN FRONT OF ALL THOSE TV CAMERAS.

THIS IS ABOUT PRESERVING OUR TRADITIONS OF *JUSTICE.*

CORRECTIONAL FACILITY

YOUR ORDERS ARE THAT YOUR WEAPON IS NOT TO BE TAKEN, NOR ARE *YOU* TO BE TAKEN.

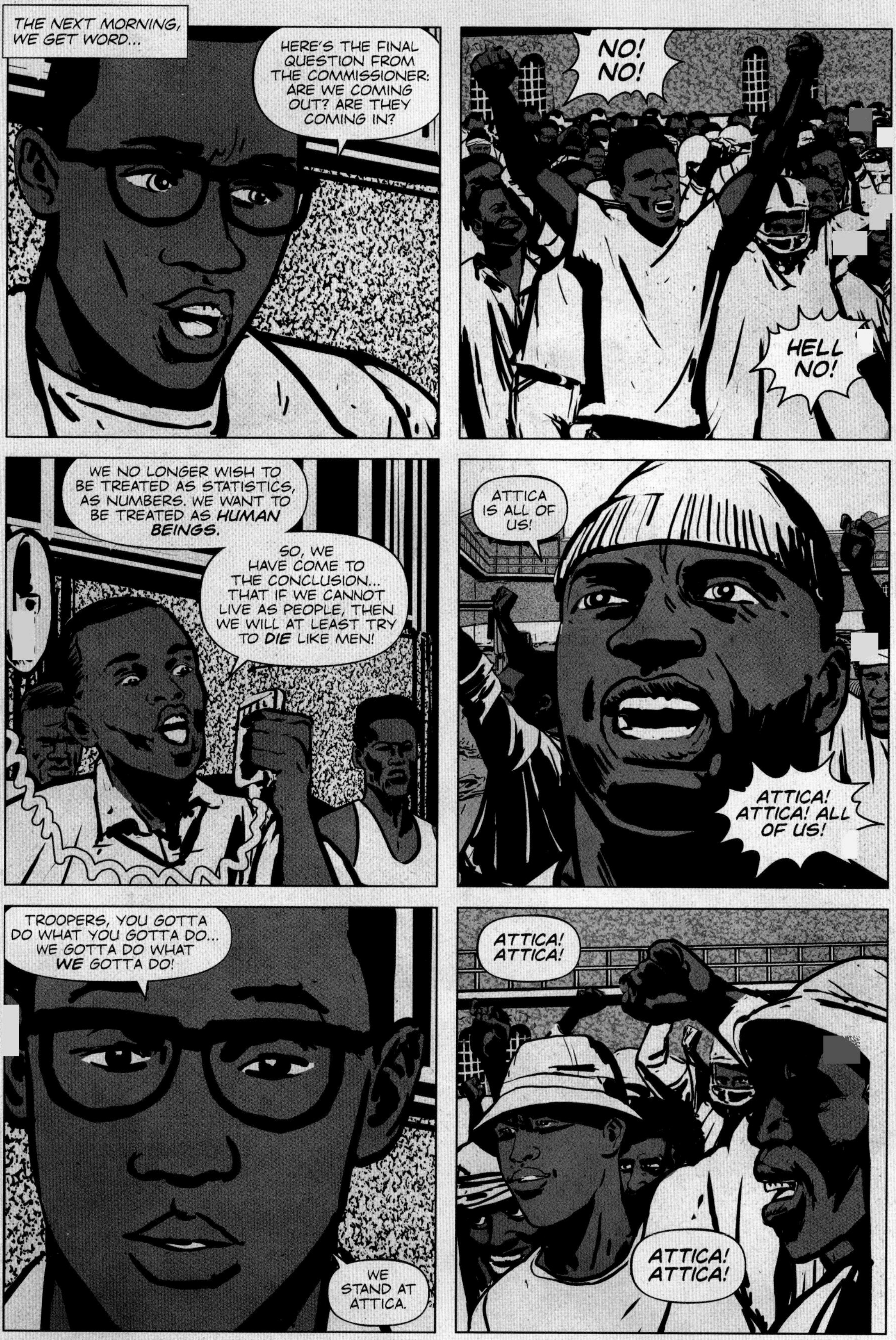
THE NEXT MORNING, WE GET WORD...
HERE'S THE FINAL QUESTION FROM THE COMMISSIONER: ARE WE COMING OUT? ARE THEY COMING IN?
NO! NO!
HELL NO!
WE NO LONGER WISH TO BE TREATED AS STATISTICS, AS NUMBERS. WE WANT TO BE TREATED AS HUMAN BEINGS.
SO, WE HAVE COME TO THE CONCLUSION... THAT IF WE CANNOT LIVE AS PEOPLE, THEN WE WILL AT LEAST TRY TO DIE LIKE MEN!
ATTICA IS ALL OF US!
ATTICA! ATTICA! ALL OF US!
TROOPERS, YOU GOTTA DO WHAT YOU GOTTA DO... WE GOTTA DO WHAT WE GOTTA DO!
WE STAND AT ATTICA.
ATTICA! ATTICA!
ATTICA! ATTICA!

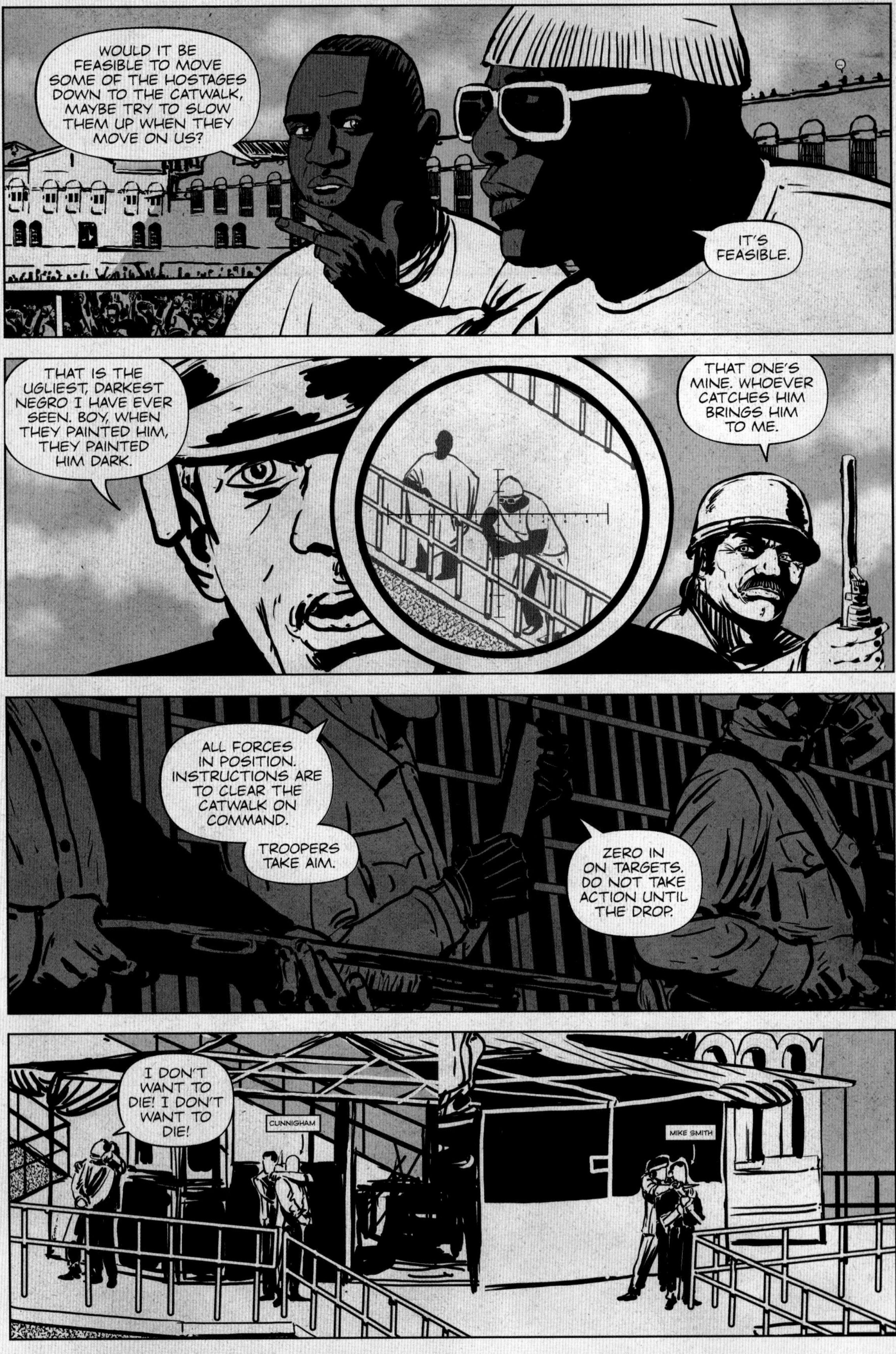
WOULD IT BE FEASIBLE TO MOVE SOME OF THE HOSTAGES DOWN TO THE CATWALK, MAYBE TRY TO SLOW THEM UP WHEN THEY MOVE ON US?
IT'S FEASIBLE.
THAT IS THE UGLIEST, DARKEST NEGRO I HAVE EVER SEEN. BOY, WHEN THEY PAINTED HIM, THEY PAINTED HIM DARK.
THAT ONE'S MINE. WHOEVER CATCHES HIM BRINGS HIM TO ME.
ALL FORCES IN POSITION. INSTRUCTIONS ARE TO CLEAR THE CATWALK ON COMMAND.
TROOPERS TAKE AIM.
ZERO IN ON TARGETS. DO NOT TAKE ACTION UNTIL THE DROP.
I DON'T WANT TO DIE! I DON'T WANT TO DIE!
CUNNIGHAM
MIKE SMITH

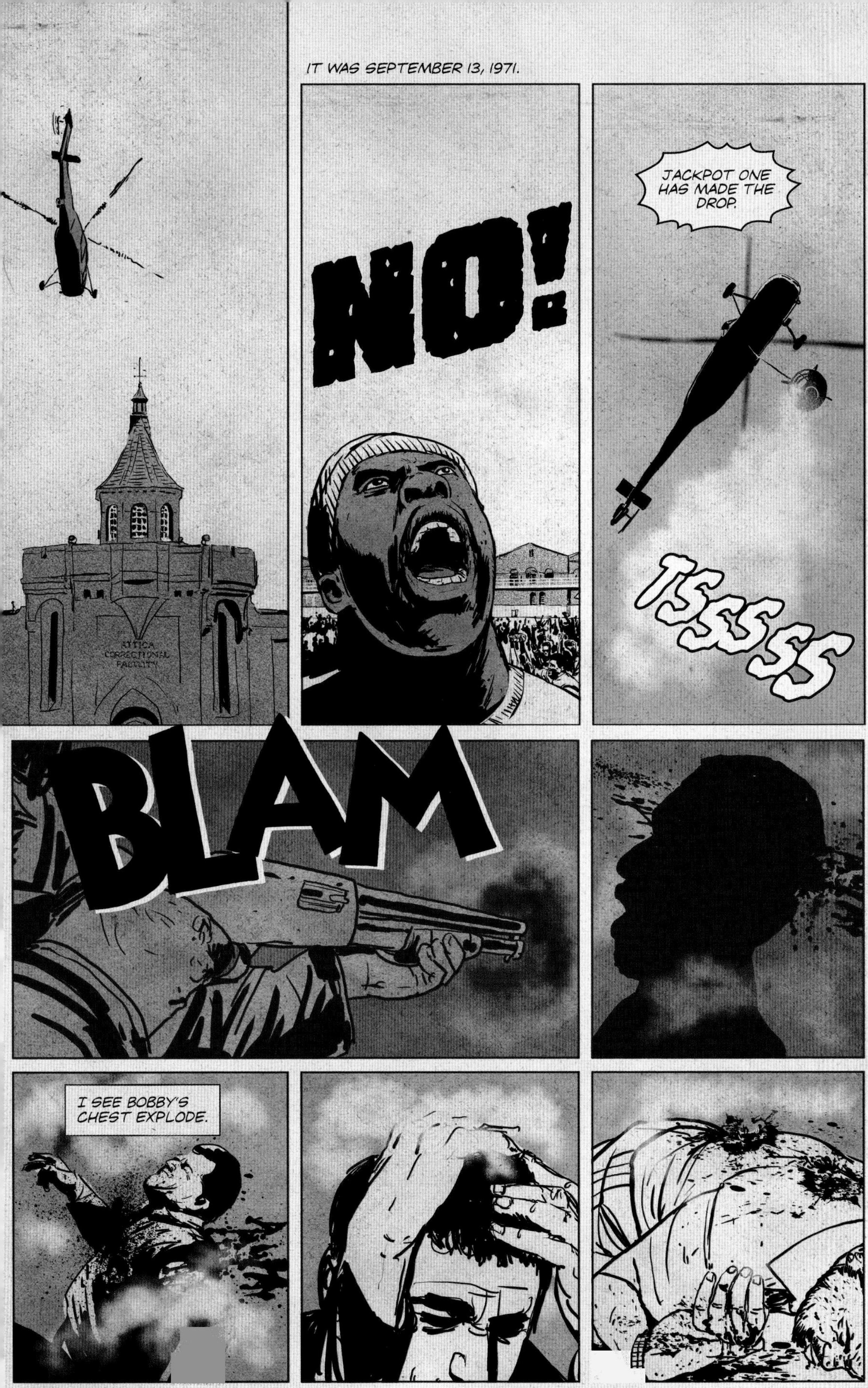
IT WAS SEPTEMBER 13, 1971.
ATTICA CORRECTIONAL FACILITY
NO!
JACKPOT ONE HAS MADE THE DROP.
TSSSSS
BLAM
I SEE BOBBY'S CHEST EXPLODE.

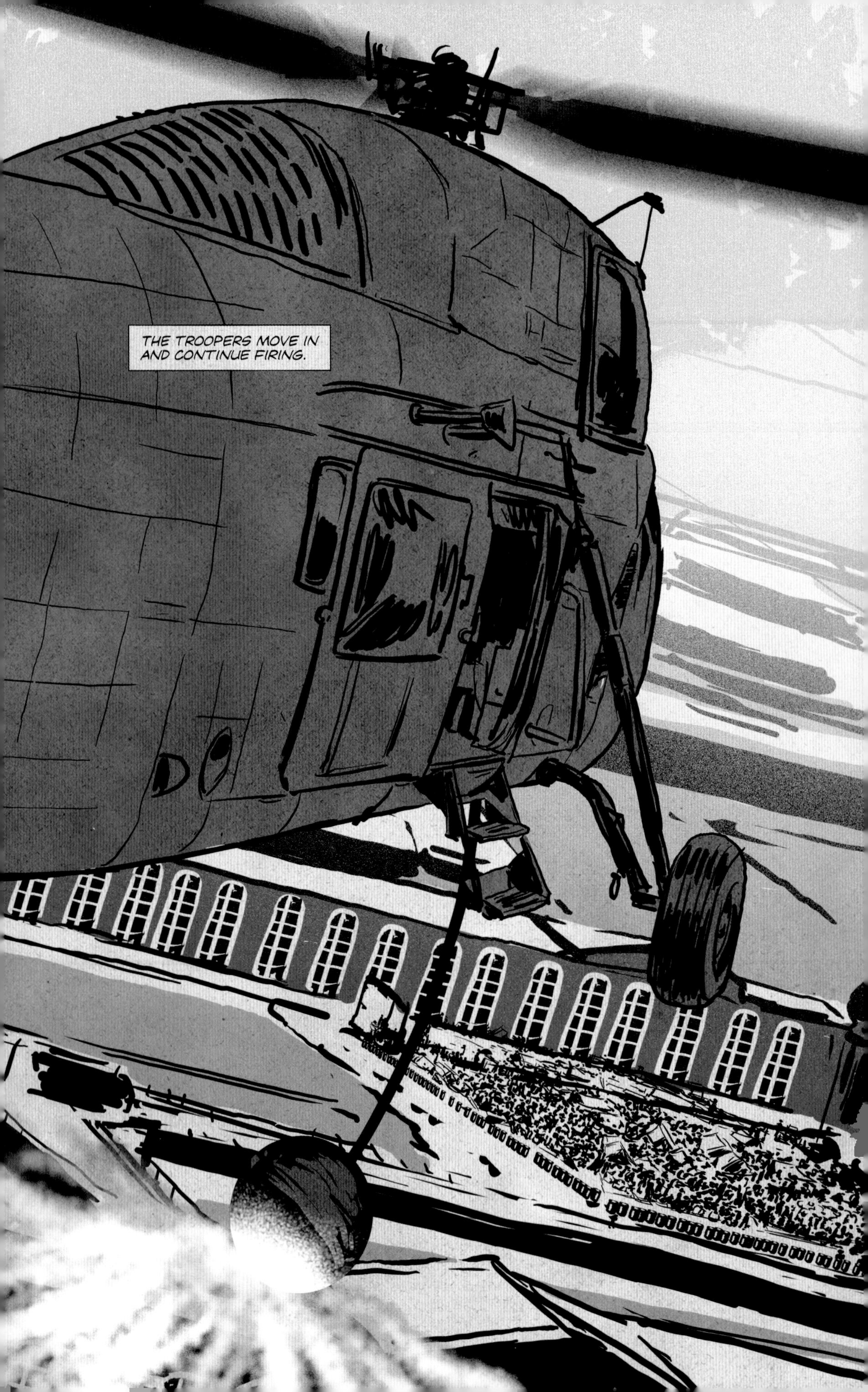
THE TROOPERS MOVE IN AND CONTINUE FIRING.

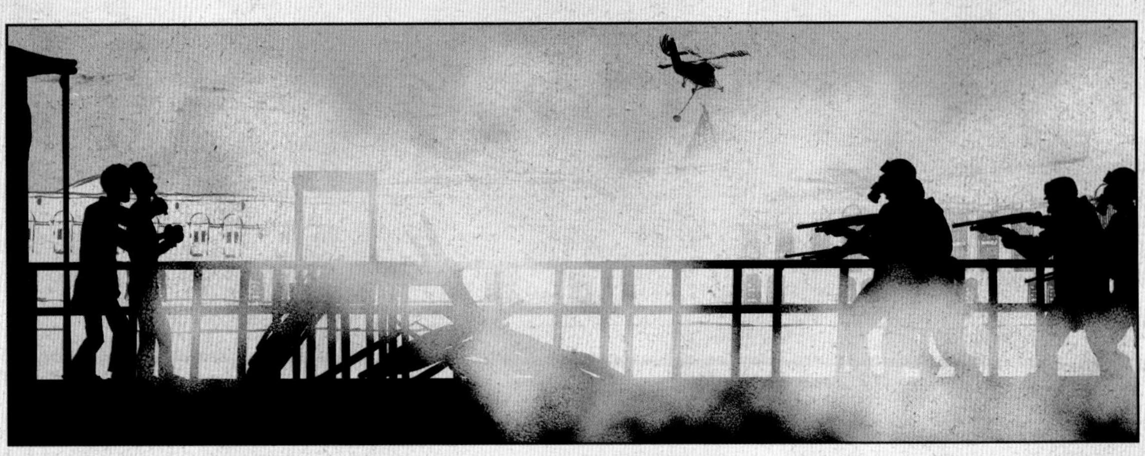

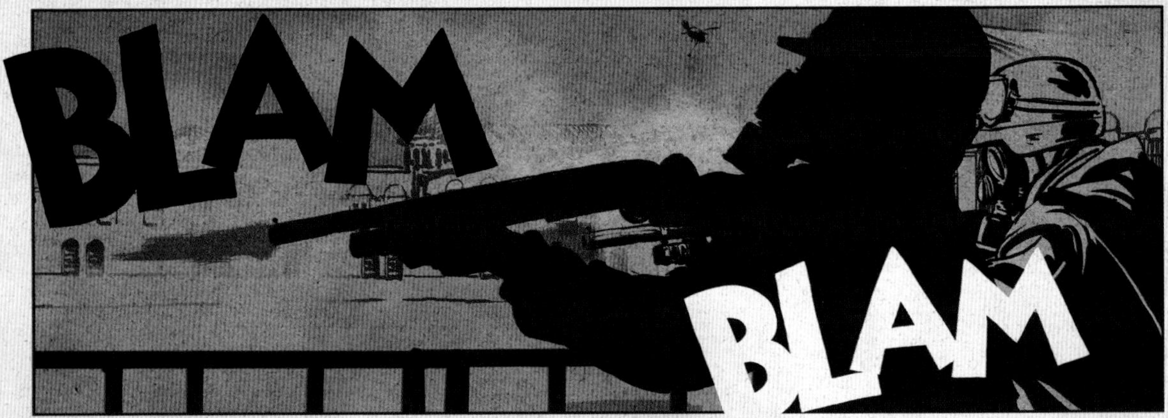
BLAM
BLAM

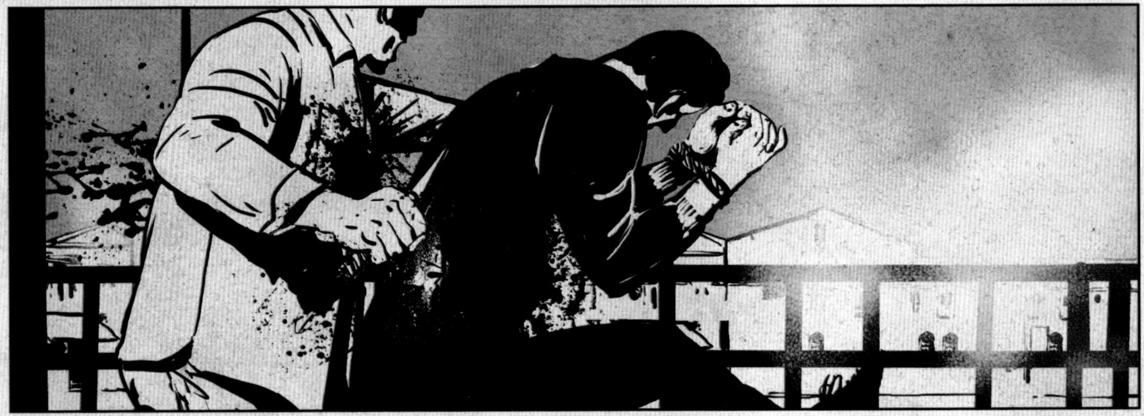

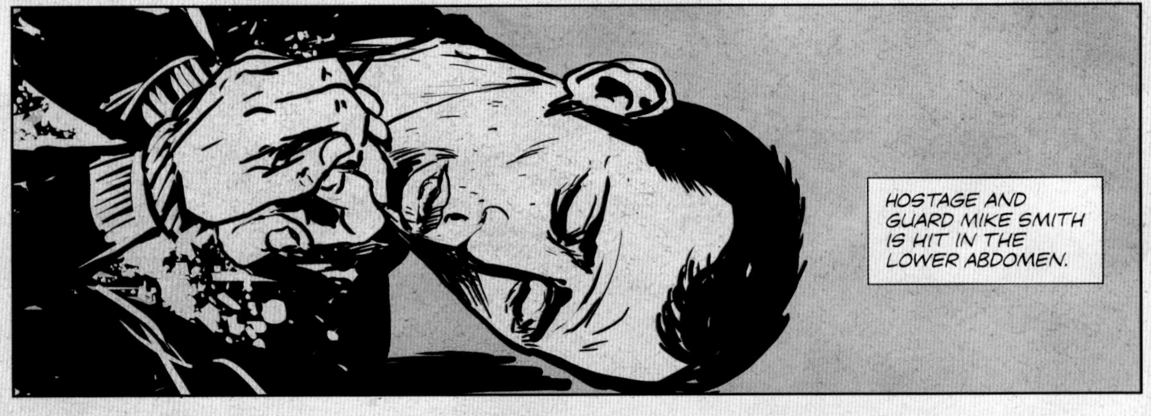
HOSTAGE AND GUARD MIKE SMITH IS HIT IN THE LOWER ABDOMEN.

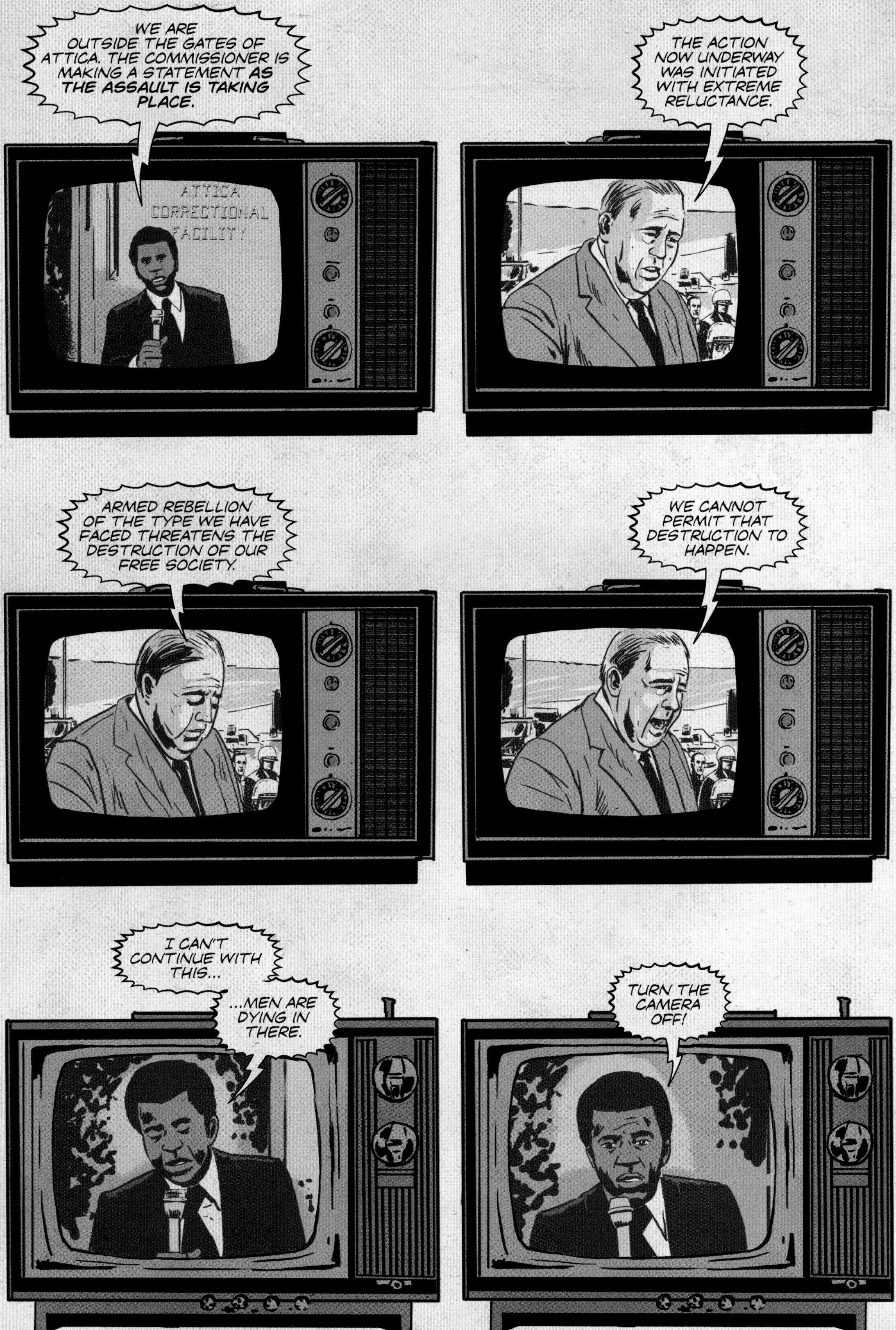
WE ARE OUTSIDE THE GATES OF ATTICA. THE COMMISSIONER IS MAKING A STATEMENT AS THE ASSAULT IS TAKING PLACE.
ATTICA CORRECTIONAL FACILITY
THE ACTION NOW UNDERWAY WAS INITIATED WITH EXTREME RELUCTANCE.
ARMED REBELLION OF THE TYPE WE HAVE FACED THREATENS THE DESTRUCTION OF OUR FREE SOCIETY.
WE CANNOT PERMIT THAT DESTRUCTION TO HAPPEN.
I CAN'T CONTINUE WITH THIS...
...MEN ARE DYING IN THERE.
TURN THE CAMERA OFF!

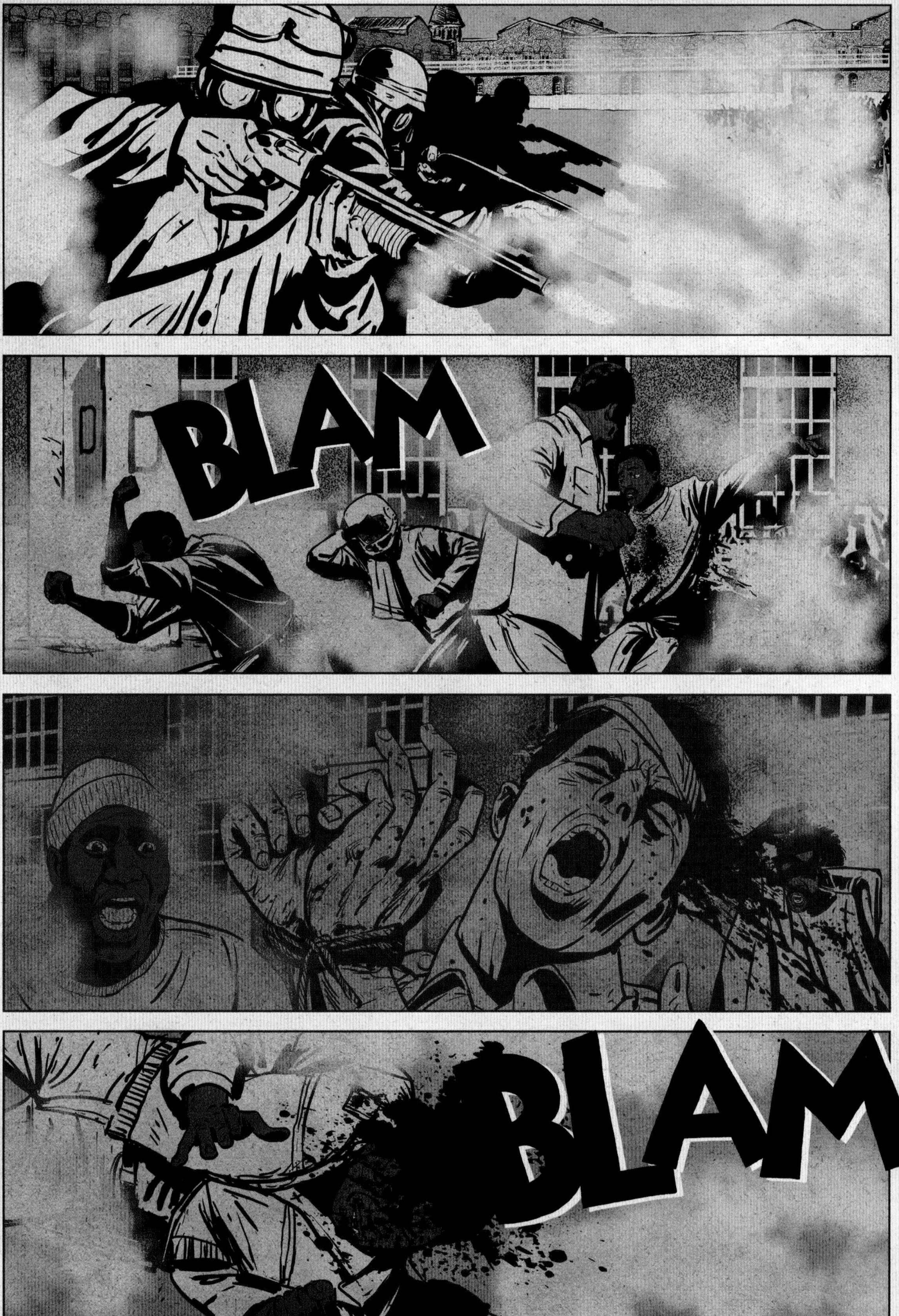
BLAM
BLAM

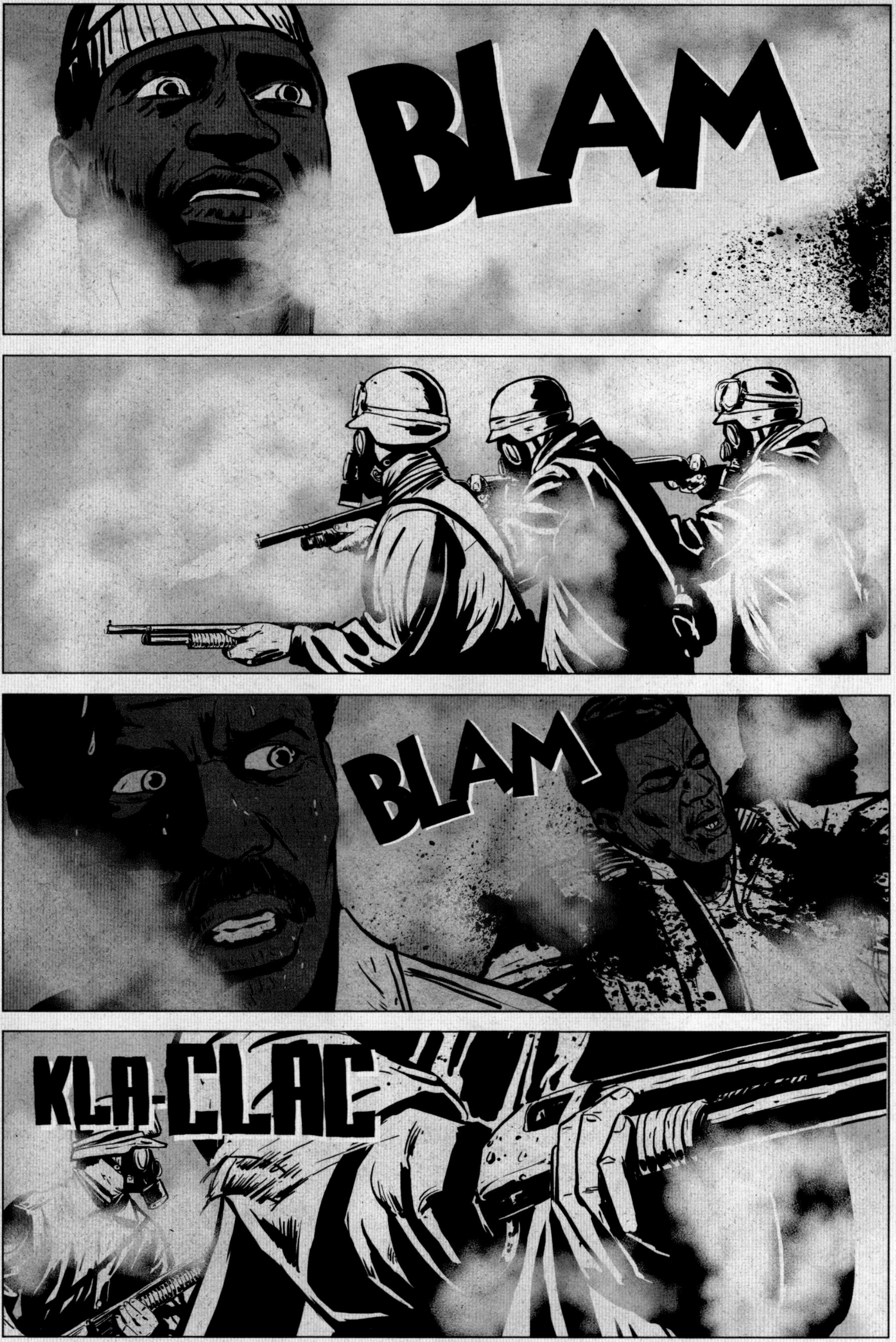
BLAM
BLAM
KLA-CLAC

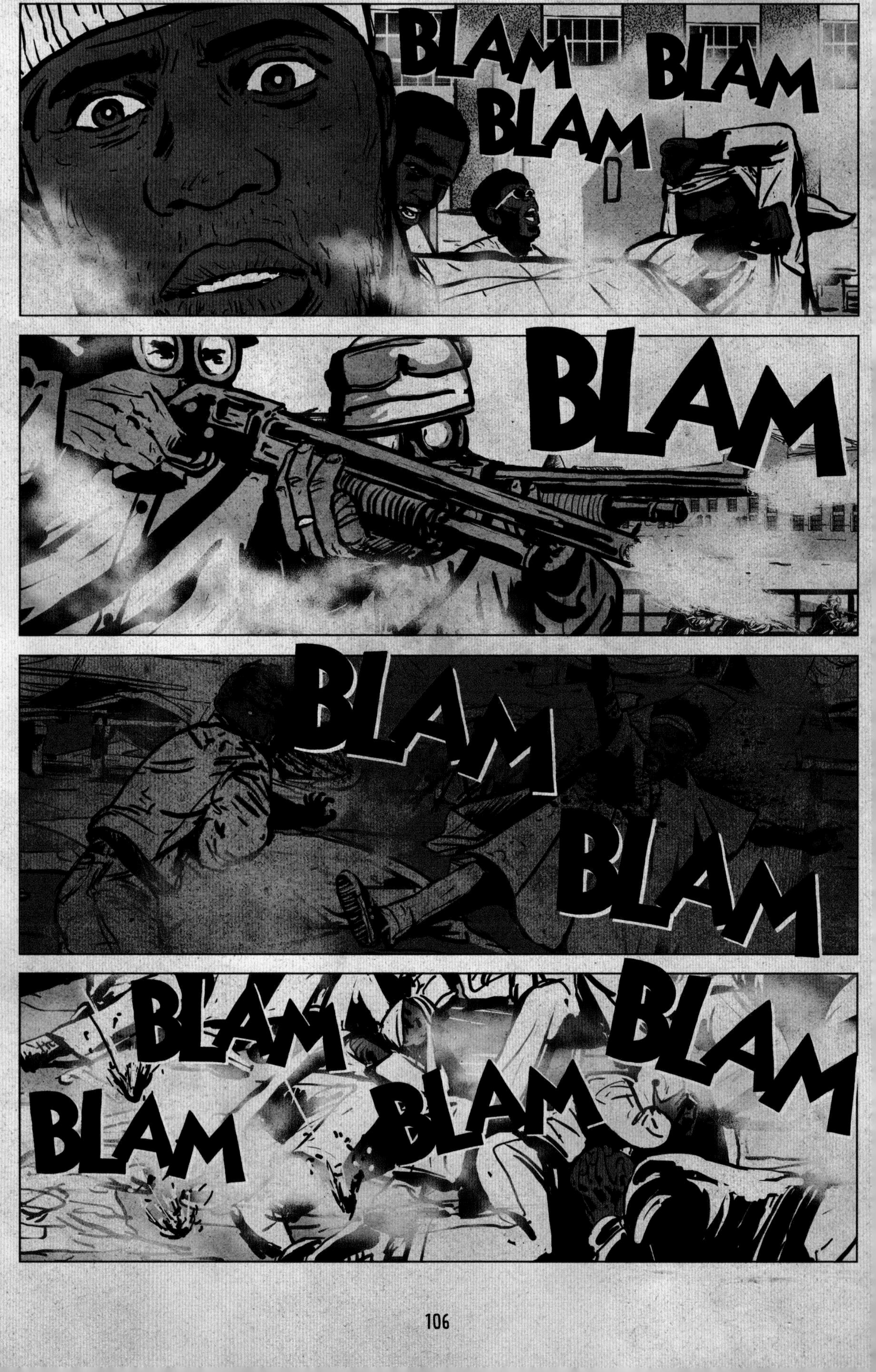
BLAM
BLAM
BLAM
BLAM
BLAM
BLAM
BLAM
BLAM
BLAM
BLAM

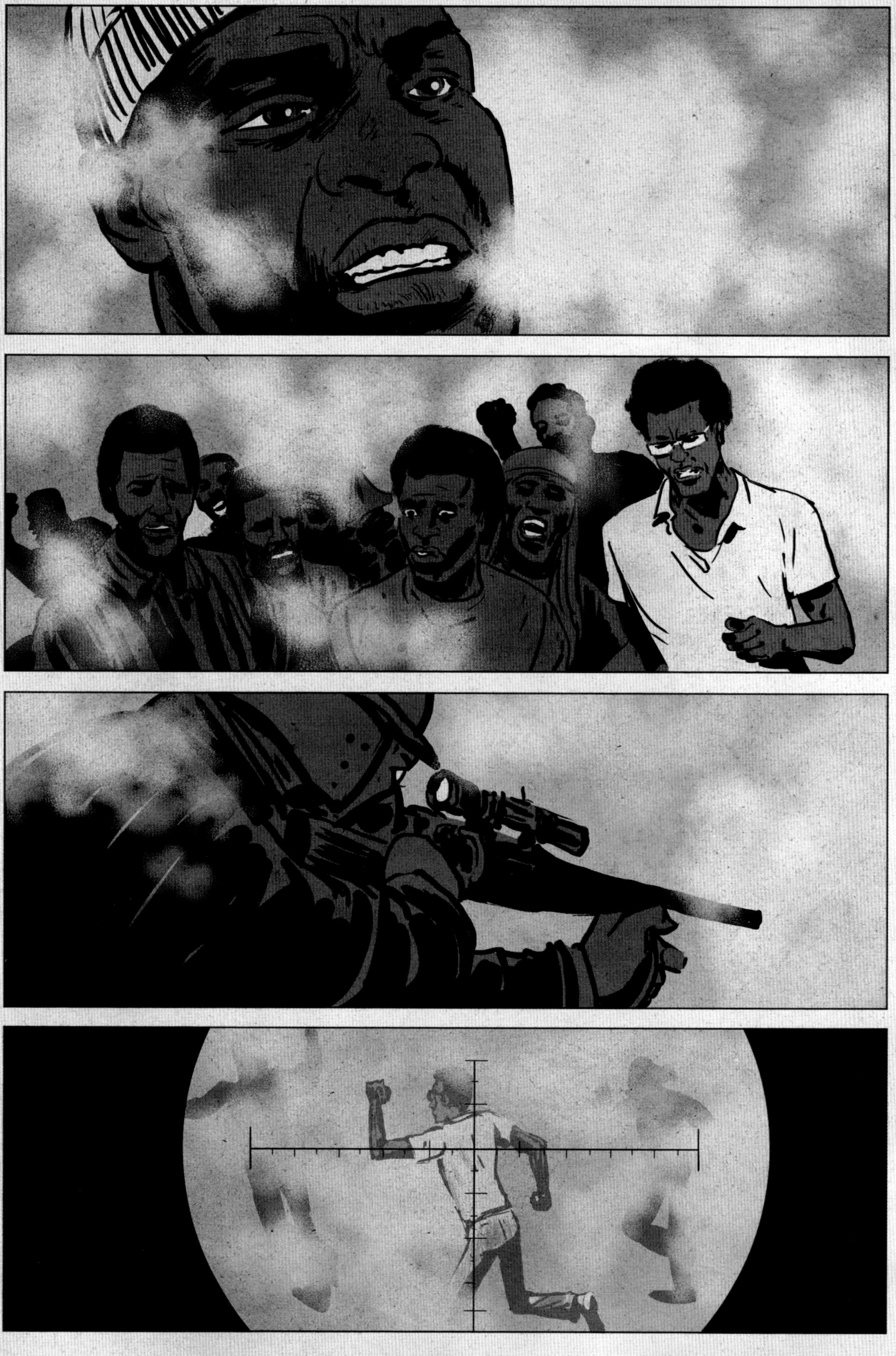

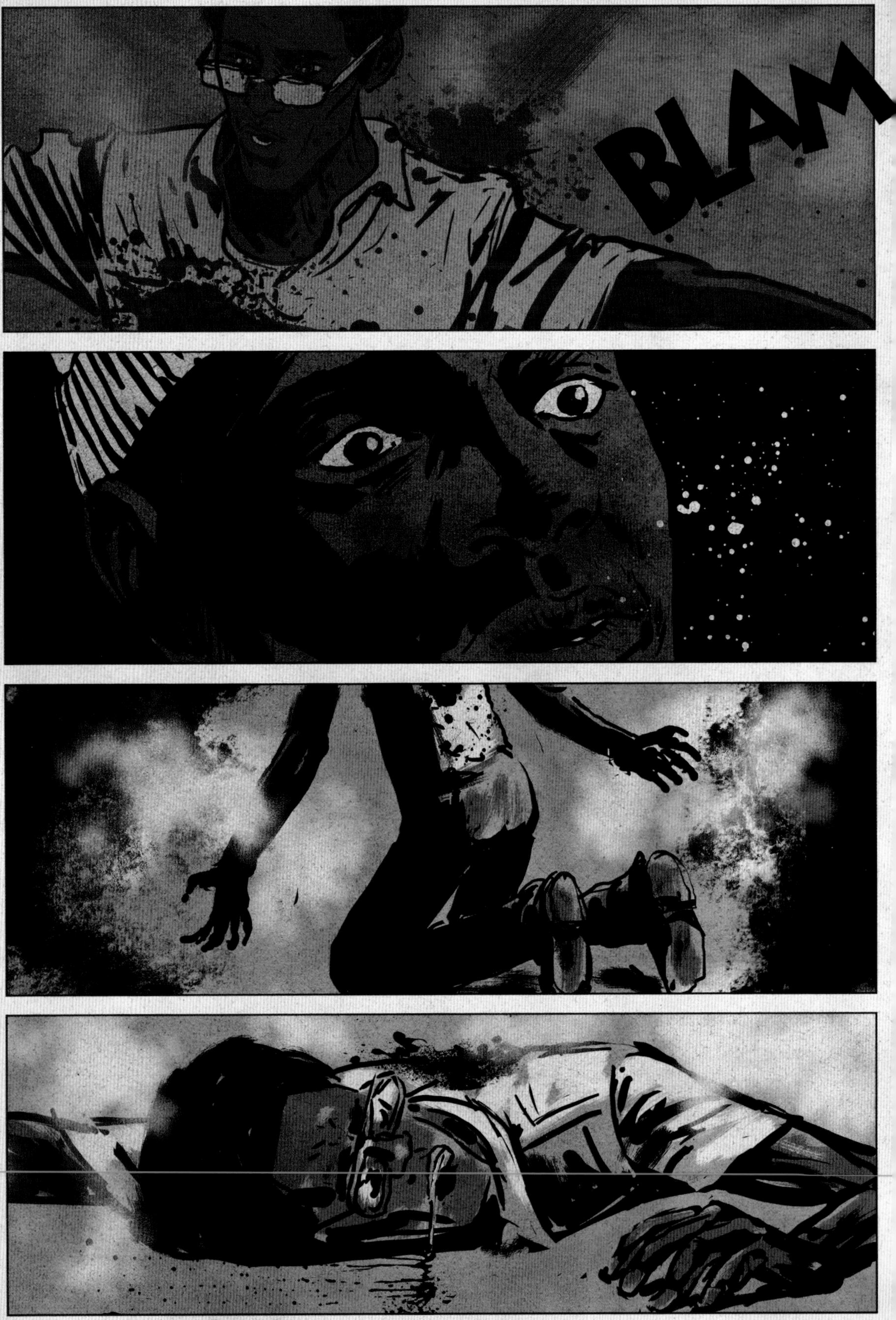
BLAM

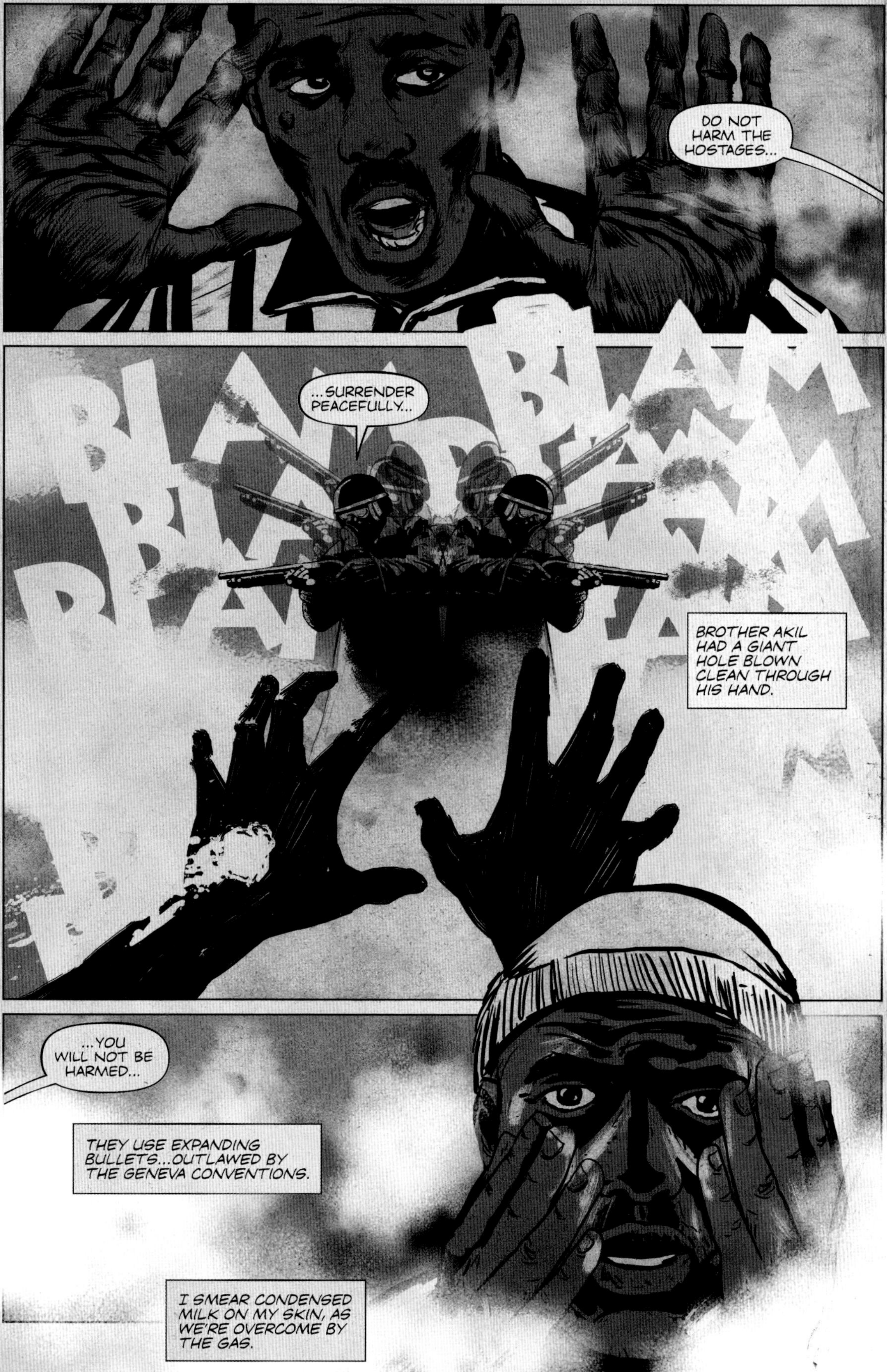

DO NOT HARM THE HOSTAGES...
BLAM BLAM BLAM BLAM BLAM BLAM
...SURRENDER PEACEFULLY...
BROTHER AKIL HAD A GIANT HOLE BLOWN CLEAN THROUGH HIS HAND.
...YOU WILL NOT BE HARMED...
THEY USE EXPANDING BULLETS...OUTLAWED BY THE GENEVA CONVENTIONS.
I SMEAR CONDENSED MILK ON MY SKIN, AS WE'RE OVERCOME BY THE GAS.

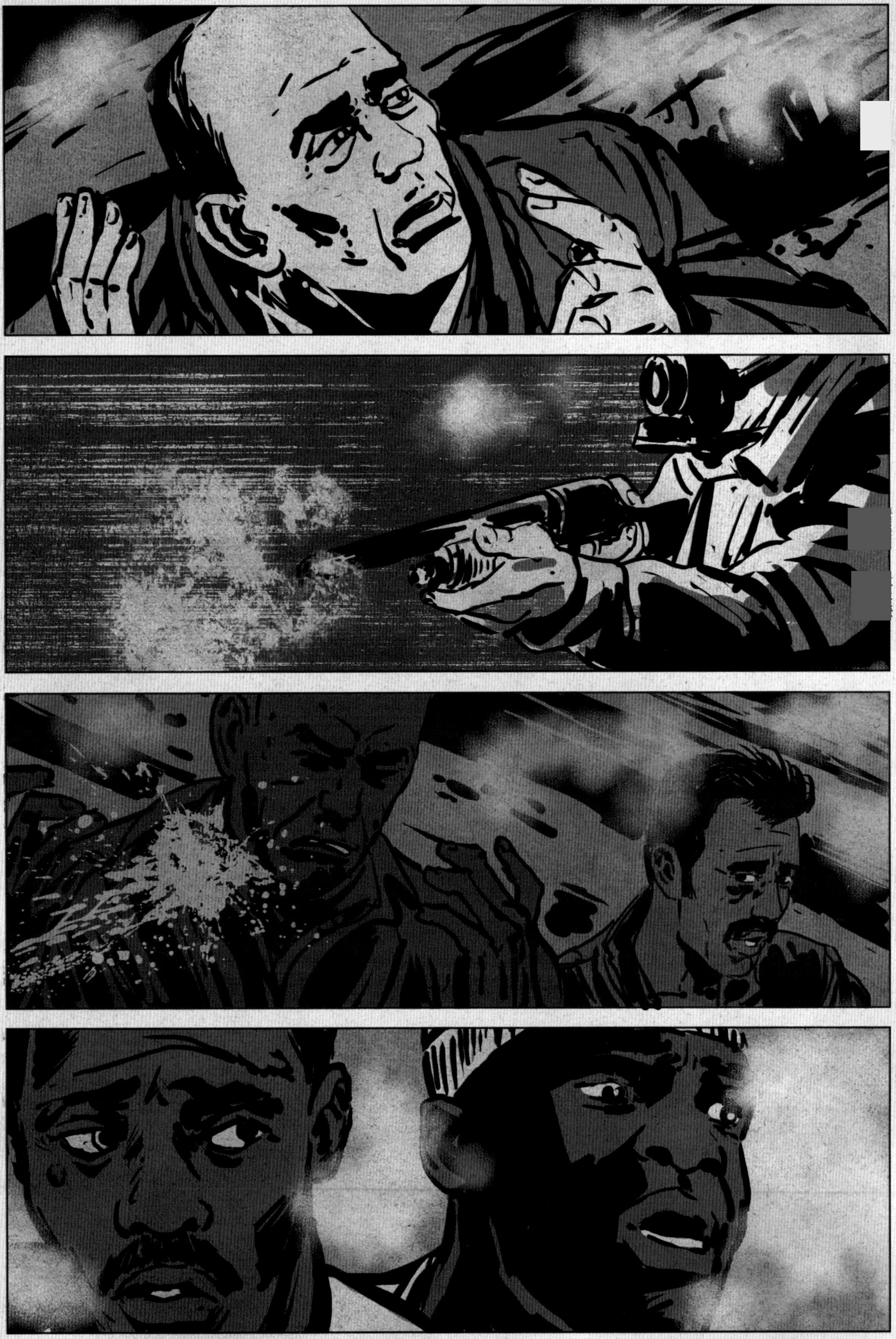

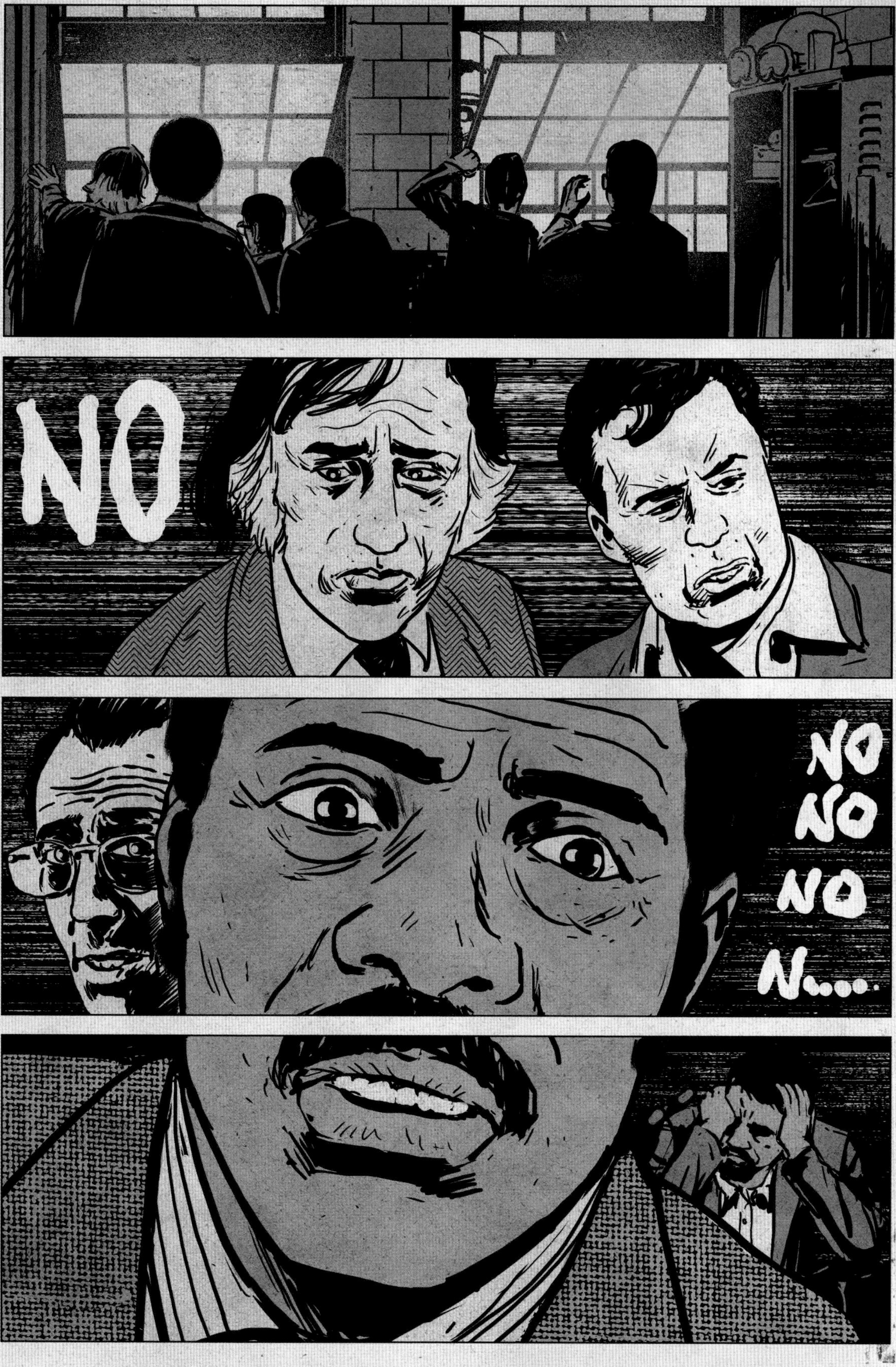
NO
NO
NO
NO
N....

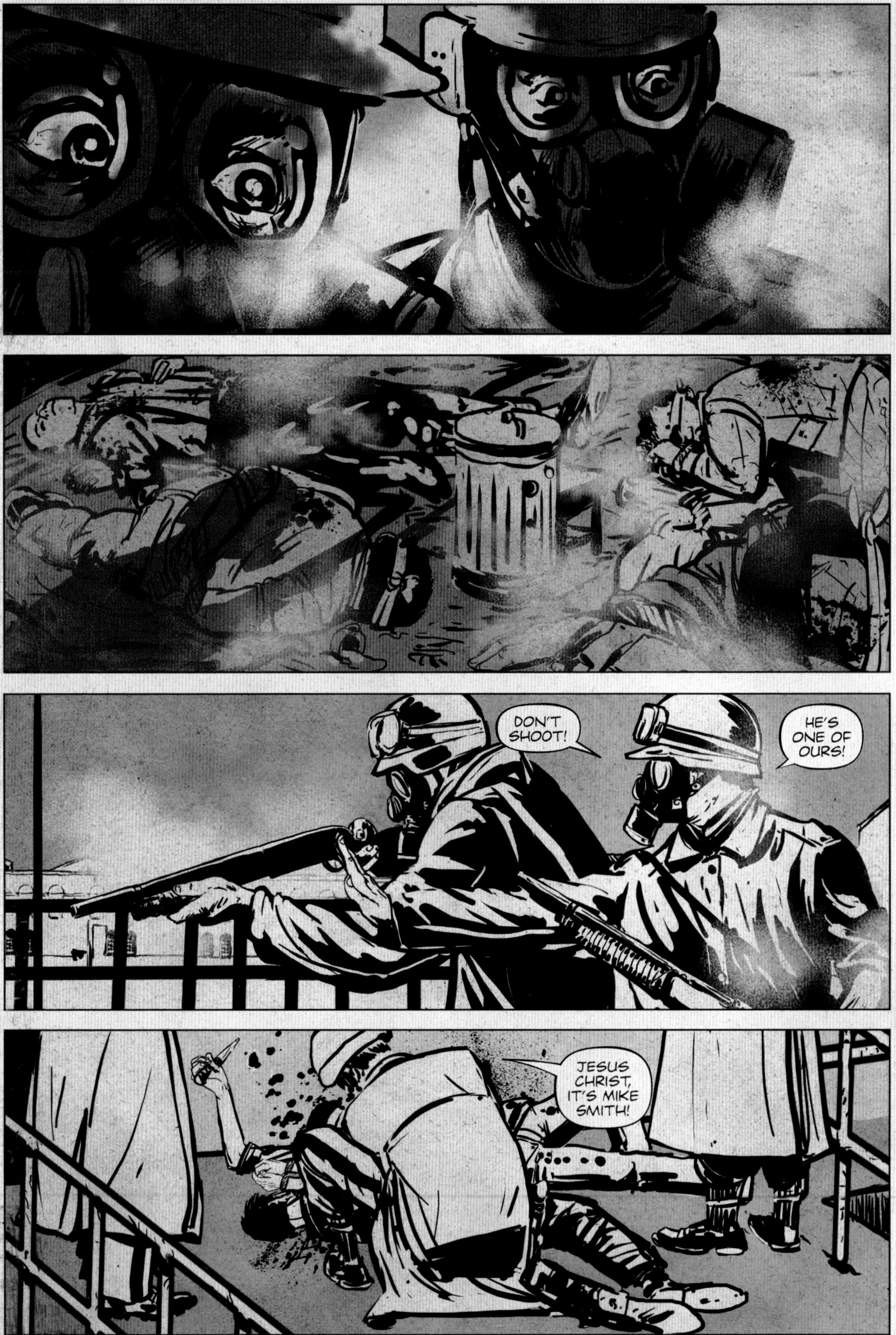
DON'T SHOOT!
HE'S ONE OF OURS!
JESUS CHRIST, IT'S MIKE SMITH!

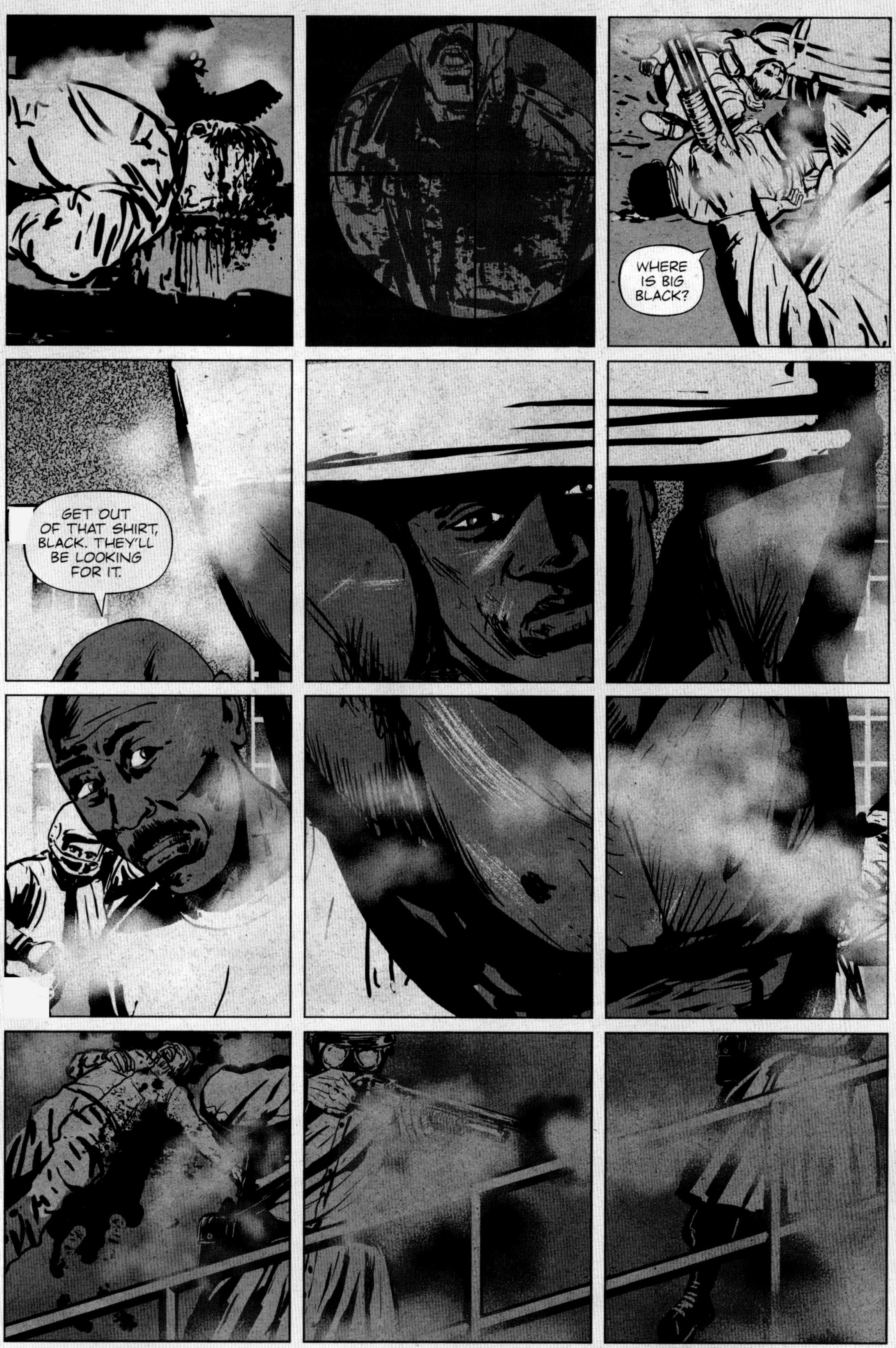
WHERE IS BIG BLACK?
GET OUT OF THAT SHIRT, BLACK. THEY'LL BE LOOKING FOR IT.

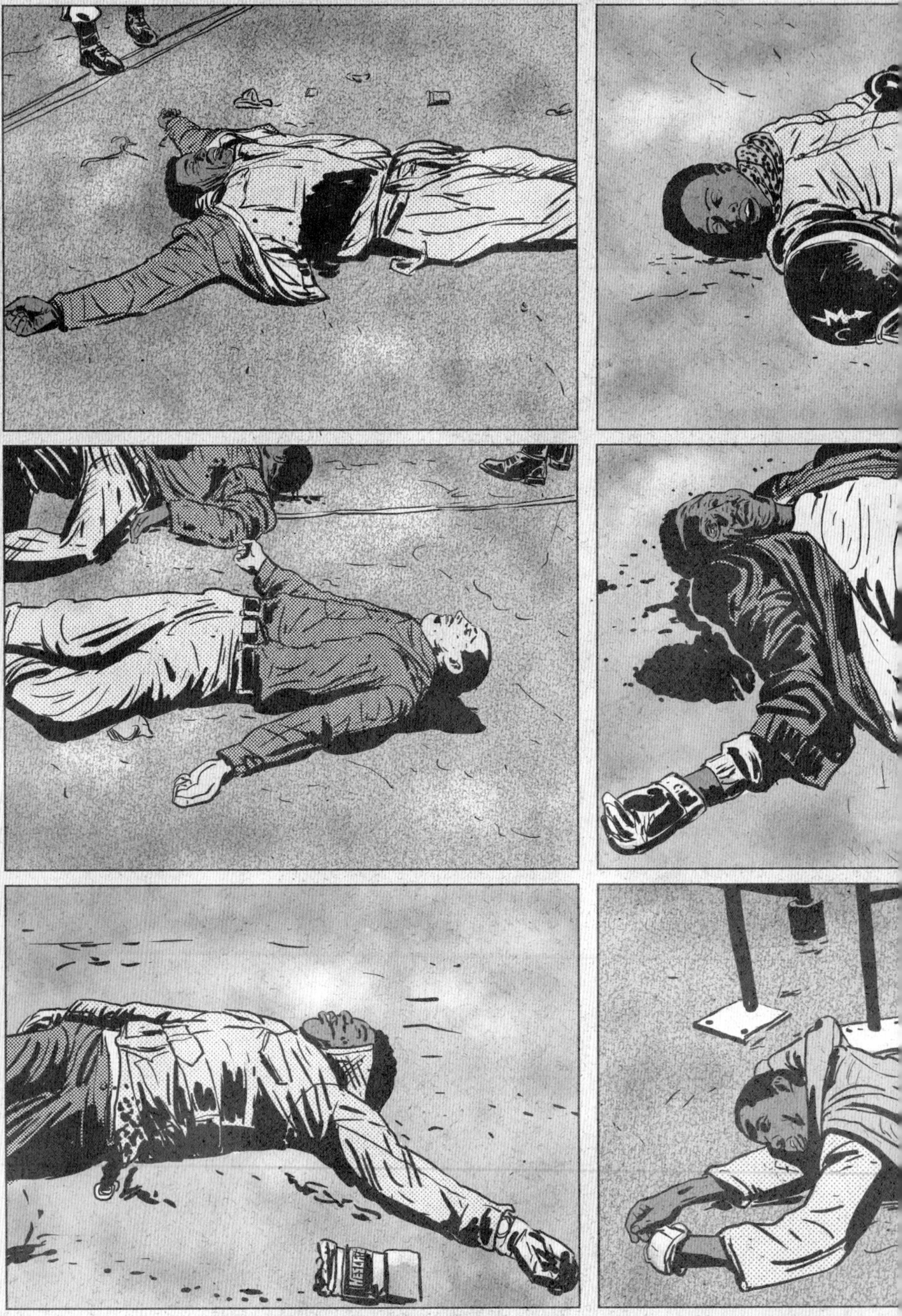

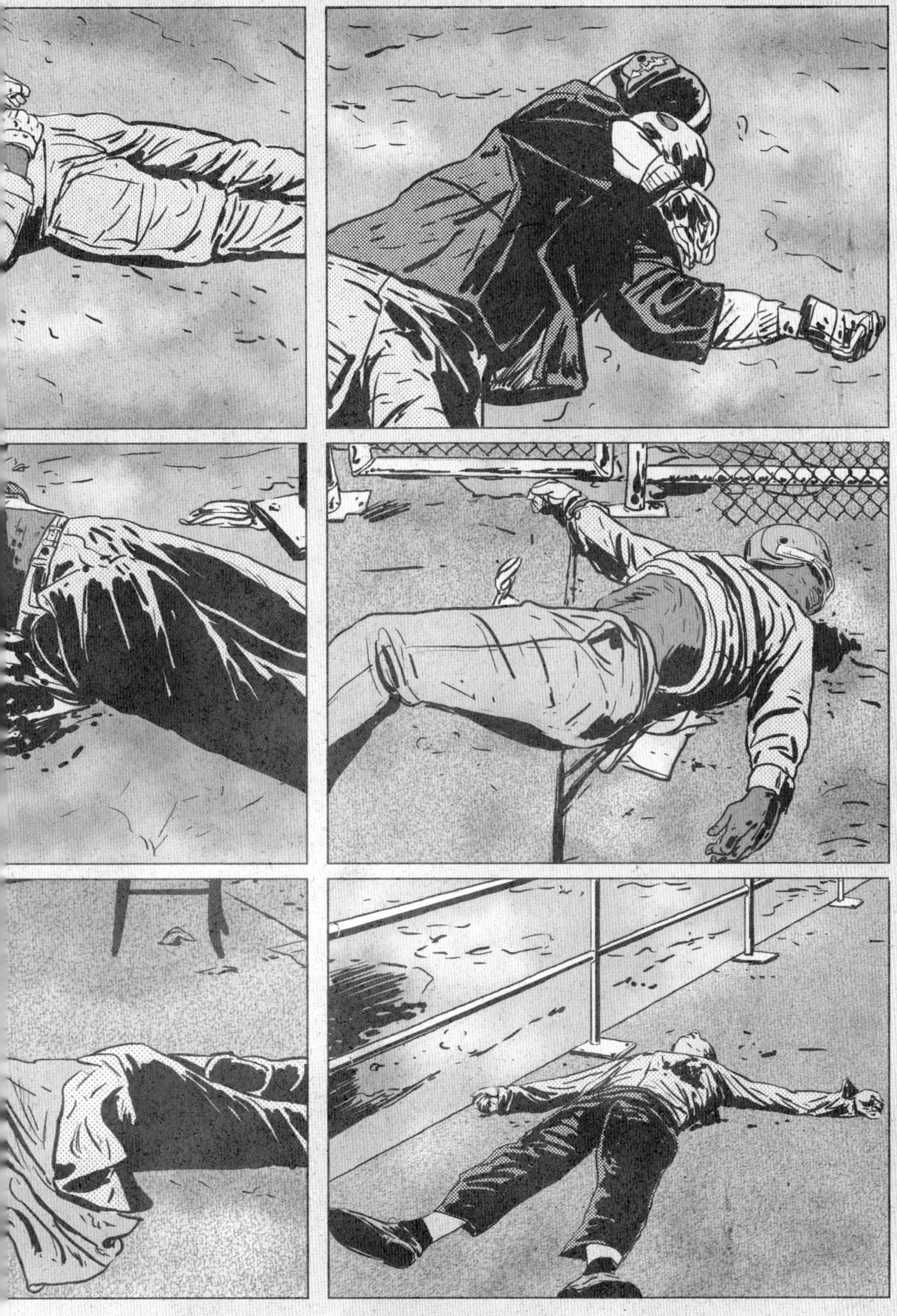

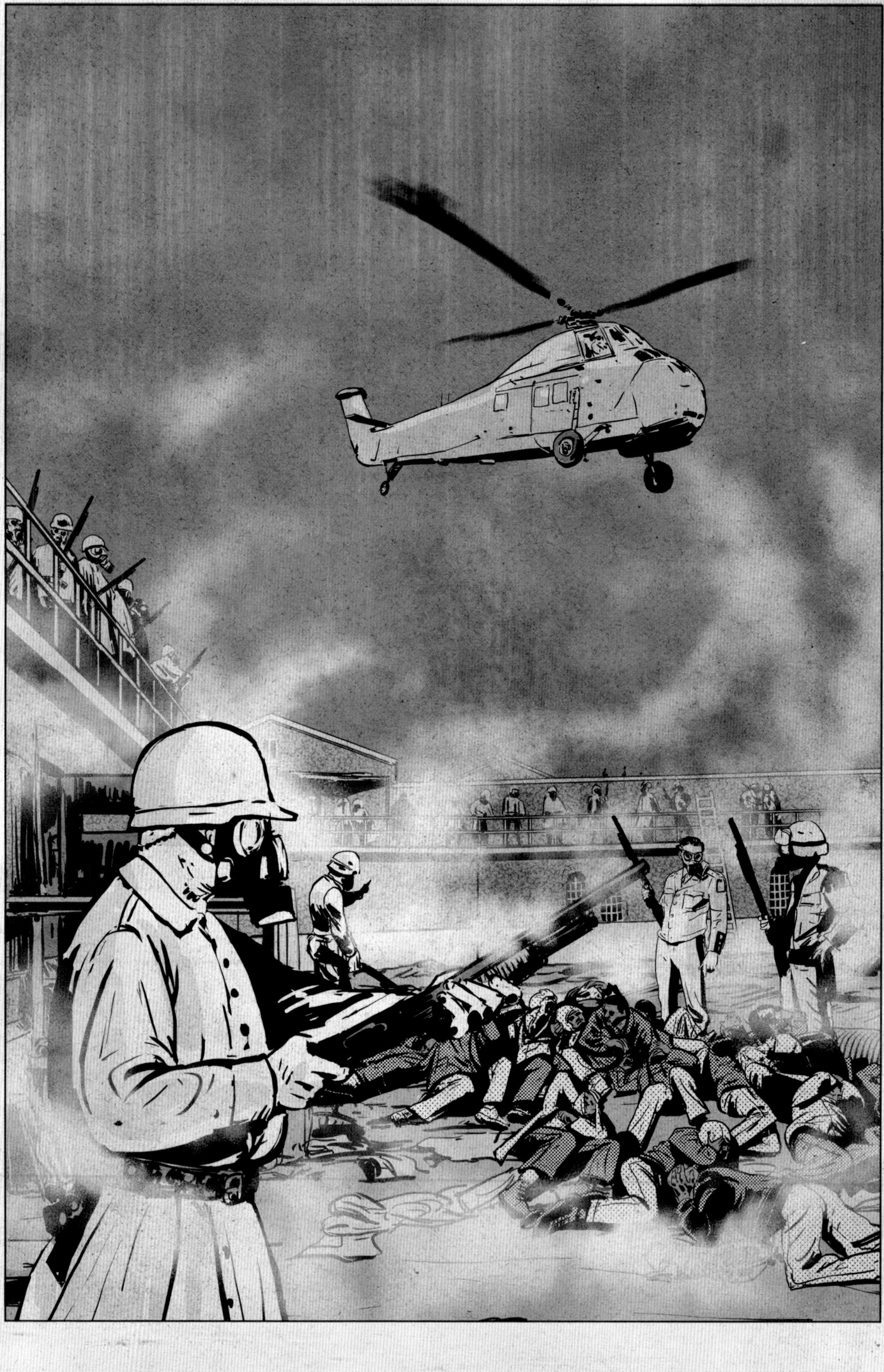

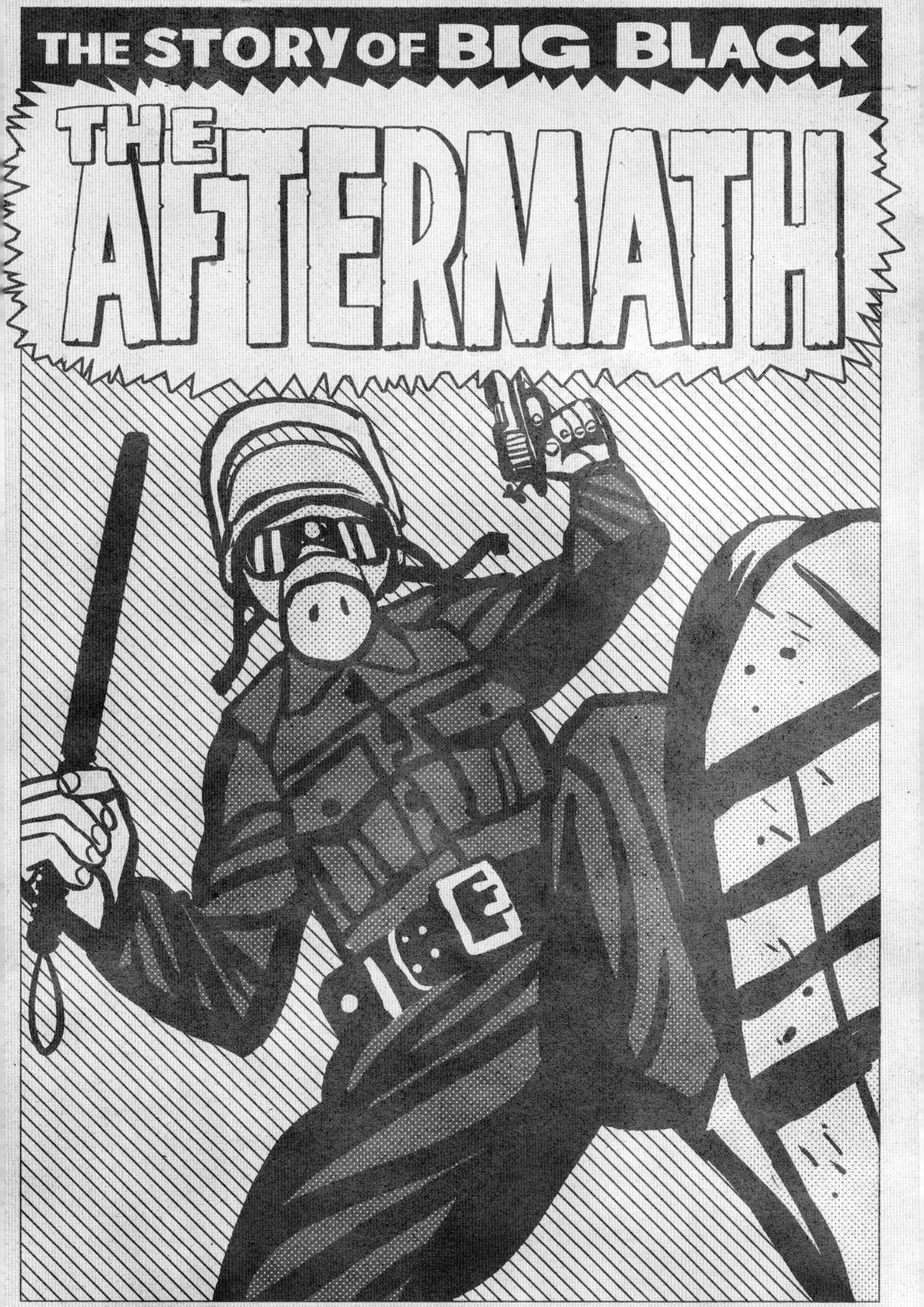
THE STORY OF BIG BLACK
THE AFTERMATH

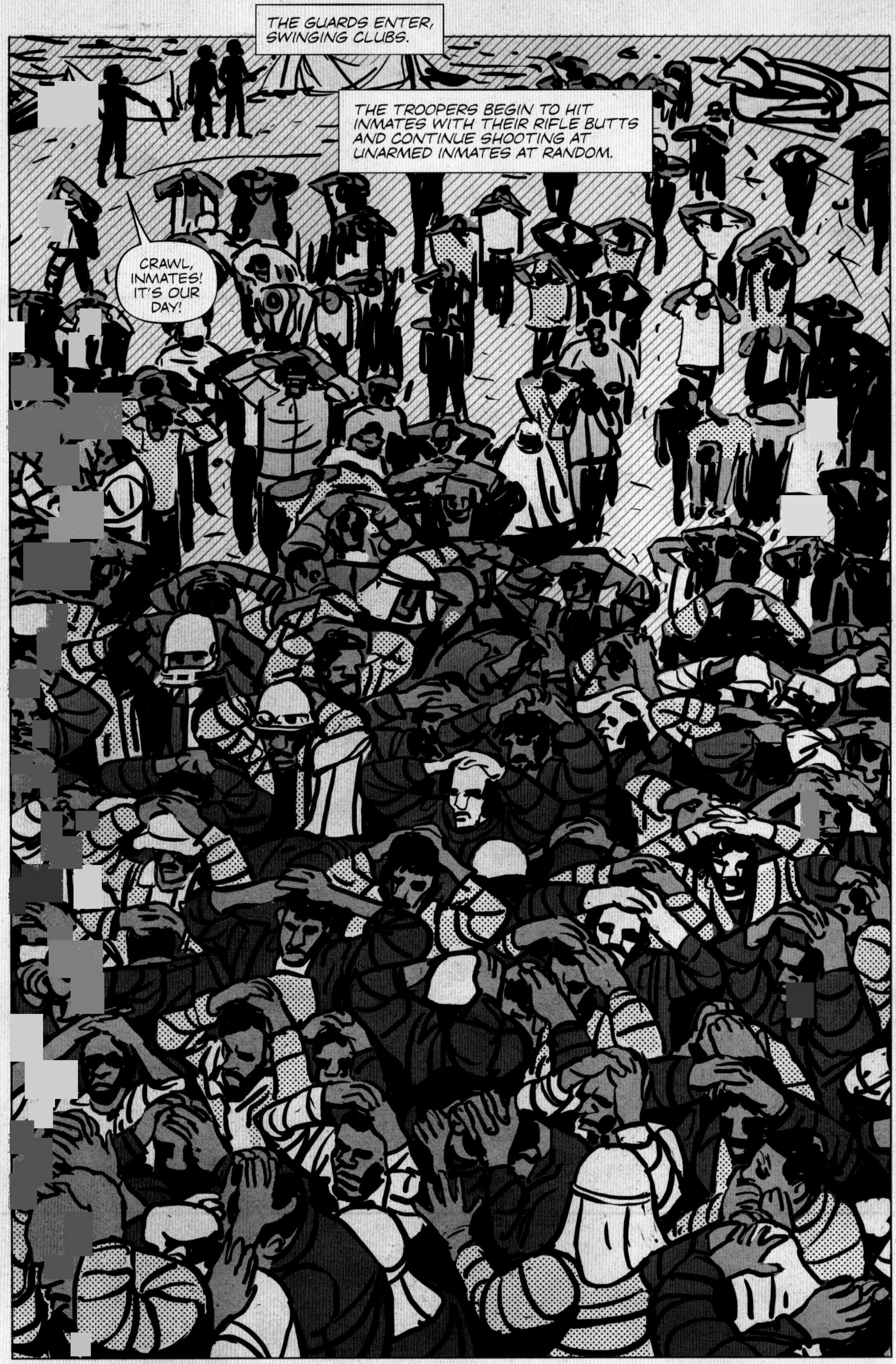
THE GUARDS ENTER, SWINGING CLUBS.
THE TROOPERS BEGIN TO HIT INMATES WITH THEIR RIFLE BUTTS AND CONTINUE SHOOTING AT UNARMED INMATES AT RANDOM.
CRAWL, INMATES! IT'S OUR DAY!

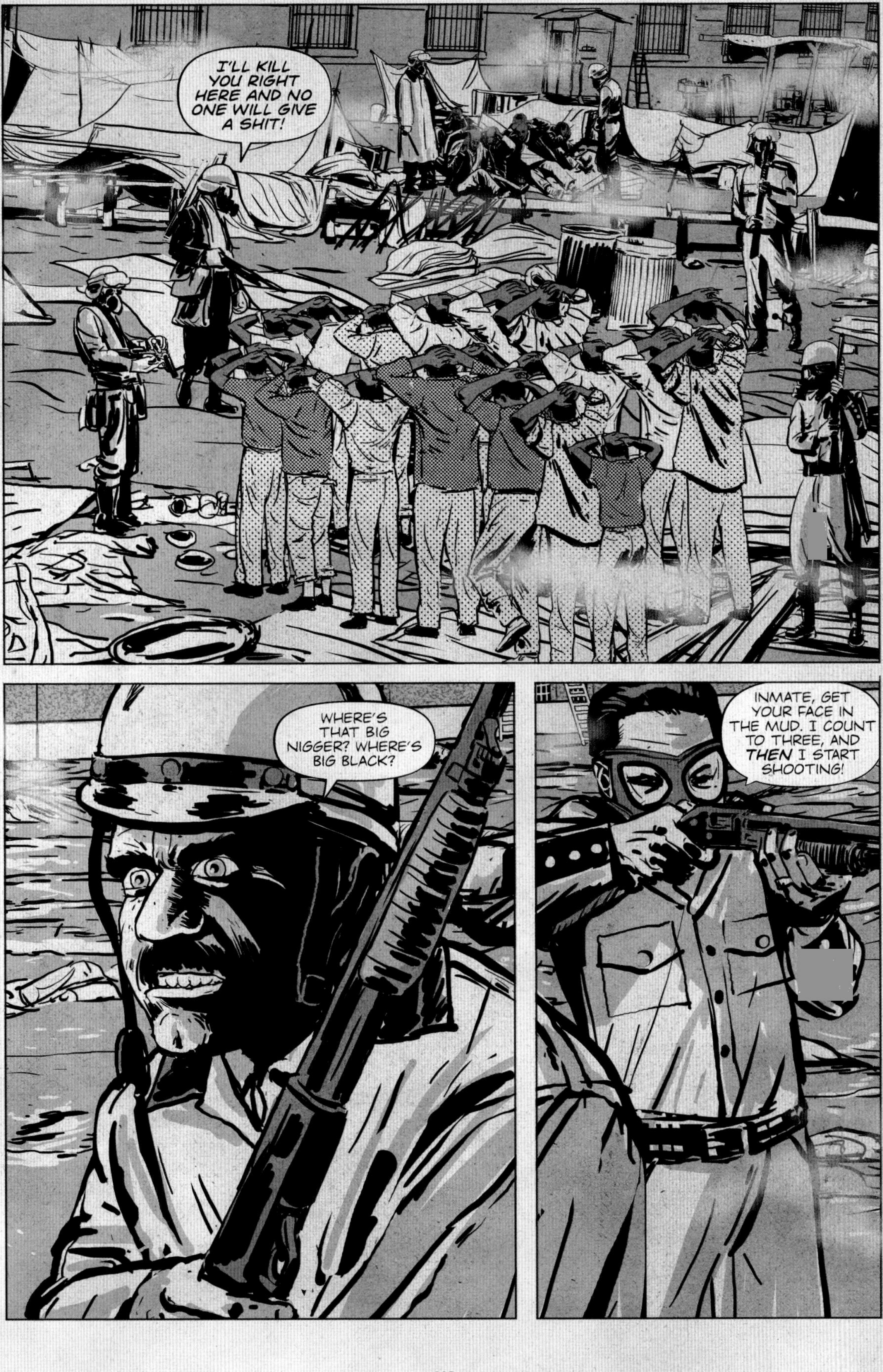
I'LL KILL YOU RIGHT HERE AND NO ONE WILL GIVE A SHIT!
WHERE'S THAT BIG NIGGER? WHERE'S BIG BLACK?
INMATE, GET YOUR FACE IN THE MUD. I COUNT TO THREE, AND THEN I START SHOOTING!

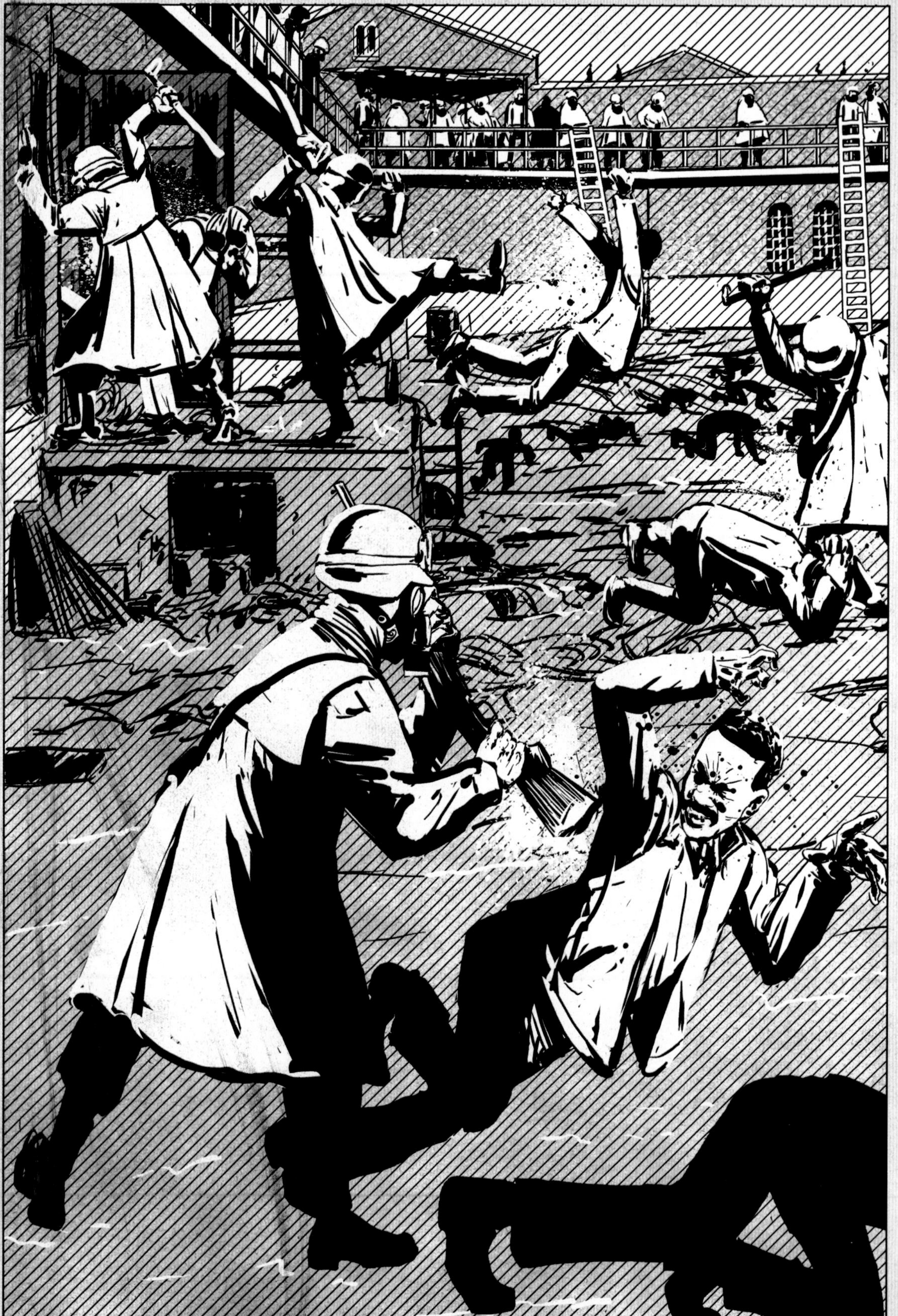

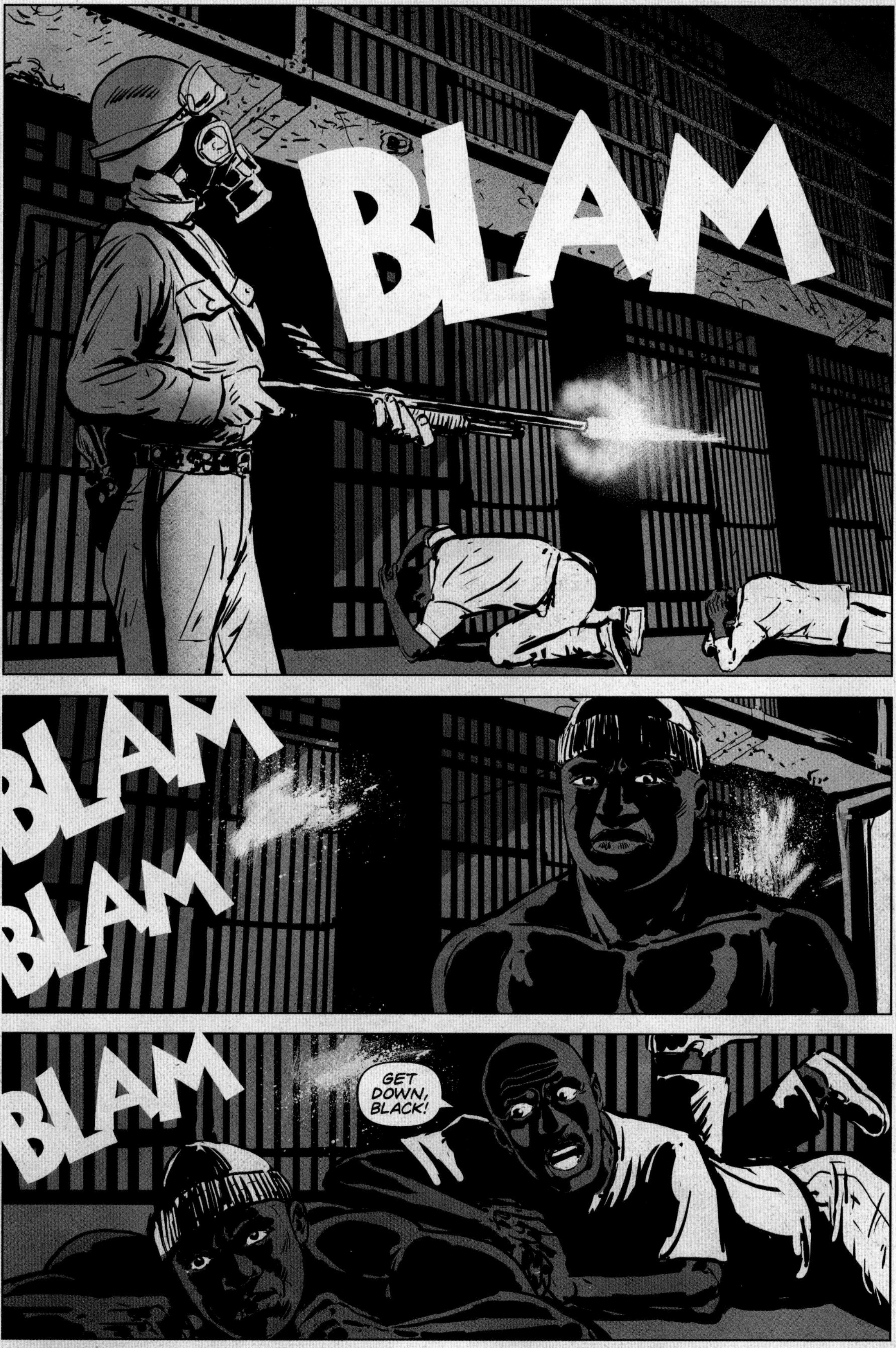
BLAM
BLAM
BLAM
BLAM
GET DOWN, BLACK!

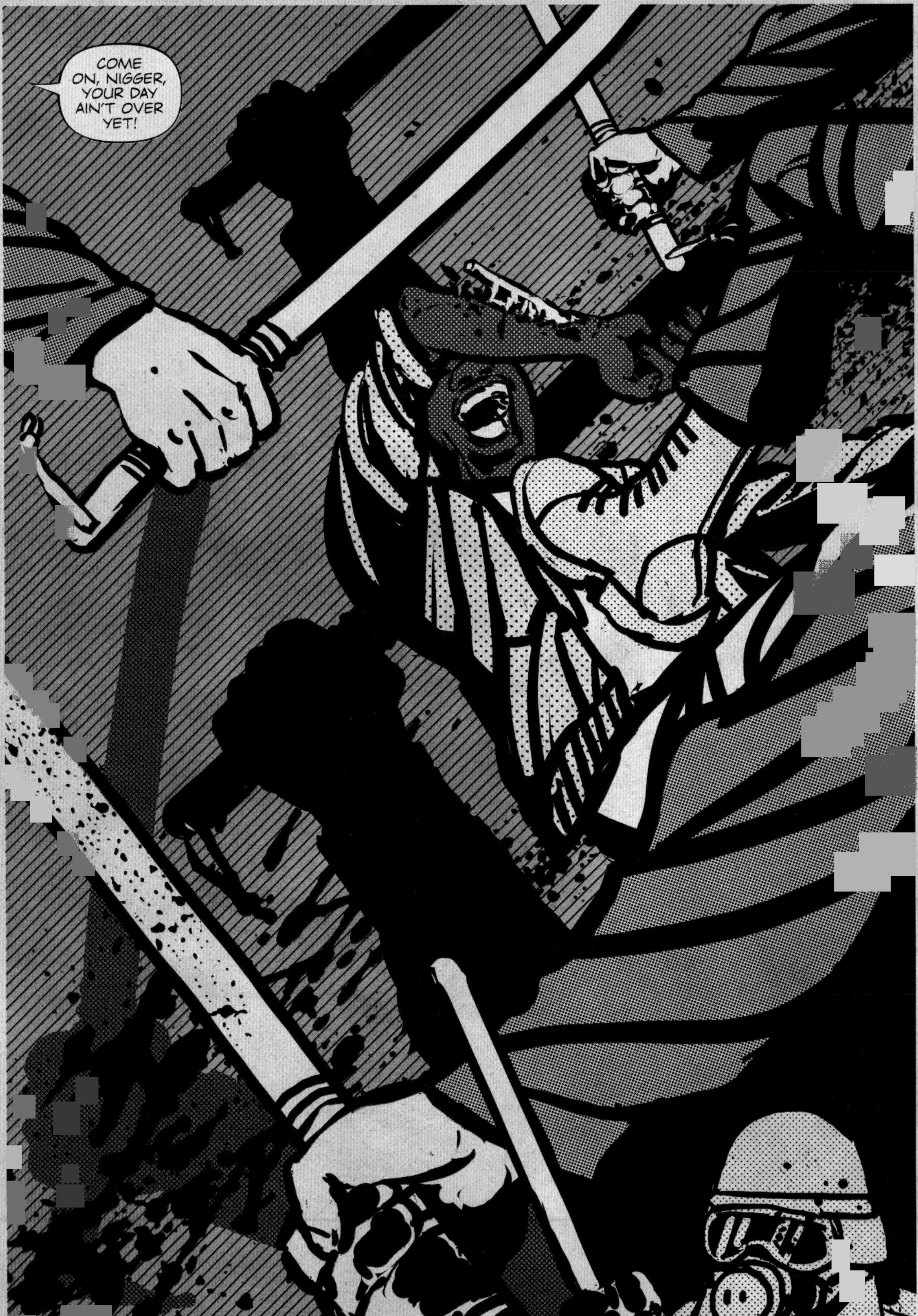
COME ON, NIGGER, YOUR DAY AIN'T OVER YET!

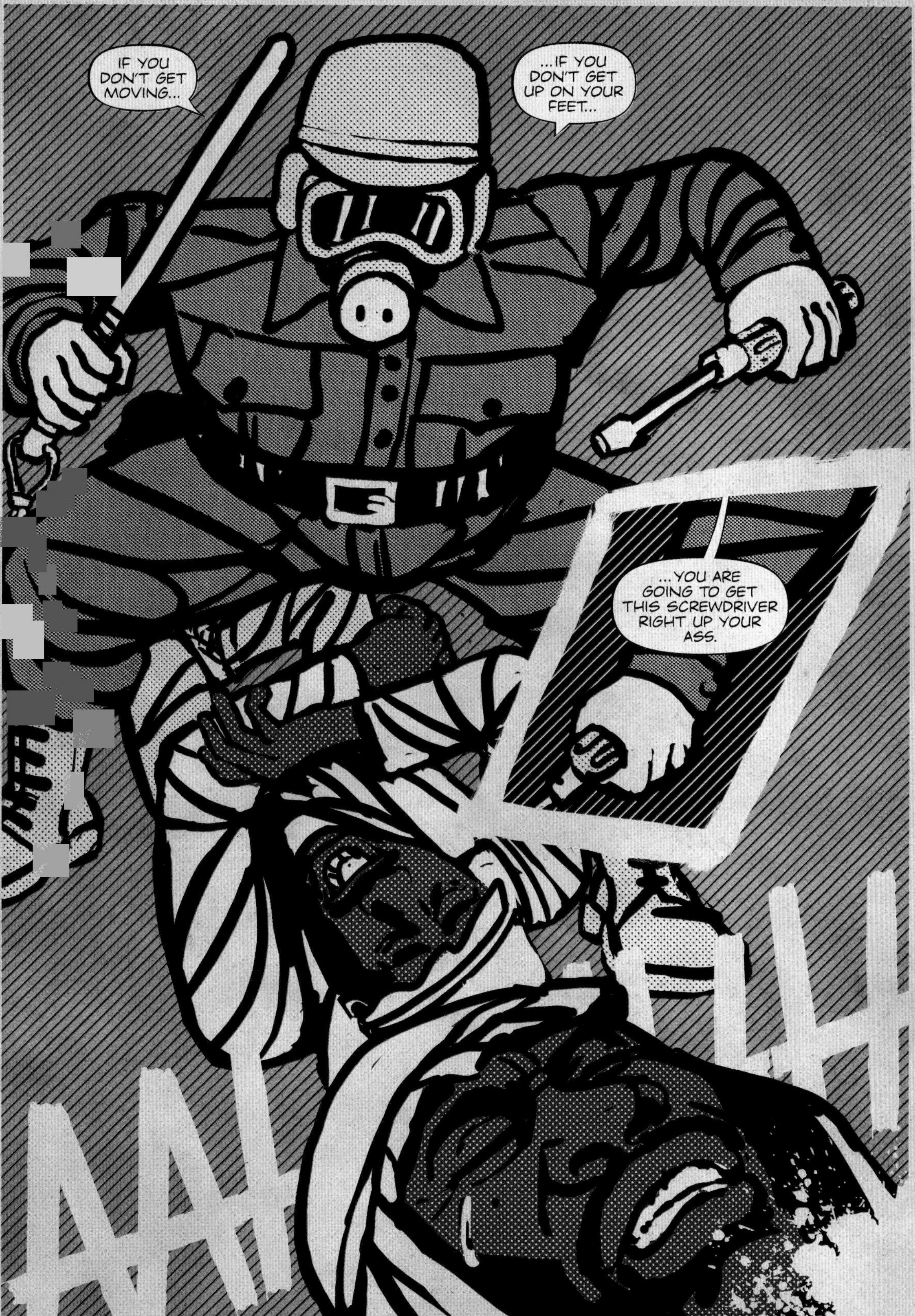
IF YOU DON'T GET MOVING...
...IF YOU DON'T GET UP ON YOUR FEET...
...YOU ARE GOING TO GET THIS SCREWDRIVER RIGHT UP YOUR ASS.

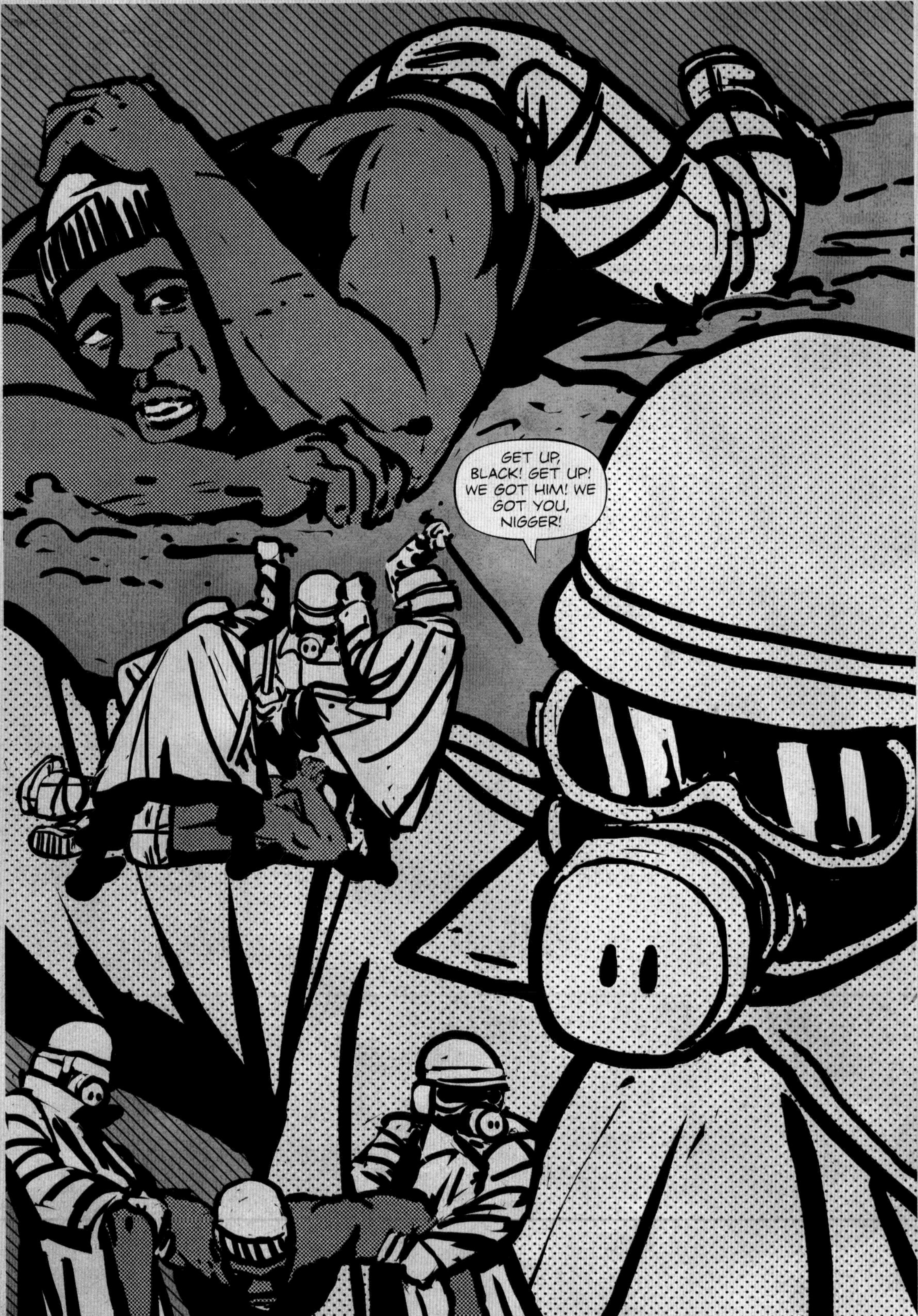
GET UP, BLACK! GET UP! WE GOT HIM! WE GOT YOU, NIGGER!

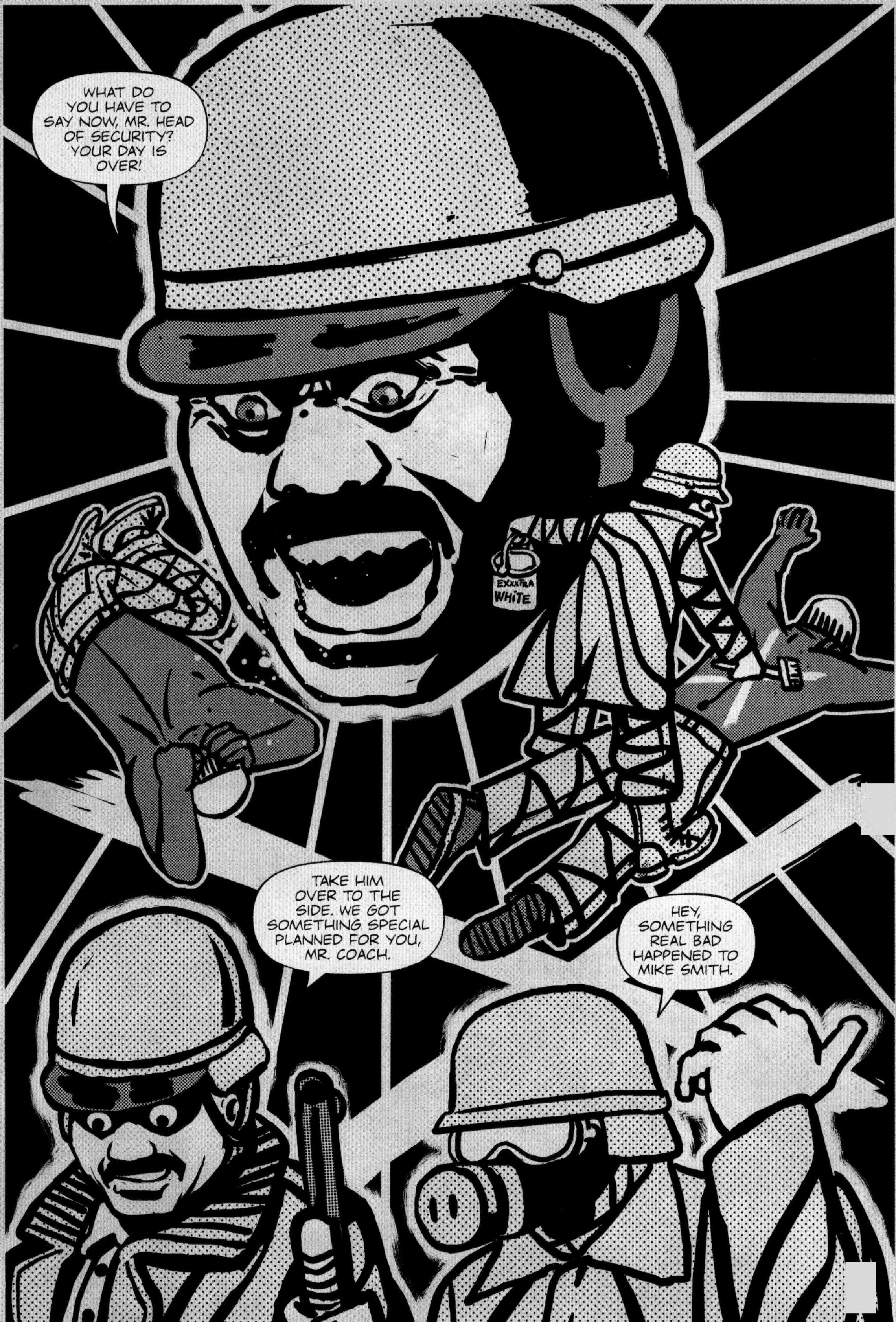
WHAT DO YOU HAVE TO SAY NOW, MR. HEAD OF SECURITY? YOUR DAY IS OVER!
EXXXTRA WHITE
TAKE HIM OVER TO THE SIDE. WE GOT SOMETHING SPECIAL PLANNED FOR YOU, MR. COACH.
HEY, SOMETHING REAL BAD HAPPENED TO MIKE SMITH.

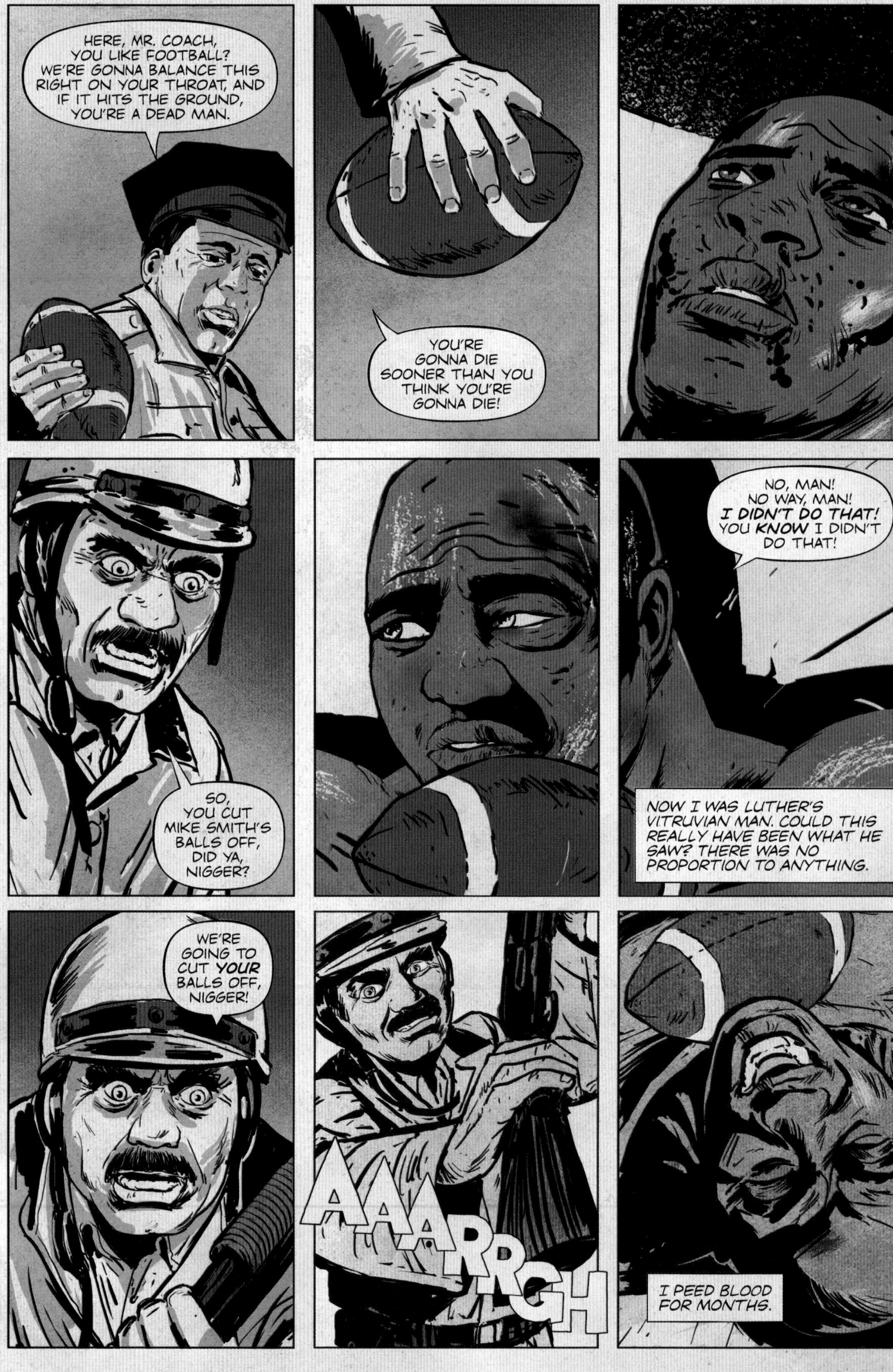
HERE, MR. COACH, YOU LIKE FOOTBALL? WE'RE GONNA BALANCE THIS RIGHT ON YOUR THROAT, AND IF IT HITS THE GROUND, YOU'RE A DEAD MAN.
YOU'RE GONNA DIE SOONER THAN YOU THINK YOU'RE GONNA DIE!
SO, YOU CUT MIKE SMITH'S BALLS OFF, DID YA, NIGGER?
NO, MAN! NO WAY, MAN! I DIDN'T DO THAT! YOU KNOW I DIDN'T DO THAT!
NOW I WAS LUTHER'S VITRUVIAN MAN. COULD THIS REALLY HAVE BEEN WHAT HE SAW? THERE WAS NO PROPORTION TO ANYTHING.
WE'RE GOING TO CUT YOUR BALLS OFF, NIGGER!
AAAARRGH
I PEED BLOOD FOR MONTHS.

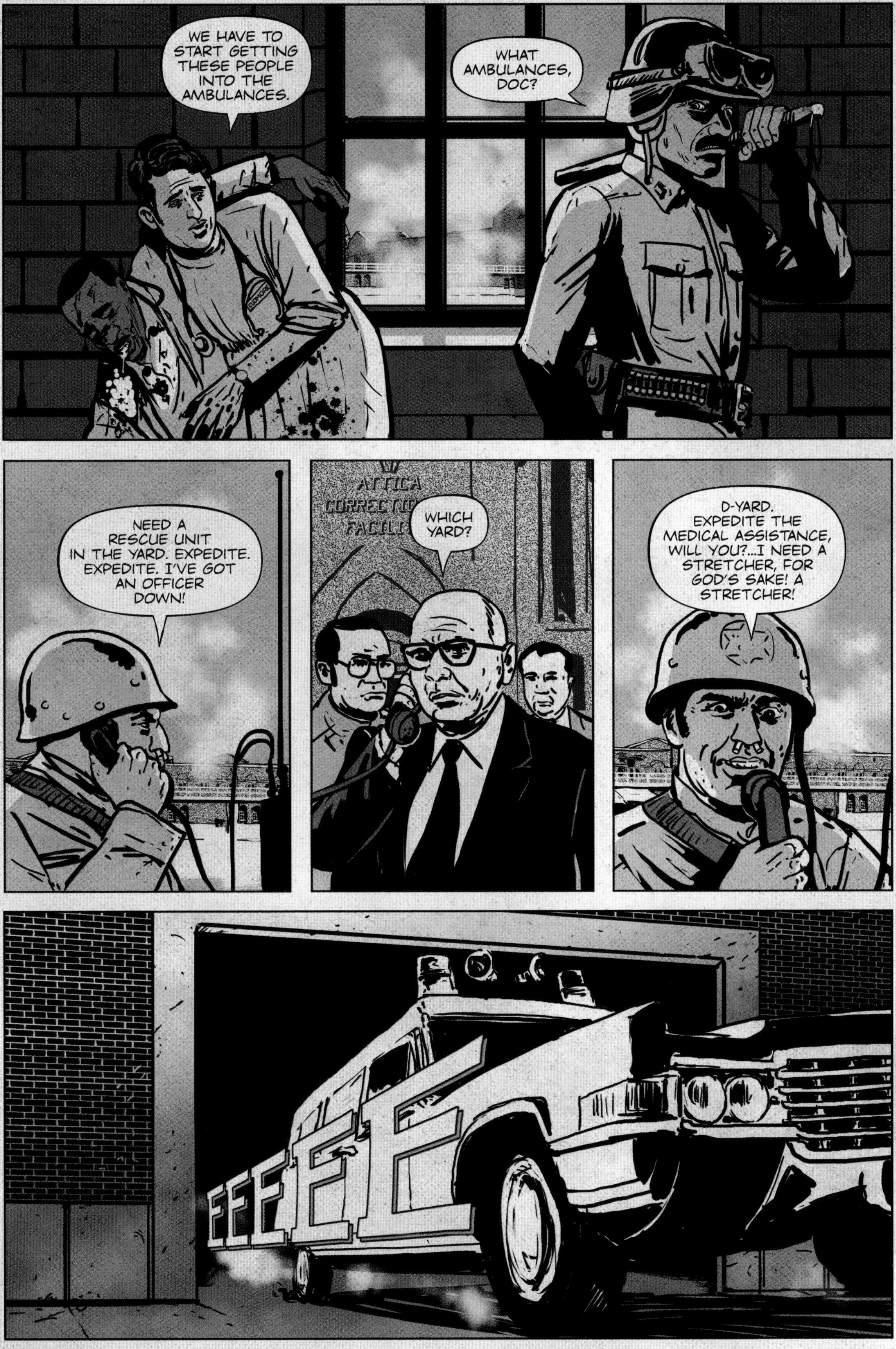
WE HAVE TO START GETTING THESE PEOPLE INTO THE AMBULANCES.
WHAT AMBULANCES, DOC?
NEED A RESCUE UNIT IN THE YARD. EXPEDITE. EXPEDITE. I'VE GOT AN OFFICER DOWN!
WHICH YARD?
D-YARD. EXPEDITE THE MEDICAL ASSISTANCE, WILL YOU?...I NEED A STRETCHER, FOR GOD'S SAKE! A STRETCHER!

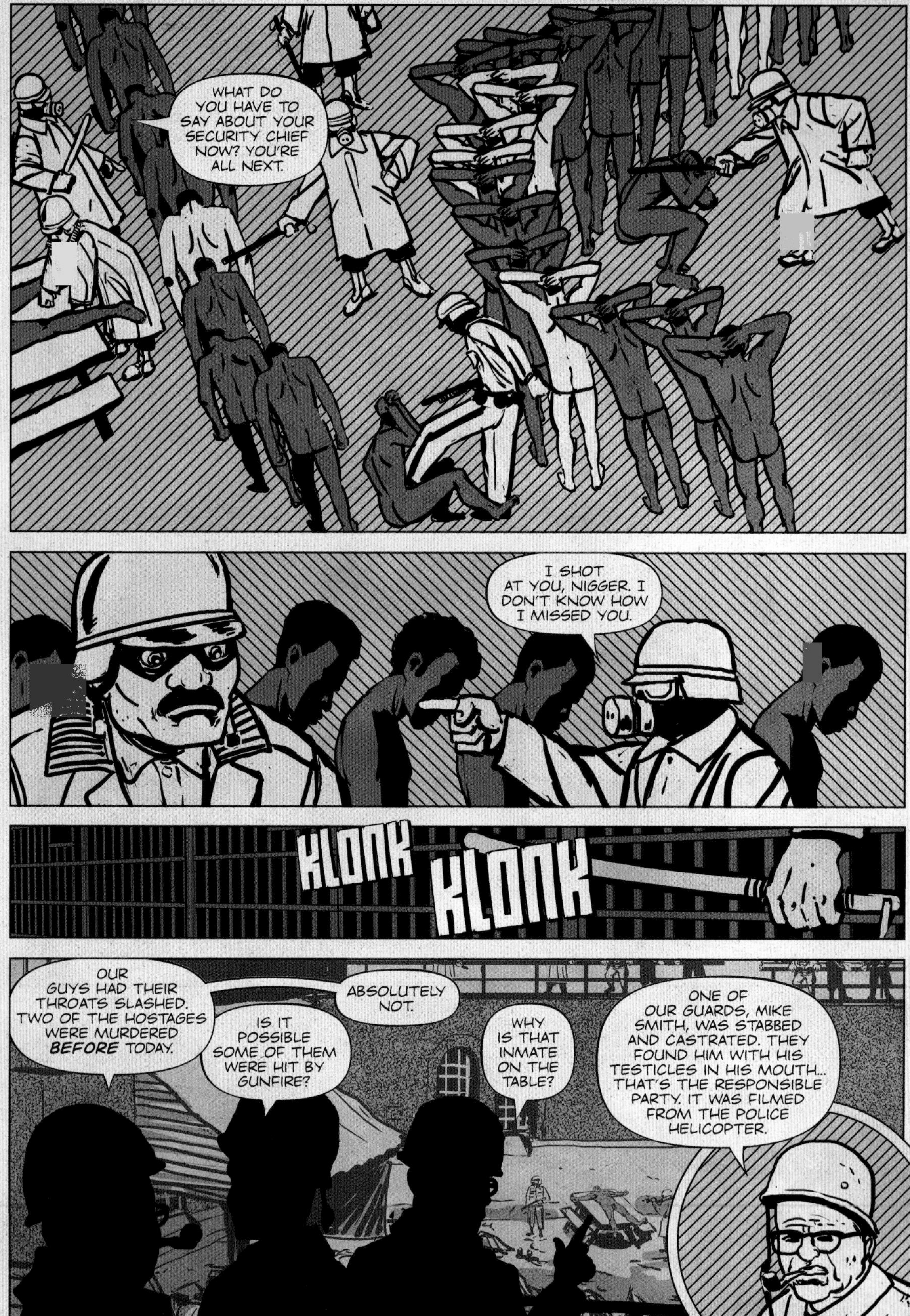
WHAT DO YOU HAVE TO SAY ABOUT YOUR SECURITY CHIEF NOW? YOU'RE ALL NEXT.
I SHOT AT YOU, NIGGER. I DON'T KNOW HOW I MISSED YOU.
KLONK
KLONK
OUR GUYS HAD THEIR THROATS SLASHED. TWO OF THE HOSTAGES WERE MURDERED *BEFORE* TODAY.
ABSOLUTELY NOT.
IS IT POSSIBLE SOME OF THEM WERE HIT BY GUNFIRE?
WHY IS THAT INMATE ON THE TABLE?
ONE OF OUR GUARDS, MIKE SMITH, WAS STABBED AND CASTRATED. THEY FOUND HIM WITH HIS TESTICLES IN HIS MOUTH... THAT'S THE RESPONSIBLE PARTY. IT WAS FILMED FROM THE POLICE HELICOPTER.

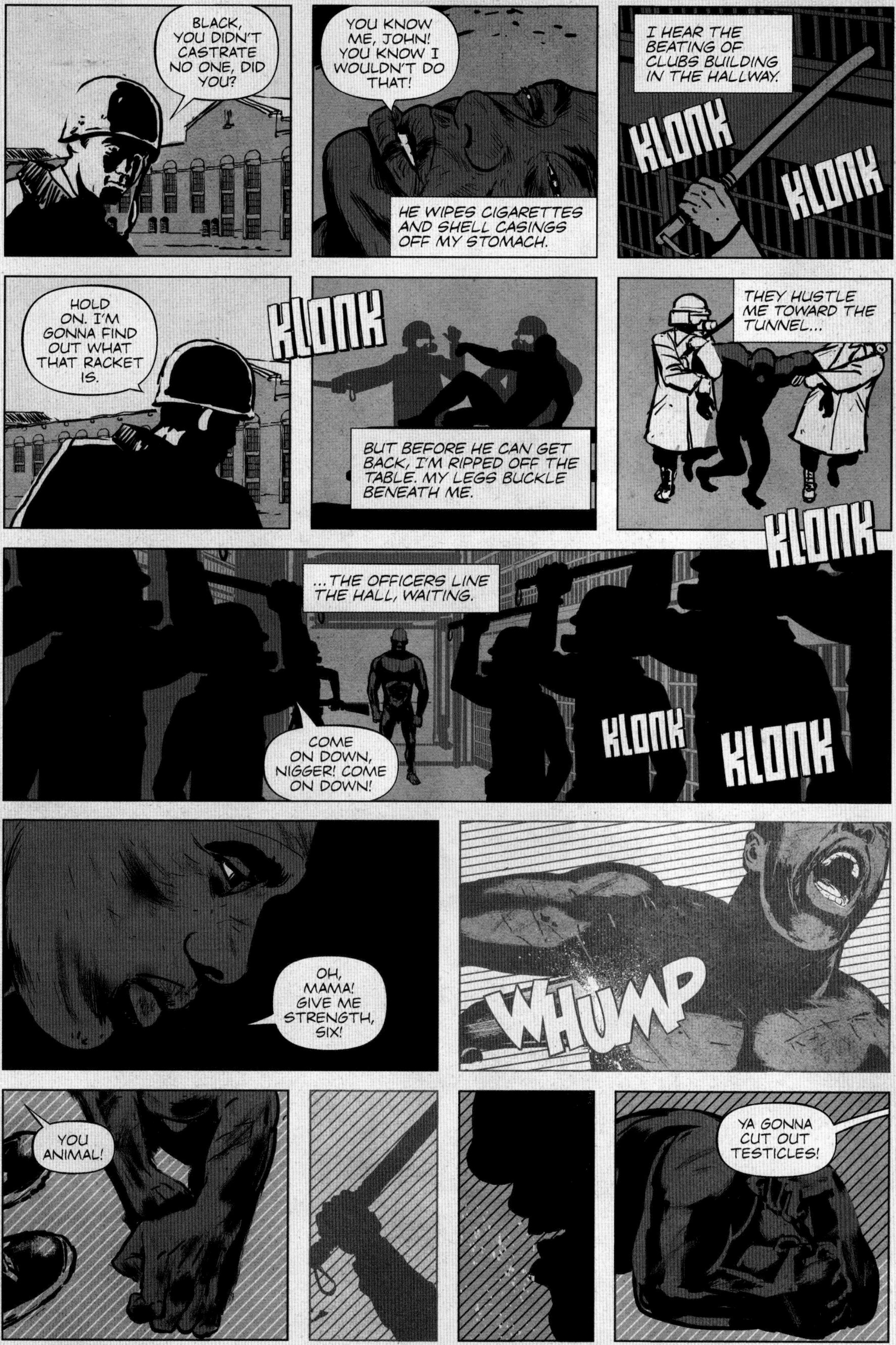
BLACK, YOU DIDN'T CASTRATE NO ONE, DID YOU?
YOU KNOW ME, JOHN! YOU KNOW I WOULDN'T DO THAT!
HE WIPES CIGARETTES AND SHELL CASINGS OFF MY STOMACH.
I HEAR THE BEATING OF CLUBS BUILDING IN THE HALLWAY.
KLONK
KLONK
HOLD ON. I'M GONNA FIND OUT WHAT THAT RACKET IS.
KLONK
BUT BEFORE HE CAN GET BACK, I'M RIPPED OFF THE TABLE. MY LEGS BUCKLE BENEATH ME.
THEY HUSTLE ME TOWARD THE TUNNEL...
KLONK
...THE OFFICERS LINE THE HALL, WAITING.
COME ON DOWN, NIGGER! COME ON DOWN!
KLONK
KLONK
OH, MAMA! GIVE ME STRENGTH, SIX!
WHUMP
YOU ANIMAL!
YA GONNA CUT OUT TESTICLES!

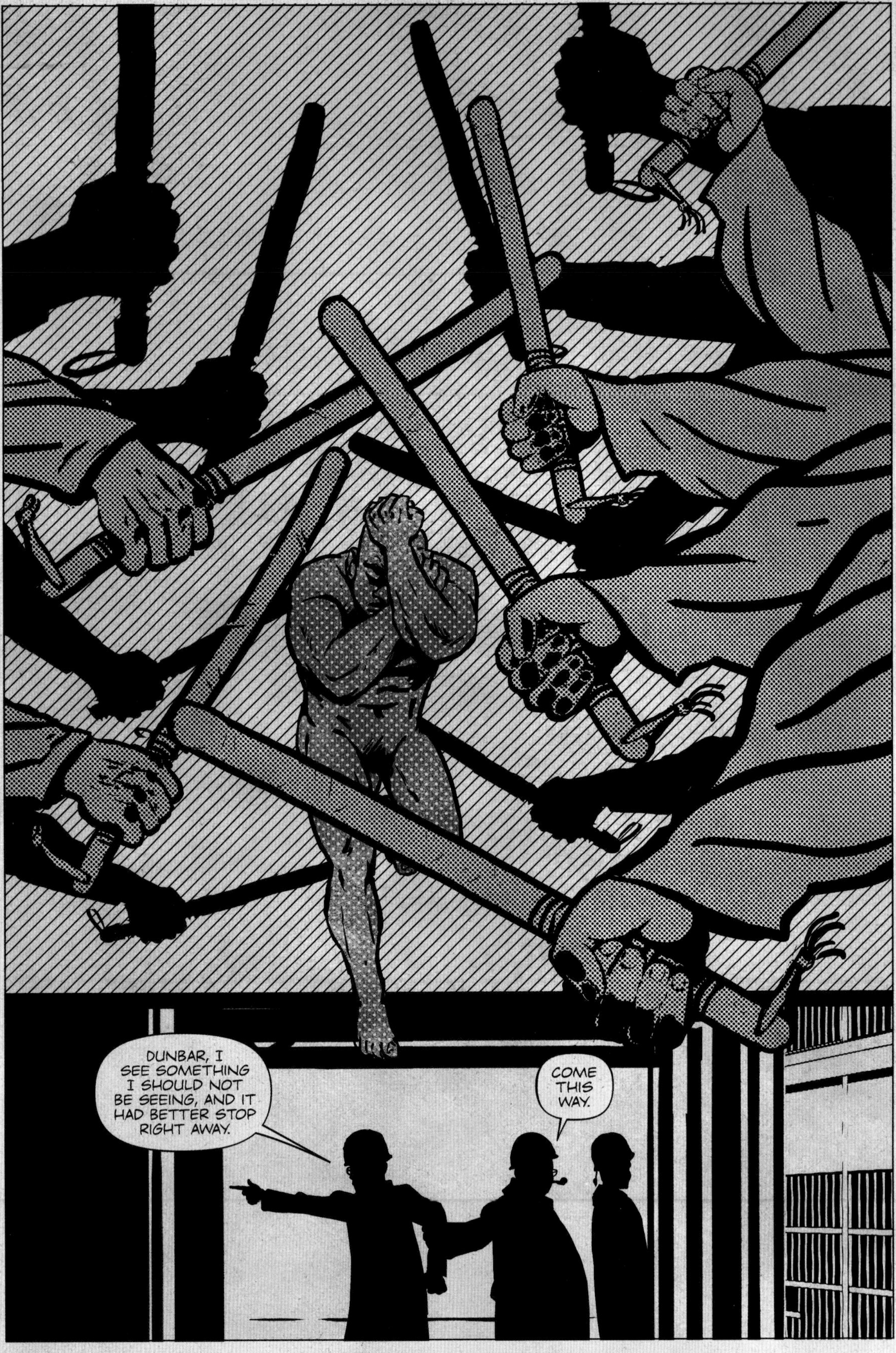
DUNBAR, I SEE SOMETHING I SHOULD NOT BE SEEING, AND IT HAD BETTER STOP RIGHT AWAY.
COME THIS WAY.

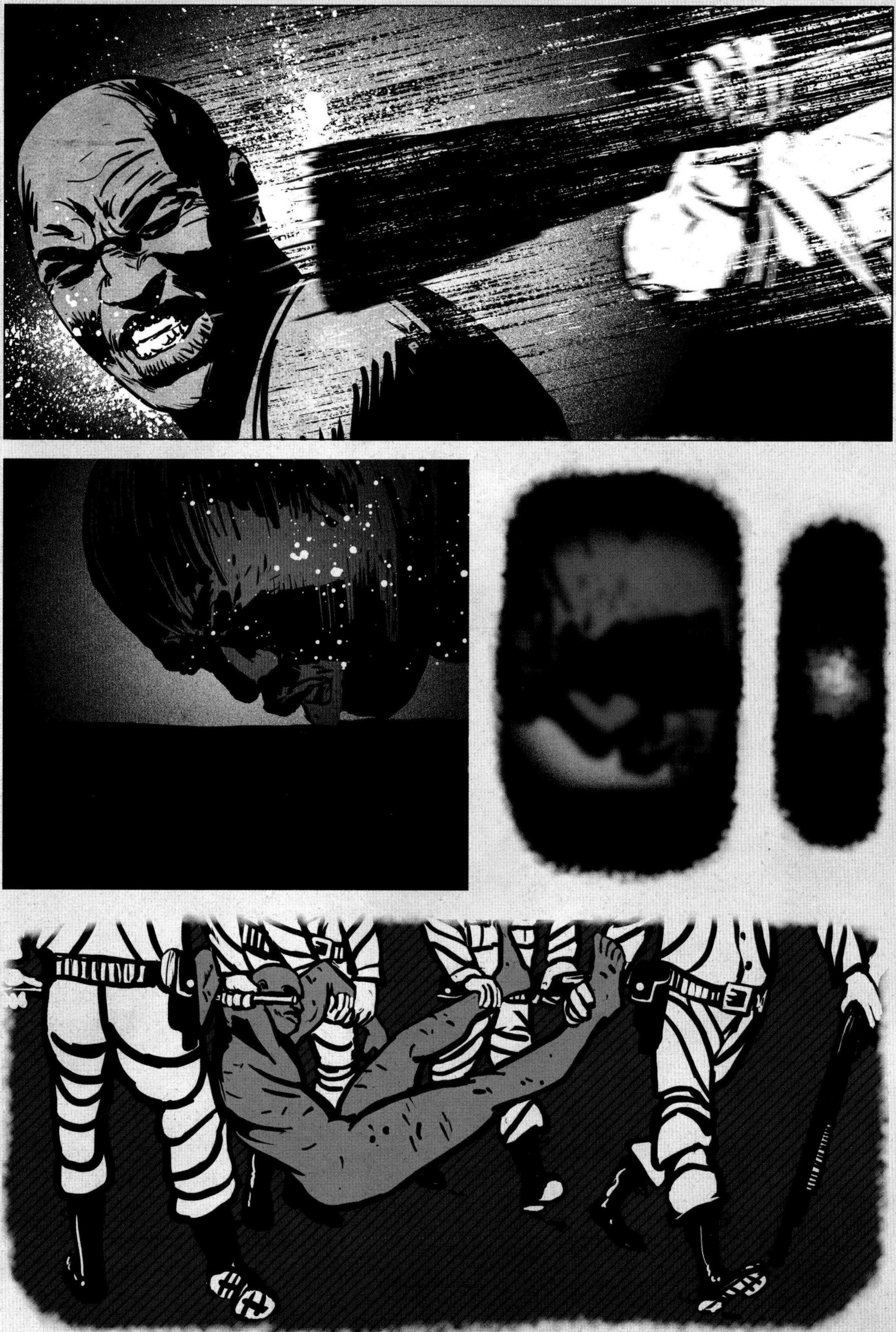

THE UGLIEST DISPLAYS OF RACISM, CRUELTY, AND BARBARISM RAN RAMPANT--BOTH **IN** AND **OUTSIDE** THE PRISON.

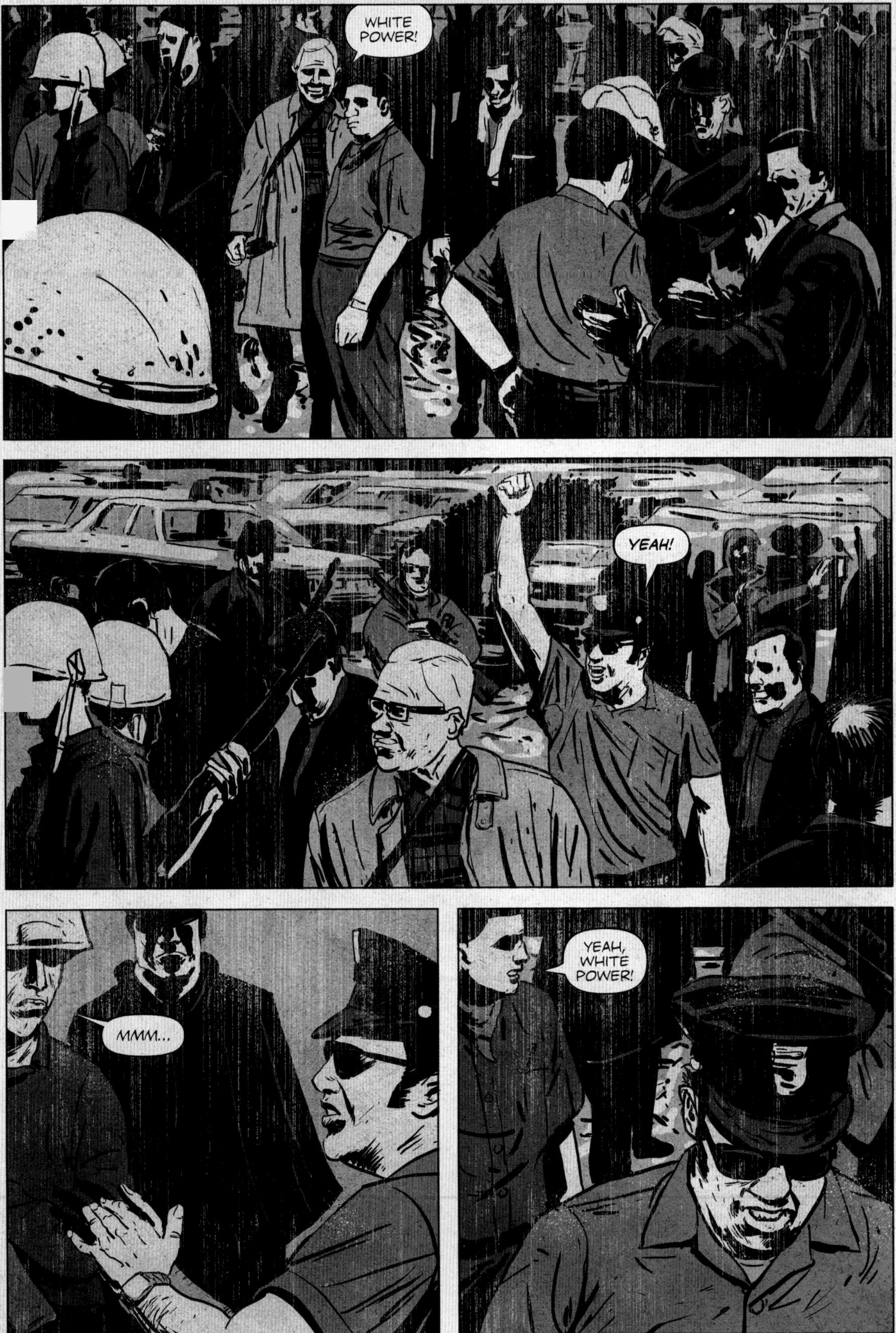
WHITE POWER!
YEAH!
MMM...
YEAH, WHITE POWER!

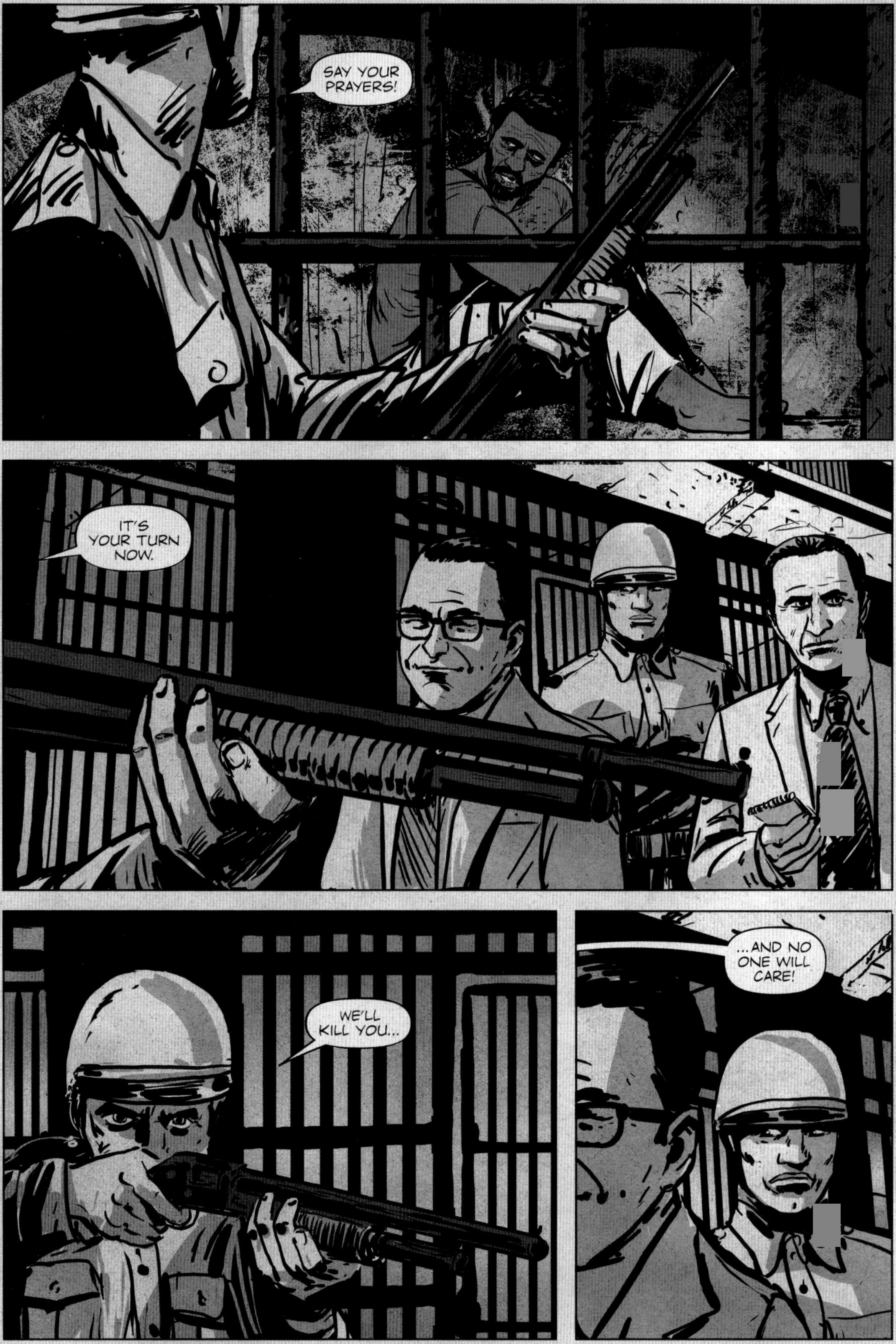
SAY YOUR PRAYERS!
IT'S YOUR TURN NOW.
WE'LL KILL YOU...
...AND NO ONE WILL CARE!

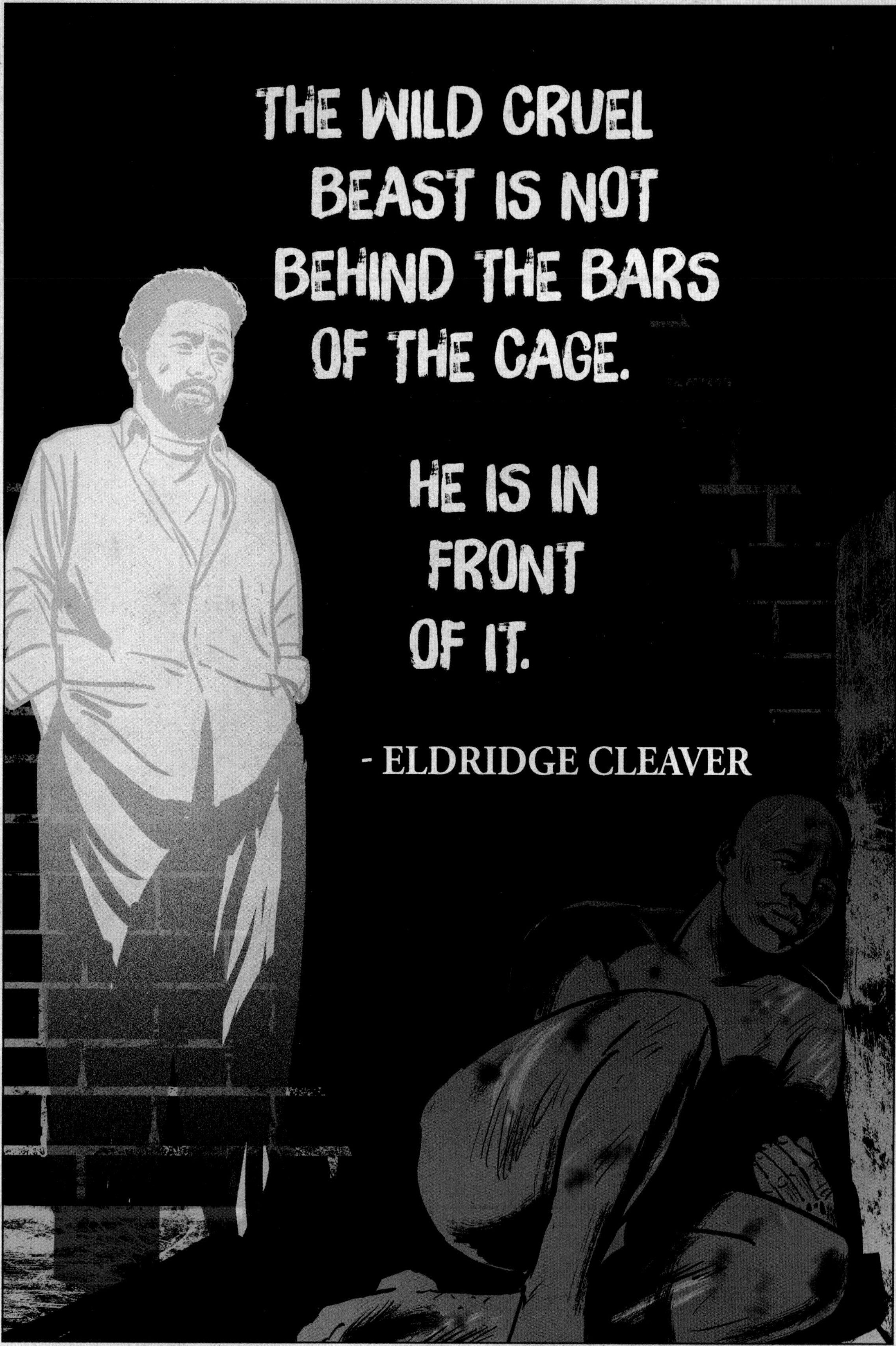
THE WILD CRUEL BEAST IS NOT BEHIND THE BARS OF THE CAGE.
HE IS IN FRONT OF IT.
- ELDRIDGE CLEAVER

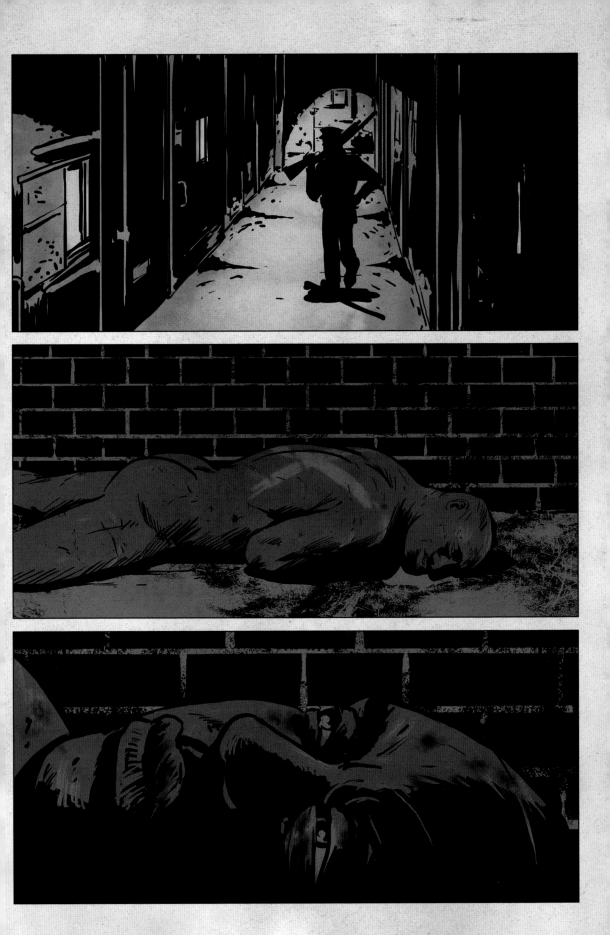

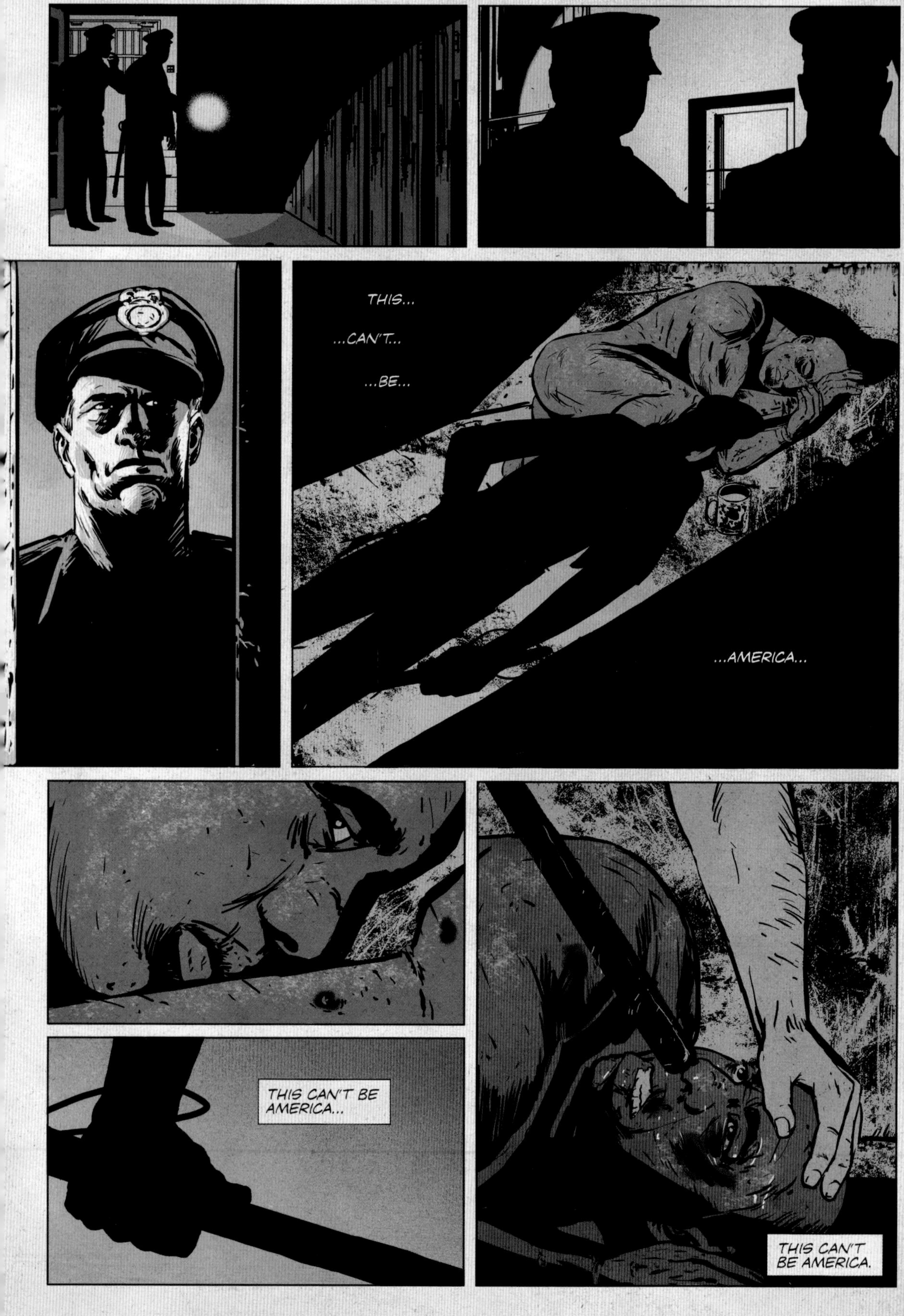
THIS...
...CAN'T...
...BE...
...AMERICA...
THIS CAN'T BE AMERICA...
THIS CAN'T BE AMERICA.

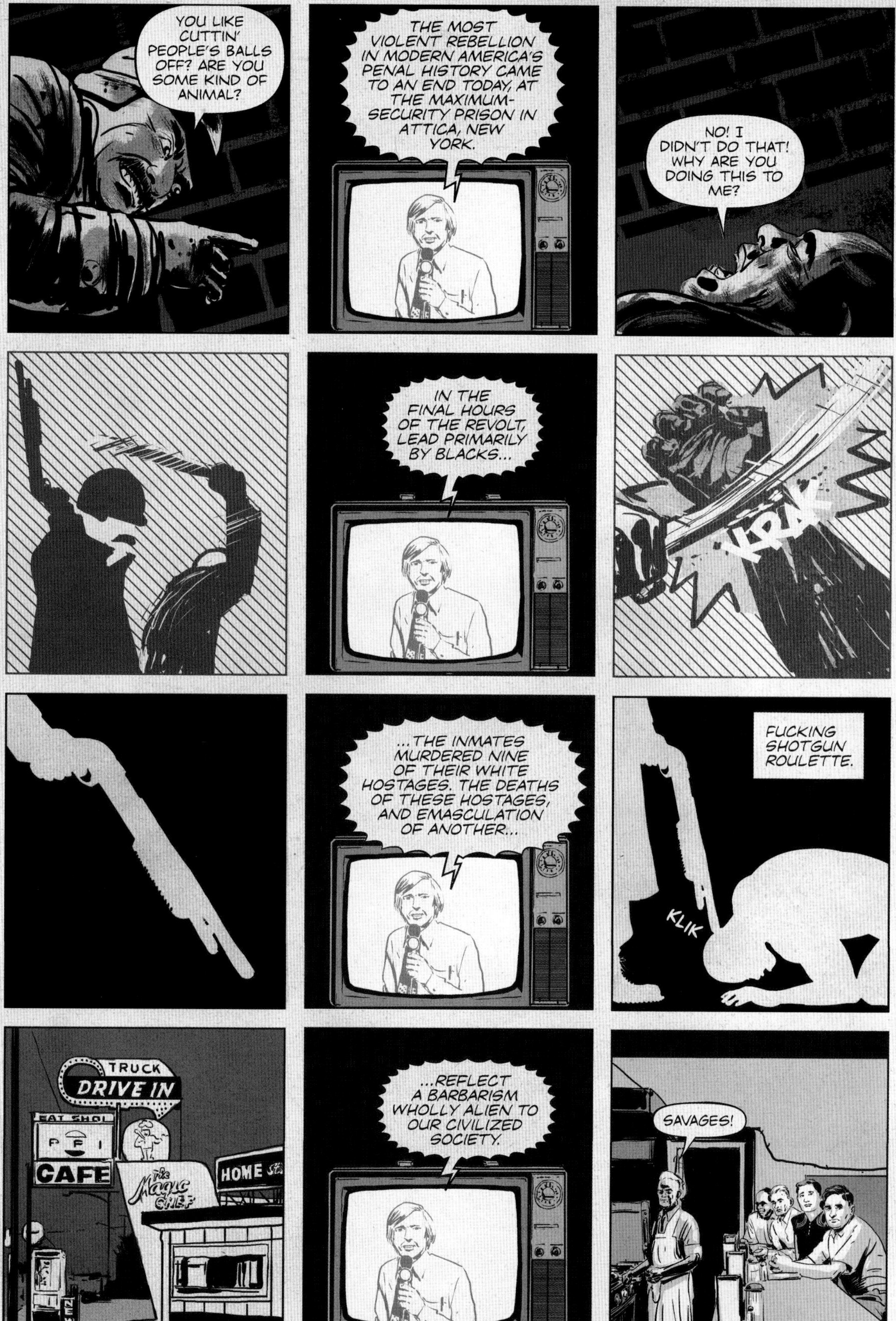
YOU LIKE CUTTIN' PEOPLE'S BALLS OFF? ARE YOU SOME KIND OF ANIMAL?
THE MOST VIOLENT REBELLION IN MODERN AMERICA'S PENAL HISTORY CAME TO AN END TODAY, AT THE MAXIMUM-SECURITY PRISON IN ATTICA, NEW YORK.
NO! I DIDN'T DO THAT! WHY ARE YOU DOING THIS TO ME?
IN THE FINAL HOURS OF THE REVOLT, LEAD PRIMARILY BY BLACKS...
KRAK
...THE INMATES MURDERED NINE OF THEIR WHITE HOSTAGES. THE DEATHS OF THESE HOSTAGES, AND EMASCULATION OF ANOTHER...
FUCKING SHOTGUN ROULETTE.
KLIK
TRUCK
DRIVE IN
CAFE
The Magic Chef
HOME
NEWS
...REFLECT A BARBARISM WHOLLY ALIEN TO OUR CIVILIZED SOCIETY.
SAVAGES!

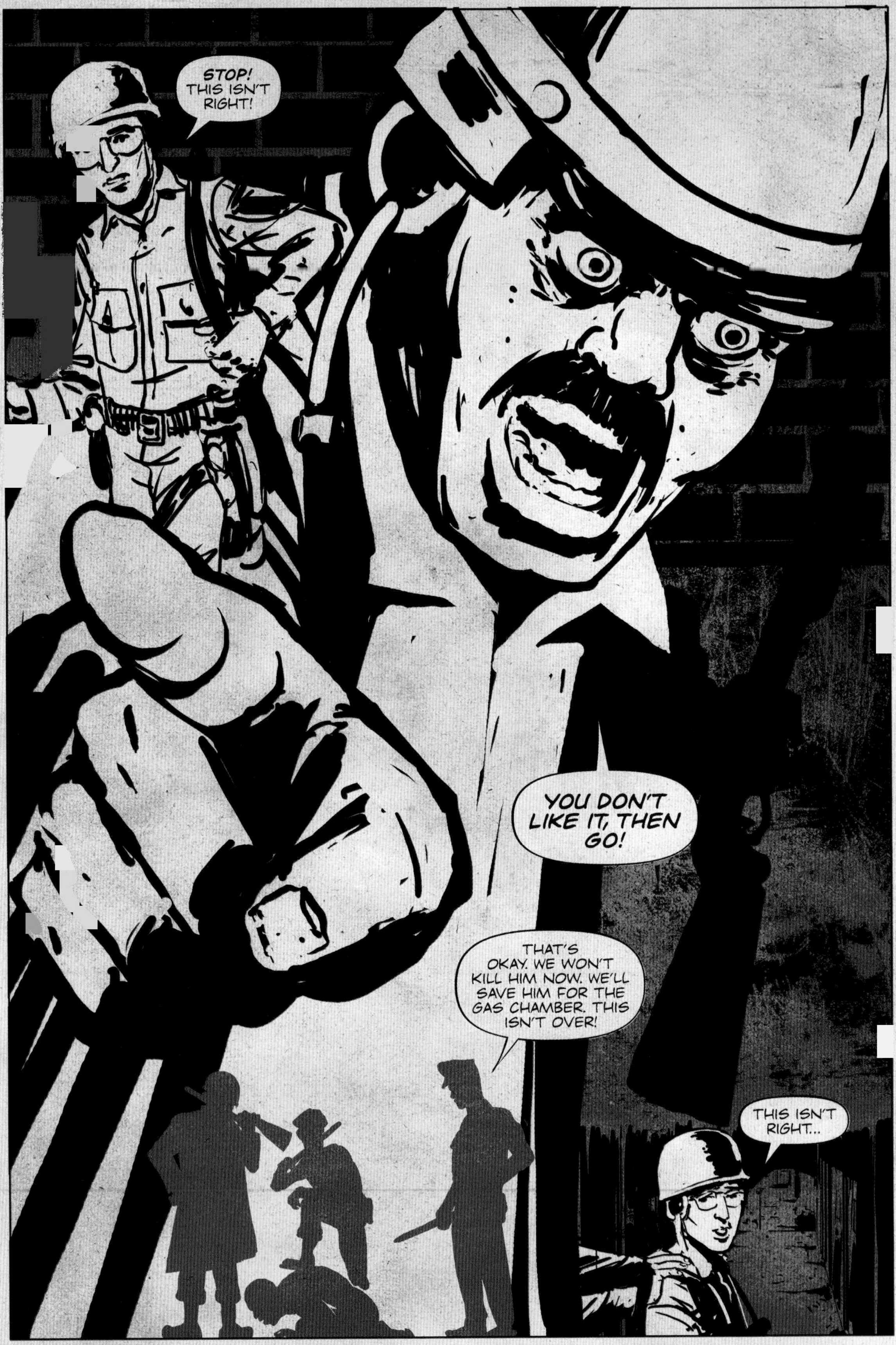
STOP! THIS ISN'T RIGHT!
YOU DON'T LIKE IT, THEN GO!
THAT'S OKAY. WE WON'T KILL HIM NOW. WE'LL SAVE HIM FOR THE GAS CHAMBER. THIS ISN'T OVER!
THIS ISN'T RIGHT...

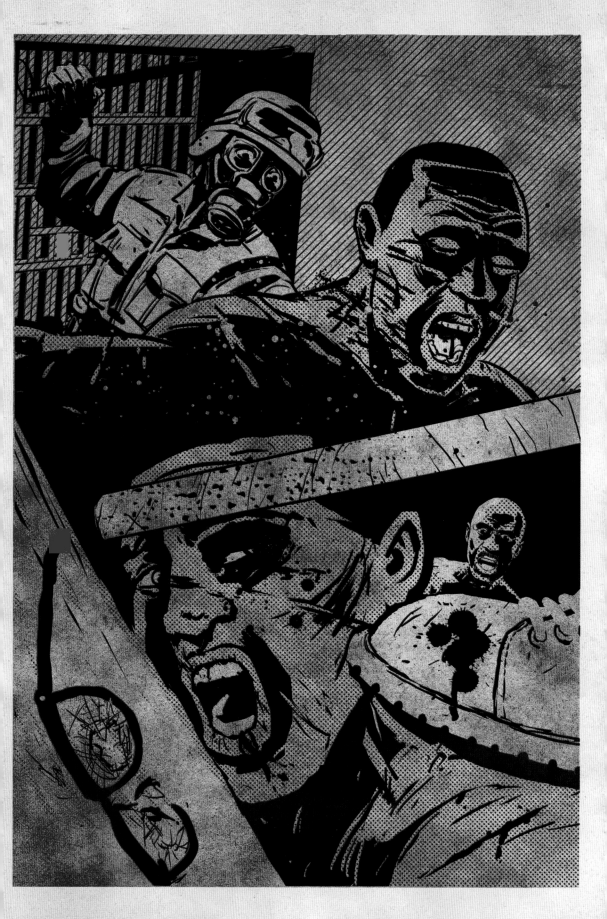

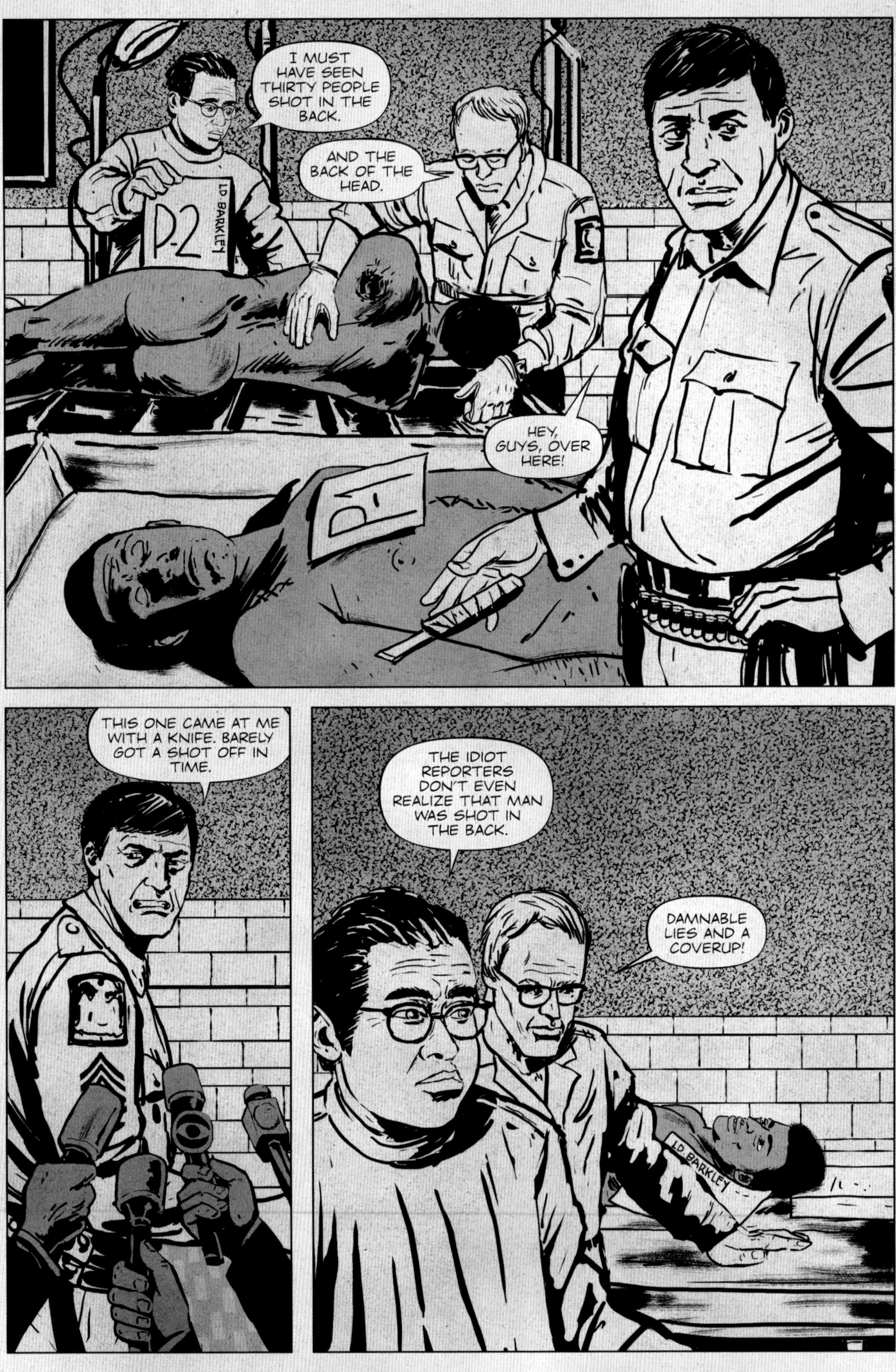
I MUST HAVE SEEN THIRTY PEOPLE SHOT IN THE BACK.
AND THE BACK OF THE HEAD.
I.D. BARKLEY
P-2
HEY, GUYS, OVER HERE!
THIS ONE CAME AT ME WITH A KNIFE. BARELY GOT A SHOT OFF IN TIME.
THE IDIOT REPORTERS DON'T EVEN REALIZE THAT MAN WAS SHOT IN THE BACK.
DAMNABLE LIES AND A COVERUP!
I.D. BARKLEY

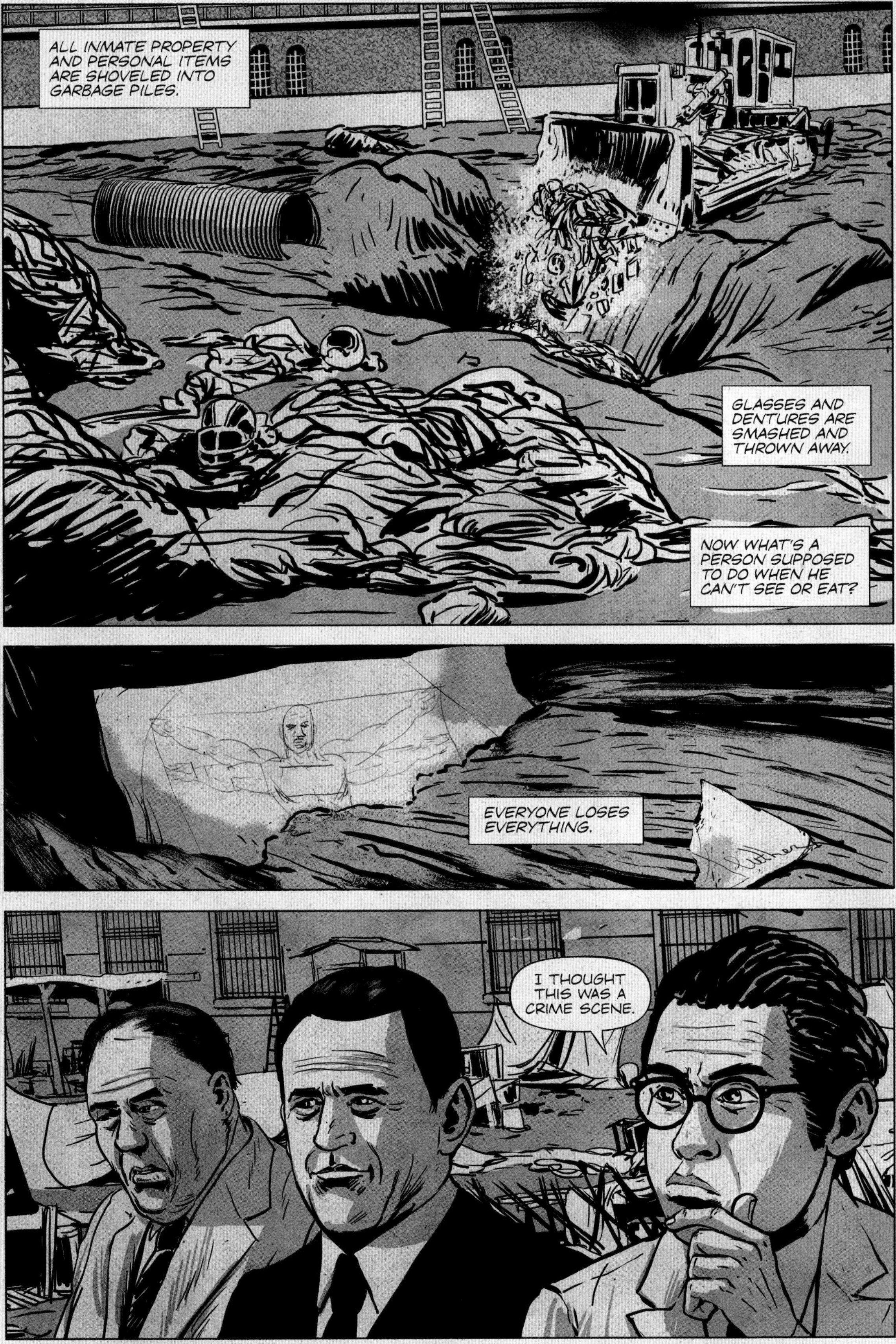
ALL INMATE PROPERTY AND PERSONAL ITEMS ARE SHOVELED INTO GARBAGE PILES.
GLASSES AND DENTURES ARE SMASHED AND THROWN AWAY.
NOW WHAT'S A PERSON SUPPOSED TO DO WHEN HE CAN'T SEE OR EAT?
EVERYONE LOSES EVERYTHING.
I THOUGHT THIS WAS A CRIME SCENE.

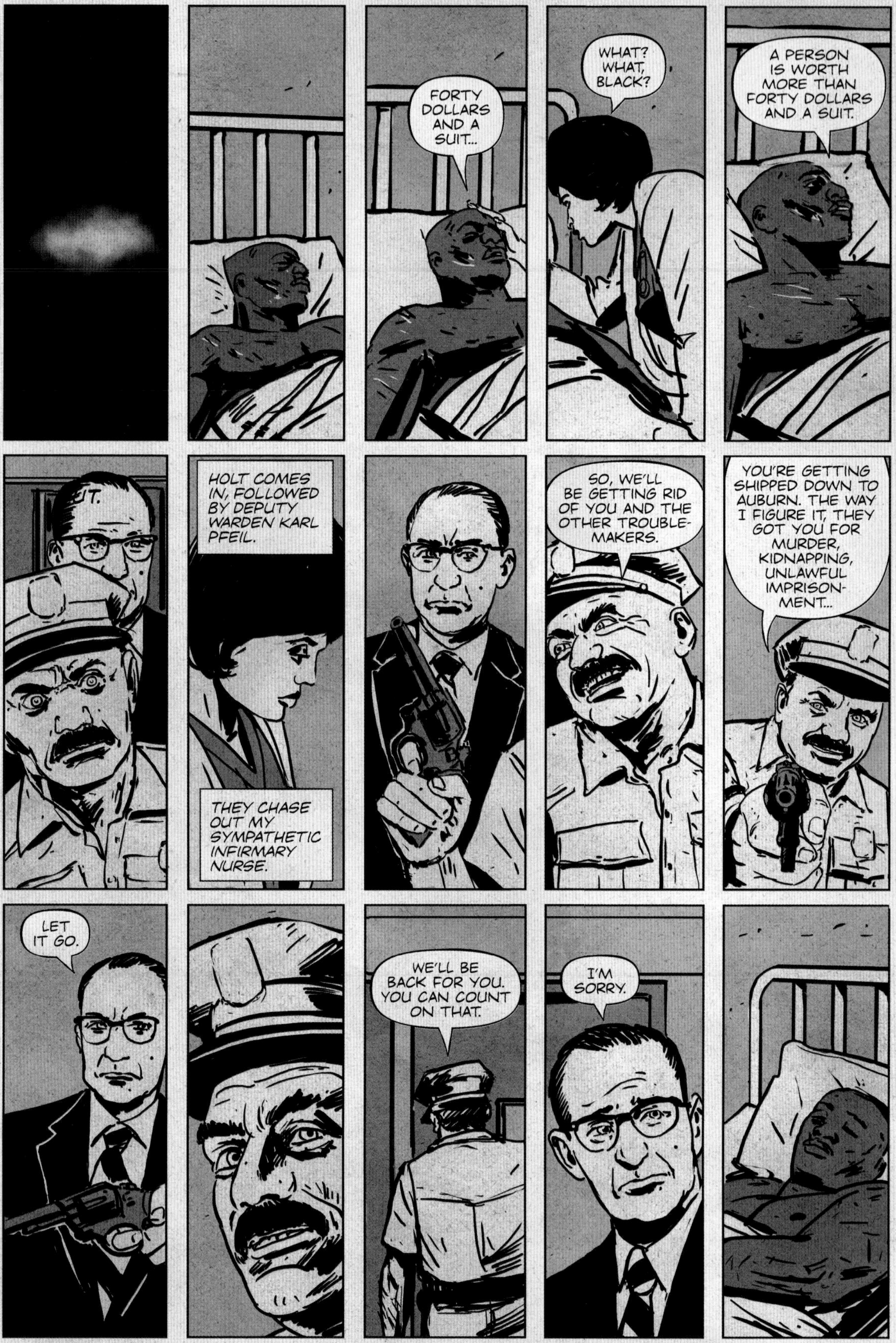
FORTY DOLLARS AND A SUIT...
WHAT? WHAT, BLACK?
A PERSON IS WORTH MORE THAN FORTY DOLLARS AND A SUIT.
HOLT COMES IN, FOLLOWED BY DEPUTY WARDEN KARL PFEIL.
THEY CHASE OUT MY SYMPATHETIC INFIRMARY NURSE.
SO, WE'LL BE GETTING RID OF YOU AND THE OTHER TROUBLE-MAKERS.
YOU'RE GETTING SHIPPED DOWN TO AUBURN. THE WAY I FIGURE IT, THEY GOT YOU FOR MURDER, KIDNAPPING, UNLAWFUL IMPRISON-MENT...
LET IT GO.
WE'LL BE BACK FOR YOU. YOU CAN COUNT ON THAT.
I'M SORRY.

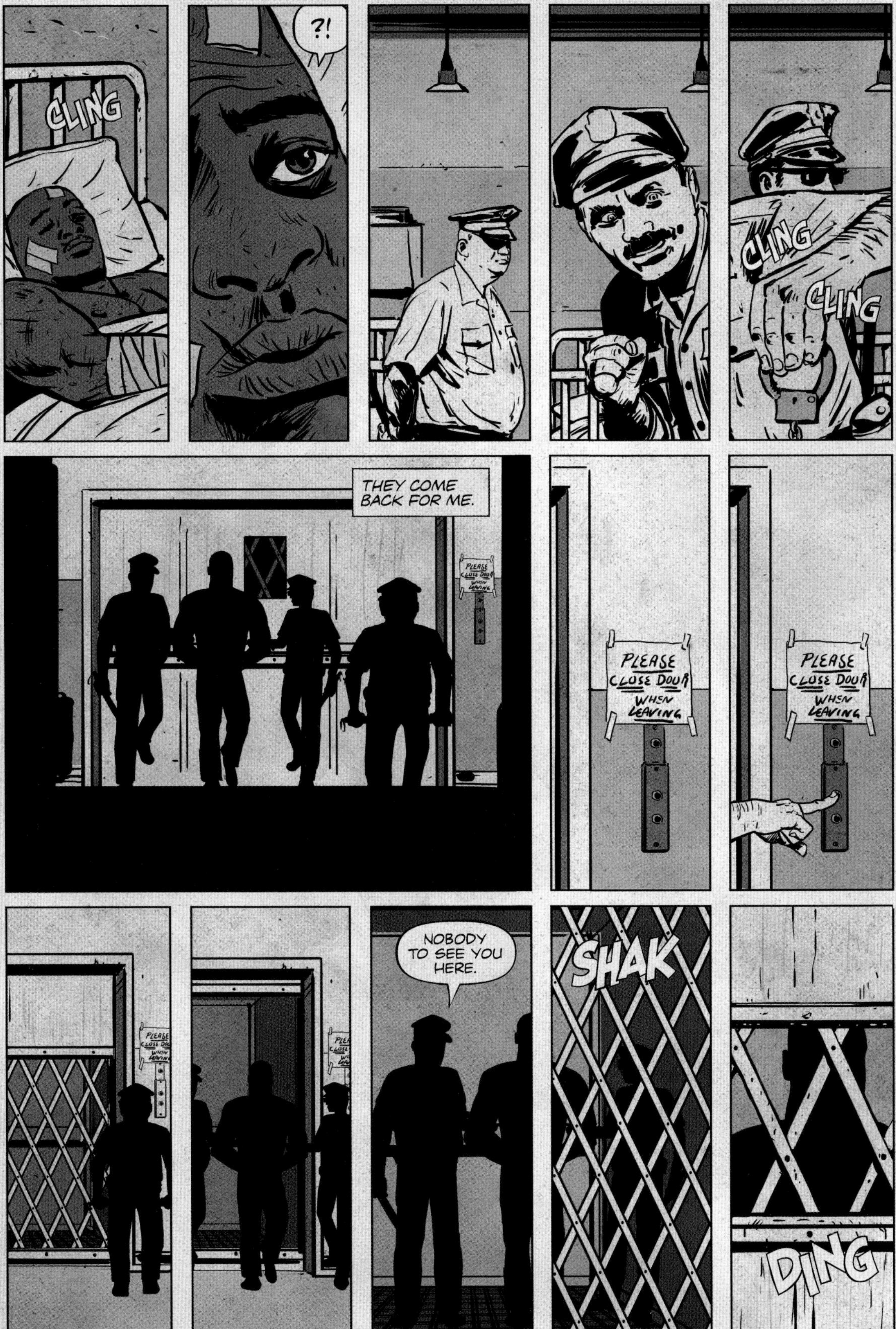
CLING
?!
CLING
CLING
THEY COME BACK FOR ME.
PLEASE CLOSE DOUR WHEN LEAVING
PLEASE CLOSE DOUR WHEN LEAVING
PLEASE CLOSE DOUR WHEN LEAVING
NOBODY TO SEE YOU HERE.
SHAK
DING

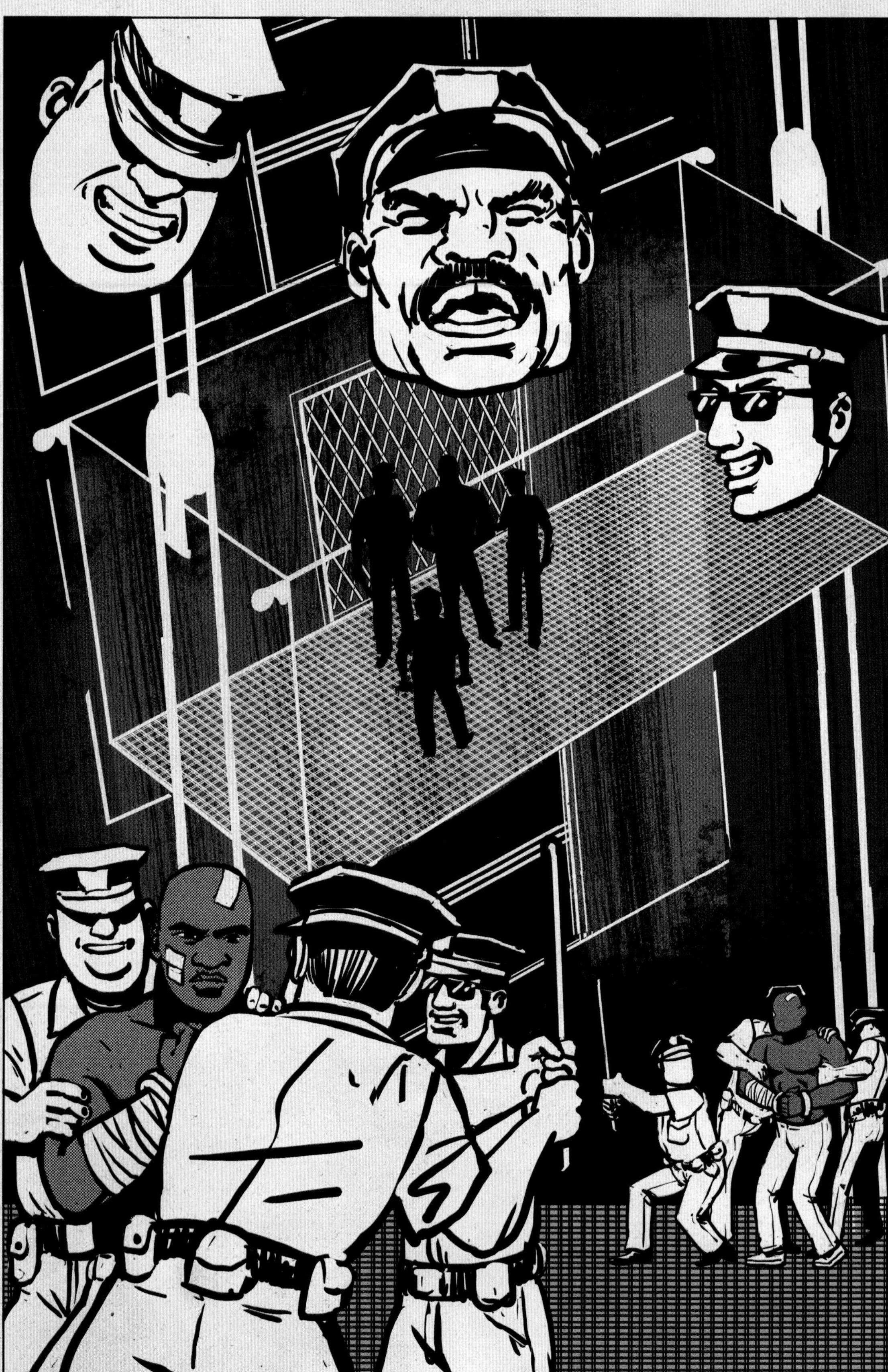

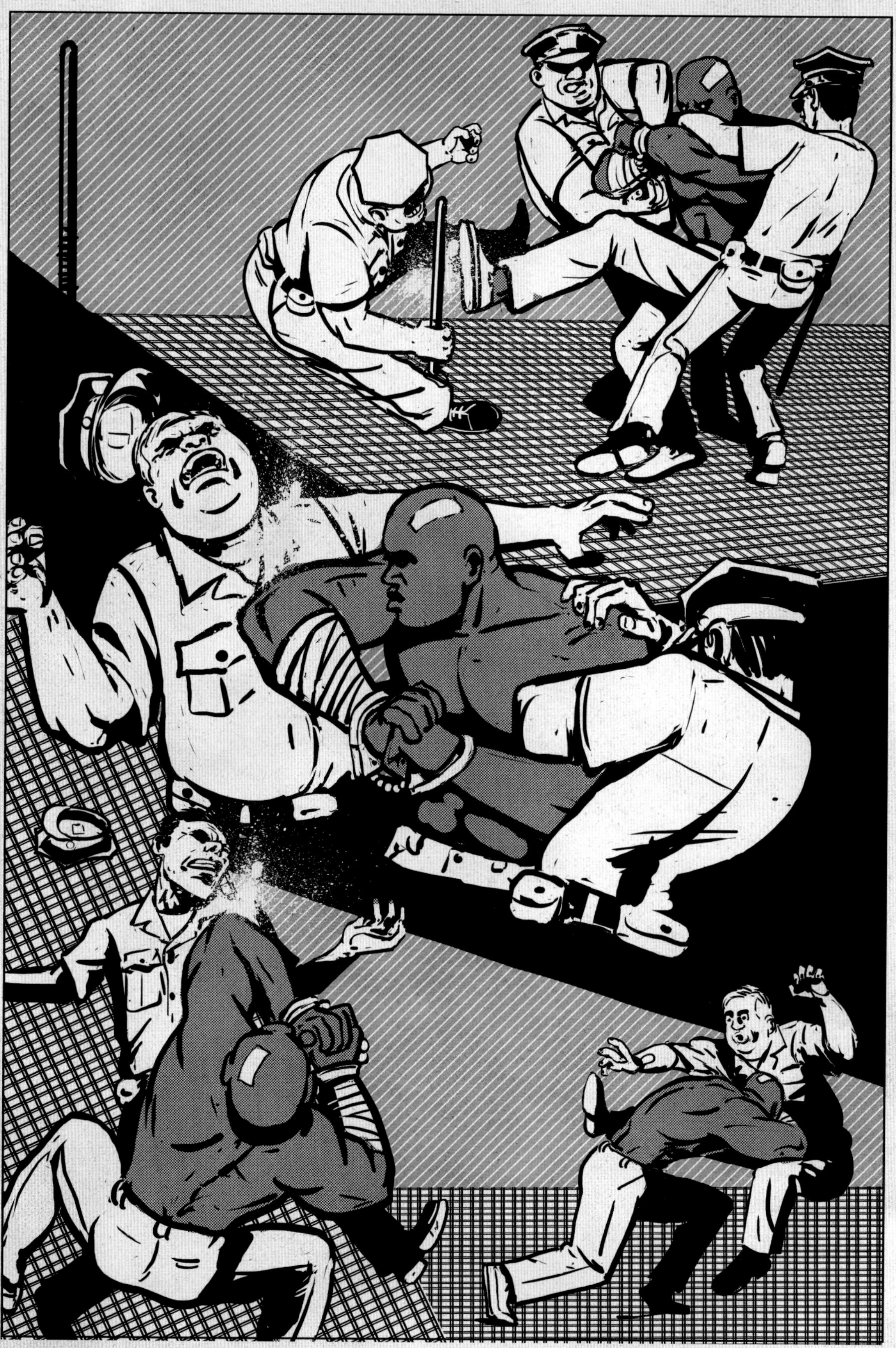

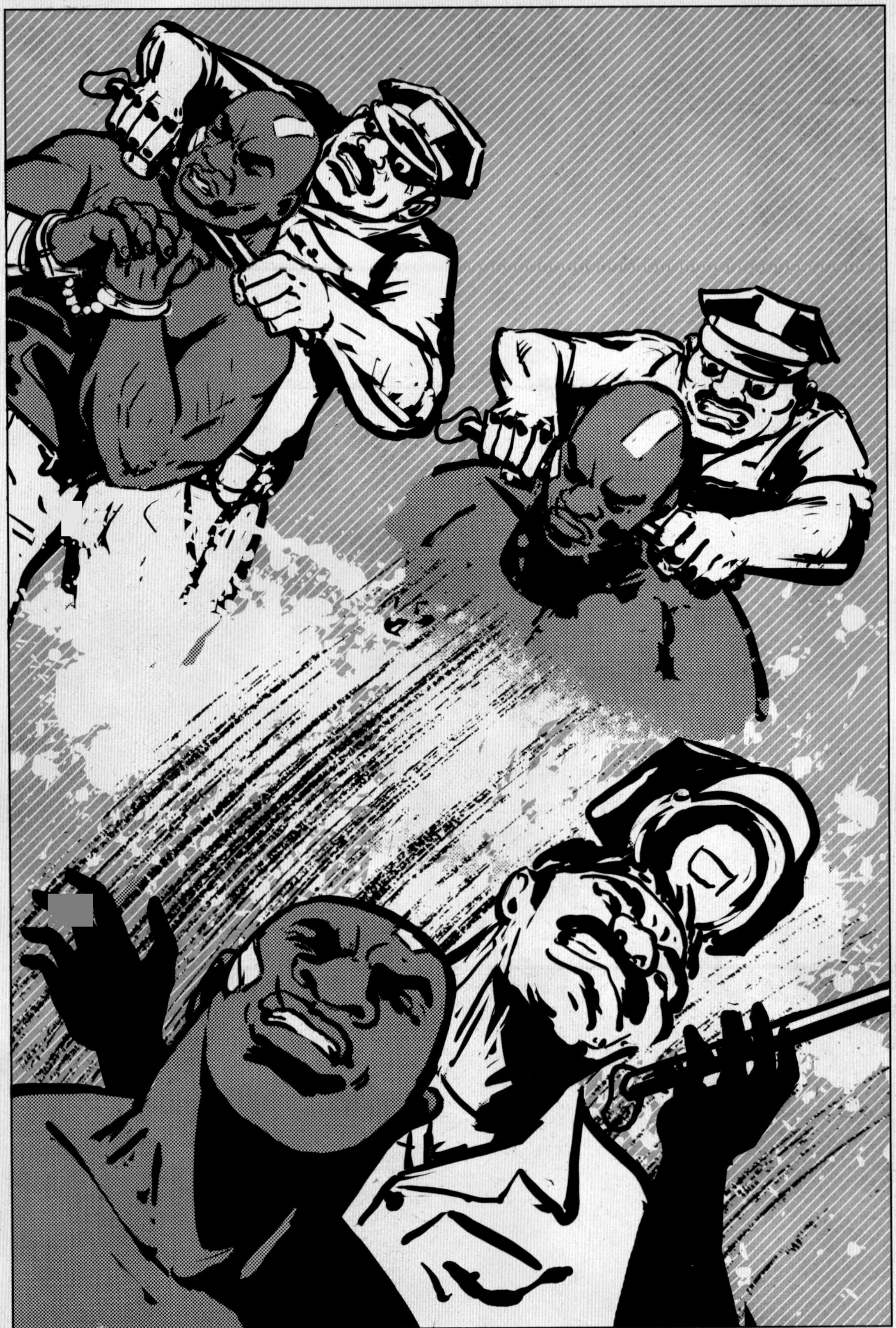

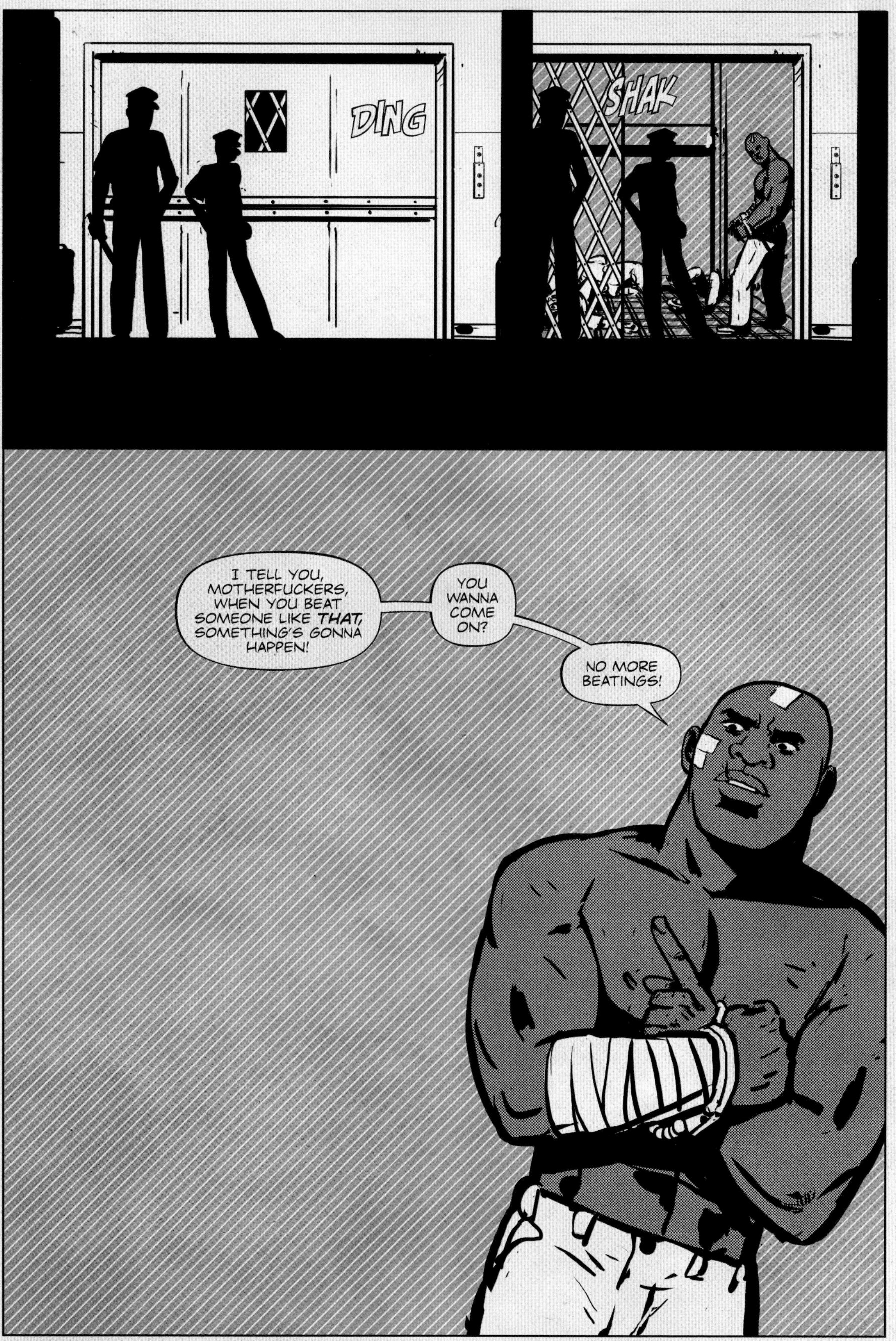
DING
SHAK
I TELL YOU, MOTHERFUCKERS, WHEN YOU BEAT SOMEONE LIKE *THAT,* SOMETHING'S GONNA HAPPEN!
YOU WANNA COME ON?
NO MORE BEATINGS!

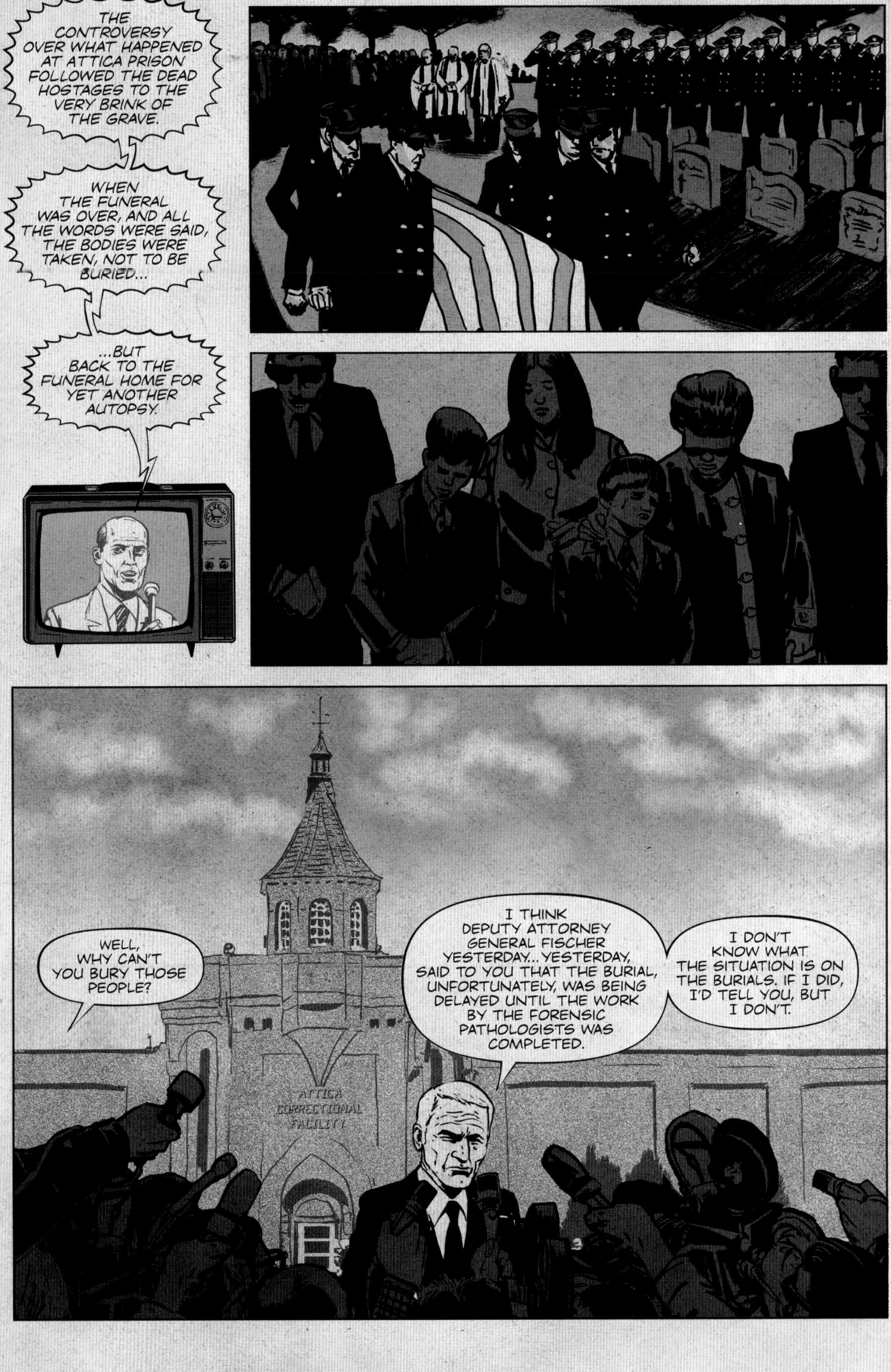
THE CONTROVERSY OVER WHAT HAPPENED AT ATTICA PRISON FOLLOWED THE DEAD HOSTAGES TO THE VERY BRINK OF THE GRAVE.
WHEN THE FUNERAL WAS OVER, AND ALL THE WORDS WERE SAID, THE BODIES WERE TAKEN, NOT TO BE BURIED...
...BUT BACK TO THE FUNERAL HOME FOR YET ANOTHER AUTOPSY.
WELL, WHY CAN'T YOU BURY THOSE PEOPLE?
I THINK DEPUTY ATTORNEY GENERAL FISCHER YESTERDAY... YESTERDAY, SAID TO YOU THAT THE BURIAL, UNFORTUNATELY, WAS BEING DELAYED UNTIL THE WORK BY THE FORENSIC PATHOLOGISTS WAS COMPLETED.
I DON'T KNOW WHAT THE SITUATION IS ON THE BURIALS. IF I DID, I'D TELL YOU, BUT I DON'T.
ATTICA CORRECTIONAL FACILITY

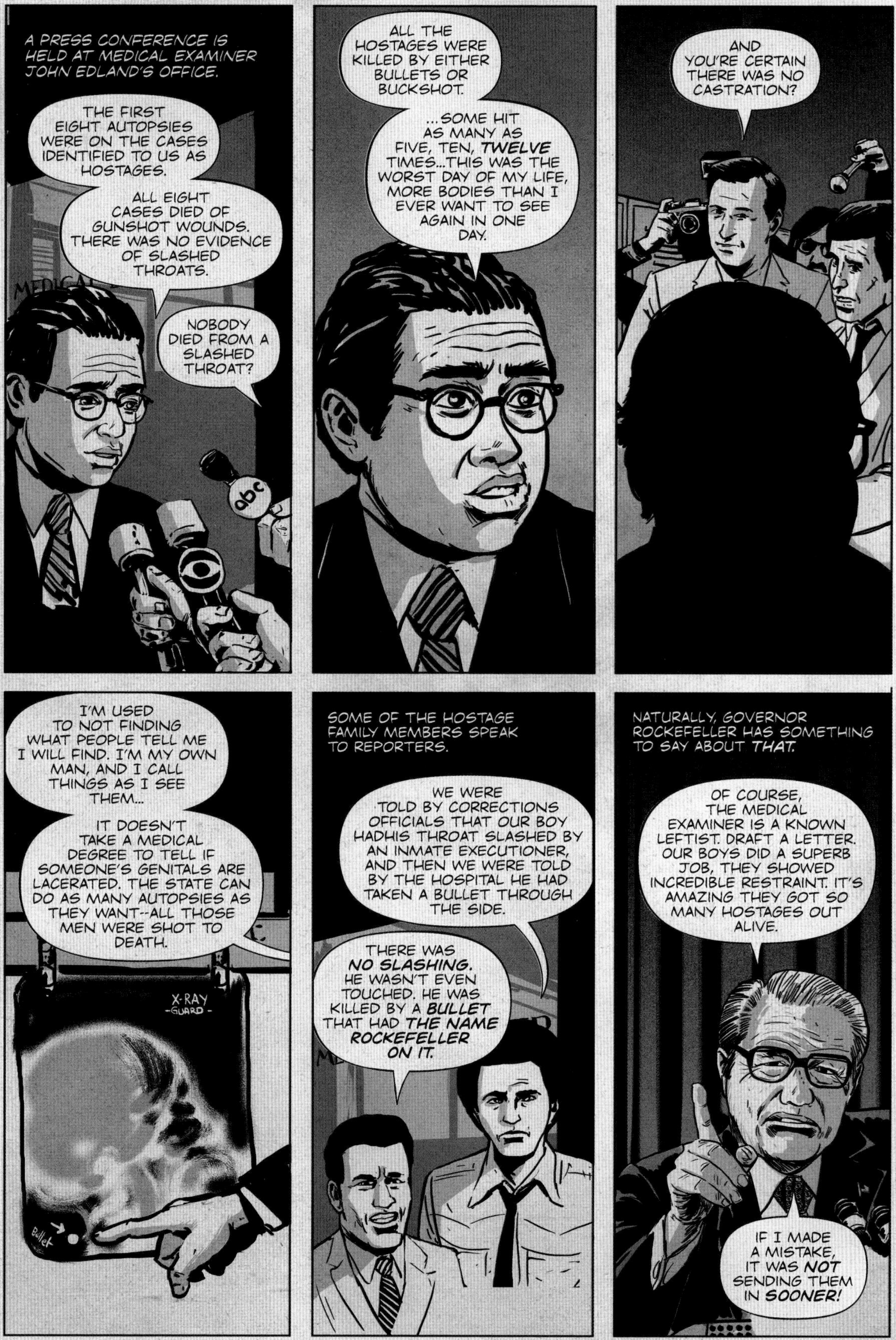
A PRESS CONFERENCE IS HELD AT MEDICAL EXAMINER JOHN EDLAND'S OFFICE.
THE FIRST EIGHT AUTOPSIES WERE ON THE CASES IDENTIFIED TO US AS HOSTAGES.
ALL EIGHT CASES DIED OF GUNSHOT WOUNDS. THERE WAS NO EVIDENCE OF SLASHED THROATS.
NOBODY DIED FROM A SLASHED THROAT?
ALL THE HOSTAGES WERE KILLED BY EITHER BULLETS OR BUCKSHOT.
...SOME HIT AS MANY AS FIVE, TEN, TWELVE TIMES...THIS WAS THE WORST DAY OF MY LIFE, MORE BODIES THAN I EVER WANT TO SEE AGAIN IN ONE DAY.
AND YOU'RE CERTAIN THERE WAS NO CASTRATION?
I'M USED TO NOT FINDING WHAT PEOPLE TELL ME I WILL FIND. I'M MY OWN MAN, AND I CALL THINGS AS I SEE THEM...
IT DOESN'T TAKE A MEDICAL DEGREE TO TELL IF SOMEONE'S GENITALS ARE LACERATED. THE STATE CAN DO AS MANY AUTOPSIES AS THEY WANT--ALL THOSE MEN WERE SHOT TO DEATH.
X-RAY -GUARD-
Bullet
SOME OF THE HOSTAGE FAMILY MEMBERS SPEAK TO REPORTERS.
WE WERE TOLD BY CORRECTIONS OFFICIALS THAT OUR BOY HADHIS THROAT SLASHED BY AN INMATE EXECUTIONER, AND THEN WE WERE TOLD BY THE HOSPITAL HE HAD TAKEN A BULLET THROUGH THE SIDE.
THERE WAS NO SLASHING. HE WASN'T EVEN TOUCHED. HE WAS KILLED BY A BULLET THAT HAD THE NAME ROCKEFELLER ON IT.
NATURALLY, GOVERNOR ROCKEFELLER HAS SOMETHING TO SAY ABOUT THAT.
OF COURSE, THE MEDICAL EXAMINER IS A KNOWN LEFTIST. DRAFT A LETTER. OUR BOYS DID A SUPERB JOB, THEY SHOWED INCREDIBLE RESTRAINT. IT'S AMAZING THEY GOT SO MANY HOSTAGES OUT ALIVE.
IF I MADE A MISTAKE, IT WAS NOT SENDING THEM IN SOONER!

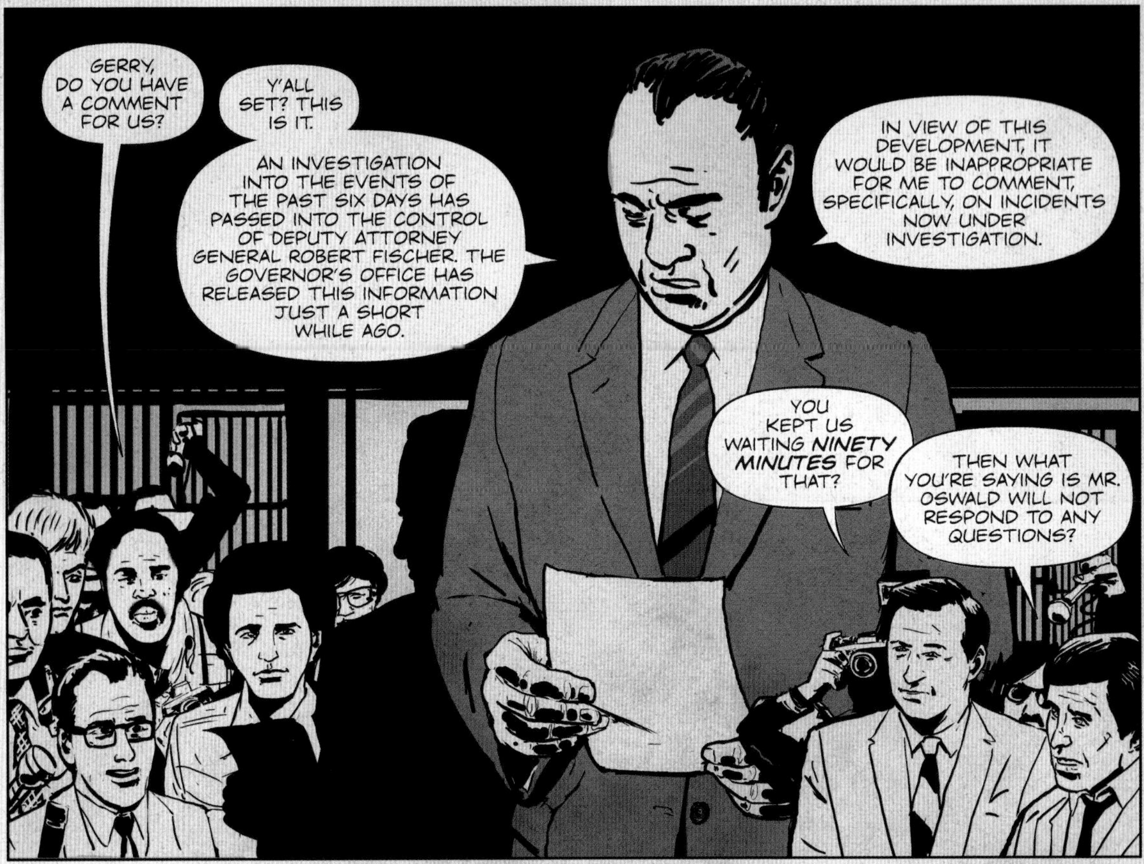
GERRY, DO YOU HAVE A COMMENT FOR US?
Y'ALL SET? THIS IS IT.
AN INVESTIGATION INTO THE EVENTS OF THE PAST SIX DAYS HAS PASSED INTO THE CONTROL OF DEPUTY ATTORNEY GENERAL ROBERT FISCHER. THE GOVERNOR'S OFFICE HAS RELEASED THIS INFORMATION JUST A SHORT WHILE AGO.
IN VIEW OF THIS DEVELOPMENT, IT WOULD BE INAPPROPRIATE FOR ME TO COMMENT, SPECIFICALLY, ON INCIDENTS NOW UNDER INVESTIGATION.
YOU KEPT US WAITING ***NINETY MINUTES*** FOR THAT?
THEN WHAT YOU'RE SAYING IS MR. OSWALD WILL NOT RESPOND TO ANY QUESTIONS?

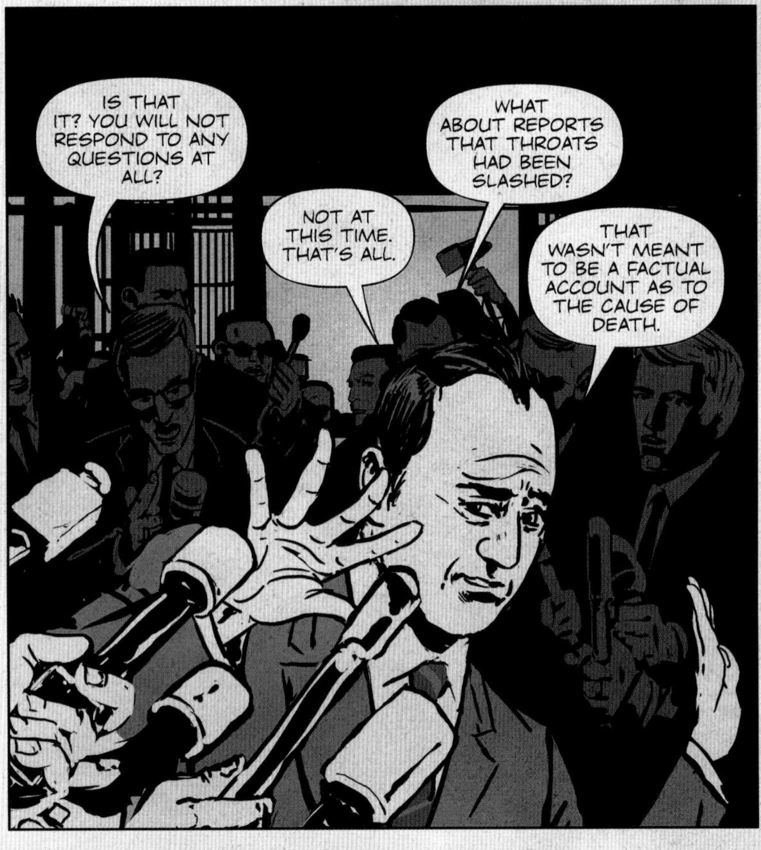
IS THAT IT? YOU WILL NOT RESPOND TO ANY QUESTIONS AT ALL?
NOT AT THIS TIME. THAT'S ALL.
WHAT ABOUT REPORTS THAT THROATS HAD BEEN SLASHED?
THAT WASN'T MEANT TO BE A FACTUAL ACCOUNT AS TO THE CAUSE OF DEATH.

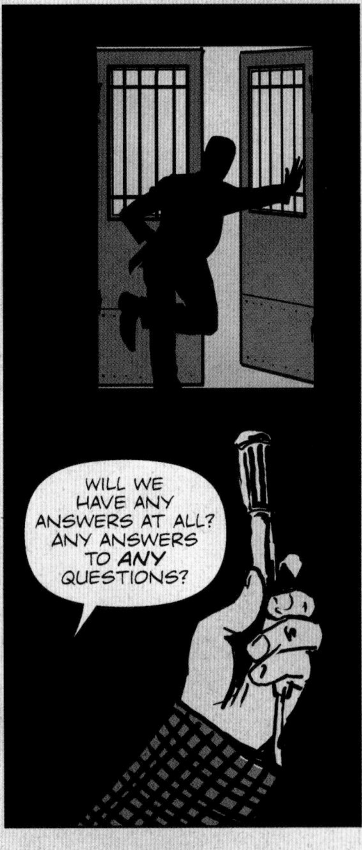
WILL WE HAVE ANY ANSWERS AT ALL? ANY ANSWERS TO ***ANY*** QUESTIONS?

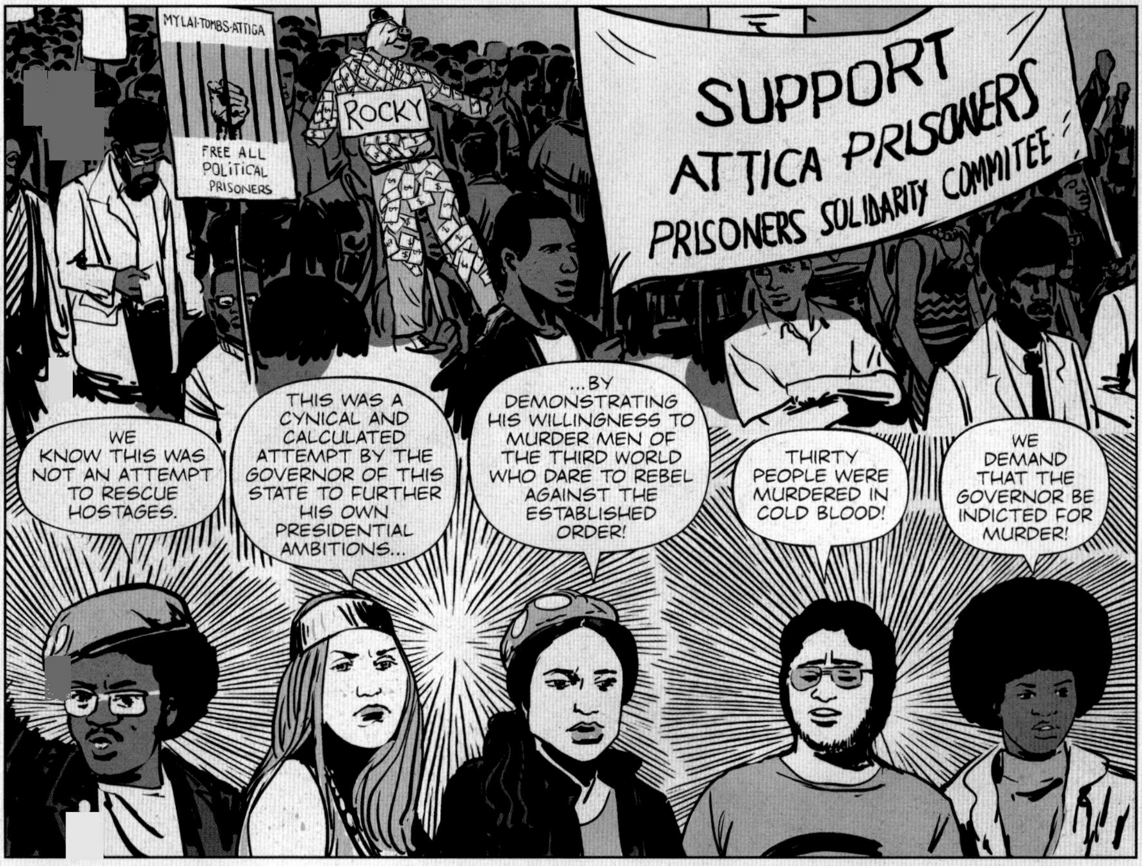
MY LAI-TOMBS-ATTICA
FREE ALL POLITICAL PRISONERS
ROCKY
SUPPORT ATTICA PRISONERS PRISONERS SOLIDARITY COMMITEE
WE KNOW THIS WAS NOT AN ATTEMPT TO RESCUE HOSTAGES.
THIS WAS A CYNICAL AND CALCULATED ATTEMPT BY THE GOVERNOR OF THIS STATE TO FURTHER HIS OWN PRESIDENTIAL AMBITIONS...
...BY DEMONSTRATING HIS WILLINGNESS TO MURDER MEN OF THE THIRD WORLD WHO DARE TO REBEL AGAINST THE ESTABLISHED ORDER!
THIRTY PEOPLE WERE MURDERED IN COLD BLOOD!
WE DEMAND THAT THE GOVERNOR BE INDICTED FOR MURDER!

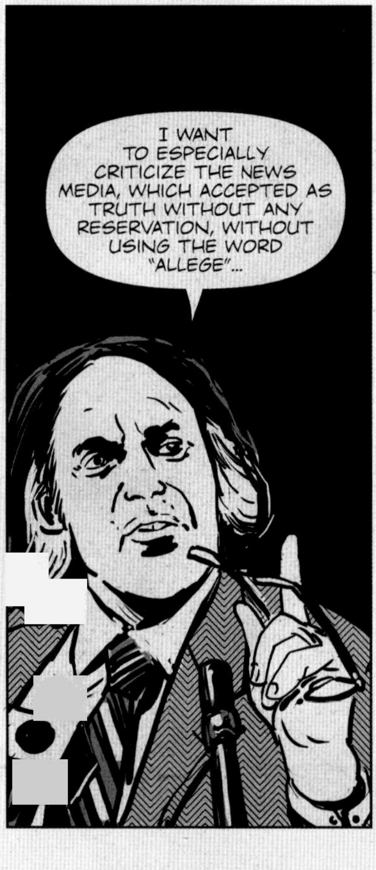
I WANT TO ESPECIALLY CRITICIZE THE NEWS MEDIA, WHICH ACCEPTED AS TRUTH WITHOUT ANY RESERVATION, WITHOUT USING THE WORD "ALLEGE"...

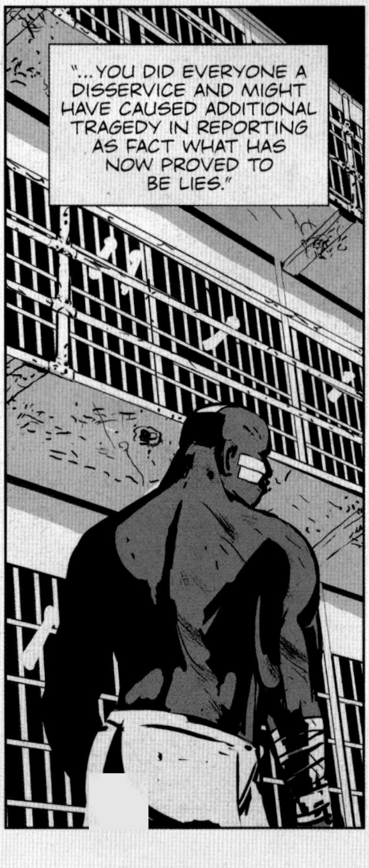
"...YOU DID EVERYONE A DISSERVICE AND MIGHT HAVE CAUSED ADDITIONAL TRAGEDY IN REPORTING AS FACT WHAT HAS NOW PROVED TO BE LIES."

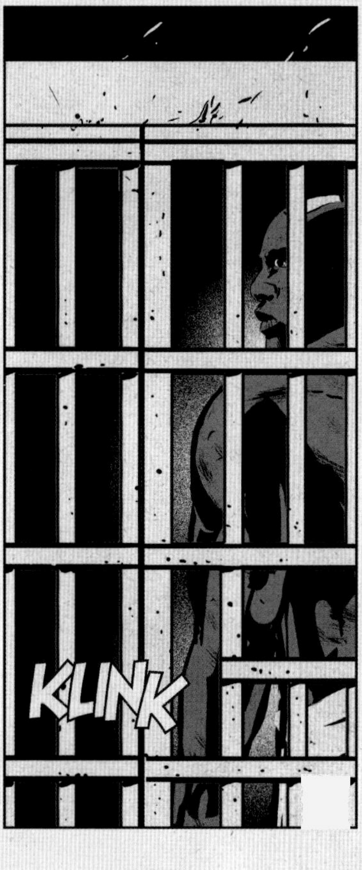
KLINK

1973

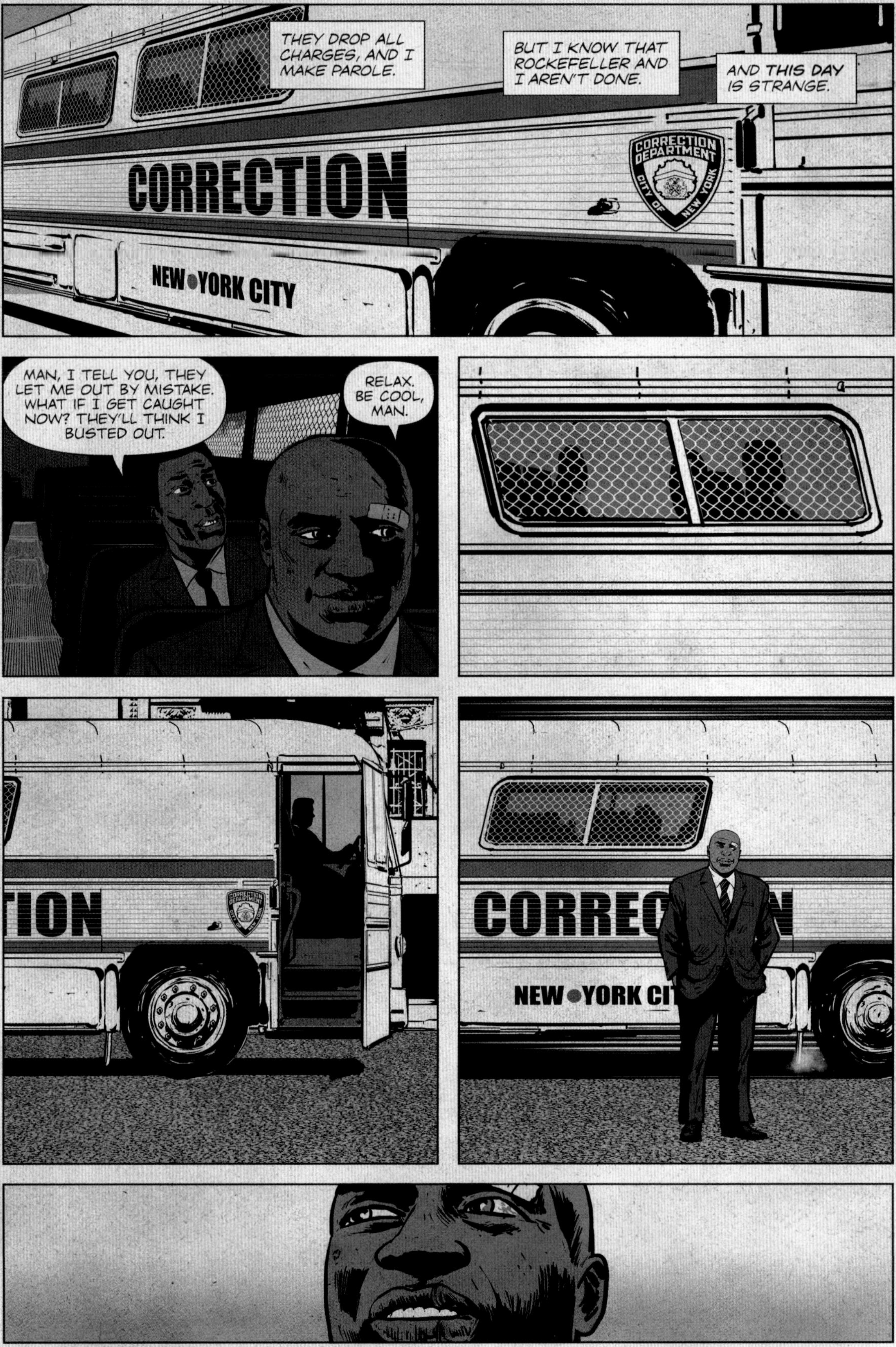
THEY DROP ALL CHARGES, AND I MAKE PAROLE.
BUT I KNOW THAT ROCKEFELLER AND I AREN'T DONE.
AND THIS DAY IS STRANGE.
CORRECTION
CORRECTION DEPARTMENT CITY OF NEW YORK
NEW YORK CITY
MAN, I TELL YOU, THEY LET ME OUT BY MISTAKE. WHAT IF I GET CAUGHT NOW? THEY'LL THINK I BUSTED OUT.
RELAX. BE COOL, MAN.
TION
CORREC N
NEW YORK CI

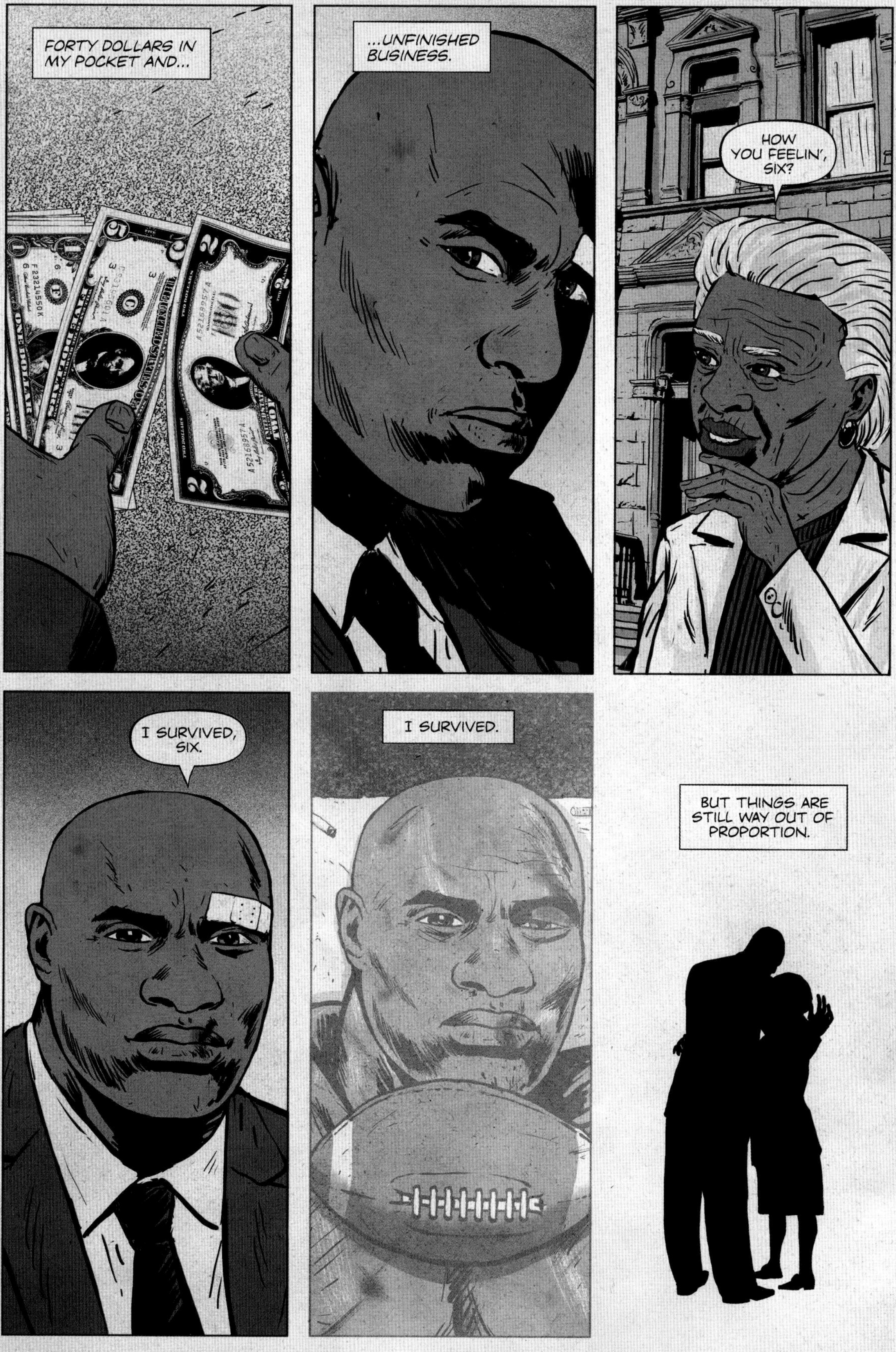
FORTY DOLLARS IN MY POCKET AND...
...UNFINISHED BUSINESS.
HOW YOU FEELIN', SIX?
I SURVIVED, SIX.
I SURVIVED.
BUT THINGS ARE STILL WAY OUT OF PROPORTION.

1974

ON AUGUST 26, THE SENATE CONFIRMATION HEARINGS ARE IN PROGRESS.

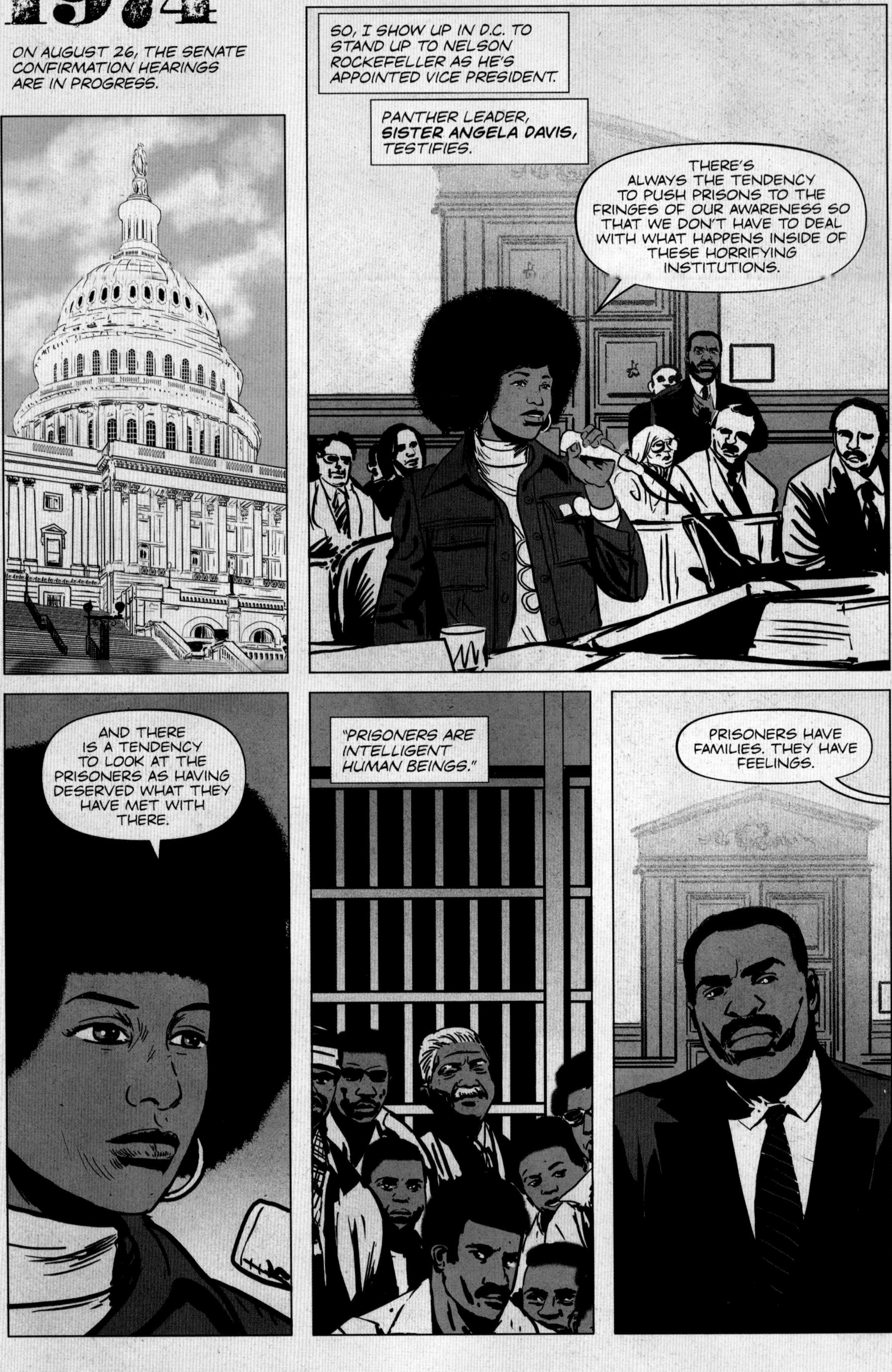

SO, I SHOW UP IN D.C. TO STAND UP TO NELSON ROCKEFELLER AS HE'S APPOINTED VICE PRESIDENT.
PANTHER LEADER, **SISTER ANGELA DAVIS,** TESTIFIES.
THERE'S ALWAYS THE TENDENCY TO PUSH PRISONS TO THE FRINGES OF OUR AWARENESS SO THAT WE DON'T HAVE TO DEAL WITH WHAT HAPPENS INSIDE OF THESE HORRIFYING INSTITUTIONS.
AND THERE IS A TENDENCY TO LOOK AT THE PRISONERS AS HAVING DESERVED WHAT THEY HAVE MET WITH THERE.
"PRISONERS ARE INTELLIGENT HUMAN BEINGS."
PRISONERS HAVE FAMILIES. THEY HAVE FEELINGS.

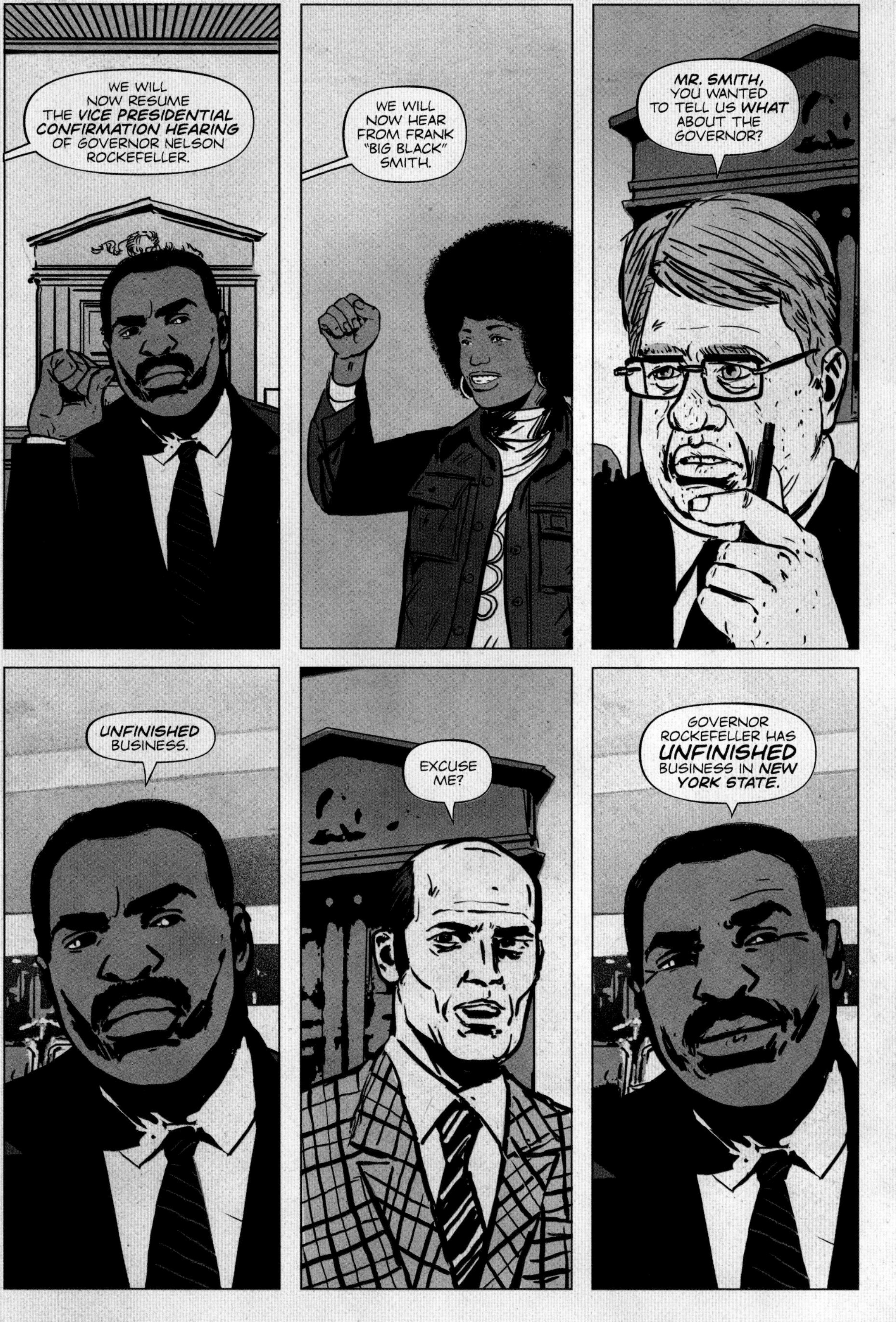
WE WILL NOW RESUME THE VICE PRESIDENTIAL CONFIRMATION HEARING OF GOVERNOR NELSON ROCKEFELLER.
WE WILL NOW HEAR FROM FRANK "BIG BLACK" SMITH.
MR. SMITH, YOU WANTED TO TELL US WHAT ABOUT THE GOVERNOR?
UNFINISHED BUSINESS.
EXCUSE ME?
GOVERNOR ROCKEFELLER HAS UNFINISHED BUSINESS IN NEW YORK STATE.

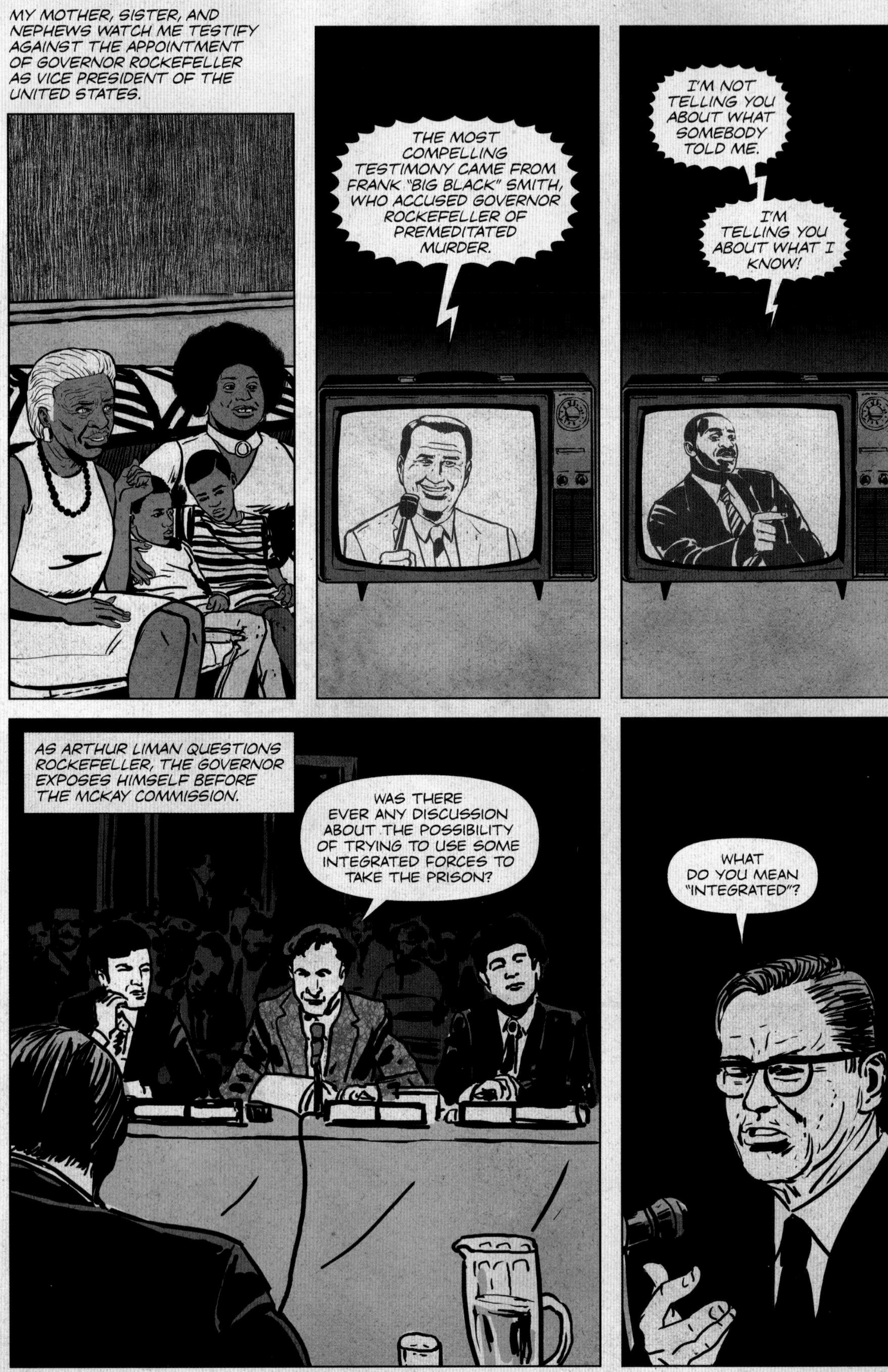
MY MOTHER, SISTER, AND NEPHEWS WATCH ME TESTIFY AGAINST THE APPOINTMENT OF GOVERNOR ROCKEFELLER AS VICE PRESIDENT OF THE UNITED STATES.
THE MOST COMPELLING TESTIMONY CAME FROM FRANK "BIG BLACK" SMITH, WHO ACCUSED GOVERNOR ROCKEFELLER OF PREMEDITATED MURDER.
I'M NOT TELLING YOU ABOUT WHAT SOMEBODY TOLD ME.
I'M TELLING YOU ABOUT WHAT I KNOW!
AS ARTHUR LIMAN QUESTIONS ROCKEFELLER, THE GOVERNOR EXPOSES HIMSELF BEFORE THE MCKAY COMMISSION.
WAS THERE EVER ANY DISCUSSION ABOUT THE POSSIBILITY OF TRYING TO USE SOME INTEGRATED FORCES TO TAKE THE PRISON?
WHAT DO YOU MEAN "INTEGRATED"?

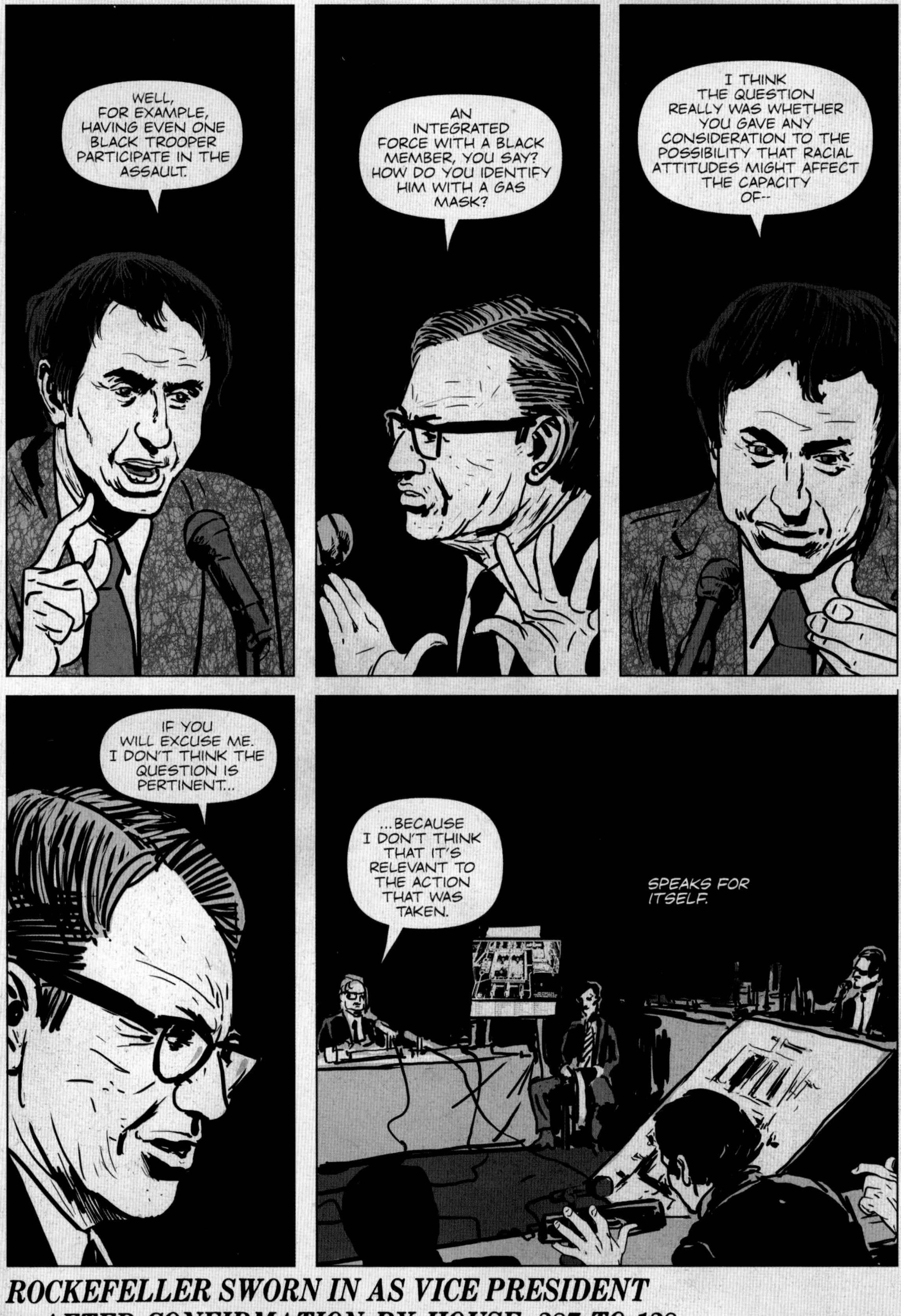
WELL, FOR EXAMPLE, HAVING EVEN ONE BLACK TROOPER PARTICIPATE IN THE ASSAULT.
AN INTEGRATED FORCE WITH A BLACK MEMBER, YOU SAY? HOW DO YOU IDENTIFY HIM WITH A GAS MASK?
I THINK THE QUESTION REALLY WAS WHETHER YOU GAVE ANY CONSIDERATION TO THE POSSIBILITY THAT RACIAL ATTITUDES MIGHT AFFECT THE CAPACITY OF--
IF YOU WILL EXCUSE ME. I DON'T THINK THE QUESTION IS PERTINENT...
...BECAUSE I DON'T THINK THAT IT'S RELEVANT TO THE ACTION THAT WAS TAKEN.
SPEAKS FOR ITSELF.

ROCKEFELLER SWORN IN AS VICE PRESIDENT AFTER CONFIRMATION BY HOUSE, 287 TO 128

ROCKEFELLER BECOMES VICE PRESIDENT, BUT ATTICA FOLLOWS HIM.

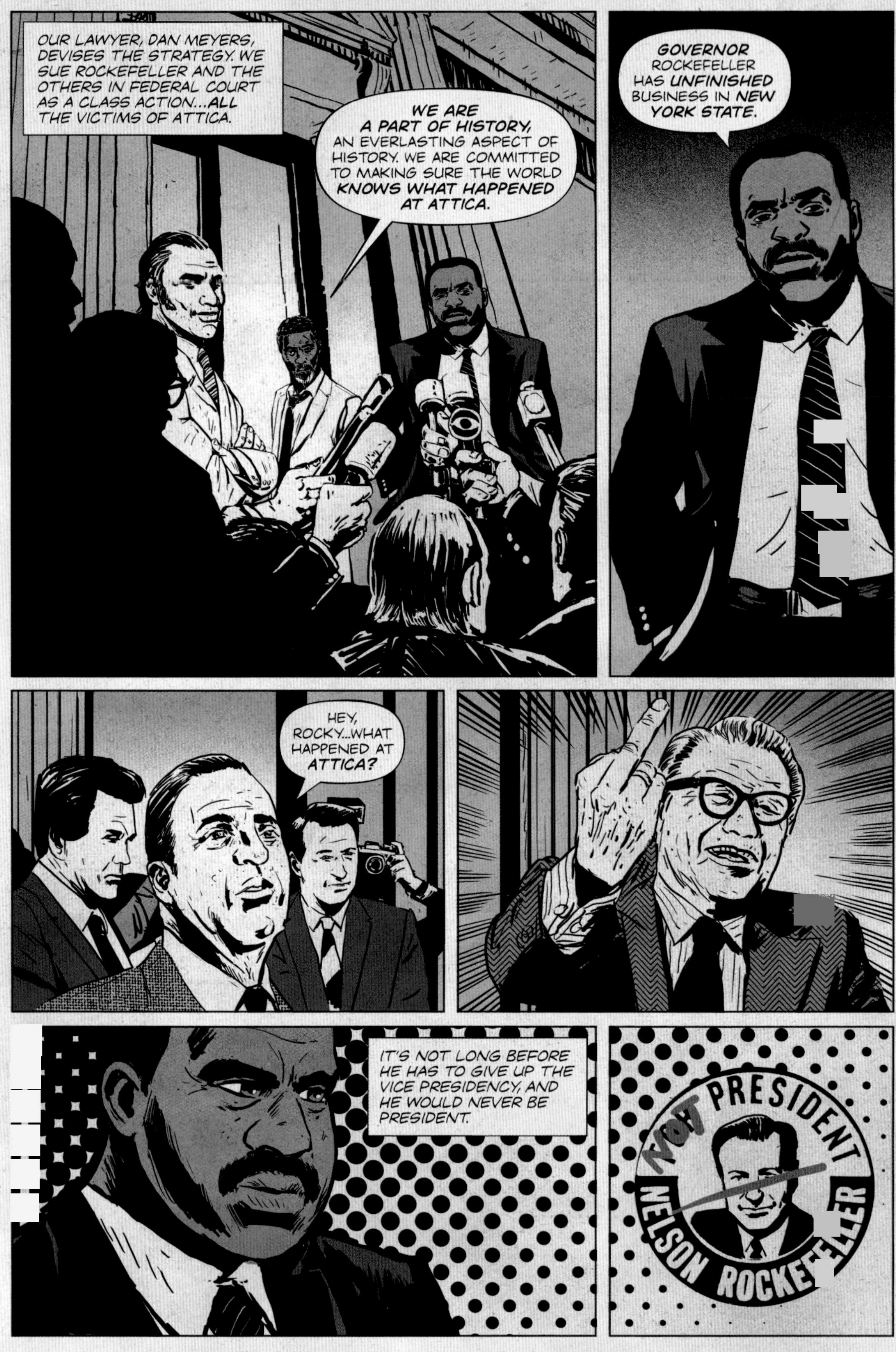
OUR LAWYER, DAN MEYERS, DEVISES THE STRATEGY. WE SUE ROCKEFELLER AND THE OTHERS IN FEDERAL COURT AS A CLASS ACTION...ALL THE VICTIMS OF ATTICA.
WE ARE A PART OF HISTORY, AN EVERLASTING ASPECT OF HISTORY. WE ARE COMMITTED TO MAKING SURE THE WORLD KNOWS WHAT HAPPENED AT ATTICA.
GOVERNOR ROCKEFELLER HAS UNFINISHED BUSINESS IN NEW YORK STATE.
HEY, ROCKY...WHAT HAPPENED AT ATTICA?
IT'S NOT LONG BEFORE HE HAS TO GIVE UP THE VICE PRESIDENCY, AND HE WOULD NEVER BE PRESIDENT.
NOT PRESIDENT
NELSON ROCKEFELLER

AMBULANCE
HE DIES OF A HEART ATTACK EARLY IN 1979.
NEW YORK POST
FINAL
ROCKY DEAD
Collapses with heart attack while working on new book

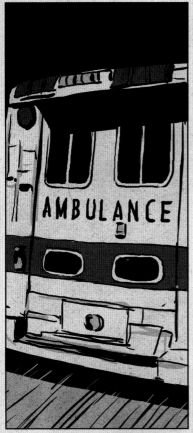

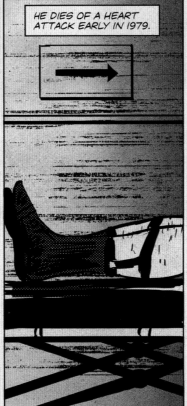

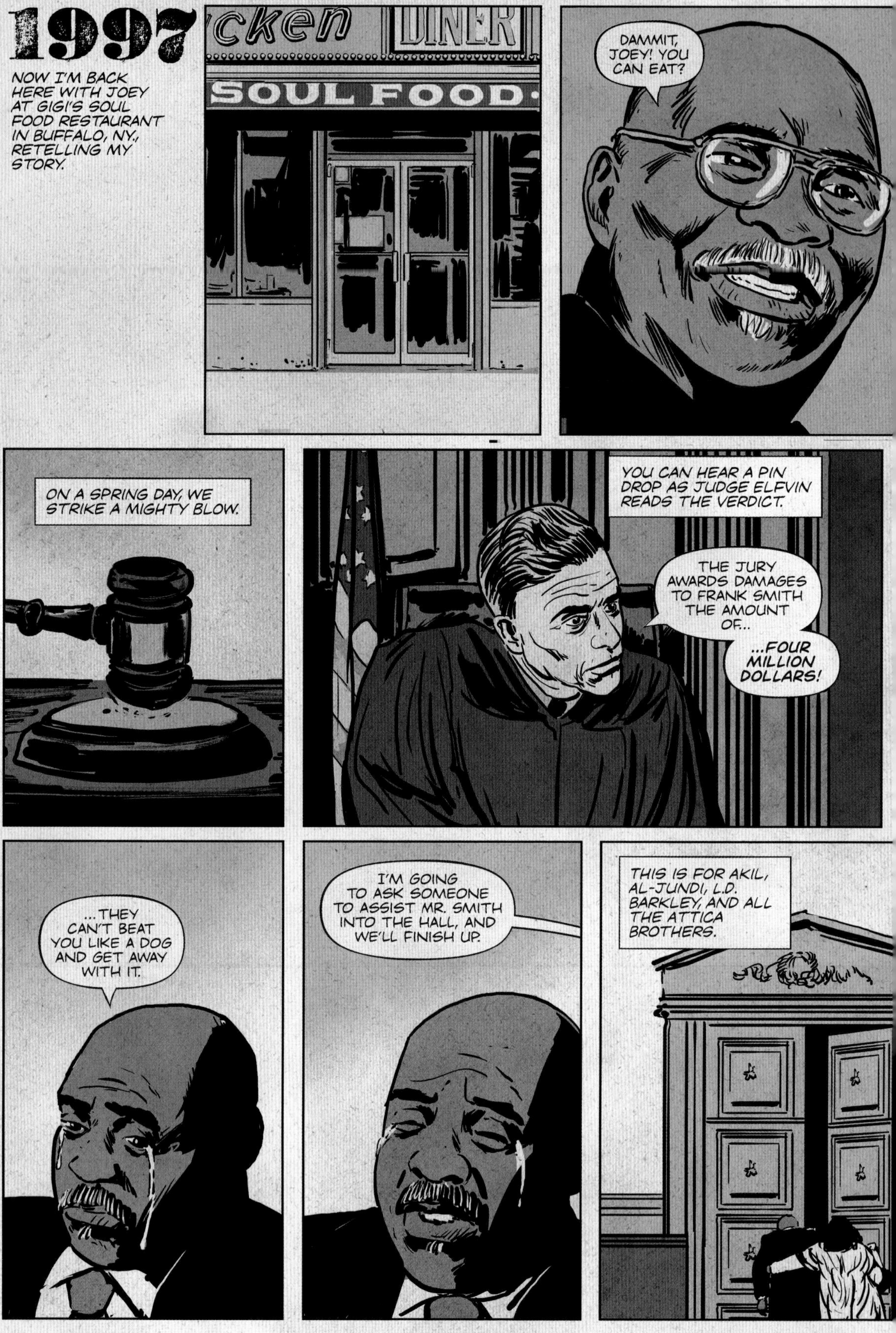
1997
NOW I'M BACK HERE WITH JOEY AT GIGI'S SOUL FOOD RESTAURANT IN BUFFALO, NY., RETELLING MY STORY.
DINER
SOUL FOOD
DAMMIT, JOEY! YOU CAN EAT?
ON A SPRING DAY, WE STRIKE A MIGHTY BLOW.
YOU CAN HEAR A PIN DROP AS JUDGE ELFVIN READS THE VERDICT.
THE JURY AWARDS DAMAGES TO FRANK SMITH THE AMOUNT OF...
...FOUR MILLION DOLLARS!
...THEY CAN'T BEAT YOU LIKE A DOG AND GET AWAY WITH IT.
I'M GOING TO ASK SOMEONE TO ASSIST MR. SMITH INTO THE HALL, AND WE'LL FINISH UP.
THIS IS FOR AKIL, AL-JUNDI, L.D. BARKLEY, AND ALL THE ATTICA BROTHERS.

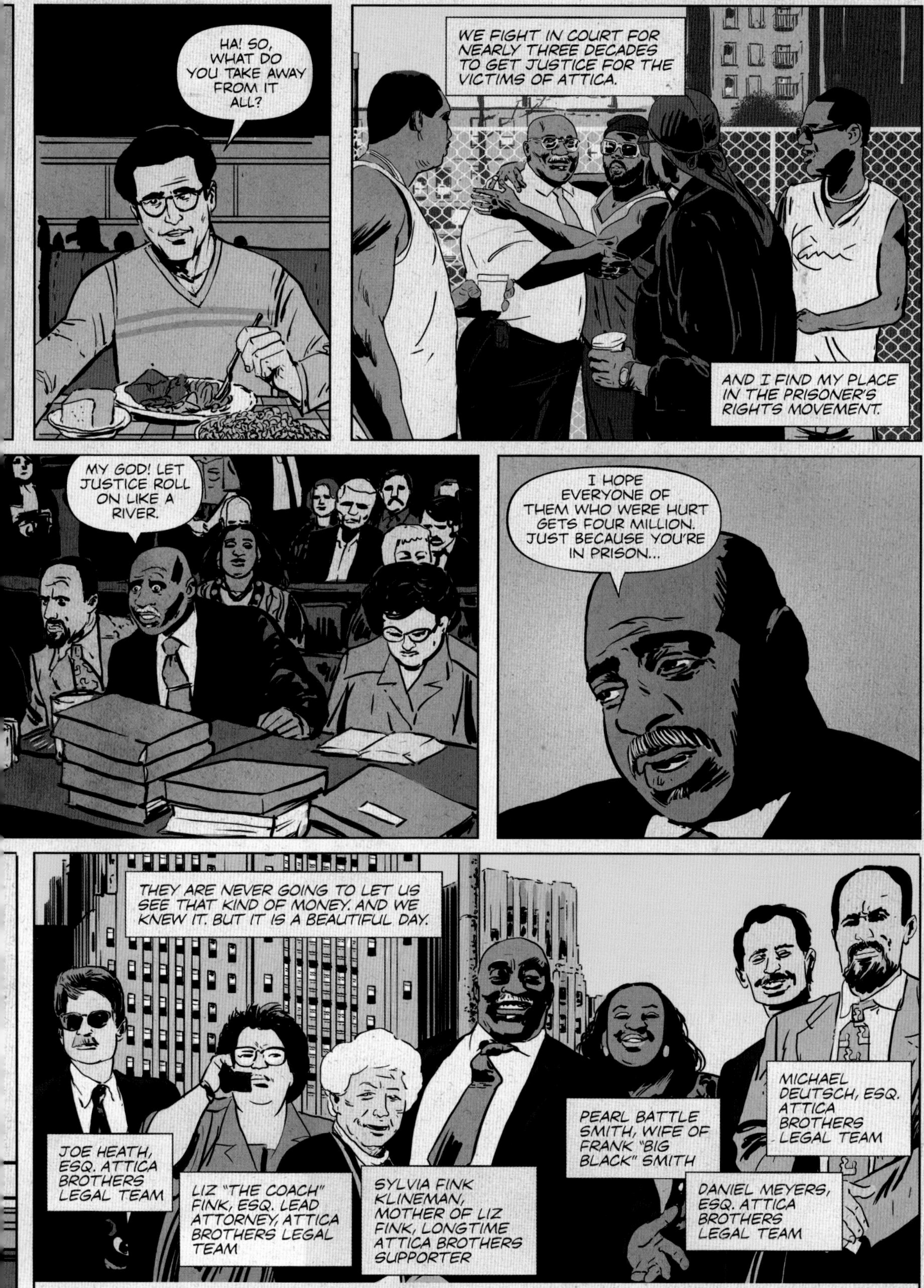
HA! SO, WHAT DO YOU TAKE AWAY FROM IT ALL?
WE FIGHT IN COURT FOR NEARLY THREE DECADES TO GET JUSTICE FOR THE VICTIMS OF ATTICA.
AND I FIND MY PLACE IN THE PRISONER'S RIGHTS MOVEMENT.
MY GOD! LET JUSTICE ROLL ON LIKE A RIVER.
I HOPE EVERYONE OF THEM WHO WERE HURT GETS FOUR MILLION. JUST BECAUSE YOU'RE IN PRISON...
THEY ARE NEVER GOING TO LET US SEE THAT KIND OF MONEY. AND WE KNEW IT. BUT IT IS A BEAUTIFUL DAY.
JOE HEATH, ESQ. ATTICA BROTHERS LEGAL TEAM
LIZ "THE COACH" FINK, ESQ. LEAD ATTORNEY, ATTICA BROTHERS LEGAL TEAM
SYLVIA FINK KLINEMAN, MOTHER OF LIZ FINK, LONGTIME ATTICA BROTHERS SUPPORTER
PEARL BATTLE SMITH, WIFE OF FRANK "BIG BLACK" SMITH
MICHAEL DEUTSCH, ESQ. ATTICA BROTHERS LEGAL TEAM
DANIEL MEYERS, ESQ. ATTICA BROTHERS LEGAL TEAM
Ex-Attica Inmate Wins $4 Million in Suit Over Reprisals After 1971 Uprising

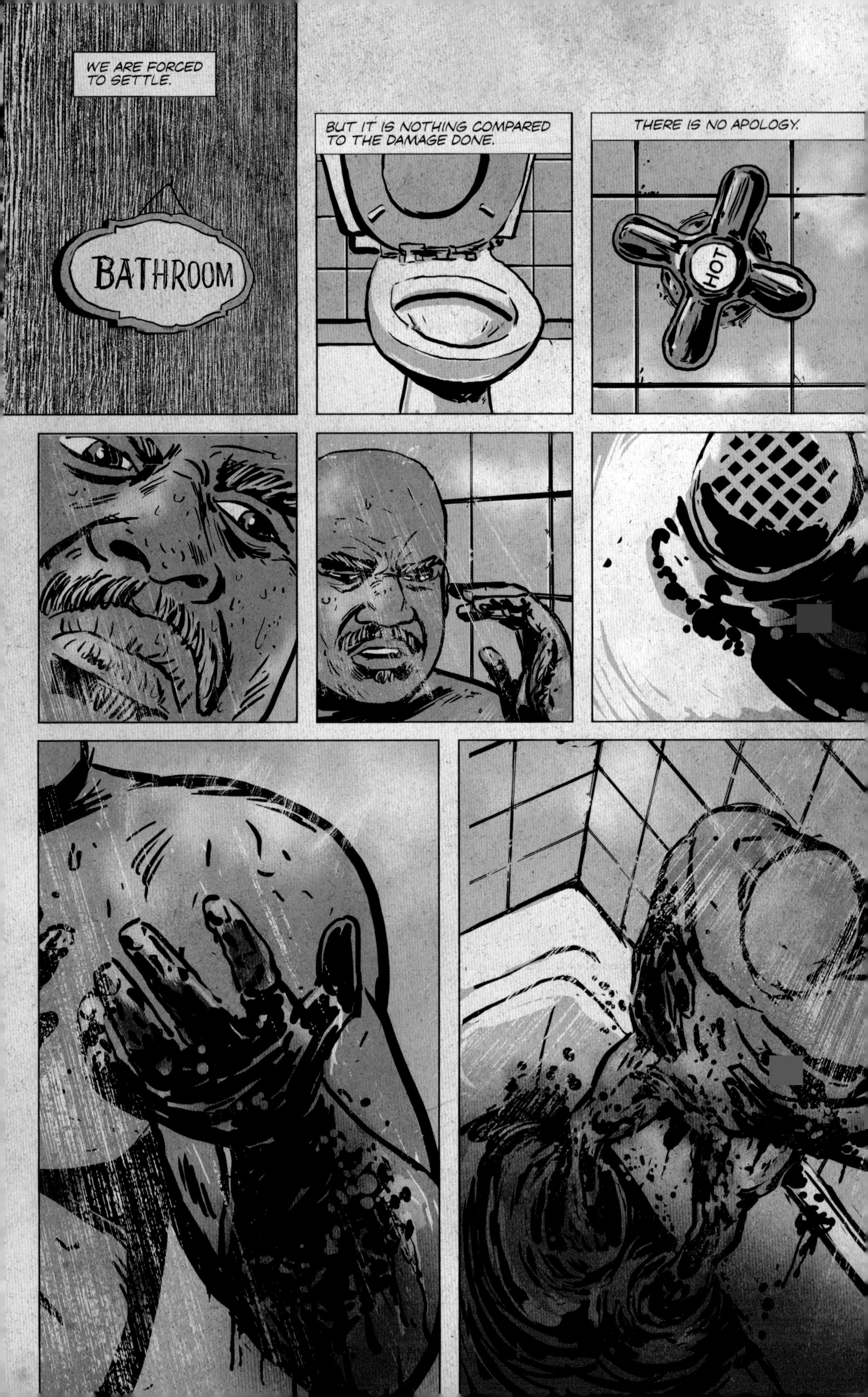
WE ARE FORCED TO SETTLE.
BATHROOM
BUT IT IS NOTHING COMPARED TO THE DAMAGE DONE.
THERE IS NO APOLOGY.
HOT

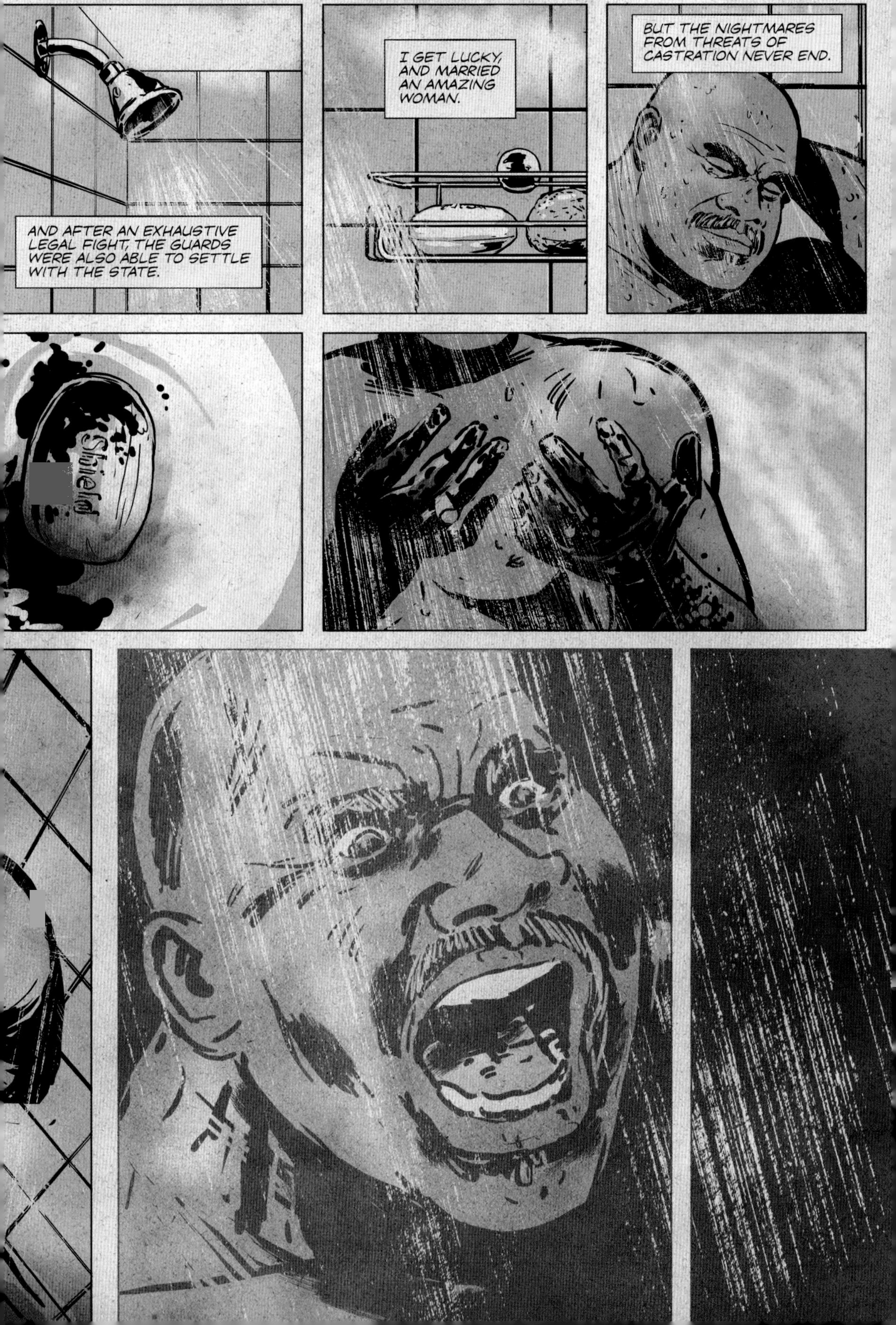
AND AFTER AN EXHAUSTIVE LEGAL FIGHT, THE GUARDS WERE ALSO ABLE TO SETTLE WITH THE STATE.
I GET LUCKY, AND MARRIED AN AMAZING WOMAN.
BUT THE NIGHTMARES FROM THREATS OF CASTRATION NEVER END.
Shield

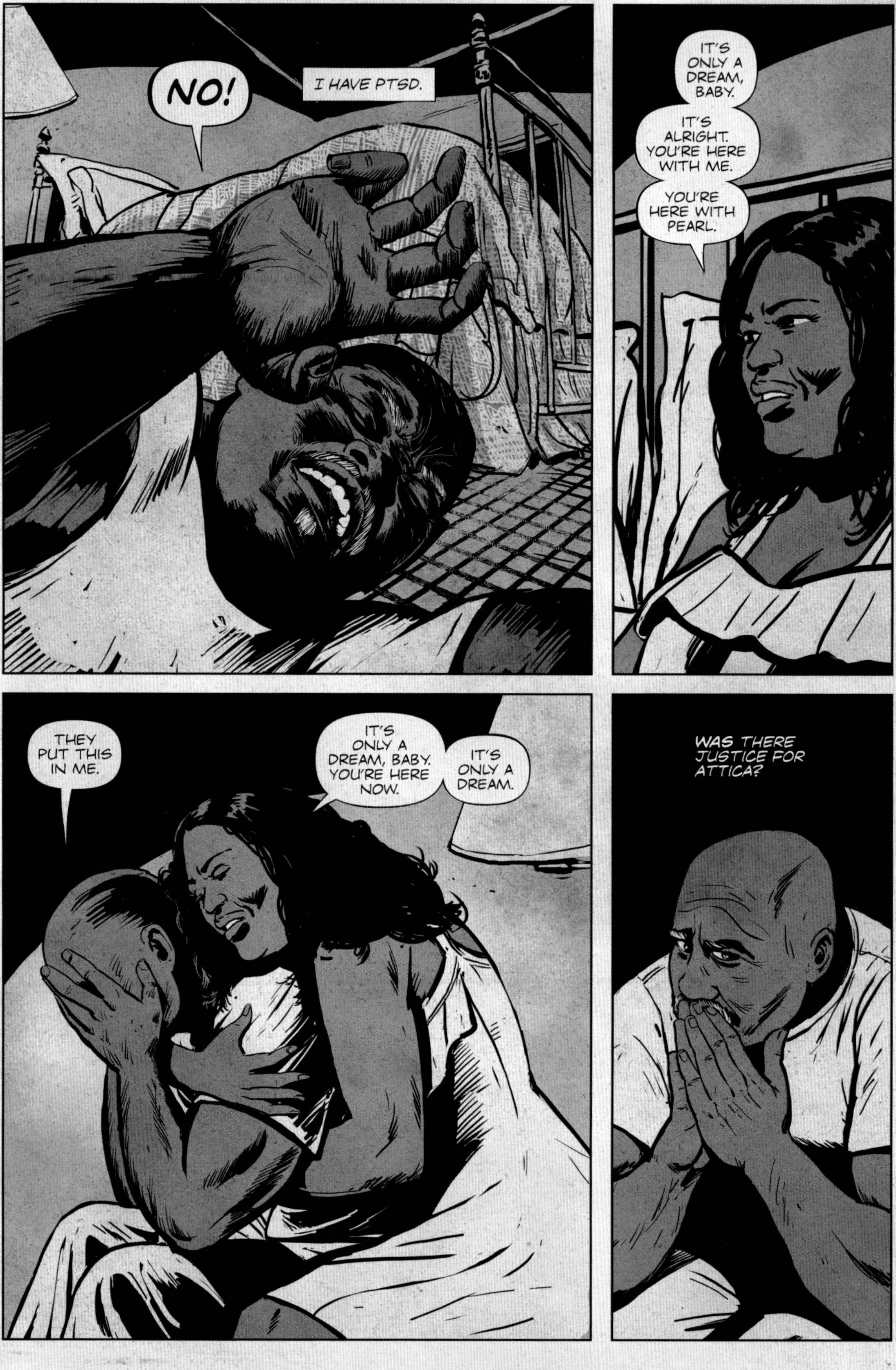
NO!
I HAVE PTSD.
IT'S ONLY A DREAM, BABY.
IT'S ALRIGHT. YOU'RE HERE WITH ME.
YOU'RE HERE WITH PEARL.
THEY PUT THIS IN ME.
IT'S ONLY A DREAM, BABY. YOU'RE HERE NOW.
IT'S ONLY A DREAM.
WAS THERE JUSTICE FOR ATTICA?

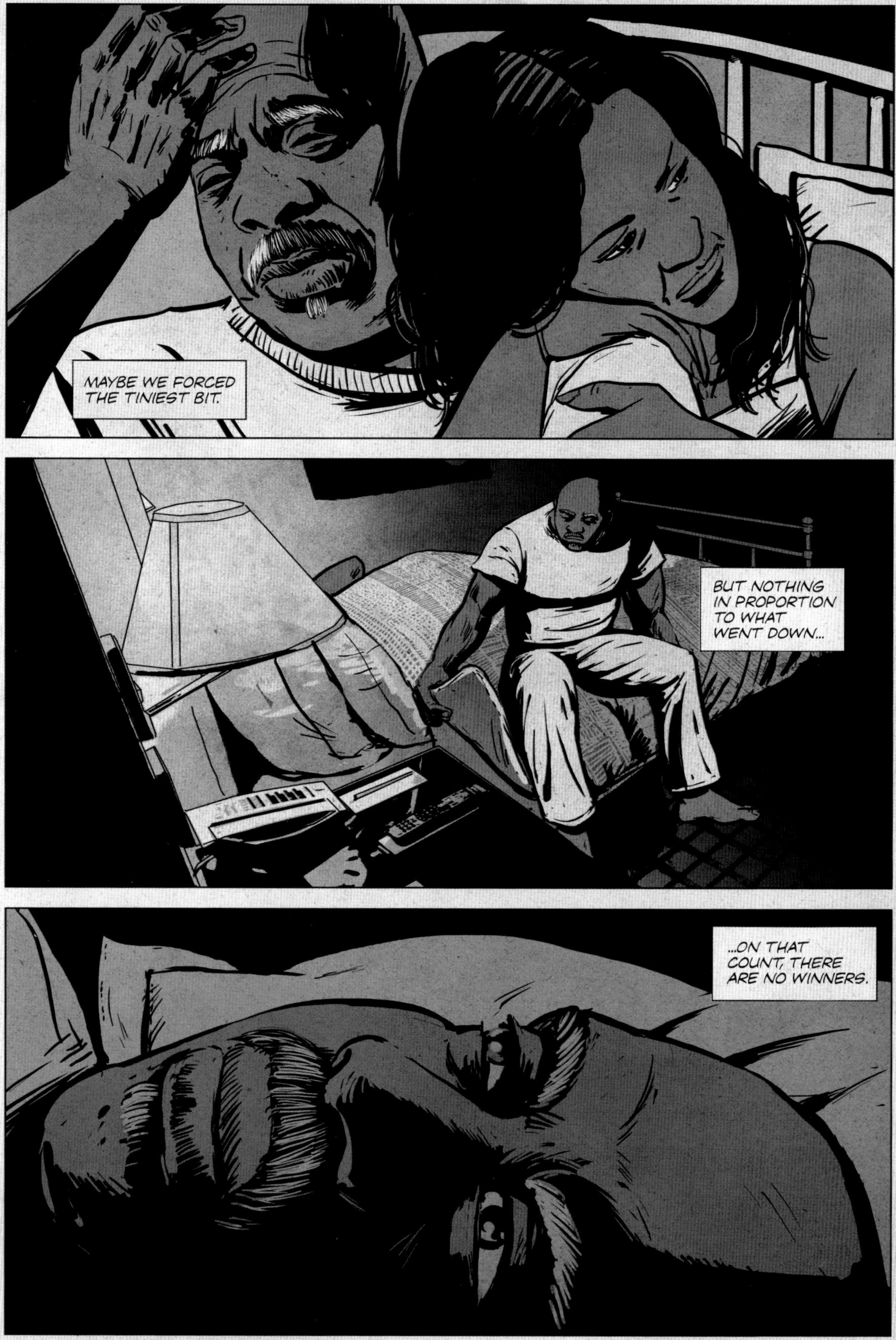
MAYBE WE FORCED THE TINIEST BIT.
BUT NOTHING IN PROPORTION TO WHAT WENT DOWN...
...ON THAT COUNT, THERE ARE NO WINNERS.

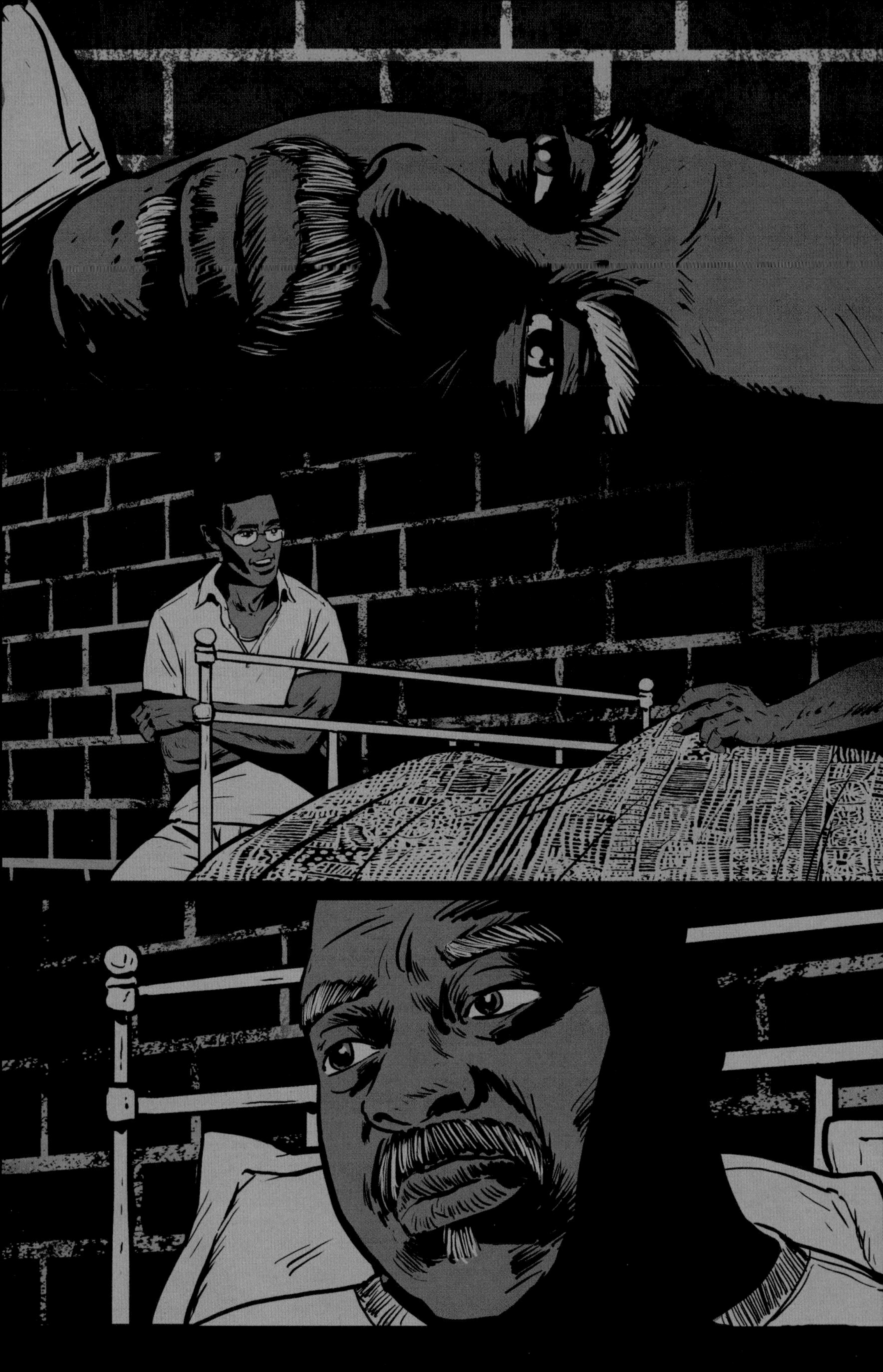

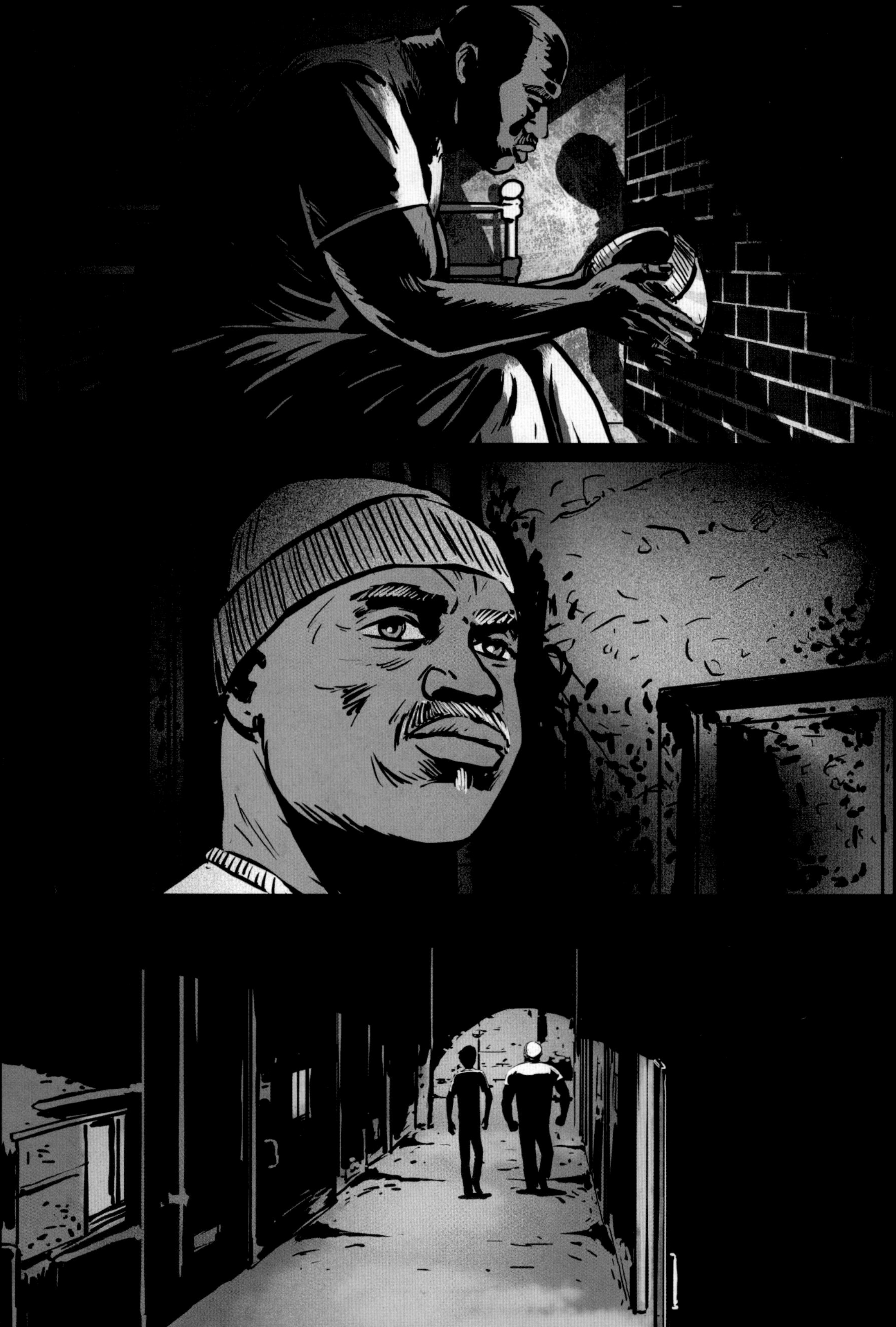

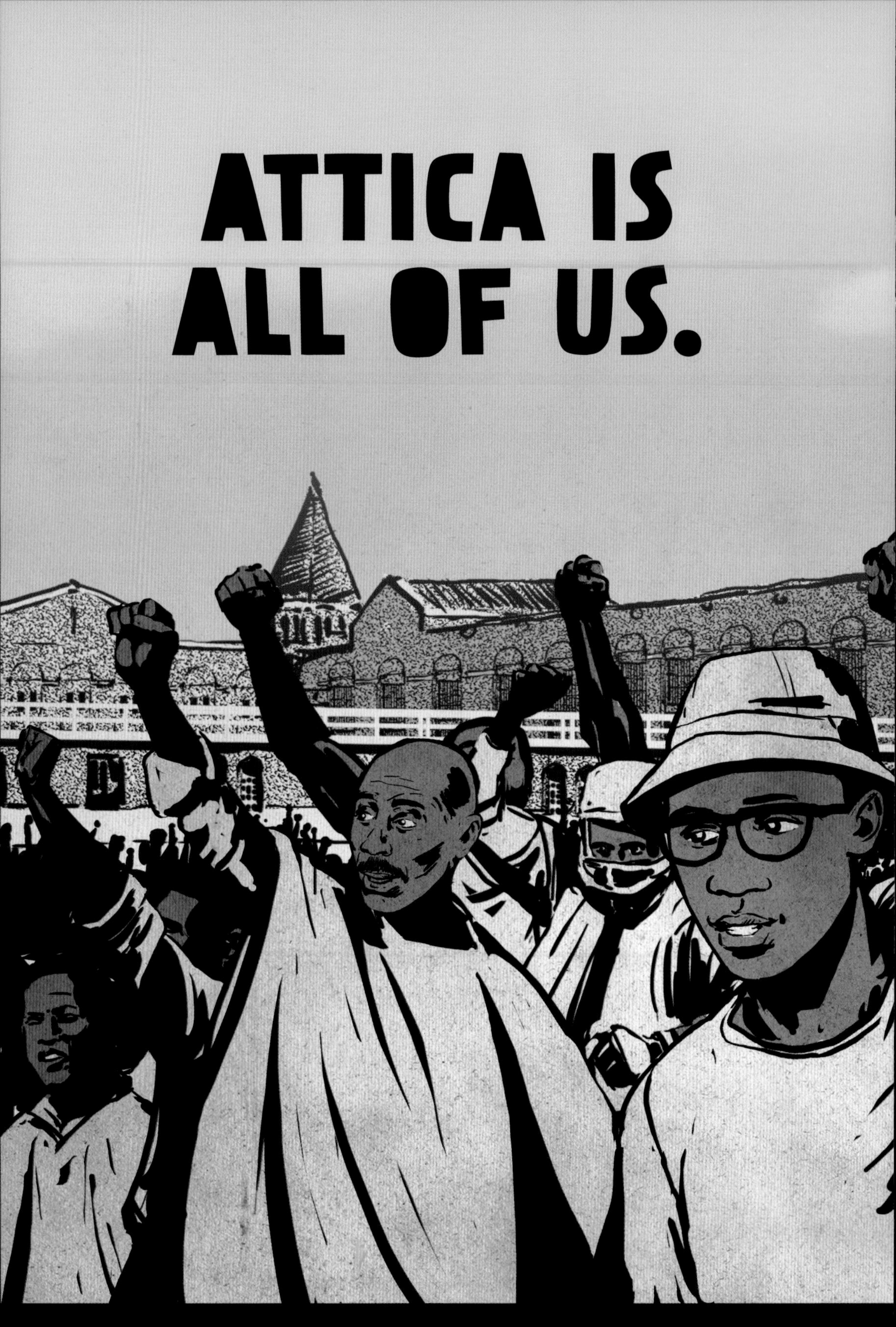
ATTICA IS ALL OF US.

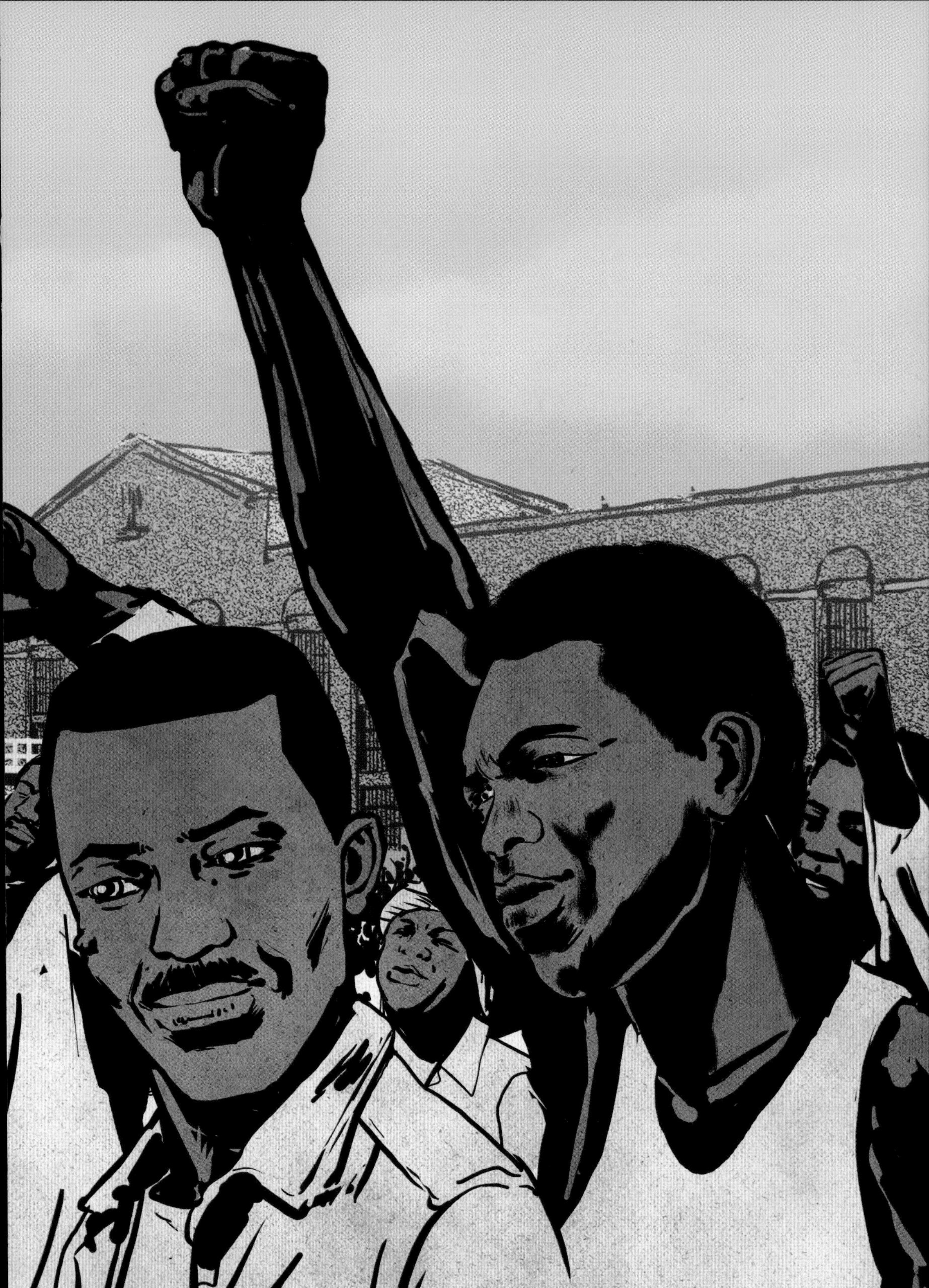

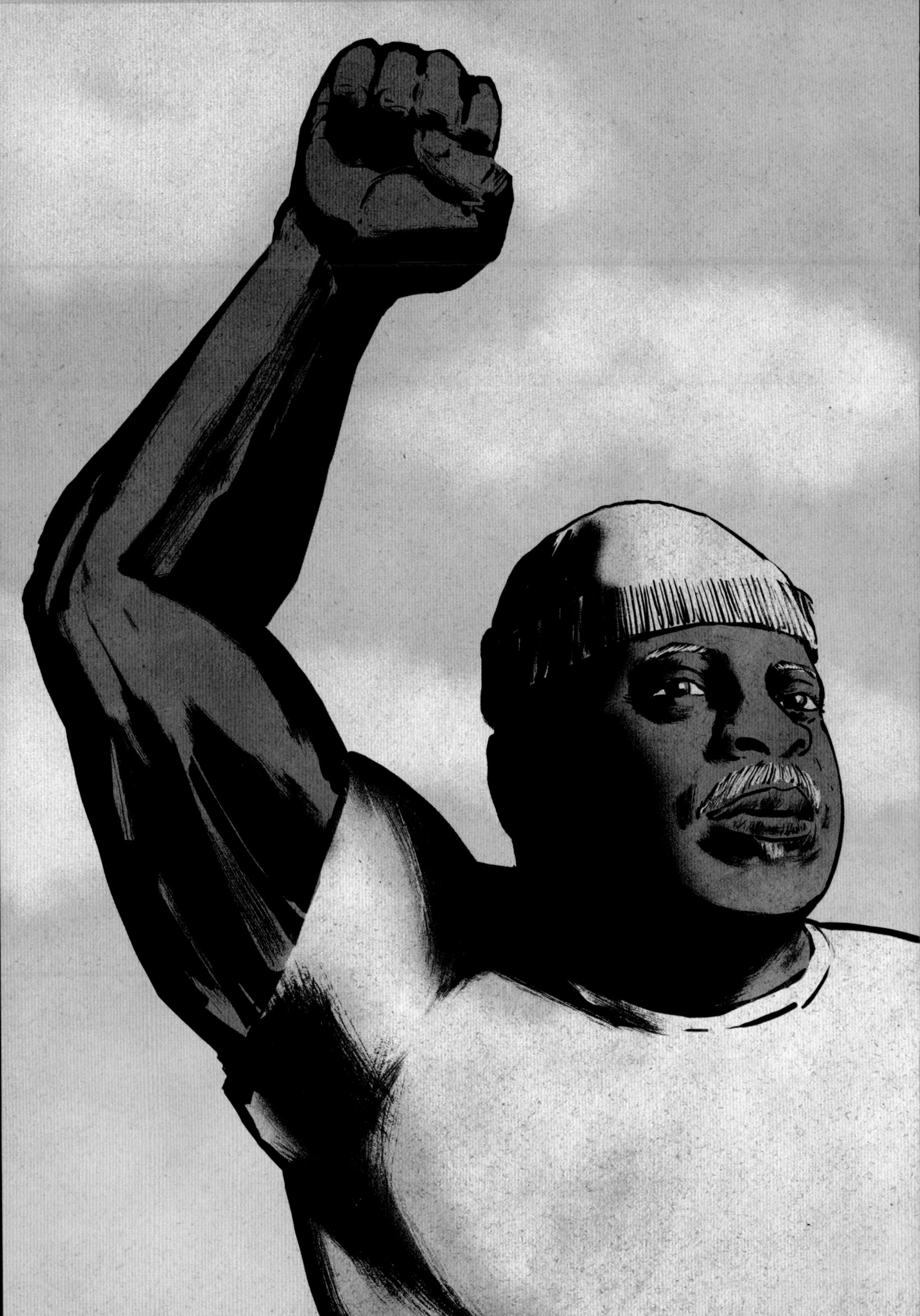

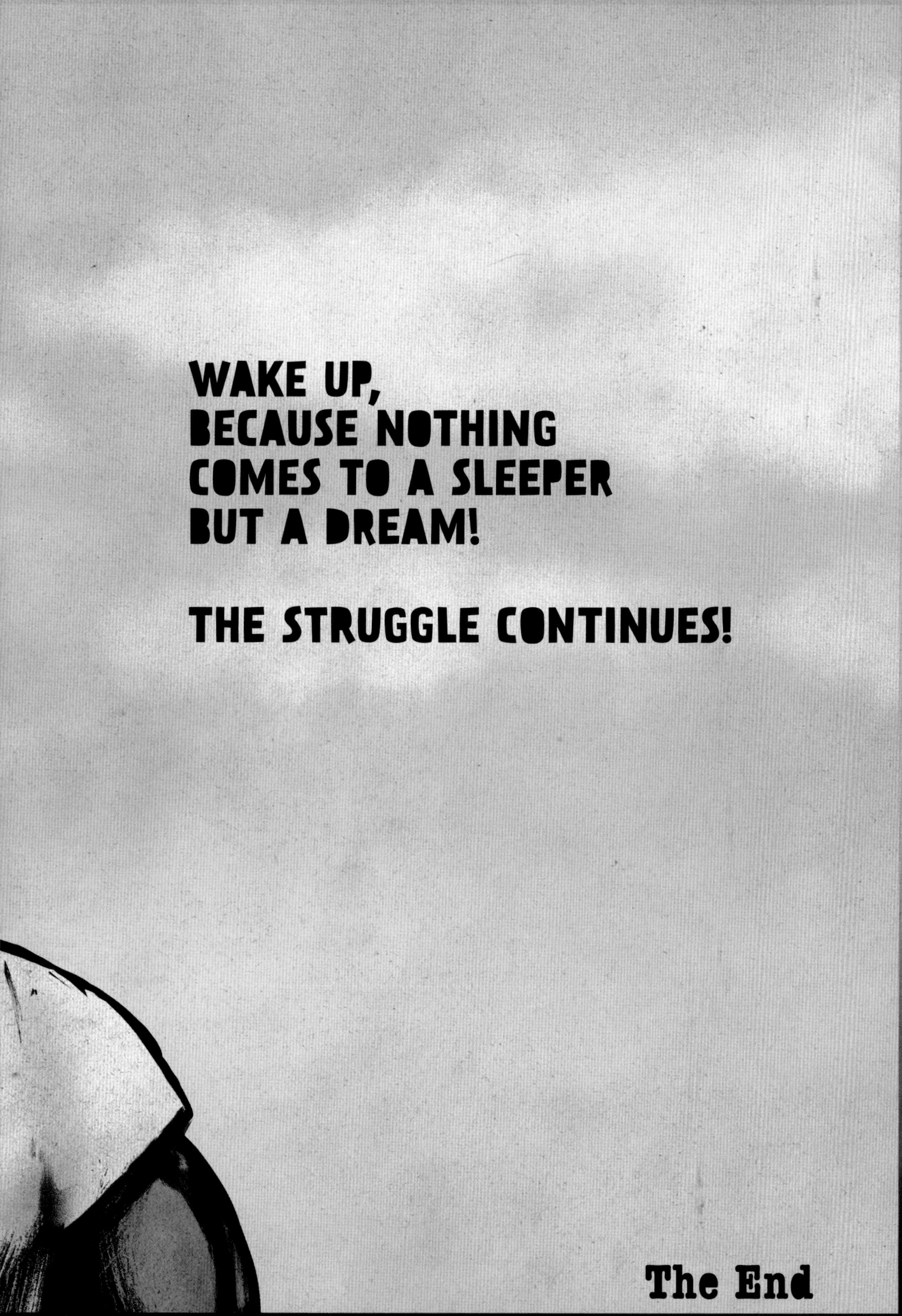
WAKE UP,
BECAUSE NOTHING
COMES TO A SLEEPER
BUT A DREAM!
THE STRUGGLE CONTINUES!
The End

WHO DIED AT ATTICA,
WE WILL NOT FORGET

William Allen

Elliott (L. D.) Barkley

John B. Barnes

Edward Cunningham (hostage)

John J. D'Arcangelo (hostage)

Bernard Davis

Allen Durham

Willie Fuller

Melvin D. Gray

Elmer G Hardie (hostage)

Robert J. Henigan

Kenneth E. Hess

Edward R. Menefee

Jose Mentijo

Milton Menyweather

John G. Monteleone (hostage)

Richard Moore

Carlos Prescott

Michael Privitiera

William E. Quinn (hostage)

Raymond Rivera

James B. Robinson

Santiago Santos

Barry J. Schwartz

FRANK "BIG BLACK" SMITH

(1933 -2004)

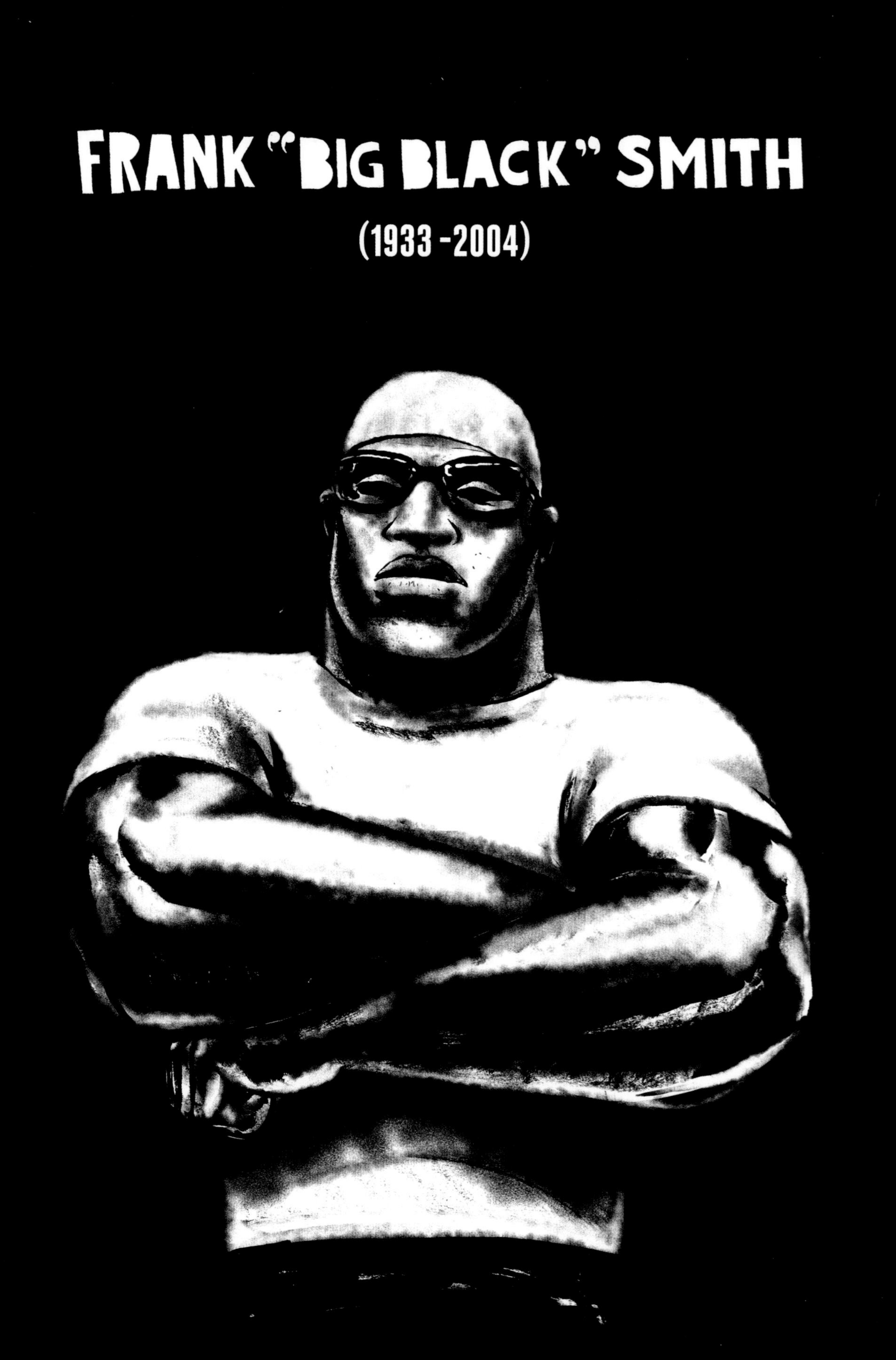

BIBLIOGRAPHY

"40 Years After Attica Rebellion, New Tapes Reveal Nixon, Rockefeller Praised Deadly Crackdown."
Democracy Now! www.democracynow.org/2011/9/16/40_years_after_attica_rebellion_new.

Attica. (Motion Picture). Tricontinental Film Center, 1974.

Bell, Malcolm. *The Attica Turkey Shoot: Carnage, Cover-up, and the Pursuit of Justice*. New York, NY: Skyhorse
Publishing, 2017.

Clark, Richard X., and Leonard Levitt. *The Brothers of Attica*. New York: Links, 1973.

Cleaver, Eldridge. *Soul on Ice*. New York, NY: Delta Trade Paperbacks, 1999.

Eyes on The Prize: Episode 12: A Nation of Law? (1968–71). PBS, 1990.

Ghosts of Attica. Icarus Films, 2001.

Jackson, George, and Jonathan Jackson. *Soledad Brother: The Prison Letters of George Jackson*. Chicago:
Lawrence Hill Books, 2006.

McKay, Robert B. *The Official Report of the New York State Special Commission on Attica*. N.Y.: Praeger, 1972.

Steele, Lewis. *The Butler's Child: An Autobiography*. New York, NY: St. Martin's Press, 2016.

Thompson, Heather Ann. *Blood in the Water: The Attica Prison Uprising of 1971 and Its Legacy*. New York:
Vintage Books, 2017.

Wicker, Tom. *A Time to Die*. Chicago, IL: Haymarket Books, 2011.

William Kunstler: Disturbing the Universe. Arthouse Films, 2009.

WE OWE OUR THANKS TO A LOT OF INCREDIBLE PEOPLE WHO LIVED AND DIED FOR THE CAUSE. WE HONOR THEM HERE.

The Attica Observers
Joseph Agovino
Akil Al-Jundi
Daniel Alterman
Richard Ashe
Ellen G. Battle
Lorenzo Battle
Otis Battle
Robert Bloom
Herbert X Blyden
Ethel Bostic
Robert Boyle
Lillie Bradford and Guy Smith
Charlotte B. Brooks
David Brosig
Haywood Burns
Bob Camp and Missy Ford
Jed Cecil
Roger Champen
Richard X Clark
Joe Corallo
Chuck Culhane
Dennis Cunningham
Nikō Davidopoulos
Jean DeMay
Michael Deutsch
Amy DiCesare and Family
Carol Dudek
Ian Moses Eaton
Soffiah Elijah
Polly Eustic

Elizabeth Fink
FJM Inc. and Families
Andrea J. Fulton
Kent Gash
Mike Gold
Christopher Golden
Judge Emily Goodman
Allen Harris
Glenn Hauman
Joseph Heath
Judy Hinchey and Family
Daryl Hochheiser and Family
Molly Jackson
Gertrude Jeannette
Peter Joseph
Marc Kandel
Joseph Kennedy
Rose Kennedy
Kimanthi
Emily Kunstler
Margaret Ratner Kunstler
Sarah Kunstler
William Kunstler
Joe R. Lansdale
Kasey Lansdale
Frank Lott
Nancy Lyall
Allen Lyons
Dirk Manning
Robert Markfield
The Max/Lewis Family

Leslie McGuire
Delia Mellis
Daniel Meyers
David Meyers and Family
Matt Meyers
Michael Meyers and Family
Sam and Carolyn Meyers
Alicia Mitchell-Foxworth
George Che Nieves
Ward Nixon
Rev. Julian & Debra Pridgen
Joan Max Reinmuth
Kriston Reinmuth and Family
William Reinmuth
Carlos Roche
Jonathan Rosenbaum
Helen Smith
Millie Smith
Pearl Battle Smith
Shakiba Smith
Stephanie Smith
J David Spurlock
Lewis Steel
Frank Stella
Alex Tichane and Kat Famera
Robert Van Lierop
Al Victory
John Wellington
Justus K. White
The White Family
Ellen Yacknin

AND TO THE ATTICA BROTHERS, THEIR FAMILIES AND SUPPORTERS (TOO NUMEROUS TO MENTION HERE)

ABOUT THE AUTHORS

FRANK "BIG BLACK" SMITH

Frank "Big Black" Smith was a former inmate at Attica prison who was tortured by officers following the deadly 1971 uprising. After his release from prison, he kicked a drug addiction and worked as a substance abuse counselor. He also devoted his life to becoming the voice of his fellow prisoners in a 26-year lawsuit against New York state. Smith later became an advocate for the Forgotten Victims of Attica, a group comprised of surviving hostages and relatives of the dead prison guards who were believed to have been encouraged to accept limited benefits which barred them from suing the state. Smith married in 1983, studied to be a paralegal, and worked as an investigator for lawyers. He passed away at 70 years old in Kingston, N.C., after a long battle with cancer. He is survived by his wife, Pearl.

JARED REINMUTH

Jared Reinmuth has worked as an actor, writer, teacher, director, and songwriter. He made his acting debut at the 1994 Dionysian International Theatre Festival in Veroli, Italy in Karen Malpede's *The Beekeeper's Daughter*. Regional and National Tour Credits include: *Cyrano de Bergerac*, *Dracula*, *Don Quixote*, Athos in *The Three Musketeers*, and Guildenstern in *Rosencrantz and Guildenstern Are Dead*. Jared made his directorial debut in 2016 at the Theater for the New City's Dream UP Festival with Andrea J. Fulton's *Roof-Top Joy*. His adaptation, *Monte Cristo*, debuted at the Hackensack Cultural Arts Center. Jared began his writing collaboration with Frank "Big Black" Smith in 1997, while assisting his step-father, famed Attica attorney Dan Meyers. In 2017, at the suggestion of friend and colleague Patrick Kennedy, he joined forces with Pearl Battle Smith and artist Améziane to turn Frank's vision into the graphic novel *Big Black: Stand at Attica*. Also in 2017, Jared began his musical collaboration with Alex Tichane, songwriting original music to accompany the book, and further explore Big Black's inspiring biography.

AMÉZIANE

Améziane grew up in Paris, France with the comics of Frank Miller and Bill Sienkiewicz, the films of Bruce Lee, and the soul music of '66/'76. Améziane worked several years as an art director, illustrator, and graphic designer. Late in 2001, he finally jump-started his comic book career by writing several scripts. He worked on the comics adaptation of *Cuatro Manos* with his favorite novelist, Paco Ignacio Taibo II. Améziane recently completed *Miss Davis* (a biopic of Angela Davis), the final installment in his Soul Trilogy, which also includes *Muhammad Ali* and *Big Black*. The *New York Times* bestseller *Muhammad Ali* was written by Sybille Titeux de la Croix and is Améziane's first comics work published in the United States. *Clan* and *CashCowboys* are available digitally, and *Big Black: Stand at Attica* is his first original production in English. Today, Améziane divides his time between his own *Noir* comics, projects with writer Sybille Titeux de la Croix, collaborations with Jared Reinmuth, and working in film. Of course, he doesn't sleep enough . . .